Step by Step

Web Database Development

Jim Buyens

PUBLISHED BY
Microsoft Press
A Division of Microsoft Corporation
One Microsoft Way
Redmond, Washington 98052-6399

Library of Congress Cataloging-in-Publication Data
Buyens, Jim.
    Web Database Development Step by Step / Jim Buyens.
       p. cm.
    Includes index.
    ISBN 0-7356-0966-7
    1. Web databases. 2. Database design. 3. Web sites--Design. I. Title.
  QA76.9.W43 B89 2000
  005.75'8--dc21   00-020240

Printed and bound in the United States of America.

1 2 3 4 5 6 7 8 9   QMQM   5 4 3 2 1 0

Distributed in Canada by Penguin Books Canada Limited.

A CIP catalogue record for this book is available from the British Library.

Microsoft Press books are available through booksellers and distributors worldwide. For further information about international editions, contact your local Microsoft Corporation office or contact Microsoft Press International directly at fax (425) 936-7329. Visit our Web site at mspress.microsoft.com. Send comments to *mspinput@microsoft.com*.

Macintosh is a registered trademark of Apple Computer, Inc. ActiveX, Developer Studio, FrontPage, JScript, Microsoft, Microsoft Press, MS-DOS, PowerPoint, Visual Basic, Visual C++, Visual InterDev, Visual J++, Windows, and Windows NT are either registered trademarks or trademarks of Microsoft Corporation in the United States and/or other countries. Other product and company names mentioned herein may be the trademarks of their respective owners.

Unless otherwise noted, the example companies, organizations, products, people, and events depicted herein are fictitious. No association with any real company, organization, product, person, or event is intended or should be inferred.

Acquisitions Editor: Eric Stroo
Project Editor: Devon Musgrave
Technical Editor: Brian Johnson

This book is dedicated to the homeless mentally ill persons of America. Why do we lavish health care dollars on victims of other, less debilitating illnesses while condemning these unfortunates to the streets and gutters?

Contents

Part 1

Introducing Web Database Pages

Part 2

Key Concepts

Part 3

Developing Applications

Chapter 7
Running and Displaying Queries   183

Chapter 8
Updating Tables from a General Purpose Form   211

Part 6

Tuning and Debugging

Acknowledgments

Many thanks to my wife, Connie, and my children, Lorrill, Justin, and Lynessa, for their support and for putting up with all the time I spent writing this book. Thanks as well to my parents, my brothers, and their families: Harold, Marcella, Ruth, Dave, Connie, Michael, Steven, Rick, Jenny, Matt, and Claire. What a bunch we are.

At Microsoft, thanks to Eric Stroo, who set up the business details; to John Pierce, the managing editor; and to Devon Musgrave, the project editor. Thanks to Brian Johnson for his astute technical review and to Becka McKay for her sharp-eyed manuscript editing.

Thanks to Interland, Inc., and in particular to Ken Gavranovic and Jason Peoples, for their assistance in providing the *www.interlacken.com* Web site.

Most of all, thanks to you, the readers, who make an effort such as this both possible and worthwhile. I hope the book meets your expectations and that we meet again.

Introduction

This book teaches you how to create database applications that operate on the World Wide Web. If you know how to create ordinary Web pages, know a little about databases, and want to integrate the two, this book is for you.

Potential Web database applications are at least as numerous as databases. If your data can reside in a database, you can write Web pages to enter it, maintain it, and distribute it to others. Furthermore, you can do so without distributing and installing any software (other than the ubiquitous Web browser) on any computer other than your Web server.

You can certainly use Web database pages to create or access traditional business applications such as order entry, inventory, billing, and payroll, but any collection of repetitive Web pages is also a candidate for Web database development. Rather than create (and maintain) an individual Web page for each person, place, or thing, why not put the variable portion in a database and code a single Web page to display the one you want?

Developing a Web page that accesses a database (that is, a Web database page) needn't be terribly difficult. Simple cases require only twenty or so lines of code, most of which is HTML you already know. Pages that provide more functionality will naturally require more code, but that's no reason to avoid getting started.

Does the phrase "lines of code" make you cringe? It shouldn't; millions of people know how to create lines of HTML code, and millions more are proficient to some extent in Microsoft Visual Basic. This is all the background you need to complete the examples in this book and start creating Web database applications of your own.

System Requirements

Most of the Web pages in this book are Active Server Pages (or ASP pages), which means they contain script code that runs on the Web server each time a Web visitor requests the page. This code receives input from the Web visitor, accesses the database, and customizes the outgoing Web pages.

ASP is a feature of Microsoft Web servers, and your production Web server should therefore be Microsoft Windows 2000 Server running Internet Information Services or Microsoft Windows NT Server 4.0 running Internet Information Server 4.0. If your existing Web server uses any other type of software, you'll need to change servers, change providers, or use a different technique.

Accessing the database requires several layers of software, all of which come bundled in a package called Microsoft Data Access Components (MDAC). A version of MDAC comes with IIS, but more recent versions are generally available from *http://www.microsoft.com/data/*.

If you prefer developing and testing new Web pages on your desktop system, you can install versions of IIS on Windows 95, Windows 98, Windows NT Workstation, and Windows 2000 Professional. To install IIS on Windows 95 or Windows NT Workstation, download and install the Windows NT 4.0 Option Pack. To install IIS on Windows 98, install the Windows component titled

Personal Web Server. To install IIS on Windows 2000 Professional, install the Windows component titled Internet Information Services.

You can access almost any type of database from a Web database page, but the database used in this book is created with Microsoft Access. The decision to use Access was based on ease of use and accessibility; Access is easily the most prevalent and easiest to use database system around. If, however, your application requires high transaction volumes or extremely high reliability, the book also explains how to access Microsoft SQL Server databases.

There is no requirement to use a particular HTML editor; you can use Microsoft FrontPage, Microsoft Visual InterDev, Notepad, or any other editor you prefer. Just make sure it doesn't treat ASP code—that is, code enclosed in <% and %> tags—as a syntax error.

With the exception of a few pages that use eXtensible Markup Language (XML), the Web pages in this book are browser-neutral. This means they'll work with almost any browser your visitors are likely to have, including older versions of Microsoft Internet Explorer and Netscape Navigator. Browser independence is a major advantage of server-side scripting.

How This Book Is Organized

The book consists of six parts, organized as follows:

- **Part 1, "Introducing Web Database Pages,"** provides a high-level introduction to the material and explains how to create a simple Web database page. In short, this is a preview of everything that follows.

- **Part 2, "Key Concepts,"** provides key background on the design and use of databases, on the interfaces between server-side scripts and databases, on the interface between a server-side script and the Web server, and on Visual Basic, Scripting Edition (VBScript), the programming language most often used for server-side scripts. It concludes with a chapter on setting up a Web database development environment.

  This part of the book contains a lot of reference material you might want to scan or skip on the first pass. You can always return for additional detail as needed.

- **Part 3, "Developing Applications,"** is the heart of the book—the part that explains how to create practical, real-world applications. Four chapters explain how to create a simple catalog application that includes browsing, searching, and three kinds of item maintenance.

  The Web pages in these chapters aren't rudimentary examples; they're reasonably full-featured pages with features you're likely to want in your own site. After all, you want your site to be more full-featured than a textbook example. This leads to a certain amount of complexity but, hopefully, nothing that's overwhelming.

- **Part 4, "Advanced Topics,"** explains how to access Microsoft Index Server from a Web server. Index Server is a text search engine that comes with Microsoft's higher-end Web servers. This is useful for word-searching documents of any type, including Web pages, and also as an example of how to use a nonrelational database.

This part also explains how to use the IIS Session object for accumulating data as Web visitors traverse multiple pages within your site.

- **Part 5, "Exchanging Data with XML,"** introduces XML and provides practical working examples that involve both the browser and the Web server.

  If you haven't worked with XML before, these chapters will likely be a surprise. XML tags denote the *structure* of data, not its appearance. Using XML to display data is thus a two-step process: first getting the data in XML format and then converting the XML data to some other format (such as HTML) for display. This part of the book explains several ways to perform each of these steps.

- **Part 6, "Tuning and Debugging,"** provides a series of tips for improving the performance of Web database pages and for diagnosing pages that run amuck. The last but not least topic in the book explains how to start interactive debugging sessions that execute Web database pages a statement at a time, highlighting the current statement and providing access to all current values and properties.

Contacting the Author

Hearing from happy readers is always a welcome and pleasant experience, and hearing from the less-than-satisfied is important as well. Please write in English. My e-mail address is

buyensj@primenet.com

I'm most interested in your impressions of this book: what you liked or disliked about it, what questions it did or didn't answer, what you found superfluous, and what you'd like to see added in the next edition. I'll post errors, omissions, and corrections on my Web site at

http://www.interlacken.com/webdb/errata.htm

You can find additional information at the Microsoft Press support page:

http://mspress.microsoft.com/support/

I can accept enhancement requests only for this book and not for the Microsoft software. The e-mail address for suggesting product enhancements is

mswish@microsoft.com

Please understand that I'm just one person and I can't provide technical support or debugging assistance, even for readers. Please try other channels, including the Microsoft Developer Network library and the Microsoft support Web site at

http://msdn.microsoft.com/library/
http://support.microsoft.com/directory/

If all else fails, please write. While I can't promise to answer each message, I'll try to provide at least a useful suggestion. Even when I can't answer your e-mail messages directly, I find it instructive to learn what problems users like you are experiencing—and therefore how I can make this and future books more useful to everyone.

Chapter 1

Getting Started with Web Databases

Chapter Objectives	Estimated Time: 40 minutes

In this chapter, you'll learn how to

- Create a new ASP file.

- Write code to read a database.

- Install and run an ASP file on your Web server.

Use of the World Wide Web to present and accumulate data has grown far beyond simple page display. The days are long past when Web designers who needed to present items in a collection created a separate Web page for each item. Such pages were difficult to organize initially and almost impossible to keep updated over time.

Increasingly, the volume and structure of data presented on the Web warrants storing and organizing it into databases, and then generating Web pages based on those databases. The range of sites that can benefit from this approach is staggering. Any Web site (or portion of one) that presents information about a collection of like items is a candidate for using a Web database. These like items could be products for sale, personal photographs, hyperlinks, or almost anything you can think of.

The general approach is to define a database (perhaps in Microsoft Access), add a record for each item, and then query the database to generate Web pages on the fly. A menu page in ordinary HTML becomes a multirecord database query. A subordinate page becomes a detailed display of one database record. Additional advantages are

- The database is much easier to maintain than all the individual Web pages.

- Using a database facilitates searching for desired items.

- A database makes it easy to present the same data in different ways: by category, by description, by age, or by any other field in the database.

The appeal of disseminating or collecting information via Web pages is universal. It makes no difference whether your organization is large or small; whether it's business, government, educational, or personal; or whether it's profit or nonprofit. The same techniques apply whether the items are antiques, used cars, rare stamps, art prints, carpool riders, homes for sale, or missing children. If you think that creating a static Web page for each of many items seems tedious, error-prone, and difficult to organize and maintain, Web database pages are for you.

Unfortunately—despite at least 20 years of trying—no one has yet found a way to construct database applications by using either WYSIWYG or point-and-click technology. At best, such development systems automate only a subset of the requirements for a specific type of application. For developing database applications of any kind—Web, client/server, or mainframe—code reigns supreme.

The Internet Information Services (IIS) component of Microsoft Windows 2000 and Internet Information Server for Microsoft Windows NT 4 provides a powerful collection of technologies for developing Web database applications quickly, easily, and with minimal code. If you're even moderately familiar with these technologies, you can develop Web database applications for yourself, your department, or your company. A list of the technologies you'll need to know follows. Except for the basics of HTML and Microsoft Visual Basic, which you should already know, this book will explain every one of them.

- **HTML**   Despite its many limitations, Hypertext Markup Language remains the fundamental technology for controlling the structure and appearance of Web pages. This book assumes you're comfortable enough with HTML to hand-code simple Web pages.

- **Microsoft Active Server Pages (ASP)**   This is a simple, server-side scripting facility that Microsoft supplies with all its Web servers. When a Web visitor requests a page that contains server-side scripting, the script customizes the page before it leaves the server. This book presumes no prior knowledge of ASP on your part, but your Web server will need this capability to run the examples and any similar code you write yourself. Chapter 5, "Customizing Web Content with Server-Side Scripting," will explain this.

- **Microsoft Visual Basic Scripting Edition (VBScript)**   This is the programming language of choice for Active Server Pages. To understand this book, you don't need great knowledge of Visual Basic, but you should be at least somewhat comfortable with Visual Basic structure and syntax. For example, you should recognize an *If Then...Else...End If* structure or a *While...Wend* loop when you see one. See Chapter 5.

> **Note**   Many Web developers avoid using VBScript within Web pages because Netscape Navigator doesn't support it. However, because ASP pages run on the Web server rather than on the browser, lack of Netscape browser support isn't an issue.

- **Database design and implementation**   The first step in using any database is, of course, designing its tables and fields. The second step is implementing this structure with the database software. The third and fourth steps are adding and querying data—which are totally dependent on the first two steps.

You don't need to be an expert database designer to develop Web database pages, but you do need to understand how to create the necessary databases. Chapter 2, "Understanding Database Concepts and Terms," and Chapter 3, "Accessing Databases with ADO and ODBC," should offer enough assistance to get you started.

- **Microsoft ActiveX Data Objects**   Accessing any database from a programming language obviously requires some sort of software interface. Microsoft Web servers provide such an interface—ActiveX Data Objects. Opening databases and reading records is a matter of performing the following steps:

  - Instantiating (creating active copies of) the necessary ADO objects

  - Setting their properties

  - Invoking their methods (some would say commands)

  - Receiving the results

  Chapter 3 explains how ADO gets installed on your Web server. Nearly every example in the book will show how to use ADO in one way or another.

- **Structured query language**   Virtually all database systems accept commands from applications in a format called structured query language (SQL). Neither Access—the primary database system covered in this book—nor Microsoft SQL Server are exceptions. ADO accepts SQL commands from the application code and sends them to the database software, which executes them.

  Most Web database pages construct their own SQL statements, often incorporating options or search values received from the Web visitor. Developing database pages thus requires at least a passing knowledge of SQL. Chapter 2 provides an introduction to SQL and shows how Access can write most of your SQL statements for you.

Comprehensive books on all these topics are widely available, but as a group they're too expensive and too intimidating for beginning Web database developers. Beginners need only a small subset of this information, but they need it clearly explained in an integrated, cohesive way. In short, they need a cookbook.

Web Database Development Step by Step is that cookbook. Using simple yet practical examples, the book shows how to take a database you've designed in Access, copy it to a Web server, and write Web pages for query and update. The emphasis here is on learning by example—not on long, monotonous text.

Creating a Simple Web Database Display

Speaking of examples, let's try one now. If you're at all like most readers, you'll agree that nothing is better than a concrete, working example for grasping the key concepts of an unfamiliar technology. The example will read the

Access database shown in Figure 1-1 and produce the Web page shown in Figure 1-2. Creating this example involves four fundamental steps:

1. Create a new ASP file.
2. Add code to read the database and write corresponding HTML.
3. Copy the ASP file and the database onto the Web server.
4. Run the page and view the results.

playerid	jersey	fname	sname	position	birthday	height	weight	birthcity	birthstate
adamlem	12	Mike	Adamle	RW	9/21/85	73	197	Stamford	CT
adamles	17	Scott	Adamle	D	3/1/99	70	184	Columbus	OH
armanova	31	Arkady	Armanov	LW	10/25/98	71	197	Minsk	RU
boolea	8	Alexi	Boole	RW	9/14/97	72	194	Kiev	UK
choakd	11	Dominick	Choak	RW	2/22/97	72	196	Prague	CZ
clobberk	24	Kilroy	Clobber	D	6/21/86	73	200	Bangor	ME
clubbes	7	Sam	Clubbe	LW	7/26/99	75	190	Paramus	NJ
finleyp	14	Peter	Finley	D	6/8/87	76	194	Denver	CO
fiskj	25	Jerke	Fisk	D	11/25/85	71	193	Helsinki	FI
gruberh	29	Hans	Gruber	D	2/11/91	70	175	Munich	DE
grunwala	6	Allan	Grunwald	C	10/17/90	74	189	Buffalo	NY
ivanow	4	Valerei	Ivanovich	C	9/20/79	72	175	Moscow	RU
jeffriea	30	Angus	Jeffries	G	11/8/95	70	185	Springfield	MA
jonesr	35	Robert	Jones	C	5/22/97	73	189	Hartford	CT
lexourb	9	Bruce	Lexour	D	9/5/88	75	198	Quincy	IL
lunds	93	Steven	Lund	D	5/22/97	71	193	St. Paul	MN

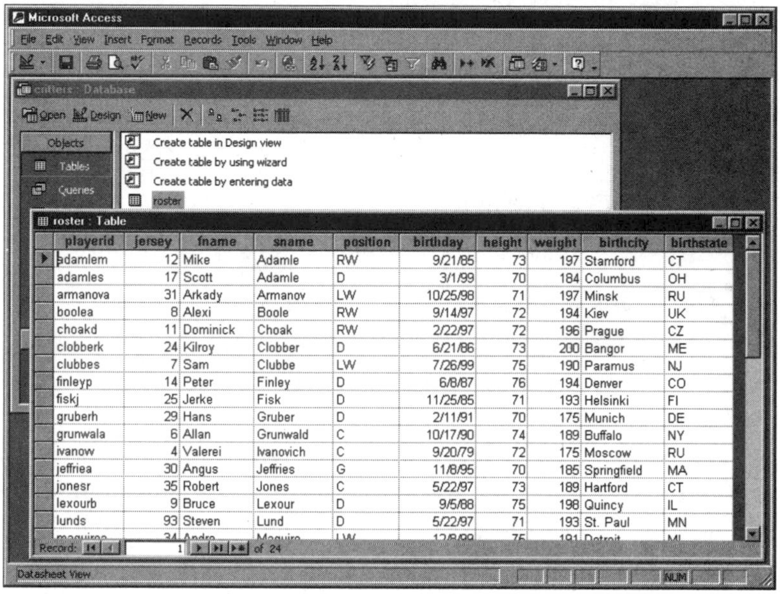

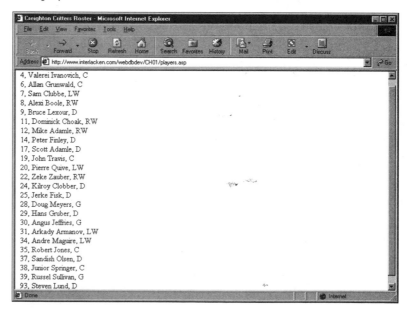

Figure 1-1 *The roster table in this database contains a list of hockey players to display.*

Figure 1-2 *Here's how the hockey roster should appear on the Web. For this introductory example, simplicity is more important than elaborate formatting.*

Create a new ASP file

Creating a Web database page begins the same as creating any other type of Web page. This process should already be familiar to you, but in any case here it is.

1. Start your favorite HTML editor. This can be a simple text editor, such as Notepad, a WYSIWYG editor such as Microsoft FrontPage or Microsoft Visual InterDev, or anything in-between.

2. If you choose a WYSIWYG editor, switch it to a view that shows the HTML code.

> **Tip** If you prefer not to type the code for this example, you can copy it from this book's companion CD-ROM. The location is *d*:\webdbdev\ch01\players.asp; *d* is your CD-ROM drive letter.

3. Create a new file.

   If the following statements aren't already present, add them. Case doesn't matter.

```
<html>
<head>
</head>
<body>
</body>
</html>
```

For detailed information about Active Server Pages, see Chapter 5, "Customizing Web Content with Server-Side Scripting."

Add code to read the database and write corresponding HTML

This is the good part—the part you bought this book to see. You'll enter the code that extracts the roster from the database and presents it as HTML. Chapter 3 and Chapter 4 ("Accessing Tables and Records with ADO") will more fully explain the ADO technology that's introduced here.

1. Enter the following code between the <body> and </body> tags.

```
<p>
<%
%>
</p>
```

   The first and fourth lines mark the beginning and end of an HTML paragraph. The second and third lines mark a block of VBScript code that will execute on the Web server whenever a Web visitor requests the page.

2. To read the database, you must first open it. Therefore, enter the following code between the <% and %> tags you entered in step 1.

```
openStr = "driver={Microsoft Access Driver (*.mdb)};" & _
          "dbq=" & Server.MapPath("critters.mdb")
Set cn = Server.CreateObject("ADODB.Connection")
cn.Open openStr
```

(continued)

```
' Code to open and read a table will go here.
cn.Close
Set cn = Nothing
```

Note The ampersand (&) operator in Visual Basic joins two strings. The following expressions are equivalent:

```
"a" & "b"
"ab"
```

The underscore (_) operator continues a line. That is, it tells Visual Basic to ignore the next end-of-line following the underscore.

The first two lines define the *connection string* for opening the database. The *driver=* portion specifies that this is an Access database; the *dbq=* portion specifies its file location. These are the two pieces of information ADO needs to open the database.

The expression *Server.MapPath("critters.mdb")* in the second line warrants a bit of explanation. Any filename you specify in the *dbq=* portion of a connection string must be a local, fully qualified filename such as F:\InetPub\wwwroot\webdbdev\ch01\cri9tters.mdb. This presents a problem because in most cases you don't know where in the Web server's file system your Web site begins. You do, however, know the URL of every file in your site, and this is where the *Server.MapPath* method comes in. *Server.MapPath* converts a relative URL to a local, fully qualified file location.

The third line tells the server to create an ADODB Connection object, and to store a reference to it in the variable *cn*. *ADODB* stands for ADO database. An ADODB Connection object manages the connection to an open database.

The fourth line tells the Connection object created in the previous line to open the database you specified in the first two lines. This line invokes the *cn* object's *Open* method and specifies the connection string from the first two lines as an argument.

The fourth and fifth lines, respectively, close the database connection and destroy the database Connection object. It's always best to be tidy and clean up any objects you use.

3. With the database open, it's now possible to issue a query and retrieve some records. To accomplish this, enter the following code between the *cn.Open* and *cn.Close* statements you entered in step 2.

```
sql = "SELECT jersey, fname, sname, position " & _
      "FROM roster " & _
      "ORDER BY jersey; "
Set rs = Server.CreateObject("ADODB.Recordset")
rs.Open sql, cn, 3, 3
' Code to read through the table will go here.
rs.Close
set rs = Nothing
```

The first three lines define a SQL statement that retrieves the necessary records and fields in the desired sequence.

The fourth line creates an ADODB Recordset object and stores a reference to it in the variable named *rs*. An ADODB Recordset object provides access to the results of a query—that is, to the set of records that the query retrieved.

The fifth line opens the recordset by using, naturally enough, the *Open* method of the *rs* Recordset object just created. It accepts as parameters the SQL statement created in the first three lines, the database connection established in step 2, and two parameters discussed in Chapter 4, *CursorType* and *LockType*. For now, set these values to 3.

Step 4 will supply the code for reading the recordset, but for now you should again be tidy by closing the recordset and destroying the Recordset object. If you delay coding these kinds of tasks, you'll find yourself forgetting them.

4. To read through the records retrieved in step 3, enter the following code between the *rs.Open* and *rs.Close* statements:

```
On Error Resume Next
rs.MoveFirst
Do While Not rs.EOF
'   Code to process each record will go here.
    rs.MoveNext
Loop
```

The first statements tells the server to keep running the code even if something goes wrong. Up until now, if something doesn't work, ADO will send the Web visitor an error message and the server will stop running the script. The statement *On Error Resume Next* tells the server that if something goes wrong with one statement, it should simply continue with the next.

The second line positions the recordset in *rs* to the first record. Having just been opened, the recordset should be at this position anyway; nevertheless, it's best to be sure.

The third and sixth lines mark the beginning and end of a loop that keeps running until it reads past the end of the *rs* recordset. Reading past the end of any recordset sets its *EOF* property to *True*.

The fifth line is the statement that advances from one record in the *rs* recordset to the next. It does this, naturally enough, using the *rs* recordset object's *MoveNext* method.

5. The only piece of code left to write is the code that writes the database values into HTML for transmission to the Web visitor. Here it is—you should put it just before the *rs.MoveNext* statement.

```
Response.Write Server.HTMLEncode(_
    rs.Fields("jersey") & ", " & _
    rs.Fields("fname") & " " & _
```

(continued)

```
        rs.Fields("sname") & ", " & _
    rs.Fields("position")) & "<br>" & vbCrLf
```

It's best to consider this code from the inside out. First, the four expressions like *rs.Fields("jersey")* each retrieve data values from the current record in the *rs* recordset. The names within parentheses specify which database fields to retrieve from that (current) record.

Server.HTMLEncode is a method that inspects text strings, locates any characters reserved by HTML, and replaces them with symbolic equivalents. That is, it replaces any less than (<) characters with *<*, any greater than (>) characters with *>*, and so on. This ensures that if any database values contain reserved HTML characters, the browser will simply display them and not interpret them as HTML.

The *Response.Write* method writes any supplied argument string into the Web page delivered to the Web visitor. The string appears in place of the <% and %> range that contains *Response.Write* statement. Neither the <% and %> tags nor the code between them goes out to the Web visitor.

The *
* literal and the *vbCrLf* built-in constant provide an HTML line break and an ASCII end-of-line, respectively, after each hockey player's displayed information.

Here's the completed Web page, including the code from the five steps shown earlier. Now that you understand each piece, the page should make sense when assembled.

```
<html>
<head>
</head>
<body>
<p>
<%
openStr = "driver={Microsoft Access Driver (*.mdb)};" & _
          "dbq=" & Server.MapPath("critters.mdb")
Set cn = Server.CreateObject("ADODB.Connection")
cn.Open openStr

sql = "SELECT jersey, fname, sname, position " & _
      "FROM roster " & _
      "ORDER BY jersey; "
Set rs = Server.CreateObject("ADODB.Recordset")
rs.Open sql, cn, 3, 3

On Error Resume Next
rs.MoveFirst
Do While Not rs.EOF
   Response.Write Server.HTMLEncode(_
       rs.Fields("jersey") & ", " & _
       rs.Fields("fname") & " " & _
```

```
        rs.Fields("sname") & ", " & _
        rs.Fields("position")) & "<br>" & vbCrLf
    rs.MoveNext
Loop

rs.Close
Set rs = Nothing

cn.Close
Set cn = Nothing
%>
</p>
</body>
</html>
```

If you're satisfied that you entered the page correctly, save it as players.asp. Note that the file name extension is .asp. If you save the file with a .htm file name extension, the server won't recognize or execute the VBScript code.

Copy the Web page and the database onto the Web server

To see the database Web page in action, you must copy both the players.asp file and the critters.mdb database to a properly configured location on your Web server. You can find details about setting up your Web server in Chapter 6, "Organizing Your Web Environment."

There are two requirements for proper configuration:

- The Web server software must be one of those listed in Table 1-1. Other servers lack the software to process the VBScript code, the software to process the Access database, or both.

- The Web server folder where you put the players.asp file must be flagged as *executable*. This is something the server's administrator must do.

Note   You can find a copy of the critters.mdb database on the companion CD-ROM. Its location is *d*:\webdbdev\ch01\critters.mdb; *d* is your CD-ROM drive letter.

Caution   When you copy files from a CD-ROM to your hard disk via Windows Explorer, Explorer marks the resulting file as read-only. This is unacceptable for Access databases. To turn off the read-only attribute, right-click the file, choose Properties from the pop-up menu, uncheck the Read-Only box, and then click OK. If you use the installer on the CD, you don't need to worry about this because the read-only attribute will be set to False automatically.

As long as you upload players.asp and critters.mdb to an executable location on a supported Web server, the upload method doesn't matter. You can keep doing whatever you've been doing to upload ordinary Web pages.

Table 1-1   Web Servers that Support Active Server Pages

Operating System	Web Server
Windows 95 or Windows 98	Microsoft Personal Web Server 4 or later
Windows NT Workstation 4	Microsoft Personal Web Server 4 or later
Windows NT Server 4	Internet Information Server 4 or later
Windows 2000 Professional, Server, and Advanced Server	Internet Information Services

Note   For Active Server Pages to work, the Web server has to be properly configured. If someone else administers your Web server—perhaps someone at your Internet Service Provider or someone in your organization's Information Technology department— you'll need to know what to ask for. If you administer your own Web server—anything from a full-blown production server to a test server running on your own PC—you'll need to know which settings to configure. Chapter 5 provides guidance in this area.

Run the page and view the results

Once you've uploaded your page, you can test it simply by typing its URL into your browser. If all goes well, you'll get the results shown in Figure 1-1.

Three results you shouldn't get are

- A Web page displaying your VBScript code

- A Web page containing no database information

- A prompt asking if you'd like to download the page

These errors are usually the result of your Web server not executing an ASP page as a program, but instead delivering it like an ordinary Web page. If this happens to you, either move the players.asp and critters.mdb files to an executable folder or ask the server administrator to mark the existing folder as executable.

You'll also get incorrect results by using your browser to open the players.asp file directly from disk. The scripts in an ASP page need to be processed and executed by a Web server; it's the result of that execution that you finally see in the Web browser.

Figure 1-3 shows typical results from a typing error in the VBScript code. There are far too many error messages to describe in a book this size, but in most cases the message will supply a line number or an object name to identify the location of the error.

If you get an error message involving an invalid or unknown database format, there's probably a mismatch between the version of Access that created the database and the version of the Access drivers on the Web server. Such mismatches have two possible solutions. First, you can convert your database to the correct version. Second, the server administrator can upgrade or backlevel the Access drivers on the Web server.

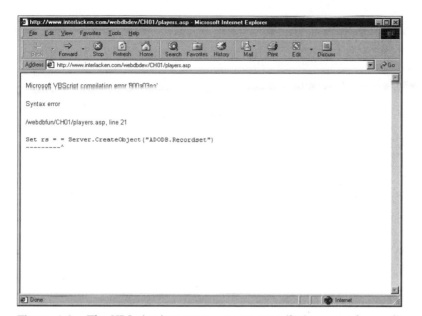

Figure 1-3 *The VBScript interpreter reports compilation errors by sending an error page to the Web visitor.*

Once you get correct output, it's interesting to use your browser's View Source command and look at the HTML received. As shown in Figure 1-4, the browser receives not the ASP code, but ordinary HTML. The Web server executes the ASP code before transmitting the Web page to the Web visitor. Therefore, instead of receiving the ASP code, the browser receives any HTML the ASP code generates.

```
players[1] - Notepad
File  Edit  Search  Help
<html>
<head>
<title>Creighton Critters Roster</title>
</head>
<body>
<p>
4, Valerei Ivanovich, C<br>
6, Allan Grunwald, C<br>
7, Sam Clubbe, LW<br>
8, Alexi Boole, RW<br>
9, Bruce Lexour, D<br>
11, Dominick Choak, RW<br>
12, Mike Adamle, RW<br>
14, Peter Finley, D<br>
17, Scott Adamle, D<br>
19, John Travis, C<br>
20, Pierre Quive, LW<br>
22, Zeke Zauber, RW<br>
24, Kilroy Clobber, D<br>
25, Jerke Fisk, D<br>
28, Doug Meyers, G<br>
29, Hans Gruber, D<br>
30, Angus Jeffries, G<br>
31, Arkady Armanov, LW<br>
34, Andre Maguire, LW<br>
35, Robert Jones, C<br>
37, Sandish Olsen, D<br>
38, Junior Springer, C<br>
39, Russel Sullivan, G<br>
93, Steven Lund, D<br>
</p>
</body>
</html>
```

Figure 1-4 *After requesting an ASP page, the browser receives no ASP code. It only receives the HTML produced by executing the ASP page on the server.*

What's Next?

This chapter obviously skipped over a great many details in introducing the players.asp example. You might be wondering, for example:

- What if my Web server isn't one of those listed in Table 1-1?

- How do I test ASP pages on my own PC?

- How do I create the database and organize the tables within it?

- Querying records is fine, but how do I insert, update, and delete records?

- How can I query and update databases by using HTML forms?

- Can I watch my ASP code as it runs, pause the execution, and inspect data values?

- What's XML, the Extensible Markup Language, and how does it apply to Web databases?

Well, you're in luck—the rest of the book is specifically designed to answer these questions and many more.

Chapter Summary

This chapter introduced the concept of Web database pages, itemized the basic technologies involved, and described the general level of knowledge you'll need to benefit from this book. It also presented a simple Web database example.

The next part of the book—Part 2, "Key Concepts"—consists of five chapters full of background material. Depending on your background, you can study them judiciously, skim them for good parts, or ignore them for now and come back as needed. Part 3, "Developing Applications," will get back to coding complete Web pages.

Part 2

Key Concepts

This section of the book explains the nature of databases, how to design databases, how to implement databases in Microsoft Access, how to code Web pages that access these databases, and how to configure Web servers so that those Web pages can run. In short, it provides all the background information you'll need to understand and emulate the practical examples that comprise the rest of this book.

Like all background material, and despite your author's best efforts, this information might at times seem a bit abstract or even downright boring. Don't let this slow you down too much. If you do get bogged down, you can always skip ahead to Part 3 and return to this section when the mood or the need strikes you.

Chapter 2

Understanding Database Concepts and Terms

Estimated Time: 60 minutes

In this chapter, you'll learn

- The basic concepts of a relational database.

- How to design a database—that is, how to properly arrange the fields in an application into appropriate tables.

- How to give a database physical reality by defining it in Microsoft Access.

- About structured query language (SQL), the language most often used for manipulating information in databases.

Databases exist to serve the needs of *applications*. An application, in turn, is a unit of software that exists to serve the needs of some *activity*: a business system, a game, a public service, an advertisement, or almost any real-world process you can imagine. In a perfect world, the needs of the activity determine the requirements of the application, and the needs of the application determine the requirements of the database. The applications in this book are Web pages that distribute or collect data to or from visitors on the World Wide Web.

The job of a database designer is first to implement all requirements derived from the application, and second to avoid placing reverse requirements (that is, restrictions) on the application or the activity.

The basic idea of a database is to store data in an organized way. This has two benefits. First, the data is readily available for a variety of uses throughout your organization. Second, because the database has a known structure, the system that stores it can provide powerful tools for extending its use. If you've never used databases before, you might be surprised at how quickly these simple ideas can become complicated.

Almost all the examples in this book use Microsoft Access 2000 databases. Access 2000 isn't the most powerful, the fastest, or the most flexible database in the world, but it could easily be the most available. Millions of copies have been sold with the various versions of Microsoft Office. In addition, Access 2000 doesn't require expensive licenses per user or per server.

If your application requires high reliability or high transaction volumes, you'll want to consider an industrial-strength solution such as Microsoft SQL Server. Even then, migrating from Access to SQL Server is a fairly straightforward process if you're suitably prepared.

The Nature of Relational Databases

Although databases physically consist of computer files, applications that use databases don't manipulate these files directly. Instead, applications send commands to and receive responses from a *database management system* (DBMS). SQL Server and Access are examples of database management systems. A DBMS relieves the programmer of many tedious and intricate tasks involved in processing the database and guards against the introduction of invalid data.

Nearly all modern databases conform to the so-called *relational model*. This is what makes them *relational databases*.

The basic unit of organization in any relational database is the *table*. The columns in a table represent *fields*, and the rows are *records*. Table 2-1 illustrates a simple table representing the members of an Internet-based coin-collecting club.

Table 2-1   *members* **Table**

memberid	fname	sname	position	phone	email
buchanan	Steven	Buchanan	M	206-555-1189	steven@sselhtrow-23.net
davolio	Nancy	Davolio	M	206-555-9857	nancy@gnihton-55.gov
fuller	Andrew	Fuller	P	206-555-9482	andrew@hcliz-07.net
lever	Janet	Leverling	V	206-555-3412	janet@ytpme-33.com
peacock	Margaret	Peacock	S	206-555-8122	margaret@sselesu-62.net

In this table, the first field in each record contains the same kind of data: a member identification code called *memberid*. The second field of every record contains the member's first name; the third field always contains the member's surname, and so on. There's nothing special about the order of the fields; you could rearrange fields, add fields, or delete fields without affecting the functionality of the table in any way. However, within the same table, you can't make *memberid* the first field in one record and the second field of another, nor can you make one record contain a field (for example, spouse's license plate number) that another record doesn't.

All relational DBMS's must provide the following three functions for accessing data:

When used as database commands, the words select, project, and join are all verbs. Therefore, pronounce project like the first two syllables in projector and not like the word project in Microsoft Project.

- **Select**   Presents a view of a table showing only those records having specified values in specified fields. In English, the following command would request a select operation: "Please retrieve all records from the *members* table where *position* is M."

- **Project**   Presents a view of a table that doesn't include all its fields. A project command might be: "Please retrieve only the *fname* and *sname* fields from the *members* table."

- **Join**   Presents a combined view of two tables as if they were one table. The result is like a temporary table that the DBMS builds by matching record values in one table to record values in another and then combining fields from both matching records.

To show an example of a join requires a second table, such as Table 2-2—the *forsale* table. This table contains a list of coins offered for sale by members. Notice that the *members* table shown previously and the *forsale* table shown here both contain a *memberid* field. You could therefore tell the DBMS to: "Match the *forsale* table and the *members* table based on *memberid*, and show me a view that includes *forsale.country*, *forsale.coiname*, *forsale.year*, *forsale.qty*, *forsale.price*, *members.memberid*, and *members.email.*"

Note   The notation *members.memberid* means, "The *memberid* field from the *members* table." This is a common notation when working with tables and fields—one you should learn quickly.

Table 2-2   *forsale* Table

country	coiname	year	qty	memberid	price
USA	20 GOLD	1890	2	fuller	$100.00
USA	NICKEL	1999	100	peacock	$0.06
USA	PENNY	1850	1	lever	$1.05
USA	PENNY	1850	4	fuller	$1.00
USA	PENNY	1850	5	davolio	$0.95

Table 2-3 shows the results of this join operation. Notice that the results consist of multiple records called a *result set*. Some of the fields come from the *forsale* table and some from the *members* table, but the records in each case contain equal values in the *memberid* field.

The result of a join is always called a result set, *even if it's empty or contains a single record.*

Table 2-3   *itemsforsale* Query

forsale. country	forsale. coiname	forsale. year	forsale. qty	forsale. price	members. memberid	members. email
USA	20 GOLD	1890	2	$100.00	fuller	andrew@hcliz-07.net
USA	NICKEL	1999	100	$0.06	peacock	margaret@sselesu-62.net
USA	PENNY	1850	5	$0.95	davolio	nancy@gnihton-55.gov
USA	PENNY	1850	4	$1.00	fuller	andrew@hcliz-07.net
USA	PENNY	1850	1	$1.05	lever	janet@ytpme-33.com

If you have sharp eyes, you might have noticed that these join results don't show all the fields from both tables. This is because the query didn't ask for all the fields, even though it could have. In fact, this query joins two tables and projects the results. This is perfectly acceptable; in fact, you can combine select, project, and join operations at will.

Designing a Database

A single relational database can contain any number of tables. This raises questions of how many tables a database should have and what fields belong in what tables. Such decisions are the basis of database design. A good design makes the database easy to work with and provides flexibility to support future requirements. A poor design gets in the way of select, project, and join operations, making the database inflexible and hard to work with.

Like so many things in life, database design is part art and part science. This means you can approach database design informally, armed with experience and rules of thumb, or formally, applying rigorous scientific methods. The informal approach will be first.

Informal Database Design

The approach detailed in the following steps—each described in a separate section—will generally produce a fairly workable database design. This is the approach most database designers use for real work. The formal approach described later serves more often to check and validate an informal design than to generate a design from scratch.

Identify the major entities in the application

Every application involves a number of entities whose properties and relationships are fundamental to the application. Here are some examples:

- **Class Scheduling System** Teachers, Students, Classrooms, Curriculums, and Class Sessions

- **Airline Ticket System** Customers, Crew Members, Flights, Airplanes, Seats, Airports, Gates

- **Sports League** Players, Teams, Venues, Scheduled Games, Player Game Statistics, Coaches, Referees

- **Order Entry System** Customers, Orders, Order Line Items, Bills of Lading, Bill of Lading Line Items, Customer Invoices, Customer Invoice Line Items, Stocked Items, Warehouses, Warehouse Bins, Suppliers, Purchase Orders, Purchase Order Line Items, Receiving Tickets, Receiving Ticket Line Items, Supplier Invoices, Supplier Invoice Line Items

Note that at this point in the process, you should only be interested in the application's high-level objects . Some thinking ahead is smart, but for the most part you should delay worrying about the attributes of each entity for now.

Create a table for each major entity

The next step is to initialize a table for each major entity in your application. You can do this on paper, in any sort of electronic document, or in a DBMS such as Access or SQL Server—it really doesn't matter at this point. Give each table a succinct name that's easy to remember and easy to spell. For example, if you create a table to define and describe salable products, you might name it *products*.

Choose a key for each major entity

Now, for each table you've defined, define one or more fields that will uniquely identify each record in the table. This will be the table's *primary key*. A primary key can never be blank, and every record in the table must have a different primary key. Putting this another way, requesting a record by means of its primary key should return one and only one record.

The computer doesn't care what you use for a key, but human beings do. Therefore, it's best to identify entities with *natural keys* wherever possible. A natural key is one that already identifies the entity to human beings or other applications. For example, it probably makes sense to identify each book in a *books* table by its International Standard Book Number (ISBN) rather than by some new code you invent.

On the other hand, some natural keys make very poor database keys. Keys that are long, that are case-sensitive, or that contain spaces or punctuation generally make poor database keys. If the natural key has one or more of these defects, you should probably create a new key of your own. A system that manages medical clinics, for example, shouldn't identify clinics by means of clinic names such as, "Central Barnesville Clinic," "First Avenue Clinic," and "North Ellerby Medical Center." Getting the application's user to correctly spell such keys will be a never-ending battle. Instead, assign clinic codes such as 1, 2, and 3.

Add entity attributes to each major entity table

To begin this step, think about the information your application needs to know about each major entity you've defined (that is, for each table). A *customer* table would probably have a *customer number* field, of course, but it would also have fields such as *name*, *street address*, *city*, *state*, *country*, *postal code*, *e-mail address*, *phone number*, *fax number*, and so on.

It's not critical at this point to identify every single field your application needs, but the sooner you identify a field, the easier adding it to your database design will be. If the application involves printed forms of any kind, you can probably discover what fields you need by looking at those forms. In fact, any sort of sample document serves the same purpose.

You should expect that every application will have a different combination of tables—and different fields within each table. There's no such thing as a single, universal database design suitable for all applications.

Create additional tables for repeating attributes

While you add the entity attributes, you'll probably discover some attributes that occur more than once for each primary key. In the coin club system, for example, you might consider recording committee membership by adding a *committee* field to the *members* table. Then, you might discover that some members belong to more than one committee. In a training class system, some instructors might have more than one assigned class. In a classified ad system, some advertisers might have more than one ad.

One solution, although a poor one, is to define a series of fields such as *committee1*, *committee2*, and *committee3* in the *members* table. However, this approach has three problems. First, on some records in the *members* table, one or more of these fields might be blank. Blank fields are usually a clue that something isn't organized correctly. Second, having multiple committee fields in the same record makes it hard to select, project, and join based on committee. Which of the three committee fields should you use, and what about the data still contained in the others? Third, what if some member decides to join four committees? The database can't accommodate more than three.

A better solution is to create a committee membership table containing one record for each member on each committee. Such a table would probably have a primary key consisting of two fields: a *committeeid* and a *memberid*. This design is flexible because it supports the concept of one member belonging to zero to many committees, and also the concept of one committee having zero to many members. If any additional data pertains to the assignment of a particular member to a particular committee—such as date joined—the same record can easily accommodate it.

Make sure each field is truly an attribute of the primary key

To complete this phase of the design, you should review each field in each table and verify that the table's primary key provides reasonable lookup for that field. To see how this works, first suppose you've tentatively designed a committee membership table with the following fields. Then play the old game: which of these objects doesn't belong?

- Committee ID (first field of primary key)
- Member ID (second field of primary key)
- Date Joined
- Committee Name

If you guessed that *Committee Name* is the object that doesn't belong, you're right. The *Committee Name* field isn't a property of a committee membership, it's a property of the committee and therefore belongs in a *committees* table (whose primary key would be only a *committeeid* field).

Here's another way of looking at this. Finding a committee name shouldn't require supplying both a *committeeid* and one of its *memberid* values; supplying a *committeeid* value alone should be sufficient. Therefore, *Committee Name* doesn't belong in a table whose primary key is both *committeeid* and *memberid*.

What if you needed to know the committee names for a given committee member? You'd join the *committee members* and *committees* tables based on *committeeid*.

Review the relationships among the tables

As a final step, review all the tables in your proposed database, identify those that have real-world relationships, and make sure you've provided a way to join them. In essence, this means verifying that any tables you'll need to join have fields in common that you can use as keys.

Note that the keys in a join needn't have exactly the same names. In theory you can join tables based on any fields you want. In practice, however, joins are almost always between like fields: *employeeid* in one table to *employeeid* in another, for example. It just doesn't make sense to join two tables based on part numbers from one table equaling street addresses in another.

Tip If two fields in different tables have the same meaning, it's good practice to give them the same name. Calling the same field *employeeid* in one table and *employeenum* in another only creates confusion, even though the database itself will still work.

This is a good time to think about code tables. If you've created or used any code values in your database design, it's often valuable to have a table relating code values to code descriptions. Among other things, you can use such tables in joins to display meaningful descriptions rather than obscure codes, and in HTML forms to populate drop-down list boxes. In the coin club example, it would probably make sense to create code tables for at least the *committeeid* and *position* fields.

The section "Implementing a Database Design in Access 2000," later in this chapter, will explain how to make your database design a physical reality. In the meantime, you might be interested in reviewing the formal rules behind the informal approach.

Formal Database Design

A true relational database is one that follows the so-called *relational model* first articulated by E. F. Codd, a research fellow at IBM. The relational model describes databases, tables, records, fields, and operators like select, project, and join in a formal, mathematical way. One of the relational model's great strengths is that it's *mathematically complete*—a term that in common English means it contains no inconsistencies or missing links. The result is a database model with unprecedented applicability to an extremely wide range of problems.

In relational technology, the process of organizing fields into tables is called *normalization* because with each step, the design approaches the relational standard (that is, the relational norm) more closely. Experts have proposed many degrees of normalization, but everyone seems to agree on the first five:

- **First normal form**   A given field in a given record can only contain one value. This prohibits any sort of repeating group within a single record. To implement repeating groups properly, design a table with repeating records.

    In the preceding section, creating *committee1*, *committee2*, and *committee3* fields would have violated first normal form. Creating a separate committee members table satisfies this form.

- **Second normal form**   Every nonkey field must depend on all the fields in the primary key. Recall, for example, the committee membership table whose primary key consisted of two keys: *committee id* and *memberid*. For this table to contain a *committee name* field would violate second normal form because *committee name* depends on only one of the two keys: *committeeid*. The solution is generally to move the offending field to a more appropriate table.

This form also specifies that two or more tables can't have the same primary key. If your design has two or more tables with the same primary key, you should combine those tables into one.

- **Third normal form**   No nonkey field depends on another nonkey field. Recall that the *members* table contains a *position* field. This contains P for president, V for vice president, S for secretary, or M for member. Third normal form maintains that you shouldn't put a *position description* field in the *members* table because *position description* depends not on *memberid*, the table's primary key, but on another nonkey field: namely *position*!

  As with second normal form, achieving third normal form requires moving any noncompliant fields to a more appropriate table.

- **Fourth normal form**   This form prohibits multiple, independent, one-to-many relationships between primary key fields and nonkey fields. To understand this form, recall that the database needs to keep track of multiple coins for sale by a given member, and also multiple committees for the same member. Occurrences of coins for sale and occurrences of committees have nothing to do with each other—they're independent—and so you shouldn't try to accommodate both repeating groups in the same table. To achieve fourth normal form, you need to create a separate table for each independent one-to-many relationship.

- **Fifth normal form**   This form is very extreme and frequently ignored. It requires breaking a table into the smallest possible pieces to eliminate all redundancy. For example, suppose the coin club has a catalog of convention posters and all posters cost either $10, $15, or $20. This means the *posters* table will have dozens, hundreds, or thousands of records containing one of these three values. Fifth normal form says you should create a price table keyed by some code—perhaps a high, medium, low code—and then put the price code, rather than the actual price, in the catalog table.

As you might have noticed, the normal forms are more like auditing rules than procedures. In theory, you could start with any random assortment of fields, repeatedly apply the normalization rules, and end up with a logically correct design. In practice, this is extremely tedious and boring.

Achieving normal form is generally a matter of breaking large tables into multiple smaller ones until all data in each table is clearly and uniquely associated with other data in the same table. This makes the data easier to maintain and the application easier to code. You can always use the join operation to reassemble tables you've split apart in the pursuit of normalization.

After they've designed and normalized a number of databases, most developers acquire a certain mindset and no longer subject each table to a sequential normalization process. When the need to accommodate another field develops, they automatically put it in the right table or, if required, create a new table. Such is the nature of experience.

Implementing a Database Design in Access 2000

Once you've designed your database, you'll naturally want to enter its structure into your DBMS and populate it with some data. To provide an example, you'll define an Access 2000 database that contains the *members* and *forsale* tables shown earlier in this chapter.

Create a blank database

Access databases consist of a single file with an .mdb filename extension. No matter how many tables, queries, forms, reports, macros, and modules you create, they all reside within that one file. Therefore, the first step in any Access project is to initialize a blank database. Here's the procedure:

1. Start your copy of Access 2000.

2. When the opening screen appears, select the Blank Access Database option and click OK. Figure 2-1 illustrates this action.

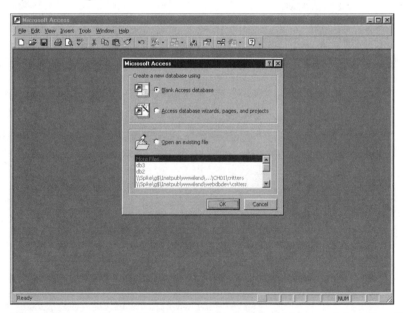

Figure 2-1 *Creating a blank Access database provides a container for all tables, queries, and other objects in an application.*

3. Once you click the OK button in Figure 2-1, Access will prompt you for a filename as shown in Figure 2-2. For this example, name the database coinclub.mdb, select a convenient folder, and click the Create button.

Figure 2-2 *This dialog box prompts you for the filename and folder location of a new Access database.*

Create a new table

Access 2000 provides three ways to create a new table. Each way provides a different degree of automation, but they all produce essentially the same results.

- **Create Table In Design View** This approach displays a grid listing all the fields in a table. Initially, of course, the grid is empty. To add a field, first type its name into any blank line and then set its properties.

- **Create Table By Using Wizard** This approach starts by presenting a list of commonly used tables and associated fields. From this list, select the fields you want in your new table. Access then creates the table, asks about any relationships with other tables, and offers to open the table for data entry.

- **Create Table By Entering Data** This option opens an unnamed table in a view that resembles a spreadsheet. If you already have some data prepared, you can use the File menu to import it or the Edit menu to paste it. When you close the unnamed table, Access will examine the data in each field and do its best to determine appropriate field properties. Access will also prompt you for a meaningful table name.

Among these three options, Design View provides the least automation but the most control over results. Design View is also the best way to add, modify, or delete fields in existing tables. This example therefore uses Design View.

1. Locate the Database window in Access, and double-click Create Table In Design View.

2. When the Table window shown in Figure 2-3 appears, click the first cell under Field Name and enter the field name *memberid*.

If you'd rather look at the completed coinclub.mdb database than build it, open the sample file ch02\ coinclub.mdb.

Tip When you create your own fields, avoid field names that are overly long or contain spaces, punctuation, or mixed case.

Tip It's good practice to make key fields the first fields in a database record, placing the most significant fields first. When arranging nonkey fields, put the most-used fields closer to the top and keep related fields (such as *city, state*, and *zip code*) together.

---

3. Click the drop-down list button just right of the field name you just entered and select the most appropriate data type. For the *memberid* field, choose Text. For key fields, select only Text, Number, Date/Time, or AutoNumber.

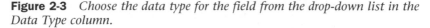

Figure 2-3 *Choose the data type for the field from the drop-down list in the Data Type column.*

4. Review the property settings in the lower half of the Table window, particularly the following. Some of these properties don't occur for certain field types.

- ***Field Size*** This property controls the maximum size content the field can contain. For text, this is a maximum number of characters. For numbers, it refers to the internal storage format: *Byte* means 8 bits, *Integer* means 16 bits, *Long Integer* means 32 bits, *Single* and *Double* mean floating point, and so on.

   For numeric data types, there will also be a *Decimal Places* property that controls the number of digits stored at the right of the decimal.

- **Default Value**   If you enter a value here and an application later tries to create a record without supplying a data value, Access will assign this value.

- **Allow Zero Length**   If you set this property to No and an application later tries to create a record with the field left blank, Access will refuse to save the record and return an error code.

- **Required**   Many database systems, including Access, differentiate between fields that have empty values (such as zero or a null string) and fields that have no value at all. If a field's *Required* property is Yes, Access will reject any records that have no value at all in the given field.

5. For each remaining field in the table, enter the name in the first available cell in the *Field Name* column, and then select the type and properties for that field. The remaining field names for the *members* table are *fname*, *sname*, *position*, *phone*, and *email*. The data type for each of these fields is Text.

6. Once you've entered all the field names, select the fields that will form the table's primary key, then select Primary Key from the Edit menu. Figure 2-4 illustrates this operation. To select multiple fields, hold down the Shift or Ctrl key while clicking.

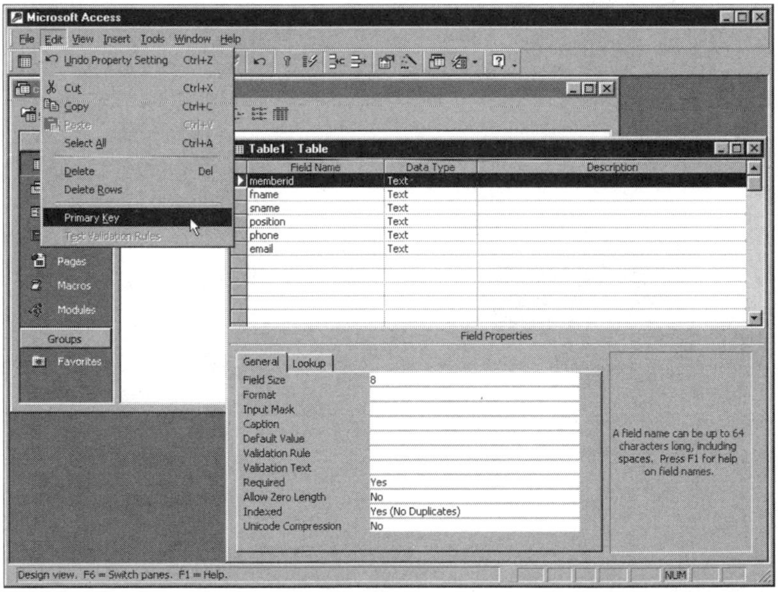

Figure 2-4   *To assign a table's primary key, first select the desired fields and then select Primary Key from the Edit menu.*

7. Save the table by choosing Save from the File menu. Access will prompt you for the table's name. Type **members** and press Enter.

Repeat the steps above, and create a new Access table for the *forsale* table (Table 2-2) in the coinclub.mdb database. The data types for *year* and *qty* should be Number, and the type for *price* should be Currency. The others should be Text. Select all the fields in the table except *price*, and make them primary keys. When you're finished, close the table.

Add data to the new table

Immediately or soon after creating a table, you'll probably want to put some data in it. There are several ways to do this. To add the data from the *members* table (Table 2-1), follow these steps:

1. Select Tables in the Objects bar.

2. Locate the desired table in the resultant listing.

3. Double-click the desired table.

4. Access will display the table in Datasheet view, which makes the table resemble a spreadsheet.

5. To create a new record, enter whatever field values you want in the last line of the grid (that is, the one with an asterisk in the leftmost gray column).

6. To save the new record, either press Enter while the cursor is anywhere within the record or simply move the cursor to another record.

Follow steps 5 and 6 to enter each value for the fields in the *members* table. You can see these values in Table 2-1. When you're finished, your table should look like the one in Figure 2-5. Repeat the process for items in the *forsale* database (Table 2-2).

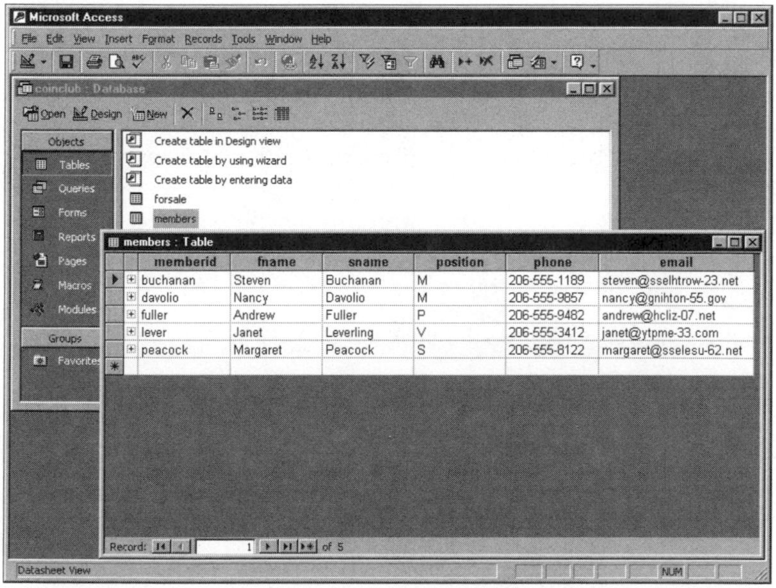

Figure 2-5 *Datasheet view offers a simple, spreadsheet-like interface for entering data values into a table.*

If you're working with data that already exists in another source, you can paste it right into any table you've opened in Datasheet view. To paste data from a spreadsheet, follow these steps:

1. Open the table in Datasheet view.

2. Open the spreadsheet or other source of data.

3. Make sure the fields in the source data and the fields in Access are arranged exactly the same, from left to right. The first column you copy from the source data will appear in the first Access column, the second column from the source data in the second Access column, and so on.

4. Select the source data, and copy it to the Windows clipboard. Typically, this involves dragging the mouse across the data and then choosing Copy from the Edit menu.

5. In Access, make sure the window for the correct table is highlighted, and then choose Paste Append from the Edit menu.

6. If your source data contained any lines or records that Access couldn't add to the database, Access will create a new table called Paste Errors and put the errant records there. If necessary, you can open that table, correct the faulty records, copy them to the clipboard, and then repeat step 5.

Datasheet view is also quite handy for changing and deleting records. To change a record, highlight the data in any field and just start typing. To delete a record, click anywhere within it and then choose Delete Record from the Edit menu.

Document relationships among tables

Most applications require the use of several—perhaps even dozens—of tables. Although not required, it's usually a good idea to document the relationships you intended these tables to have when you designed them. If you like, Access can then enforce these relationships and maintain consistency among your tables.

Just as Figure 2-4 showed the structure of the *members* table introduced as Table 2-1, Figure 2-6 shows the structure of the *forsale* table introduced as Table 2-2. These tables are related through the *memberid* field in two ways:

*   A given *members* record can have zero, one, or many *forsale* records.

*   A given *forsale* record must have exactly one *members* record, identified by an existing *memberid*.

Here's the procedure to tell Access about this relationship:

1. Open the coinclub.mdb database in Microsoft Access.

2. Choose Relationships from the Tools menu.

3. The first time you open Relationships for a database, Access will display the Show Table dialog box shown in Figure 2-7.

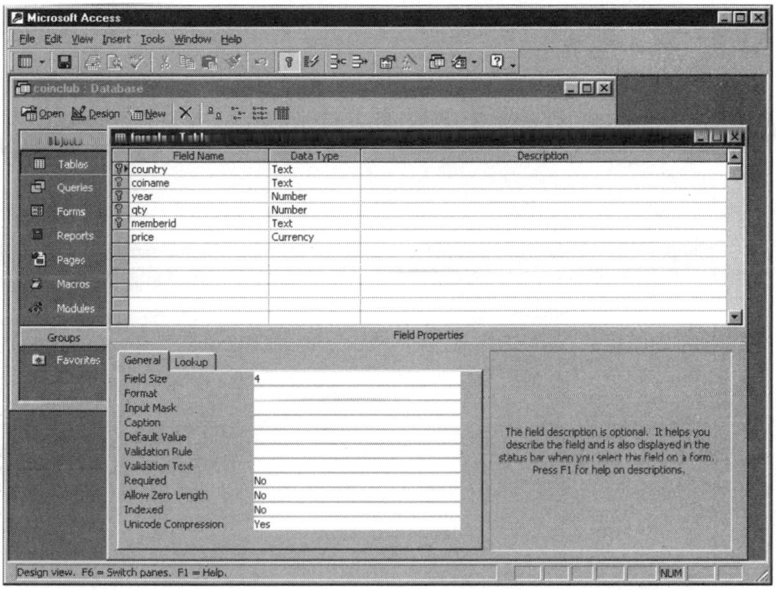

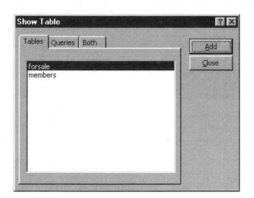

Figure 2-6 *Here's the* forsale *table first shown in Table 2-2, now implemented in Access.*

Note If you've previously opened Relationships for the current database, Access won't display the Show Table dialog box automatically. Instead, it will just show the Relationships window. To display the Show Table dialog box, either right-click the Relationships background area and choose Show Table from the pop-up menu, or choose Show Table from the Relationships menu.

Figure 2-7 *Use the Show Tables dialog box for adding tables to the Relationships window.*

4. Add any tables with relationships you want to document. To do this, either double-click a table name in the Show Table dialog box or select the table and click the Add button. For this example, double-click the *members* table and the *forsale* table.

5. Close the Show Table dialog box.

6. Drag and drop the *memberid* field from the *members* table onto the *memberid* field in the *forsale* table. Access will display the Edit Relationships dialog box, as shown in Figure 2-8. Check the Enforce Referential Integrity check box, and click OK.

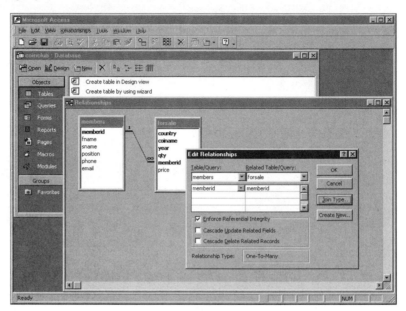

Figure 2-8 *The Relationships section of an Access database documents (and, optionally, enforces) relationships among the tables in the database.*

7. Close the Relationships window.

Access makes use of relationship information in two ways. First, whenever you select two or more tables for making a query, the default relationships will be the ones you defined in the Relationships window.

The second use of Relationships occurs only if you turn on the Referential Integrity option. Doing so tells Access that no records should exist in the table named in the Related Table/Query (right-hand) side of the Edit Relationships dialog box unless a matching record exists in the corresponding table named in the Table/Query (left-hand) side of the Edit Relationships dialog box. If this seems confusing, refer again to Figure 2-8 and consider the following points.

- Turning on the Enforce Referential Integrity box tells Access to reject the addition of any *forsale* record whose *memberid* value isn't present as a *memberid* value in the *members* table.

- Turning on the Cascade Update Related Fields box tells Access that if someone changes the *memberid* field of a *members* record, Access should change the *memberid* field of all matching *forsale* records.

- Turning on the Cascade Delete Related Records box tells Access that if someone deletes a *members* record, Access should automatically delete any *forsale* records having the same *memberid*.

Relationships and their implementation involve complex ideas that might take you some time to appreciate, let alone debug. Suppose, for example, that you established the cascading deletes between the *member* and *forsale* tables. If the club secretary then deleted and recreated a *member* record, deleting the *member* record would automatically delete all that member's *forsale* records. If the secretary then complained about missing *forsale* records, you could stare at the member maintenance code for hours and never suspect it would affect the *forsale* table. Regardless of the type of database, referential integrity, cascading updates, and cascading deletes are famous for their unexpected consequences.

Given all that, you might choose not to deal with Relationships at all. As your experience grows, however, you will find Relationships a more and more valuable tool, and it's good to know Access is ready when you are.

Create a query

Given the frequent mention thus far of the relational operators select, project, and join, you might be wondering how Access makes use of them. The following example joins the *members* table and the *forsale* table based on *members*, projects some of the fields into a grid, and selects all records from the results. Here's the procedure:

1. Start Microsoft Access, and open the coinclub.mdb database.

2. Locate the coinclub Database window, and click the Queries icon in its Objects bar.

3. Locate the Create Query In Design View option, and double-click it. Access will display a Show Table dialog box much like the one shown in Figure 2-7. Double-click each of the tables to add them to the query, and click the Close button.

4. Make sure a relationship is in effect—indicated by a connecting line— between the *memberid* field in the *members* table and the *memberid* field of the *forsale* table. If not, establish one by dragging the *memberid* field from the *members* table and dropping it on the *memberid* field in the *forsale* table.

5. Drag the following fields from the diagram in the top half of the Select Query window to the field grid in the bottom half. Drop them in order from left to right: *forsale.country, forsale.coiname, forsale.year, forsale.qty, forsale.price, forsale.memberid, members.email*.

6. To display the query results in *country* order, click anywhere in the Sort field beneath the *country* field. A drop-down list button will appear. Click the button, and select Ascending from the resulting list. Do that for any other field you want. The Select Query window should now resemble that shown in Figure 2-9. Save the query as *itemsforsale*. Once you've saved a query, opening it at any time reruns the query using current data. In addition, you can use saved queries as if they were tables when you create other queries.

7. To run the query and view the results, select Datasheet View from the View menu. You should get the results shown in Figure 2-10.

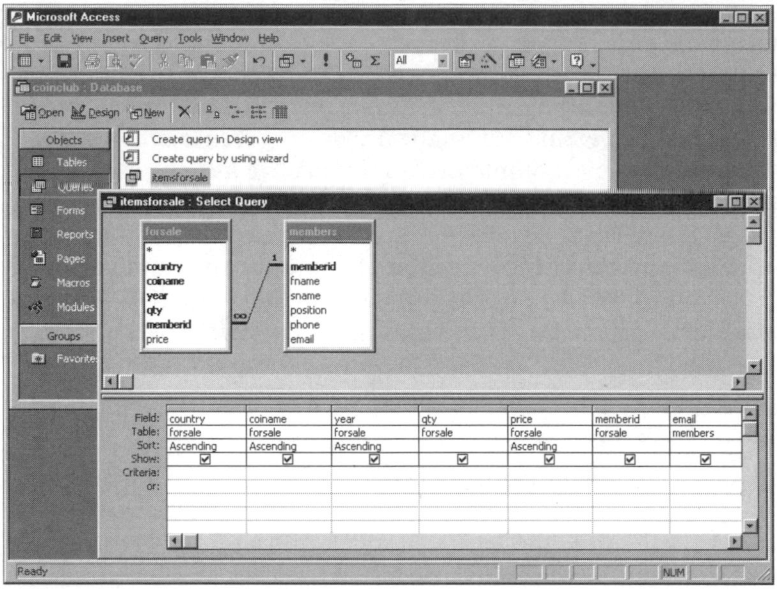

Figure 2-9   *This query joins two tables and projects the fields shown in the lower grid.*

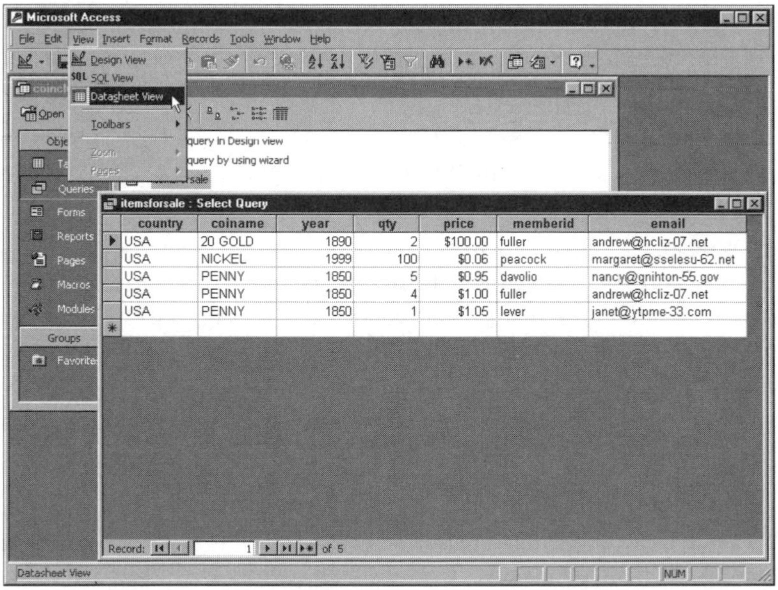

Figure 2-10   *Datasheet view displays the results of a query in tabular form.*

Create a parameter query

In speech, most database experts pronounce the acronym SQL like the word "sequel."

Many queries involve record selection criteria, or as you might call them, search values. In SQL parlance, this is a select. To make the query you just created perform a select operation, enter the value you want in the Criteria row of the Select Query window in Figure 2-9.

Selecting based on constants is a valuable technique, but one that's some-times awkward for recurring use. Specifically, every time you want to query a different value, you have to open Design View, locate the proper column, and update the Criteria value. It would be much more convenient to tell Access that it needed to prompt you for one or more Criteria values every time it ran the query. Access could then run the query with the values you specified. Parameter queries provide exactly this facility.

To see a parameter query in action, refer to Figure 2-11. This query retrieves all records from the *members* table having a given value in the *sname* field. A parameter named *qsname* specifies the desired value. The entry that makes this happen is the value *[qsname]* where the Criteria row and the *sname* column intersect.

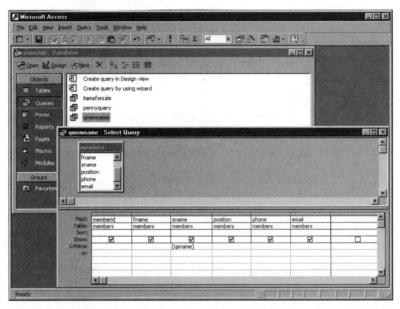

Figure 2-11 *Specifying [qsname] as the criteria for the* sname *field tells Access to prompt for and substitute a value named* qsname *whenever it runs this query.*

The square brackets around *qsname* identify this entry as a database field. If you entered just the characters *qsname* in the Criteria row, Access would, by default, treat your entry as a constant, surround it with quotation marks, and retrieve all member records with an *sname* value of "qsname". Surrounding an expression with square brackets tells Access (and SQL) that the expression names a database field.

Of course, *qsname* isn't the name of any field in any table involved in the query. Because of this, Access assumes that *qsname* is the name of a parameter you plan to supply whenever you run the query. (If you've ever hand-typed a field name, misspelled it, and then wondered why Access displayed an Enter Parameter Value prompt, now you know.)

Figure 2-12 shows what happens when you try to run this query (that is, when you switch the query window to Datasheet view): the query won't run until you supply a value for the *qsname* parameter. If you supply the value *davolio*, the query displays only records having that value in the *sname* field. Figure 2-13 illustrates this result.

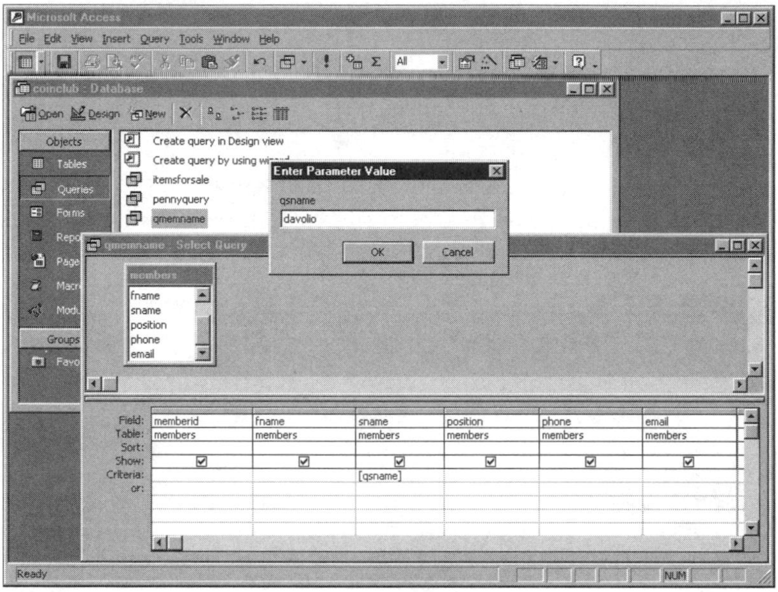

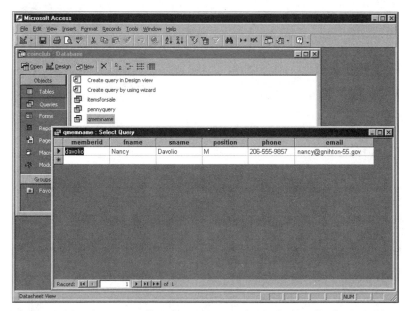

Figure 2-12 *When you switch to Datasheet view, Access prompts for the* qsname *value.*

Figure 2-13 *Access applies the* qsname *criteria before displaying this result set.*

Chapter 4, "Accessing Tables and Records with ADO," explains how to run a parameter query from a Web page. This approach has two advantages:

- You can develop a query in Access and provide it to Web visitors without ever looking at a SQL statement.

- All the queries for an application are in the database rather than in the Web pages. If you ever have to change the database structure, queries stored in the database are much easier to find and correct than queries widely scattered through Web pages and other application programs.

The primary disadvantage of using stored parameter queries in Web pages is the additional complexity required to invoke them. Chapter 4 explains this as well.

SQL Concepts and Syntax

Figure 2-14 shows a modified version of the query from Figure 2-9. It selects only those records in which *coiname* equals PENNY.

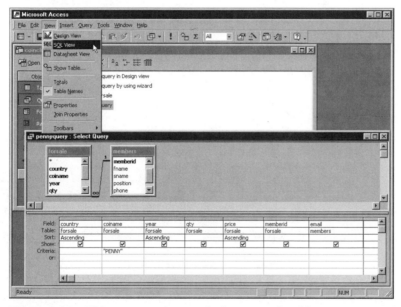

Figure 2-14   *This query retrieves only those records with a* coiname *value equal to PENNY.*

Figure 2-14 also shows that the View menu contains more than just Design View and Datasheet View, which you've seen before. It also provides a third view—called SQL View—that displays the structured query language (SQL) statement that corresponds to the current specifications in Design View. Figure 2-15 shows this feature in action.

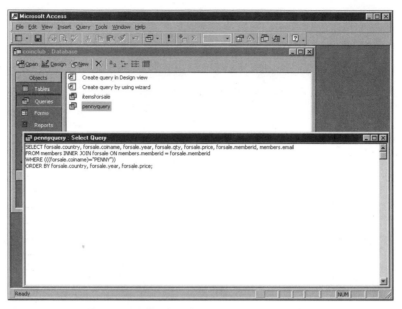

Figure 2-15 *Access can display the SQL statement corresponding to a query you build in Design View.*

Structured query language—SQL—is the way that applications usually send commands to relational databases. SQL is a powerful and complex language deserving whole books of explanation; the material in this section is therefore just an overview. Nevertheless, it describes most of the SQL used for Web database pages.

Table 2-4 lists SQL's most fundamental commands. Of these, SELECT is by far the most common—for two reasons.

- First, most modern database systems provide graphical tools for data definition and data administration. These tools are so easy to use that few developers use the CREATE, DROP, GRANT, and REVOKE commands.

- Second, all the data manipulation commands except INSERT process sets of records. To process individual records, a programmer must use application programming interfaces (APIs). As it turns out, inserting, modifying, and deleting records is frequently easier using these APIs than it is with SQL commands, Therefore, many developers seldom use the INSERT, UPDATE, and DELETE commands.

    Chapter 3, "Accessing Databases with ADO and ODBC," and Chapter 4 explain these APIs.

After excluding CREATE, DROP, GRANT, REVOKE, INSERT, UPDATE, and DELETE, only the SELECT statement remains. The rest of this section therefore concentrates on explaining SELECT statements.

Table 2-4 Fundamental SQL Commands

Category	Command	Description
Data definition	CREATE	Creates a new database, table, index, or stored query
	DROP	Deletes an existing database, table, index, or view
Data administration	GRANT	Permits specified users to perform a given action
	REVOKE	Rescinds permission for specified users to perform given actions
Data manipulation	DELETE	Removes all records matching given criteria
	INSERT	Adds a new record
	SELECT	Returns a set of all records that match given criteria
	UPDATE	Changes the value of specified fields in all records that match given criteria

Note   An index is a table of presorted record values. Having an index speeds up access or sorting based on the corresponding fields.

To clarify this, let's consider an example. Suppose a coin club Web visitor wants to know if any United States pennies from 1850 are for sale. The SELECT statement to perform this query looks like this:

```
SELECT country, coiname, year, qty, price, memberid
FROM forsale
WHERE (country="USA") AND (coiname="PENNY") AND (year=1850);
```

This statement selects all records from the *forsale* table whose *country, coiname,* and *year* fields equal USA, PENNY, and 1850, respectively. For each matching record, it shows the six fields named in the first line.

Queries like the one above are all well and good, but SQL provides no way for your program to access the resulting records—and keep in mind that there can be more than one. You need some way other than SQL to read those records one at a time and to get the field values into your Active Server Pages (ASP) code so that you can format them into a Web page.

Each database system has its own way of doing this; Access and SQL Server have more than one way. This book uses an approach called ActiveX Data Objects (ADO), which it explains in Chapter 3. For now, it's enough to know that when a SELECT statement returns data, you need to use programming methods (APIs) other than SQL for examining the returned records.

The following sections introduce the main parts of a SELECT statement.

Understanding the SELECT Statement

SELECT identifies the command, initiates it, and identifies the fields the command should return. Here's how to code the arguments for a SELECT statement.

- After the word SELECT, specify the fields you want to appear in the result set. Separate multiple fields with commas, and arrange them in the order you want them to appear.

- If the same field name appears in more than one table mentioned in the FROM clause (described below), specify it as *tablename.fieldname*.

- If a table name or field name contains spaces or special characters, enclose it in square brackets (for example, *members.[first name]*).

- To include all field names from a table, use an asterisk (for example, *forsale.**).

- With most database systems, you can specify functions and formulas as if they were field names. For example, to get the absolute value of the *balance* field from the *account* table, you could code

```
abs(account.balance) AS absbal
```

This would add a field named *absbal* to the result set, with data values equal to the absolute value of the *balance* field from the *account* table. If the SELECT statement contains a GROUP BY clause (described below), the SELECT clause can include aggregate functions such as *sum*, *avg*, *count*, *min*, *max*, *first*, and *last*.

Understanding the FROM Clause

FROM identifies the table or join to use in formulating the result set. To select fields from an existing table, specify its name. To select from a join of two tables, specify an expression of the form:

FROM left-table jointype right-table
    ON left-table.joinfield = right-table.joinfield

That is, for example:

```
FROM forsale INNER JOIN members
    ON forsale.memberid = members.memberid
```

There are three common JOIN types:

- INNER JOIN. The result set will only contain records in which the joined fields from both tables are equal.

- LEFT JOIN. The result set will contain all records from the left table and only those records from the right table in which the joined fields are equal.

When a record from the left table has no matching record in the right table, the result set will contain nulls in any field sourced from the right table.

- RIGHT JOIN. The result set will contain all records from the right table and only those records from the left table in which the joined fields are equal.

   When a record from the right table has no matching record in the left table, the result set will contain nulls in any field sourced from the left table.

Understanding the WHERE Clause

WHERE specifies criteria for selecting records. Most criteria have the form *field name, operator, value*, as in

```
forsale.country = "USA"
```

As shown in the preceding code, quotation marks identify text constants. Pound signs identify date constants, as in *#12/31/1999#*. Numeric constants have no surrounding delimiters, as in *year=1950*.

You can group criteria using parentheses, the AND operator, and the OR operator.

Understanding the GROUP BY Clause

GROUP BY, when present, tells the database system to consolidate like records based on equal values in a supplied list of fields. If you specify *GROUP BY country, coiname, year*, the database system will, before presenting the result set, consolidate all records having the same set of values in those fields.

Understanding the HAVING Clause

HAVING works a lot like WHERE, except that it operates after applying the GROUP BY clause. Suppose, for example, you code the following SELECT statement for the *forsale* table in the coin club database.

```
SELECT country, coiname, year, sum(qty) as totqty
    FROM forsale
    GROUP BY country, coiname, year
```

If you coded *WHERE qty > 5*, the database system would first select all *forsale* records whose *qty* field was greater than 5, and then aggregate them.

If you coded *HAVING totqty > 5*, the database system would first aggregate all *forsale* records by *country, coiname ,*and *year* and then, from those results, select any records whose aggregate *totqty* value was greater than 5.

Understanding the ORDER BY Clause

ORDER BY controls the order of records in the result set. You can specify any fields in the result set, separated by commas and in any order, and the database system will sort the result set accordingly: first field first, second field second, and so forth. To sort any field in descending sequence, specify the keyword DESC after its field name. Here's a typical ORDER BY clause:

```
ORDER BY country, coiname, year, price DESC
```

Let Access create your SQL statements

If this still seems a bit difficult, take heart. In most cases, you can follow these steps to get Access to create your SQL statements for you:

1. Start Access, and open your database.

2. Create a query as described under "Create a query" earlier in this chapter. This example will use the query shown in Figure 2-14.

3. When the query is producing the results you want, choose SQL View from the View menu.

4. As you already saw in Figure 2-15, Access will display the SQL statement that produced the successful query from step 3. Select the SQL code and copy it to the clipboard.

5. Open the ASP page where you need to use the query.

6. Within any ASP script block, enter a line of code, such as

```
strSQL = ""
```

7. Set the cursor between the two quotation marks, and then paste the SQL statement you copied in step 5. Now you will have

```
strSQL = "SELECT forsale.country, forsale.coiname,
forsale.year, forsale.qty, forsale.price, forsale.memberid,
members.email FROM members INNER JOIN forsale ON
members.memberid = forsale.memberid WHERE
(((forsale.coiname)="PENNY")) ORDER BY forsale.country,
forsale.year, forsale.price;"
```

8. Locate every quotation mark you pasted from Access, and change each one to an apostrophe. The example statement now reads

```
strSQL = "SELECT forsale.country, forsale.coiname,
forsale.year, forsale.qty, forsale.price, forsale.memberid,
members.email FROM members INNER JOIN forsale ON
members.memberid = forsale.memberid WHERE
(((forsale.coiname)='PENNY')) ORDER BY forsale.country,
forsale.year, forsale.price;"
```

Note that apostrophes, rather than quotation marks, now surround the value PENNY.

Note Although SQL is supposed to be a standardized language, each database system tends to implement it a little differently. That's why experienced database developers talk about *dialects* (that is, linguistic variations) of SQL. The dialect of SQL found in Access requires quotation marks to denote text constants, but the dialects used in ODBC and ADO use apostrophes (single quotes) for this purpose. This is inconvenient when you copy code out of Access and paste it into an ADO application (such as a Web database page, for example), but it's very convenient when you write code that creates SQL statements on the fly. Because VBScript uses double quotes to delimit text constants, the single quotes required by ADO are easy to code as literals.

---

9. An optional final step is to format the VBScript statement so that the SQL code is easily readable. To do this, break long constants like those in step 8 into smaller segments, join the segments with concatenation characters (ampersands), and insert continuation characters and line endings as required. Finally, indent each line so that the code takes on a tabular appearance. Here's an example:

```
strSQL = "SELECT forsale.country, " & _
            "forsale.coiname, " & _
            "forsale.year, " & _
            "forsale.qty, " & _
            "forsale.price, " & _
            "forsale.memberid, " & _
            "members.email " & _
        "FROM members INNER JOIN forsale " & _
          "ON members.memberid = forsale.memberid " & _
        "WHERE (((forsale.coiname)='PENNY')) " & _
      "ORDER BY forsale.country, " & _
            "forsale.year, " & _
            "forsale.price;
```

The number-one mistake when performing this step, by the way, is omitting the space before the ending quote on each line. (This assumes, of course, that you're breaking lines between words.)

At this point, the world is your oyster. Your code can replace any portion of the SQL statement, or even all of it, with whatever options or values you like. Perhaps, for example, you'd like to replace the literal 'PENNY' with an expression containing a value received from your Web visitor. Perhaps you'd like to generate different ORDER BY strings, depending on the setting of a list box or a set of radio buttons. Go for it. Later chapters, particularly Chapters 7 through 12, will provide further instruction and numerous examples.

Of course, there's more to developing database Web pages than knowing a few things about SQL statements, knowing how to copy and paste SQL statements generated by Access, and knowing how to construct SQL strings in VBScript. You still need to know how to send SQL statements to the database software, how to obtain the results in your VBScript code, how to collect input from the Web visitor, and how to send results to the same visitor. Chapters 3 through 6 will explain the technology to do all these things and more, and Chapters 7 through 12 will provide a number of practical examples. What could be more fun than that?

Chapter Summary

This chapter introduced the basic concepts of relational databases and explained how to design such databases and implement them in Access. It also explained the fundamentals of SQL.

Chapter 3 will introduce ActiveX Data Objects, which provide the interface between script code in a Web page and information in a database. Chapter 4 will continue that discussion by explaining how to open database tables and manipulate data records.

Accessing Databases with ADO and ODBC

In this chapter, you'll learn

- The key concepts behind ActiveX Data Objects, which provides a general-purpose way for scripts and other programs to store and retrieve data.

- The basics of open database connectivity, which provides a way for ADO to access databases.

- How a Web page can use ADO and ODBC to open a database.

Designing and implementing databases are worthy tasks, and certainly a necessary part of implementing any sort of Web database application. However, you have still more techniques to learn. One of the most important is how applications—particularly ASP pages—can send commands to the database system and then receive results. This involves the following key concepts and components:

- A *data source* is a software component that provides access to data in a structured way.

- Microsoft ActiveX Data Objects provides a programming interface between a Web database page and various data sources. Akin to the underlying data source, ADO provides a broad assortment of objects, methods, and properties.

- Open database connectivity is a data source that provides access to many relational database systems, including Microsoft Access and Microsoft SQL Server.

This chapter explains how this software works in applications where Web pages provide the visual interface.

Introducing ADO and ODBC Concepts

Figure 3-1 diagrams the information flow that occurs when processing a Web database page. As you can see, it's a multistep, multilayer process.

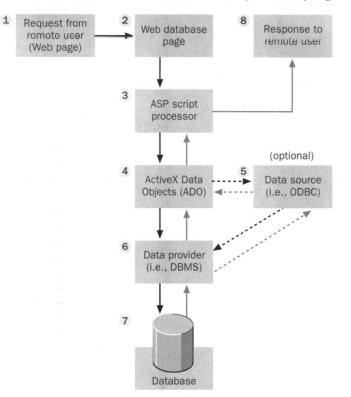

Figure 3-1 *Processing a Web database page involves several layers of software.*

1. A Web visitor initiates the process by submitting a request to the Web server. Typically, the Web visitor does this by clicking a hyperlink or clicking a Submit button displayed in the browser.

2. The Web server receives the request, notices that the requested Web page has a .asp filename extension, and starts the Active Server Pages script processor.

3. The ASP script processor reads through the requested page and executes any server-side script code it finds within.

4. The server-side script code loads (that is, creates instances of, or *instantiates*) various ADO objects. The script code then uses methods exposed by these objects (that is, it invokes software commands) to access any data sources available on the server.

5. ODBC is one such data source. ADO accesses most, but not all, relational database systems through ODBC. The ODBC data source provides ways to open databases, open tables, process SQL commands, and carry out other tasks.

6. Eventually, ADO—working directly on its own or indirectly through a data source—sends commands to a *data provider*. The data provider can be a DBMS such as Microsoft SQL Server or the Jet database engine used by Microsoft Access 2000. It can also be a nonrelational data source such as a full-text search engine or a Lightweight Directory Access Protocol (LDAP) network-accessible directory.

7. Finally, the data source accesses the database and sends results back to the calling module.

Once the provider accesses the data, it sends the result set back—either directly, or indirectly via ODBC—to ADO. ADO immediately sends the ASP code a status code. In addition, if the issued command produced a result set, ADO provides methods to move through it, inspect or update the contents of each record, or delete records. Of course, once the database processing is complete, the ASP page responds to the Web visitor by sending a customized Web page.

Obtaining and Installing ADO

ADO isn't something you buy or download and then install by itself. It's part of a larger group of programs called Microsoft Data Access Components (MDAC). MDAC contains a mixed bag of database software modules—database drivers, ODBC drivers, and of course ADO—all installed by a single setup program.

New versions of MDAC tend to appear whenever there's an upgrade to any one of its components. A new version of Access leads to a new version of MDAC. A new version of SQL Server leads to a new version of MDAC. A new version of ODBC leads to...well, you get the picture.

By default, installing a Microsoft Web server on your computer also installs ADO. This applies to Microsoft Internet Information Services (IIS), built in to Microsoft Windows 2000, as well as to Internet Information Server on Microsoft Windows NT Server and Microsoft Personal Web Server on Windows NT Workstation, Windows 98, and Windows 95. Chapter 4, "Accessing Tables and Records with ADO," addresses Web server components in more detail, but for now just remember not to turn off any options that mention ADO, MDAC, or data access when installing a Microsoft Web server.

Microsoft database products, Windows 2000, Windows NT, Microsoft Developer Studio applications, and Microsoft Internet Explorer all come with versions of MDAC. This can lead to some confusion as to which version of what components end up residing on your computer. When you're in doubt, the best procedure is usually to download and install the latest version of MDAC.

The best place to start looking for new versions of MDAC is the Microsoft Universal Data Access page at *http://www.microsoft.com/data/*. From there, choose Downloads, and then follow the usual links and prompts. The download is usually a single executable you can click to start.

Locating ADO Documentation

At the time of this writing, the exact URL for ADO documentation was *http://msdn.microsoft.com/library/psdk/dasdk/ados4piv.htm*. Unfortunately, like all URLs, this one tends to change from time to time. What's worse, the longer the URL, the greater the likelihood for change, and this URL is definitely on the long side. Here's how to find the ActiveX Data Objects start page from a more stable point of entry.

1. Load the page *http://msdn.microsoft.com/library/*.

2. Wait for this page to load fully, and then open the following items in sequence in the Table of Contents tree:

   Platform SDK
     Data Access Services
       Microsoft Data Access Components (MDAC) SDK
         Microsoft Data Access 2.5 SDK
           Microsoft ActiveX Data Objects (ADO)

   Don't be deterred if the current wording or version numbers you find on the Web are slightly different from those listed here; constant revisions are both the boon and the bane of the Web. Figure 3-2 shows the path to the ActiveX Data Objects start page.

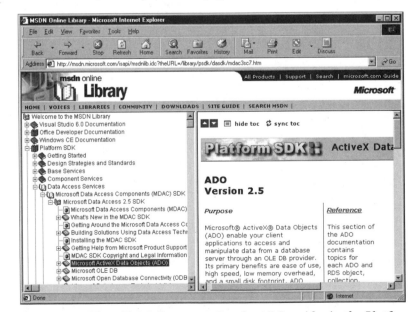

Figure 3-2   *The official documentation for ADO resides in the Platform SDK library.*

Another entry point for ADO information, documentation, and downloads is the Universal Data Access home page

http://www.microsoft.com/data/.

This is another excellent place to start looking for documentation. And if all else fails, try searching for the phrase ActiveX Data Objects start page at one of these locations: *http://www.microsoft.com/search* or *http://msdn.microsoft.com/search.*

Understanding ADO Objects

Despite their power, ADO objects are relatively few in number. The ADO objects are listed in Table 3-1. Figure 3-3 shows the hierarchy of the various ADO objects used in this book.

Table 3-1   Top-Level ADO Objects

Object	Appears in collection	Parent	Description
Connection			Provides a pathway that other objects can use to access a database provider
Recordset		Connection	Provides access to the result set of a query or other database operation
Field	Fields	Record	Provides access to individual fields in the current record of a Recordset
Property	Properties	Connection Command Recordset Field	Provides access to any characteristic of an ADO object
Command		Connection	Holds a command—and optionally command parameters—that will execute through a database connection
Parameter	Parameters	Command	Holds a named value that the database provider will merge into a predefined query or stored procedure
Error	Errors	Connection	Contains information about errors reported by the database provider
Record			Represents one row of a recordset, or a directory or file in a file system
Stream			Represents a binary stream of data

(continued)

Table 3-1 *continued*

Object	Description
The following objects are part of Remote Data Services, a technology not discussed in this book.	
DataControl	Binds a data query recordset to one or more controls (for example, a text box, grid control, or combo box) to display the recordset data on a Web page
DataFactory	Implements methods that provide read/write data access to specified data sources for client-side applications
DataSpace	Creates client-side proxies to custom business objects located on the middle tier

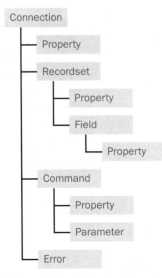

Figure 3-3   *This diagram shows the relationships that exist among the ADO objects used in this book.*

The remainder of this section contains a brief overview of each ADO object type commonly used in Web database pages. Subsequent sections will cover each object in considerably more detail.

- The highest-level ADO object is the Connection object. A Connection object handles all interactions with a data provider; thus, all other ADO objects depend on it. Using a Connection object requires two steps: loading (instantiating) the object, and then opening it. When you open a Connection object, you must supply a connection string that specifies which provider to open.

- An ADO Recordset object provides access to the result set from a database operation. Creating the Recordset object and obtaining a result set are two distinct operations, and you must perform them in that order. You can obtain a result set in two ways: by using the *Open* method of a Recordset object or the *Execute* method of a Command object.

- ADO creates a Field object for each field in a result set. This provides access to the field's value and other properties. Because ADO automatically creates Field objects when it creates recordsets, you'll seldom, if ever, need to create Field objects yourself.

- ADO automatically creates Property objects as well. Any sort of readable or settable information about an object actually resides in a Property object. As with Field objects, you normally don't need to worry about the fact that Property objects exist; you just use their names and values.

- An ADO Command object holds a command—and optionally parameters—that you plan to send to a data provider. To actually send the command, you must use the Command object's *Execute* method. For performing ordinary queries, the Recordset object's *Open* method is easier to use and requires less coding than the Command object's *Execute* method. However, the Command object supports two functions that the Record object doesn't: parameter queries and commands that don't produce a recordset.

Note A parameter query is similar to an ordinary SQL statement, but the developer modifies portions of it to accept replaceable parameters. This provides a way to store SQL statements centrally within the database instead of distributed throughout many programs. Individual programs can still supply variable information.

- An ADO Parameter object holds one replaceable parameter for use by an ADO Command object. For each parameter you want a Command object to supply, you must first create an ADO Parameter object, assign values to it, and then append the Parameter object to the Command object.

- The ADO Error object provides a collection of errors reported by a database provider. Every time you access a provider through its Connection object, ADO first clears the Error object's Errors collection, and then appends each error, if any, the provider reports. When control returns to your ASP code, you can then inspect the Error object to see if anything went wrong.

Using ADO Objects

Now that you have a basic understanding of the major ADO objects, the following sections will describe how to use them. For the sake of practicality, the text includes some code fragments.

Using ADO Named Constants

When invoking or explaining ADO services, most documentation—and most examples in this book—use named constants rather than literals. For example, instead of

```
rsMbrs.Open sql, cnn1, 0, 1, 1
```

you will see

```
rsMbrs.Open sql, cnn1, adOpenForwardOnly, adLockReadOnly, adCmdText
```

The second form is obviously more descriptive and easier to understand, but it does require *constant declarations*—such as the following—in your code:

```
Const adOpenForwardOnly = 0
Const adLockReadOnly = 1
Const adCmdText = &H0001
```

It's always best to use the adovbs.inc file that came with the version of MDAC installed on your Web server. If that's not possible, try using the adovbs.inc file supplied with the sample files.

Fortunately, installing ADO also installs a file that contains all the constant declarations needed for all the ADO properties and methods. It's called adovbs.inc and you can usually find it in a location such as C:\Program Files\Common Files\System\ado\adovbs.inc.

Here's how to use this file with your Web pages:

1. Copy the file adovbs.inc from its installed location to somewhere handy on your Web server. For example, if you're using a Microsoft FrontPage Web, copy it into the Web's root folder.

2. In each Web page that uses ADO named constants, include the following line before the first block of server-side script code. That is, insert it before the first <% tag.

   ```
   <!-- #include file="../adovbs.inc" -->
   ```

   Notice that the *file=* argument—the value inside the quotes—is a relative URL. You might need to adjust its path portion ("../" in the example) depending on the location of the adovbs.inc file relative to your Web page.

Using Server-Side Includes

Statements such as the following involve a technique called *server-side includes* that temporarily replaces a special statement in one file with the complete contents of another file.

```
<!-- #include file="../adovbs.inc" -->
```

When the Web server processes an ASP page that contains this statement, the ASP processor "sees" the entire contents of the adovbs.inc file and not the statement above. Note that the location is a relative URL and not a physical location in the server's file system.

If you have a single block of statements that needs to appear in many Web pages, it's handy to code those statements once, in a single file, and then *include* them wherever needed. If you ever need to update that code, you need to do it in only one location.

Server-side includes require extra work from the Web server and therefore aren't activated by default for all page types. For example, Microsoft Web servers usually don't process server-side includes for files with .htm extensions, but they do process them for files with .asp extensions.

Using ADO Connections

Using ADO Connection objects involves only four operations, and three of them are extremely simple:

- Create the object
- Open the object
- Close the object
- Release the object

Opening the object is usually the hard part.

Create an ADO Connection object

ADO Connection objects are simple to create because there are no options to specify. The following statement does the job. The only thing you'll ever need to change is the name of the resulting object (*cnn1* in this example), and even that's just a matter of preference.

```
Set cnn1 = Server.CreateObject("ADODB.Connection")
```

If you've worked with objects in other forms of Microsoft Visual Basic, the statement above might be a surprise. Did you expect the following statement instead?

```
Dim cnn1 as New ADODB.Connection
```

Both statements create an ADO Connection object, but the first form is the one required by Microsoft Visual Basic, Scripting Edition (VBScript). VBScript is the form of Visual Basic that ASP uses. In the first form, Server is an object that's built into the ASP scripting environment, and *CreateObject* is a method that—unsurprisingly—creates objects! The literal *ADODB.Connection* tells the *CreateObject* method what kind of object to create.

Open an ADO Connection object

Creating a Connection object doesn't automatically open communications with any database; for that, you must call the Connection object's *Open* method. To open a connection, code the following statement:

```
connection.Open ConnectionString, UserID, Password
```

Of the *Open* method's three arguments, only the first is required. You can omit the *UserID* and *Password* arguments if opening the database doesn't require logon security, or if you choose to supply this information within the *ConnectionString* argument.

Constructing a valid *ConnectionString* is the tricky part of opening an ADO connection. The connection string consists of one or more *argument=value* strings, separated by semicolons. Some of these arguments pertain to the Connection object, some to the data provider (that is, ODBC), and some to the data source (that is, Access, SQL Server, or another database). Thus, there's no single, definitive reference that tells you what belongs in a connection string.

Each layer of software scans all the arguments in the connection string it receives. If a Connection object understands what to do with a particular argument, for example, it removes that argument (and its value) from the connection string before passing it to the data provider. If the data provider knows what to do with an argument, the data provider removes it from the connection string before passing it to the data source.

Note In some cases, a software layer will receive arguments by means of application programming interfaces (APIs) and pass them to a subordinate layer by adding them to the connection string. In other cases, it does the reverse—that is, it removes connection string arguments used by a subordinate layer and passes them by means of APIs. Finally, if two layers use different argument names for the same value, either layer can translate argument names.

Table 3-2 lists the arguments an ADO Connection object will process itself and remove from the connection string it passes to a data provider. ADO removes and processes these argument names and their associated properties before passing a connection string to a data provider. If you specify any argument names not listed in the first column of Table 3-2, ADO will pass the provider both the names and the values unchanged.

Table 3-2 ADO Connection String Properties

ADO argument	ODBC equivalent	ADO default	Description
Provider	ODBC		The name of the data provider the connection should use
Data Source	DSN	DSN	An ODBC data source name the connection should use
User ID	UID		A username to supply when opening the connection
Password	PWD		A password to supply when opening the connection
File Name			The name of a provider-specific file that contains connection information
Remote Provider			The name of a provider to use when opening a client-side connection (Remote Data Services only)
Remote Server			The pathname of the server to use when opening a client-side connection (Remote Data Services only)

If you don't specify a provider, the default is Microsoft's ODBC. This is the provider you'd normally use for accessing SQL Server, Access, Oracle, Informix, and most other relational databases. Other providers, however, are certainly supported—including providers for Microsoft Index Server and for LDAP directory services.

Note Microsoft Index Server is the text-search engine that comes with Internet Information Server 4.0 and that now ships with Microsoft Windows 2000.

ADO connection arguments, ODBC arguments, further arguments unique to each DBMS, and all their acceptable values are complex and somewhat mysterious topics. Therefore, in the interests of briefness and practicality, this section shows only a small assortment of common examples. The following list includes some typical connection strings.

Several of these examples mention ODBC system data source names or, as they're more often (and more simply) called, system DSNs. System DSNs provide a way to define a database's type, location, and other settings once per computer rather than individually within each ASP page. This has obvious advantages if you ever need to relocate the database or change its supporting DBMS, but it does require an administrator working at the server's console to set it up.

See "Defining an ODBC Data Source Name" later in this chapter for more about system DSNs.

- Open a connection to an ODBC system DSN called *Pubs*.

```
Set cnn1 = Server.CreateObject("ADODB.Connection")
cString = "Pubs"
cnn1.Open cString
```

    The second statement is equivalent to

```
cstring = "Provider=ODBC;DSN=Pubs"
```

because the default provider is ODBC and the default argument name is DSN.

- Open a connection to the same source using ADO argument names. Also specify a database logon name of *sa* and a password of *pwd*.

```
Set cnn2 = Server.CreateObject("ADODB.Connection")
cString = "Data Source=Pubs;User ID=sa;Password=pwd;"
cnn2.Open cString
```

- Open a connection to the same source by using ODBC argument names.

```
Set cnn3 = Server.CreateObject("ADODB.Connection")
cString = "DSN=Pubs;UID=sa;PWD=pwd;"
cnn3.Open cString
```

- Open a connection to the same source by passing the *User ID* and *Password* as arguments to the *Open* method instead of arguments within the connection string.

```
Set cnn4 = Server.CreateObject("ADODB.Connection")
cString = "Pubs"
cnn4.Open cString, "sa", "pwd"
```

    The connection string data source defaults to DSN.

- Open a connection to a SQL Server database without using an ODBC system DSN.

```
Set cnn5 = Server.CreateObject("ADODB.Connection")
cString = "driver={SQL Server};server=bigsmile;" & _
          "uid=sa;pwd=pwd;database=pubs"
cnn5.Open cString
```

The *server* argument specifies the computer where SQL Server is running, and the *database* argument specifies SQL Server's name for the database.

- Open a connection to an Access database without using a DSN.

```
Set cnn6 = Server.CreateObject("ADODB.Connection")
cString = "driver={Microsoft Access Driver (*.mdb)};" & _
          "dbq=G:\InetPub\wwwroot\webdbdev\ch03\coinclub.mdb"
cnn6.Open cString
```

When used in an Active Server Page, the *dbq* argument must specify either a file name and path local to the Web server's file system, or a network file location in Universal Naming Convention (UNC) format. If you know the database's URL but not its file location, translate the URL by using the *Server.MapPath* method as shown here:

```
cString = "driver={Microsoft Access Driver (*.mdb)};" & _
          "dbq=" & _
          Server.MapPath ("../ch03/coinclub.mdb")
```

- Open a connection to Microsoft Index Server.

```
Set cnn7 = Server.CreateObject("ADODB.Connection")
cString = "Provider=MSIDXS"
cnn7.Open cString
```

The LDAP provider for ADO provides read-only access to directories such as Microsoft Active Directory and Novell Directory Services.

- Open a connection to any LDAP-compliant directory service.

```
Set cnn8 = Server.CreateObject("ADODB.Connection")
cString = "Provider=ADSDSOObject"
cnn8.Open cString
```

Opening an ADO connection to a database doesn't itself provide access to any records. For that, you must open and manipulate a recordset. For details, refer to "Using ADO Recordsets" in Chapter 4.

Close an ADO Connection object

Closing an ADO Connection object requires nothing more than calling its *Close* method. To close a Connection object named *cnn1*, code

```
cnn1.Close
```

If you forget to close a Connection object, the ASP scripting processor will eventually find it, close it, and remove it from memory. At least, that's the plan. In practice, your Web server will probably be more stable if you always close and release any objects you create.

Release an ADO Connection object

Even after you close a Connection object, it still remains in memory. To remove a Connection object (or any other object) named *cnn1* from memory, code

```
Set cnn1 = Nothing
```

Defining an ODBC Data Source Name

An ODBC data source name defines—in one central location per computer—the type, location, and operating parameters of any database that supports ODBC. That is quite an advantage if you ever have to move the database or upgrade to different database software. Rather than updating the connection string in each Web page, you can just update the DSN.

There are two kinds of ODBC DSNs: user and system. User data source names are in effect only when a certain user is logged in to the local system and are useless for Web database work. System data source names are in effect for all users and background processes, even when no one is logged in. Web database pages that use DSNs must use system DSNs.

The procedures needed to define ODBC data source names vary, depending on the operating system, the type of database, and the version of ODBC itself. Therefore, don't be surprised if the dialog boxes you see differ somewhat from those shown here.

Open the ODBC Data Source Administrator

The process for defining a system DSN is similar for Windows 95, Windows 98, Windows NT, and Windows 2000. However, you must be logged on to a local or Terminal Server console of the machine that will run the application, and you must be an administrator of that machine.

If you aren't the server administrator, or if the administrator isn't willing to set up DSNs for you, or if the administrator charges a large fee, you might find it simpler to use a connection string that doesn't use a DSN.

However, if you do find yourself setting up an ODBC data source name, follow this procedure:

1. Open the Control Panel, double-click Administrative Tools, and then double-click Data Sources (ODBC). If you're using Windows 95, Windows 98, or Windows NT 4, open the Control Panel and double-click the 32-bit ODBC icon.

2. The dialog box shown in Figure 3-4 will appear. Selecting the System DSN tab displays these options:

   • Clicking Add creates a new system DSN.

   • Clicking Remove deletes an existing system DSN. First select the system DSN you want to delete, and then click the Remove button.

- Clicking Configure displays (and optionally modifies) an existing system DSN. Select the system DSN you desire, and then click the Configure button. Double-clicking a listed system DSN has the same effect.

3. Click the Add button to display the dialog box shown in Figure 3-5.

4. Select the driver corresponding to the type of database you want to use, and then click the Finish button.

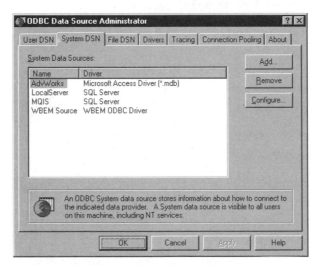

Figure 3-4   *This is the ODBC Data Source Administrator dialog box.*

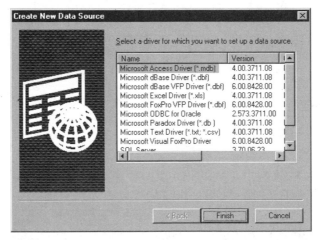

Figure 3-5   *This dialog box specifies the driver for a new ODBC system DSN.*

At this point the dialog boxes (and therefore the procedures) change depending on the type of database. The next two sections will explain the procedures for defining DSNs for Microsoft Access and Microsoft SQL Server, respectively.

Define a data source name for Microsoft Access

If the data source names an Access database, follow these steps after clicking the Finish button in Figure 3-5.

1. The ODBC Microsoft Access Setup dialog box shown in Figure 3-6 should be on display. This is the dialog box that actually defines the Access system DSN.

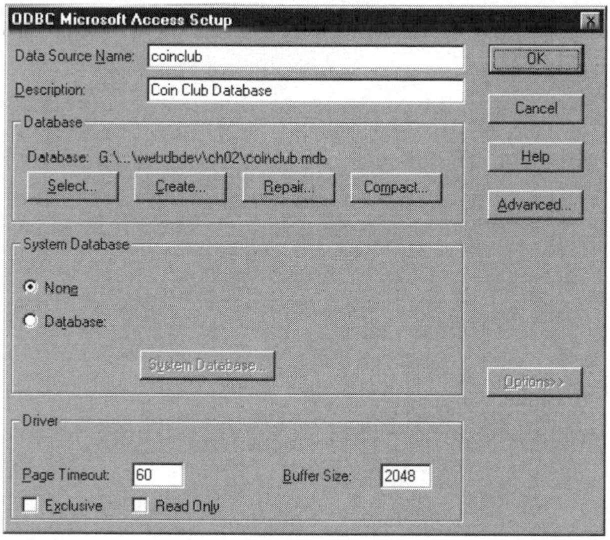

Figure 3-6 *This dialog box defines an Access ODBC system DSN.*

Enter the following options:

- **Data Source Name** supplies the name that Active Server Pages and other processes will specify to access the database. Short, meaningful names are best.

- **Description** provides a brief text description. This entry is optional.

- **Database** specifies the name of the Access database and provides certain management functions.

  - **Select** browses the local or network file system to locate and select the target Access database. An Access database normally has a .mdb filename extension.

Tip If an Access database isn't on the local system, specify a Universal Naming Convention name. Don't use mapped drive letters. Drive mappings change as different users log on and off the computer; when no one is logged on, no drive mappings are in effect at all. UNC names have the form \\<computername>\<sharename>\<path>\<filename>.

  - **Create** creates a new, empty database containing no tables.
  - **Repair** performs consistency checks and attempts to repair structural problems in the database.

- **Compact** recovers unused space from the database file.
- **System Database** controls use of a system database in conjunction with the normal Access database. The system database stores security and option settings for Access databases.
  - **None** signifies that the Access database isn't controlled through a system database.
  - **Database** signifies that a system database controls the Access database. Click the System Database button to specify the system database's location.

2. Click the Options button to expand the dialog box and display the following data fields:

- **Driver** controls operating parameters specific to the Access driver.
- **Page Timeout** specifies a time limit, in tenths of a second, for completing ODBC operations. The default value is normally adequate.
- **Buffer Size** specifies the number of bytes available for ODBC buffering. The default value is normally adequate.
- **Exclusive**, if checked, opens the database for exclusive use.
- **Read Only**, if checked, opens the database for read-only use.

3. When done, click the OK button.

Define a data source name for SQL Server

If the data source names a SQL Server database, follow these steps after clicking the Finish button in Figure 3-5.

1. The Create A New Data Source To SQL Server wizard shown in Figure 3-7 should be on display. This first screen is where you actually define the system DSN.

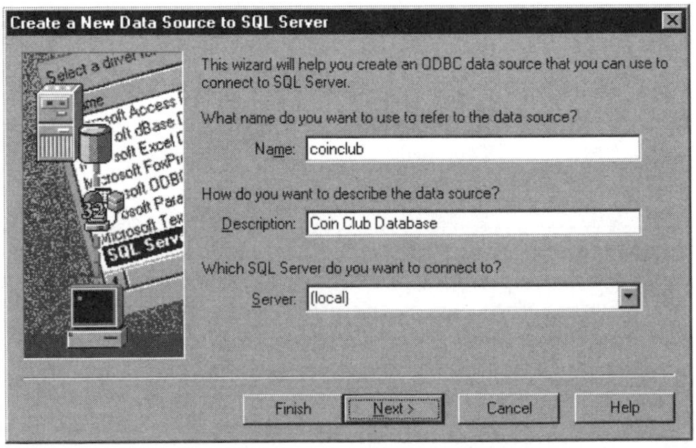

Figure 3-7   *This is the first screen of the wizard that defines a SQL Server ODBC system DSN.*

Enter the following options:

- **Name**   Give the data source a name that applications will use to identify it.

- **Description**   Specify one line of documentation regarding the DSN. This field is optional.

- **Server**   Specify the computer where the SQL Server software is running. If the computer name doesn't appear in the drop-down list, type it in.

2. Click Next to see the screen shown in Figure 3-8. This screen controls the way that SQL Server verifies the login ID used to access the database. You might need to ask the SQL Server administrator to help you complete this section.

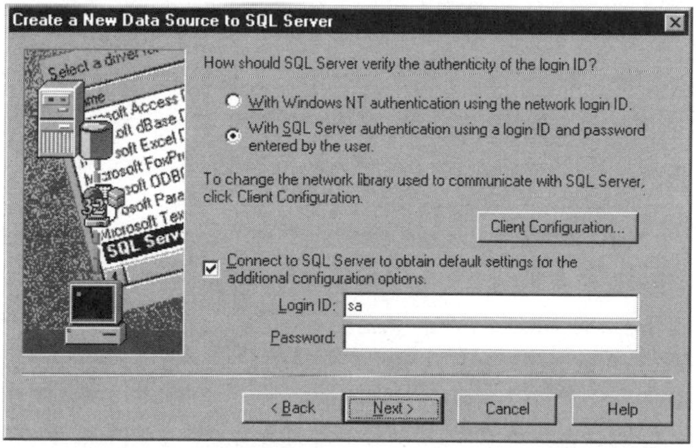

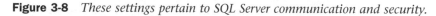

Figure 3-8   *These settings pertain to SQL Server communication and security.*

- **How Should SQL Server Verify The Authenticity Of The Login ID?**   Select With Windows NT Authentication if the SQL Server controls database access using Windows 2000 or Windows NT user accounts and passwords. Select With SQL Server Authentication if the SQL Server uses its own built-in security.

- **Client Configuration**   Click this button to select the type of network communication.

- **Connect To SQL Server To Obtain Default Settings For The Additional Configuration Options**   To obtain defaults from the server specified in step 1, check this check box and specify a login ID and password acceptable to SQL Server.

3. Click Next to continue setting up the data source. This will display the screen shown in Figure 3-9.

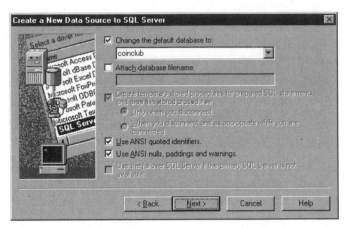

Figure 3-9 *The default database section of this screen is probably the only one you'll need to change.*

In the vast majority of cases, the only field you'll need to supply on this screen is the default database. Unless your database resides in SQL Server's *master* device, check the option box titled Change The Default Database To and then select the device that contains your database.

Note In SQL Server parlance, a *device* is a physical file that contains all the objects in a database.

As to the remaining fields on this screen, override the defaults only if the SQL Server's administrator instructs you to do so. For more information, click the Help button.

4. Click the Next button to see the screen shown in Figure 3-10. In the vast majority of cases, all the default values will be acceptable.

5. Click Finish.

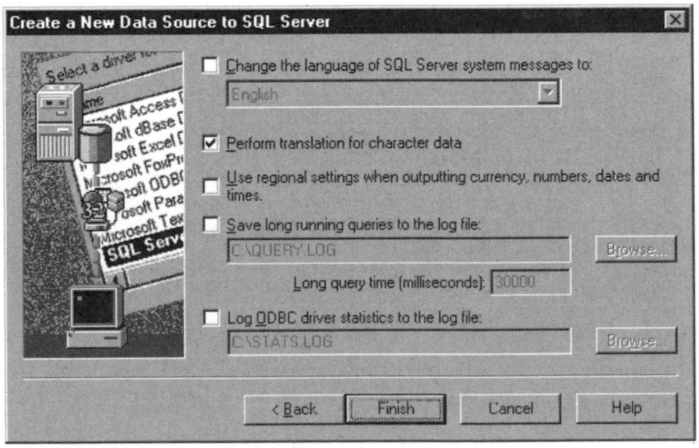

Figure 3-10 *These settings seldom require values other than the default.*

ODBC will display the information shown in the ODBC Microsoft SQL Server Setup dialog box shown in Figure 3-11. Clicking the Test Data Source button gives the new DSN a brief workout and produces the SQL Server ODBC Data Source Test dialog box, also visible in that figure.

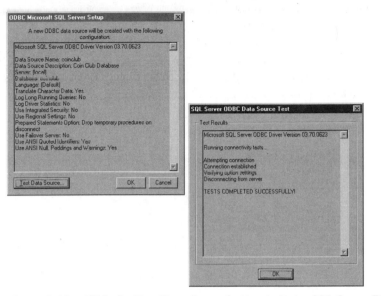

Figure 3-11   *Click the Test Data Source button to test a SQL Server DSN.*

If you get the message TESTS COMPLETED SUCCESSFULLY, assemble friends and celebrate. If you don't, recheck your entries and then go hunting for the SQL Server administrator. If you find him celebrating, tell him it's his turn to buy.

If you've forgotten how to use an ODBC data source name in an ADO Connection object, refer to "Create an ADO Connection object," earlier in this chapter.

Resolving ODBC Issues

If the data source is intended for some other type of database, use the procedures above as a general guide. Also, consult the online Help or documentation for the applicable ODBC driver.

Completing this process allows any ODBC application, including an ASP page using ADO, to open and manipulate a database in a uniform way based on a single identity—the system data source name. ODBC determines the correct driver type, physical location, and name of the database from the information you supply.

ODBC drivers are updated frequently, and new versions tend to appear whenever you install database-related software. This might result in minor changes in the dialog box options and settings described above.

The number one cause of ODBC driver failure is mismatched versions. If you run into system-related problems, click the About tab in the ODBC Data Source Administrator dialog box shown in Figure 3-4. If all the listed modules aren't the same version, replace them with a set of modules that are.

Chapter Summary

This chapter introduced the key concepts involved in using ActiveX Data Objects and open database connectivity. It also explained how to open a database from a Web page. The next chapter explains how to open tables and queries and how to retrieve and update records.

Chapter 4

Accessing Tables and Records with ADO

In this chapter, you'll learn how to

- Use the ADO Recordset object for accessing and updating the tables, records, and fields in a database.

- Use the ADO Command object for running arbitrary database commands.

- Use the ADO Parameter object for running predefined queries that incorporate replaceable parameters.

- Use the ADO Error object for getting information about any errors that occur during database operations.

As you saw in the previous chapter, opening and closing database connections are vital operations for any database application, Web-based or otherwise. However, those operations are only stepping-stones to the real heart of database applications: opening tables or queries, finding records, and displaying or updating field values. As is so often the case, the payback lies in the details.

The Recordset object is the one ADO object with the fundamental capability to process tables, records, and fields. The bulk of this chapter will therefore focus on this object. To supplement this material, the chapter will also cover three objects that work in concert with Recordset objects: the ADO Command, Parameter, and Error objects.

Using ADO Recordsets

In a practical sense, the Recordset object is the most important of all the ADO object types. The Recordset object provides the one and only ADO pathway for exchanging data between a data provider and your Web database page.

As befits its importance, the Recordset object is loaded with functionality and therefore somewhat complex. In ADO 2.5, for example, the Recordset object has 25 methods (most requiring multiple arguments) and 24 properties (most with obscure values). Describing all these methods and properties is beyond the scope of this book. Fortunately, most Web database work involves only a fraction of the Recordset object's many capabilities.

This section will explain the most common uses you're likely to make of the Recordset object. Table 4-1 summarizes the recordset methods present in ADO 2.5 and Table 4-2 summarizes the recordset properties. See "Locating ADO Documentation" in Chapter 3 ("Accessing Databases with ADO and ODBC") to learn how to find documentation that will provide further details.

Table 4-1   ADO Recordset Methods

Category *Obtaining and Discarding Result Sets*

Method	Description
Open	Obtains a result set from the data provider and makes it available for access
Clone	Creates a duplicate Recordset object from an existing one
Requery	Updates the data in a Recordset object by re-executing the query that created it
Resync	Refreshes the data in the Recordset object from the underlying database
Refresh	Updates the objects in a collection to reflect objects available from, and specific to, the provider
NextRecordset	Clears the Recordset object, tells the data provider to run the next command in its list, and makes the result set available
Close	Closes an open Recordset object and any dependent objects

Category *Movement*

Method	Description
Move	Moves the current record position forward or backward a specified number of records
MoveFirst	Makes the first record in a Recordset object the current record
MoveLast	Makes the last record in a Recordset object the current record
MoveNext	Makes the next record in a Recordset object the current record
MovePrevious	Makes the previous record in a Recordset object the current record
Find	Makes the record that satisfies a specified condition the current record
Seek	Searches a recordset's index to quickly locate the row that matches a specified condition

Category *Update*

Method	Description
AddNew	Creates a new blank record that's ready to accept field values
Update	Saves any changes made to the current record
CancelUpdate	Cancels any changes made to the current record or to a new record
Delete	Deletes the current record or a group of records

Category *Batch Update*

Method	Description
UpdateBatch	Writes all pending batch updates to disk
CancelBatch	Cancels a pending batch update

Category *Miscellaneous*

Method	Description
GetRows	Retrieves multiple records of a recordset into an array
Supports	Determines whether a specified Recordset object supports a particular type of functionality
ConvertToString	Converts a recordset to a MIME string that represents the recordset data
GetString	Returns the recordset as a string
Save	Saves the recordset in a file or a Stream object

Any specific list of ADO objects, methods, and properties can, of course, be correct only for a specific release of the software. Newer versions tend to provide additional features while still supporting old ones, but this is never certain.

The fact that ADO supports a certain method or property doesn't mean that all providers and all DBMS's support it. There are so many combinations of ADO versions, providers, DBMS's, and settings for each that no comprehensive table of supported methods and properties is possible. You can only be aware that the features available in a given configuration depend on many pieces of software and take this into account when debugging.

Batch Updating

Some applications need to perform multiple database updates on an "all or nothing" basis. The most common examples are accounting or banking systems in which every credit must have a successful and corresponding debit, and every debit must have a successful and corresponding credit. If the database accepts the credit update and then rejects the corresponding debit, the application must undo the credit update.

(continued)

Batch Updating *continued*

Most database systems support such requirements through the concept of *transactions*. A transaction is any group of "all or nothing" updates. ADO supports transaction processing through a slightly different model called *batching*. Batching multiple updates—that is, making a transaction of multiple updates—can also be useful for improving performance. If an application updates or creates dozens or hundreds of records at a time, performing such updates in a batch is often faster than performing them individually.

Table 4-2   ADO Recordset Properties

Property	Description
AbsolutePage	Identifies the page number on which the current record is located. (Refer also to the *PageSize* property.)
AbsolutePosition	Specifies the ordinal position of the current record.
ActiveCommand	Indicates the Command object that created a Recordset object.
ActiveConnection	Indicates the Connection object associated with a Recordset object.
BOF	Indicates that the current record position is before the first record.
Bookmark	Returns a value that uniquely identifies the current record. Setting this property to a value saved earlier restores the corresponding record position.
CacheSize	The number of records in a Recordset object that are cached locally in memory.
CursorLocation	Sets or returns the location of the cursor engine: client or server. Various cursor libraries provide different features for processing a recordset.
CursorType	Controls whether a recordset, while open, will reflect database additions, changes, and deletions made by other users. For more information about cursors, refer to the sidebar titled, "Cursors and Database Systems."
EditMode	Indicates whether changes to the current record are in progress.
EOF	Indicates that the current record position is after the last record.
Filter	Selectively screens out records in a Recordset object.
Index	Identifies the index currently in effect for a Recordset object.
LockType	Controls how the database will lock records (stop other users from updating them) while your code has an update in progress.

Property	Description
MarshalOptions	Controls which records from a client-side recordset get written back to the server (Remote Data Service only).
MaxRecords	Limits the number of records the provider returns from the data source.
PageCount	The number of pages of data currently in a Recordset object.
PageSize	The number of records contained in one page in the recordset.
RecordCount	Indicates the current number of records in a recordset.
Sort	Indicates one or more field names on which the recordset is sorted and whether each field is sorted in ascending or descending order.
Source	The source of the data in a Recordset object. This can be a Command object, a SQL statement, a table name, or a stored procedure name.
State	The recordset's current state (open or closed).
Status	The status of the current record with respect to batch updates or other bulk operations.
StayInSync	Indicates, in a hierarchical Recordset object, whether the reference to the underlying child records changes when the parent row position changes.

Cursors and Database Systems

When you work with recordsets, the word *cursor* has two meanings. First, it's a pointer to the current record. Second, it's the software that keeps track of and manipulates the current record position.

For performance reasons, many database systems provide several kinds of cursors having different capabilities. Some, for example, might only be able to move forward through a recordset, while others might be able to move backward as well.

In distributed applications, cursor software can run either on the client or the database server. A client-side cursor retrieves a recordset in blocks and then traverses it on the client. A server-side cursor traverses a recordset on the database server and transmits a record at a time to the client. (The client, in this sense, is the Web server that runs the ASP page, and the server is the machine that runs the database software.)

For the best performance, you should use a cursor that provides no more functionality than absolutely needed to satisfy the requirements of your Web page.

The following procedures explain how to perform the most common ADO recordset operations.

Create an ADO Recordset object

The first step in using an ADO Recordset object is to create one. The VBScript statement for this operation greatly resembles the statement that creates an ADO Connection object introduced in Chapter 3:

```
Set rsMbrs = Server.CreateObject("ADODB.Recordset")
```

You can name the recordset whatever you want, as long as the name conforms to the requirements of VBScript.

Open an ADO Recordset object

Creating a Recordset object doesn't connect it to a data provider, nor does it retrieve any records. To accomplish those ends, you must open the recordset with a statement of this form:

recordset.Open *Source, ActiveConnection, CursorType, LockType, Options*

- **recordset** is the name of the Recordset object you want to open. For this example, use the rsMbrs object created in the preceding example.

- **Source** is any expression that evaluates to a valid SQL statement, table name, stored procedure name, or Command object. The following statement puts a valid SQL statement in a variable named *sql*:

```
sql = "SELECT * FROM members"
```

    After this statement executes, the variable *sql* is suitable as a command text source argument of the Recordset.Open method. (For an explanation of the term command text, see the *Options* argument below.)

- **ActiveConnection** can be either the name of a *connection* object or an expression containing a valid connection string. For this example, use the *cnn1* connection opened in Chapter 3.

For more information about cursors, refer to the earlier sidebar titled, "Cursors and Database Systems."

- **CursorType** determines the type of cursor the provider should use. Table 4-3 lists the available types. These cursor types offer different combinations of function and performance for moving through the records in an open recordset.

- **LockType** determines what type of record locking the provider should use when processing the recordset.

    Whenever you design or code a Web database page, be aware that several Web visitors might be accessing the same record in the same database at the same time. This can lead to problems if visitors want to make updates, because only one visitor can update the same record at the same time.

    Database systems handle this situation by locking records for the duration of any update. When the first process tries to update a given record, the database system locks that record for the duration of the update. If another process tries to update the same record while the lock is in effect, that process receives an error notification.

Most Web database pages that perform updates affect only a few records per transaction—that is, only a few records, or even just one record, each time a Web visitor clicks the Submit button. In addition, most locks are in effect for a short time. Nevertheless, record locking is something you should consider whenever you open a recordset. Table 4-4 lists the record locking options that ADO supports.

- **Options** indicates what type of command the *source* argument contains and how to process it. Table 4-5 lists the available command types. These values tell the ADO *Recordset.Open* method what type of object to expect as the source argument. Table 4-6 lists the execution options, which tell the ADO *Recordset.Open* method how to execute the *Open* statement. To specify any one option, simply code its value. To specify a command type option and an execute option, add them together.

Table 4-3 Cursor Types for ADO Recordsets

Constant	Value	Description
adOpenStatic	3	**Static cursor** An unchanging copy of a set of records. While the recordset is open, it won't automatically reflect additions, changes, or deletions that other users make to the data source. Static cursors are better suited to finding and displaying data than making updates.
adOpenDynamic	2	**Dynamic cursor** The recordset will reflect additions, changes, and deletions made by other users and allow all types of movement through the recordset.
adOpenKeyset	1	**Keyset cursor** The recordset will reflect changes and deletions made by other users, but not additions. All types of movement through the recordset are allowed.
adOpenForwardOnly (default)	0	**Forward-Only cursor** Similar to a static cursor except that you can only scroll forward through records. This improves performance when you need to make only a single pass through a recordset.

Table 4-4 Lock Types for ADO Recordsets

Constant	Value	Description
adLockReadOnly (default)	1	**Read-Only** You cannot alter the data.
adLockPessimistic	2	**Pessimistic Locking, Record by Record** As soon as you start editing a record in the recordset, the provider locks it. If the record is already in use, the VBScript statement that began the edit will fail.

(continued)

Table 4-4 *continued*

Constant	Value	Description
adLockOptimistic	3	**Optimistic Locking, Record by Record** The provider doesn't lock records at the data source until your code calls the recordset's *Update* method. If the record is already in use, the VBScript statement attempting the update will fail.
adLockBatchOptimistic	4	**Optimistic Batch Updates** ADO stores up all updates you make to a recordset, and then applies them when you call the Recordset object's *BatchUpdate* method. If the provider finds that any record in the batch is already in use, the VBScript statement attempting the batch update will fail.

See "Using ADO Commands" later in this chapter for an explanation of Command objects.

Table 4-5   Command Type Options for ADO Recordsets

Constant	Value	Description
adCmdUnspecified	−1	Specifies no command type argument.
adCmdText (default)	1	The provider should evaluate the *source* argument as a textual definition of a command.
adCmdTable	2	The provider should evaluate the *source* argument as a table name.
adCmdStoredProc	4	The provider should evaluate the *source* argument as the name of a stored procedure.
adCmdUnknown	8	The type of command in the *source* argument isn't known. ADO will try sending the *source* argument to the provider in modes 1, 2, and 4.
adCmdFile	256	The provider should evaluate the *source* argument as the file name of a persistently stored recordset.
adCmdTableDirect	512	The provider should evaluate the *source* argument as a table name whose columns are all returned.

Table 4-6   Execute Options for ADO Recordsets

Constant	Value	Description
adAsyncExecute	16	The command should execute asynchronously. That is, the statement following the *Open* statement can execute without waiting for the *Open* statement to complete.
adAsyncFetch	32	After initially retrieving the number of rows specified in the *CacheSize* property, the provider should retrieve any remaining rows asynchronously.

Constant	Value	Description
adAsyncFetchNonBlocking	64	The main thread should never block while retrieving. If a requested row hasn't been retrieved, the current row automatically moves to the end of the file.
		If you open a recordset from a Stream that contains a persistently stored recordset, this option will have no effect; the operation will be synchronous and blocking.
adExecuteNoRecords	128	The command text is a command or stored procedure that doesn't return rows (for example, a command that only inserts data). If any rows are retrieved, they are discarded and not returned. This applies to the command type options *adCmdText* and *adCmdStoredProc*.
adOptionUnspecified	−1	Indicates that the command is unspecified.

Here's the completed *Open* statement for the example. In English, it says, "Open the *rsMbrs* Recordset object. Obtain its result set by submitting the command text in the variable *sql* to the data provider referenced by the *cnn1* Connection object. You don't need to support backward movement through the recordset, only forward. There's no intent to update the data producing this result set."

```
rsMbrs.Open sql, cnn1, adOpenForwardOnly, adLockReadOnly, adCmdText
```

This book's remaining examples show how to open Recordset objects with other options.

Move through an ADO recordset's result set

Once you've opened a recordset, most providers will automatically position it to the first record. This is fine if the first record is all you want, but in many cases you'll want to examine or process other records as well. To support this, the Recordset object provides five methods and four properties for moving through the result set. You can see these methods listed in Table 4-1.

The first four methods listed in Table 4-7 are the simplest and most commonly used methods for moving the current record pointers forward and backward through the records in a Recordset object. These methods require no arguments; you just code them directly as shown here:

```
rsMbrs.MoveFirst
rsMbrs.MoveLast
rsMbrs.MoveNext
rsMbrs.MovePrev
```

Table 4-7   Movement Methods for ADO Recordsets

Method	Description
MoveFirst	Establishes the first record in the result set as the current record.
MoveLast	Establishes the last record in the result set as the current record.
MoveNext	Sets the current record position forward one record.
MovePrevious	Sets the current record position back one record. Using this method will generate an error if you specified *adOpenForwardOnly* when you opened the recordset.
Move	Sets the current record position to a specific count from the start of the result set or from a bookmark.

The MoveFirst *method can be time-consuming if you specified* adOpenForwardOnly *when you opened the recordset.*

If you're already at the last record in a result set and you execute the *MoveNext* method, ADO sets the recordset's *EOF* property to *True*. Similarly, if you execute the *MovePrevious* method when you're already at the first record, ADO sets the *BOF* property to *True*. Reading all the records in a result set is therefore as easy as writing a loop such as this:

```
rsMbrs.MoveFirst
Do While Not rsMbrs.EOF
    ' Your code to process the record goes here.
    rsMbrs.MoveNext
Loop
```

If for some reason you want to process the records backward, you could code the loop like this:

```
rsMbrs.MoveLast
Do While Not rsMbrs.BOF
    ' Your code to process the record goes here.
    rsMbrs.MovePrevious
Loop
```

Of course, this will fail if the data provider doesn't support backward movement through a result set or if you specified *adOpenForwardOnly* when you opened the recordset.

The following conditions will cause a fatal error (one that halts your VBScript code and displays a cryptic message to the Web visitor):

- Using the *MoveNext* method when the *EOF* property is already *True*

- Using the *MovePrevious* method when the *BOF* property is already *True*

- Using any move method when the recordset is empty. (Both *BOF* and *EOF* will be *True* in this case.)

ADO provides a fifth method, *Move*, that works on the basis of record numbers:

recordset.Move *NumRecords, Start*

The *NumRecords* argument states the number of records to move. Positive values denote forward movement and negative values denote backward movement. The *Start* argument is optional, but if specified it can be any valid bookmark or any value from Table 4-8.

Table 4-8   ADO *Recordset.Move* Method Bookmarks

Constant	Value	Description
adBookmarkCurrent (default)	0	Start at the current record
adBookmarkFirst	1	Start at the first record
adBookmarkLast	2	Start at the last record

As with other move methods, attempting to move past the beginning or end of a result set will cause a fatal error. The same is true of any attempt to move through an empty result set.

The *Move* method has two serious limitations. First, although record numbers might seem to be a simple and useful concept, not all providers support them. Second (and this is the reason for the first limitation), record numbers change when you or other processes create or delete records in the result set or in the underlying database. This means that record number 10, for example, could within a split second become record number 9 or 11. This makes record numbers unreliable for remembering where a certain record resides and quickly returning to it later.

Bookmarks, by contrast, remain constant. The same bookmark always denotes the same record until you *Requery*, *Resync*, or *Close* the recordset.

Table 4-9 lists the properties that position and filter a recordset's current record point.

Bookmarks

A bookmark is an internally generated value that identifies each record in a result set. The bookmark value for a particular record remains constant even if you (or another process) update the record, delete other records in the same result set, or create other records in the same result set.

To save the bookmark for any current record, move to that record and then store the recordset's *Bookmark* property in a VBScript variable. To return quickly to the same record later, set the recordset's *Bookmark* property to the saved value.

You should assume that bookmark values have no significance in and of themselves. In other words, examining a bookmark value doesn't tell you (or your Web visitor) anything about the corresponding record.

You can also use the *AbsolutePosition* property to get the ordinal number of the current record.

Table 4-9   Positioning Properties for ADO Recordsets

Property	Description
AbsolutePosition	Reports the ordinal position of the current record. Changing this value changes the current record position to point to the record with the specified ordinal position.
AbsolutePage	Reports the position of the page that contains the current record. Changing this value changes the current record position to point to the first record in the indicated page.
Bookmark	Returns a system-generated value that uniquely identifies a record. Setting the *bookmark* property to a previously retrieved bookmark value sets the current record position to the corresponding record.
Filter	Restricts viewing of the current result set to records satisfying certain criteria.

Unfortunately, because the *AbsolutePosition* property uses ordinal record numbers, it shares all the limitations of the *Move* method. You're much better off sticking to bookmarks and the *MoveFirst, MoveNext, MovePrevious,* and *MoveLast* methods.

If there is no current record, that *AbsolutePosition* property will contain one of the special values listed in Table 4-10.

Table 4-10   ADO Ordinal Record Positions

Value	Constant	Description
1 to *RecordCount*	(none)	An ordinal position within the result set.
−1	*adPosUnknown*	The result set is empty, the current position is unknown, or the provider doesn't support the *AbsolutePosition* property.
−2	*adPosBOF*	The current record pointer is at *BOF*. The *BOF* property is *True*.
−3	*adPosEOF*	The current record pointer is at *EOF*. The *EOF* property is *True*.

For an explanation of the Book-mark property, see the "Book-marks" sidebar on page 75.

The *AbsolutePage* property indicates which page of the result set contains the current record. You can use an open recordset's *PageSize* property to determine the number of records in each page. To choose a different page size, store the desired value into the recordset's *PageSize* property before you open it. Frankly, it's hard to imagine what use these properties would have in a Web database page.

The *Filter* property creates a new, temporary result set that's a subset of the original one. You can filter on logical expressions such as those shown here or on any of the special criteria listed in Table 4-11.

```
position = 'M'
(position = 'P') or (position = 'V') or (position = 'S')
(position = 'M') and (sname = 'Davolio')
```

Changing a recordset's *Filter* property changes the current record position; the new current record will be the first record in the filtered result set. Removing a filter (by setting the *Filter* property to *adFilterNone*) restores all the original records to view, but doesn't restore the record position in effect before the filtering took place.

In general, it's more efficient to do any required filtering in the SQL statement that creates the original result set. There might be cases, however, when querying a large database once and then applying several filters can be more efficient than querying the large database several times.

Table 4-11 Special Values for ADO *Recordset.Filter* Property

Constant	Value	Description
adFilterNone	0	Removes the current filter and restores all records to view
adFilterPendingRecords	1	Provides access only to records that have changed but have not yet been sent to the server (only applicable for batch update mode)
adFilterAffectedRecords	2	Provides access only to records affected by the last *Delete*, *Resync*, *UpdateBatch*, or *CancelBatch* call
adFilterFetchedRecords	3	Provides access only to records in the current cache; that is, the results of the last call to retrieve records from the database

Access fields in an ADO recordset

Positioning to the record you want is all well and good, but it doesn't provide access to the information that record contains. For that, you must access the recordset's Fields collection. The Fields collection contains one Field object for each field in the recordset's result set. ADO automatically creates these Field objects whenever it opens a Recordset object.

The syntax to access a field's property is

recordset.Fields*(index).property*

where

- **recordset** is the Recordset object that contains the desired result set.

- **index** is either the field's name or its ordinal position.

- **property** is any property name listed in Table 4-12.

As you can see from Table 4-12, Field objects have quite a number of useful properties.

Table 4-12   ADO Field Properties

Property	Description
ActualSize	The current length of a field, stated in bytes.
Attributes	A bit-mapped long integer that provides the information about the field.
DefinedSize	The maximum length of a field, stated in bytes.
Name	The name of a field, typically as defined in the database or in a SQL statement.
NumericScale	The number of decimal places stored in the database (applies to numeric values only).
OriginalValue	The value held by a field when you first retrieved the record (before your code made any changes).
Precision	The maximum number of digits available to represent values.
Type	The internal format of a field.
UnderlyingValue	The current value of a field as stored in the database. ADO refreshes this property from the database every time you ask for it. If *OriginalValue* and *UnderlyingValue* are different, someone else updated the record after you opened the recordset.
Value (default)	The current value of a field, as seen or modified by your code.

The Attributes property described in Table 4-12 contains a single bit-mapped value that combines several kinds of information. It will contain the sum of all applicable values from Table 4-13. In other words, the ADO *Recordset. Field.Attributes* property contains the sum of all values listed in Table 4-13 that apply to a particular field.

Table 4-13   ADO Field Attribute Values

Constant	Value	Description
adFldMayDefer	&H00000002	The field is deferred. ADO won't retrieve the field's value unless you explicitly ask for it.
adFldUpdatable	&H00000004	You can write to the field.
adFldUnknownUpdatable	&H00000008	The provider can't determine whether you can write to the field.
adFldFixed	&H00000010	The field contains fixed-length data.
adFldIsNullable	&H00000020	The field accepts NULL values.
adFldMayBeNull	&H00000040	You can read NULL values from the field.

Constant	Value	Description
adFldLong	&H00000080	The field is a long binary field. Also, you can use the *Append-Chunk* and *GetChunk* methods on this field.
adFldRowID	&H00000100	The field contains some kind of record ID (record number, unique identifier, and so on).
adFldRowVersion	&H00000200	The field contains a time or date stamp used to track updates.
adFldCacheDeferred	&H00001000	The provider caches field values and subsequent reads are done from the cache.
adFldKeyColumn	&H00008000	The field is a part of a key.

The *Type* property described in Table 4-12 uses the values listed in Table 4-14 to indicate the internal format of a field. In most cases, however, you'll already know what kind of data each field in your application can contain. If you don't, you'll probably find it easier to view the database properties in Microsoft Access or consult your database administrator than to write a Web page that displays the field types that concern you. Testing field types in code is more useful when you write a loop that iterates through all fields in a recordset and you want to treat certain field types differently.

Table 4-14   ADO Field Types

Constant	Value	Description
adEmpty	0	No value was specified.
adSmallInt	2	A 2-byte (16-bit) signed integer.
adInteger	3	A 4-byte (32-bit) signed integer.
adSingle	4	A single-precision floating-point value.
adDouble	5	A double-precision floating-point value.
adCurrency	6	A currency value. Currency is a fixed-point number with 4 digits to the right of the decimal point. It's stored as an 8-byte signed integer multiplied by 10,000.
adDate	7	A date value. A date is stored as a double, the whole part of which is the number of days since December 30, 1899, and the fractional part of which is a fraction of a day.
adBSTR	8	A null-terminated character string.
adIDispatch	9	A pointer to an *IDispatch* interface on an OLE object.
adError	10	A 32-bit error code.

(continued)

Table 4-14 *continued*

Constant	Value	Description
adBoolean	11	A Boolean value.
adVariant	12	An Automation Variant.
adIUnknown	13	A pointer to an *IUnknown* interface on an OLE object.
adDecimal	14	An exact numeric value with a fixed precision and scale.
adTinyInt	16	A 1-byte signed integer.
adUnsignedTinyInt	17	A 1-byte unsigned integer.
adUnsignedSmallInt	18	A 2-byte unsigned integer.
adUnsignedInt	19	A 4-byte unsigned integer.
adBigInt	20	An 8-byte signed integer.
adUnsignedBigInt	21	An 8-byte unsigned integer.
adGUID	72	A globally unique identifier.
adBinary	128	A binary value.
adChar	129	A string value.
adWChar	130	A null-terminated Unicode character string.
adNumeric	131	An exact numeric value with a fixed precision and scale.
adUserDefined	132	A user-defined variable.
adDBDate	133	A date value (yyyymmdd).
adDBTime	134	A time value (hhmmss).
adDBTimeStamp	135	A date-time stamp (yyyymmddhhmmss plus a fraction in billionths).

Here's a practical example. The following expression returns the current value of the *memberid* field from the recordset named *rsMbrs*:

```
rsMbrs.Fields("memberid").Value
```

Two ADO defaults can simplify this expression even more: the Fields collection is the default object for any recordset, and the *Value* property is the default property for any field. Thus, the following expressions are all equivalent:

```
rsMbrs.Fields("memberid").Value
rsMbrs.Fields("memberid")
rsMbrs("memberid").Value
rsMbrs("memberid")
```

If it's convenient, you can also select fields by their order—numbered left to right starting with zero—as defined in the data source. For example, if you opened the *rsMbrs* recordset with a SQL statement that began

```
SELECT memberid, fname, sname, position, phone, email
FROM members ...
```

the following expressions would be equivalent:

```
rsMbrs.Fields("memberid").Value
rsMbrs.Fields(0).Value
rsMbrs(0)
```

The index values can also be variables. This means the following pairs of statements are perfectly valid:

```
fldName = "memberid"
fldValue = rsMbrs.Fields(fldName).Value

fldNum = 0
fldValue = rsMbrs.Fields(fldNum).Value
```

To iterate through all the fields in a recordset and display the value of each field in its own table cell, you could code

```
For i = 0 To rsMbrs.Fields.Count - 1
    Response.Write "<td>" & rsMbrs.Fields(i) & "</td>"
Next
```

Like most collections, the Fields collection has a *Count* property that states the number of items in the collection. In the case of the Fields collection, the *Count* property states the number of fields in the result set. The collection is zero-based, so the code must iterate from zero to the number of fields minus one.

The *Response.Write* statement sends HTML to the Web visitor's browser. The *Response.Write* statement shown above sends a <td> tag to start a table cell, the database value in field *i* of the *rsMbrs* recordset, and a </td> tag to end the table cell.

Now you have enough background information to complete the example. The annotated code follows; it should be familiar if you've understood the preceding material. Just remember the following characteristics of ASP code:

- Anything inside <% and %> tags is VBScript code that runs on the Web server.

- Nothing inside <% and %> tags gets sent directly to the Web visitor's browser.

- Code running between <% and %> tags can send text to the browser by using the *Response.Write* method. This output appears:

  - In the order that the *Response.Write* statements execute

  - In place of the <%...%> block that contains the *Response.Write* statements.

- The following statements are equivalent:

```
<%
Response.Write Server.HTMLEncode(rsMbrs("memberid"))
%>
```

   and

```
<%=Server.HTMLEncode(rsMbrs("memberid"))%>
```

In effect, the equal sign abbreviates *Response.Write*. However, this form requires that the leading <% tag, the equal sign, a single expression, and the closing %> tag all be on the same line.

- VBScript has a built-in constant called *vbCrLf* that's useful for inserting line endings. Its value always consists of two bytes: a carriage return followed by a line feed.

```
<html>
<head>
<title>members</title>
<!--Include ADO named constants -->
<!-- #include file="../adovbs.inc" -->
<%
' Open connection to Access database coinclub.mdb.
Set cnn1 = Server.CreateObject("ADODB.Connection")
openStr = "driver={Microsoft Access Driver (*.mdb)};" & _
          "dbq=" & Server.MapPath("coinclub.mdb")
cnn1.Open openStr,"",""
' Open a recordset containing all fields
' from all records in the members table.
sql = "SELECT * FROM members;"
Set rsMbrs = Server.CreateObject("ADODB.Recordset")
rsMbrs.Open sql, cnn1, adOpenForwardOnly, adLockReadOnly, adCmdText
%>
</head>
<body>
<!--Specify the heading for an HTML table. -->
<table border="1" cellspacing="0" cellpadding="3">
  <caption><b>members</b></caption>
  <tr>
    <th>memberid</th>
    <th>fname</th>
    <th>sname</th>
    <th>position</th>
    <th>phone</th>
    <th>email</th>
  </tr>
<%' Begin looping though all records.
Do While Not rsMbrs.EOF
%><!-- Start a new table row.-->
    <tr valign="TOP">
<!-- Create six table cells that contain the values
     of the memberid, fname, sname, position, phone,
     and email fields respectively. -->
<td><%=Server.HTMLEncode(rsMbrs.Fields("memberid").Value)%>
<td><%=Server.HTMLEncode(rsMbrs.Fields("fname").Value)%></td>
```

```
<td><%=Server.HTMLEncode(rsMbrs.Fields("sname").Value)%></td>
<td><%=Server.HTMLEncode(rsMbrs.Fields("position").Value)%></td>
<td><%=Server.HTMLEncode(rsMbrs.Fields("phone").Value)%></td>
<td><%=Server.HTMLEncode(rsMbrs.Fields("email").Value)%></td>
/tr)
<%
' Move to next record.
rsMbrs.MoveNext
' End of loop repeated once for each record.
Loop
' Close the recordset and discard the object.
rsMbrs.Close
set rsMbrs = Nothing
' Close the connection and discard the object.
cnn1.Close
set cnn1 = Nothing
%>
</table>
</body>
</html>
```

This code and a copy of the *coinclub.mdb* database both appear on the companion CD-ROM in the ch04 folder in the sample files. The filename is members1.asp. Figure 4-1 shows how the output looks in a browser. Figure 4-2 shows a representative portion of the HTML received by the browser.

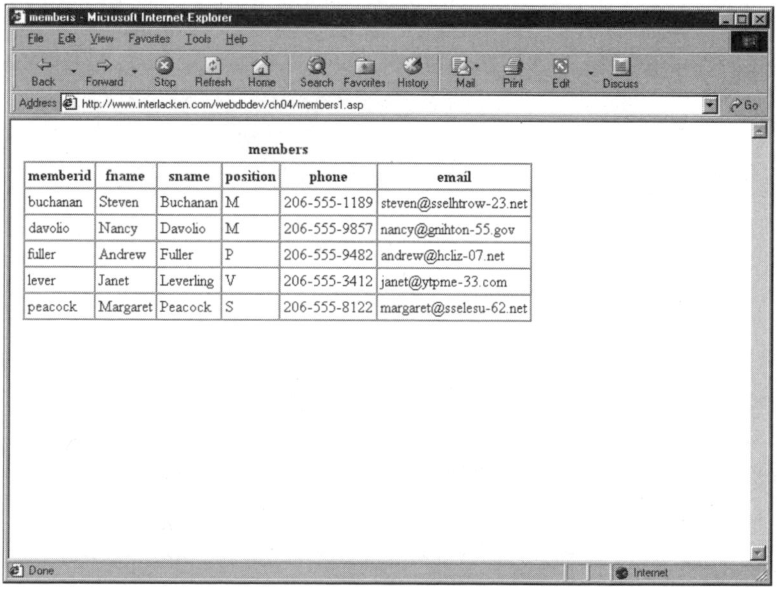

Figure 4-1 *The members1.asp example produces this Web page.*

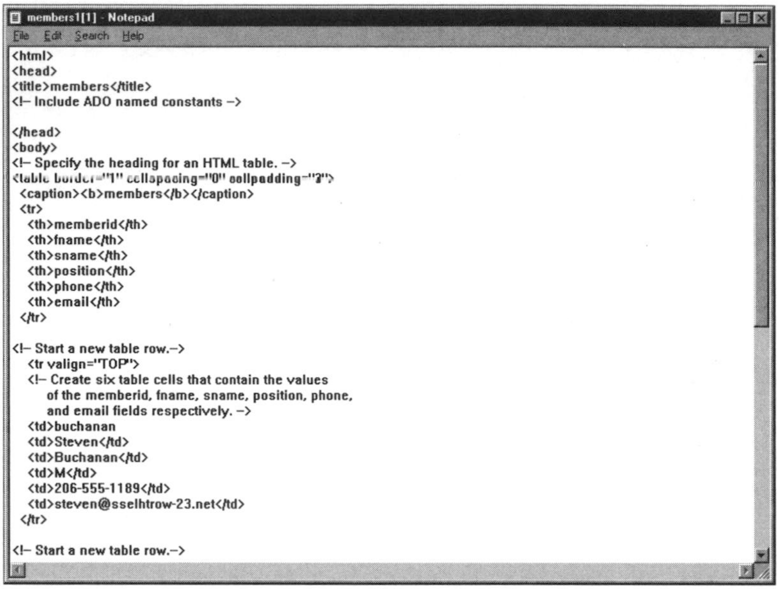

```
members1[1] - Notepad
File Edit Search Help
<html>
<head>
<title>members</title>
<!-- Include ADO named constants -->

</head>
<body>
<!-- Specify the heading for an HTML table. -->
<table border="1" cellspacing="0" cellpadding="3">
 <caption><b>members</b></caption>
 <tr>
  <th>memberid</th>
  <th>fname</th>
  <th>sname</th>
  <th>position</th>
  <th>phone</th>
  <th>email</th>
 </tr>

<!-- Start a new table row.-->
  <tr valign="TOP">
  <!-- Create six table cells that contain the values
     of the memberid, fname, sname, position, phone,
     and email fields respectively. -->
  <td>buchanan
  <td>Steven</td>
  <td>Buchanan</td>
  <td>M</td>
  <td>206-555-1189</td>
  <td>steven@sselhtrow-23.net</td>
 </tr>

<!-- Start a new table row.-->
```

Figure 4-2 *The HTML that a Web visitor receives from the members1.asp example. Note that the server-side VBScript code has disappeared and that the HTML it creates appears in its place.*

An alternative solution that generates similar results appears below. Instead of hard-coding the column headings, this solution loops through the recordset's Fields collection and uses field names from the database. Similarly, instead of hard-coding the fields in each table cell, this solution loops through each record's Fields collection.

```
<html>
<head>
<title>members</title>
<!-- #include file="../adovbs.inc" -->
<%
Set cnn1 = Server.CreateObject("ADODB.Connection")
openStr = "driver={Microsoft Access Driver (*.mdb)};" & _
          "dbq=" & Server.MapPath("coinclub.mdb")
cnn1.Open openStr,"",""

sql = "SELECT * FROM [members];"
Set rsMbrs = Server.CreateObject("ADODB.Recordset")
rsMbrs.Open sql, cnn1, adOpenForwardOnly, adLockReadOnly, adCmdText
%>
</head>
<body>
<table border="1" cellspacing="0" cellpadding="3">
  <caption><b>members</b></caption>
<%
'  Start of table row for column headings.
```

```
response.write "<tr>" & vbCrLf
' Loop through the Fields collection, and create a
' table heading cell for each field name.
For i = 0 To rsMbrs.Fields.Count-1
    Response.Write "  <th>" & _
        Server.HTMLencode(rsMbrs.Fields(i).Name) & _
        "</th>" & vbCrLf
Next
' End of table row for column headings.
Response.Write "</tr>" & vbCrLf
' Start of loop repeated for each record.
Do While Not rsMbrs.EOF
  ' Start of table row for record values.
  Response.Write "<tr>" & vbCrLf
  ' Loop through the Fields collection, and create
  ' a table cell for each field value.
  For i = 0 To rsMbrs.Fields.Count-1
      Response.Write "<td>" & _
        Server.HTMLencode(rsMbrs.Fields(i)) & _
        "</td>" & vbCrLf
  Next
  ' End of table row for record values.
  Response.Write "</tr>" & vbCrLf
  rsMbrs.MoveNext
' End of loop repeated for each record.
Loop
%>
</table>
<%
rsMbrs.Close
Set rsMbrs = Nothing
cnn1.Close
Set cnn1 = Nothing
%>
</body>
</html>
```

Chapters 5, 6, and 7 will illustrate many more examples of database queries initiated and displayed through Web pages.

Modify a record in an ADO recordset

Using ADO to modify existing records is relatively simple. At a summary level, here are the steps required:

1. Open a connection to the database.

2. Open a recordset that contains the record you want to update.

3. Position to the record you want to update.

4. Replace the contents of any fields you want to change.

5. To save your changes, use either the recordset's *Update* method or any of its move methods. To discard your changes, use the recordset's *CancelUpdate* method before using any of its move methods.

6. Close the recordset and the database connection.

To illustrate this procedure, the next example implements a hit counter that keeps its values in the coinclub database. Figure 4-3 shows the table that stores these counts. It's called the *hitcounts* table, and it contains three fields:

- The *url* field is a text field that contains the URL of a Web page. This is the table's primary key.

- The *hitcnt* field is a numeric field that contains the current hit count for the corresponding Web page.

- The *lasthit* field records the date of the most recent visit to the Web page.

The first step in developing this application is to get the URL of the current Web page. Your first thought might be to simply hard-code this, but Web pages frequently get moved around and no one usually remembers to check ASP code for hard-coded location values. In addition, gathering hit counts is an addictive process for Webmasters, and it makes sense to develop a single piece of code that works without needing modification in many different pages.

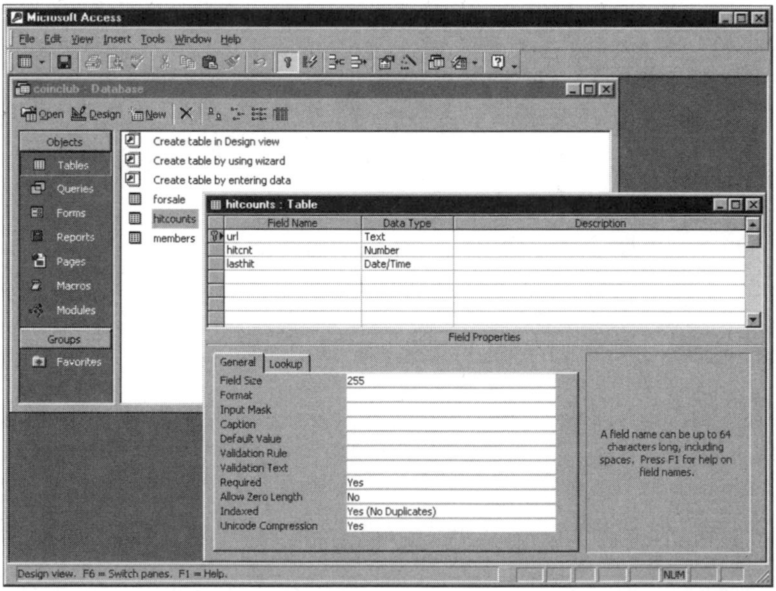

Figure 4-3 *This table accumulates hit count and date-last-visited statistics for any number of Web pages.*

As Chapter 5, "Customizing Web Content with Server-Side Scripting," explains in far more detail, the ASP environment provides five important built-in objects:

- The *Server object* provides information and resources local to the Web server.

- The *Request object* provides information about the current request for service by a Web visitor

- The *Application object* provides a common, persistent storage area shared by all Web pages in the same application (that is, by all Web pages in a designated folder tree).

- The *Session object* provides a common, persistent storage area for all transactions from the same Web visitor.

- The *Response object* sends a Web page or other response back to the Web visitor who originated the current request.

One of the Request object's properties is a collection called ServerVariables. Within this collection is a property called *PATH_INFO* that contains the URL of the current page. The following statement retrieves this information and stores it in a variable named *thisURL*.

```
thisURL = Request.ServerVariables("PATH_INFO")
```

The next statement writes this information into the Web page going back to the Web visitor. It's unlikely that any real Web page would display this information, but it's useful for debugging and understanding this example.

```
Response.Write "<p>This page's URL is: " & thisURL & _
               "</p>" & vbCrLf
```

The next 10 statements open a connection to the database, construct a SQL statement to retrieve the record containing the value in *thisURL*, and open a recordset that makes that record available. There are no new techniques in this code, except that to permit updates, it specifies *adLockPessimistic* instead of *adLockReadOnly*.

```
Set cnn1 = Server.CreateObject("ADODB.Connection")
openStr = "driver={Microsoft Access Driver (*.mdb)};" & _
          "dbq=" & Server.MapPath("coinclub.mdb")
cnn1.Open openStr,"",""

sql = "SELECT url, hitcnt, lasthit " & _
      "FROM hitcounts " & _
      "WHERE url = '" & thisURL & "';"
Set rsHits = Server.CreateObject("ADODB.Recordset")
rsHits.Open sql, cnn1, adOpenDynamic, adLockPessimistic, adCmdText
```

The next group of statements checks the recordset's *EOF* property. If it's *True*, the *hitcounts* table has no record for the current page and the script sends the Web visitor a message to that effect. If the recordset's *EOF* property is *False*, the record contains the one and only record for the requested URL. (Because the *url* field is the table's primary key, there can never be more than one record with the same URL value.)

```
If rsHits.EOF Then
    Response.Write "<p>No hit counter defined.</P>"
Else
    curCount = rsHits("hitcnt") + 1
    rsHits("hitcnt") = curCount
    rsHits("lasthit") = Now()
    rsHits.Update
    Response.Write "<p>Hits so far for this page: " &  curCount
End If
```

- The first statement after the *Else* gets the current *hitcnt* value from the database, increments it by one, and stores the results in a variable named *curCount*.

- The next statement copies the value from *curCount* back to the *hitcnt* field in the database.

- The third statement after the *Else* saves the current date and time into the *lasthit* field. (The *Now* function is a built-in feature of VBScript.)

- The fourth statement after the *Else* commits the change into the database.

- The last statement after the *Else* displays the new hit count for the Web visitor to read.

The only tasks remaining are to close and release the Connection and Recordset objects. This code should accomplish this without any surprises:

```
rsHits.Close
Set rsHits = Nothing
cnn1.Close
Set cnn1 = Nothing
```

Here's how the example looks when integrated into a complete Web page. You can find this page located within the sample files as ch04\counter1.asp. When run, it produces the results shown in Figure 4-4 on page 9. At this point, the example only updates existing hitcount records; it can't create new records for pages that lack them.

```
<html>
<head>
<title>Hit Counter</title>
```

```
<!-- #include file="../adovbs.inc" -->
</head>
<body>
<%
' Get the URL of the current page, and display it to the Web visitor.
thisURL = Request.ServerVariables("PATH_INFO")
Response.Write "<p>This page's URL is: " & thisURL & _
  "</p>" & vbCrLf
' Open a database connection.
Set cnn1 = Server.CreateObject("ADODB.Connection")
openStr = "driver={Microsoft Access Driver (*.mdb)};" & _
          "dbq=" & Server.MapPath("coinclub.mdb")
cnn1.Open openStr,"",""
' Open a recordset, and get the record for the current URL.
sql = "SELECT url, hitcnt, lasthit " & _
      "FROM hitcounts " & _
      "WHERE url = '" & thisURL & "';"
Set rsHits = Server.CreateObject("ADODB.Recordset")
rsHits.Open sql, cnn1, adOpenDynamic, adLockPessimistic, adCmdText
' If the recordset contains no records, no hit counter is available.
If rsHits.EOF Then
    Response.Write "<p>No hit counter defined.</P>"
Else
    ' Retrieve the existing hit count, and increment it by 1.
    curCount = rsHits("hitcnt") + 1
    ' Update the database with the new hit count and most recent hit date.
    rsHits("hitcnt") = curCount
    rsHits("lasthit") = Now()
    rsHits.Update
    ' Display the new hit count to Web visitor.
    Response.Write "Hits so far for this page: " & curCount & _
      "</p>"
End If
' Close and release the Recordset and Connection objects.
rsHits.Close
Set rsHits = Nothing
cnn1.Close
Set cnn1 = Nothing
%>
</body>
</html>
```

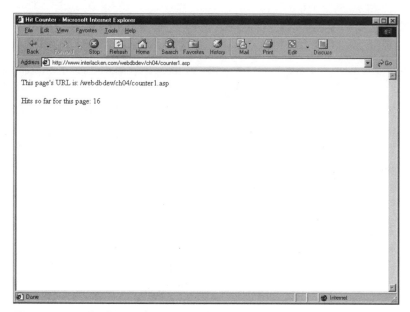

Figure 4-4   *The hit count reported on this Web page is actually a field in a database.*

Add a record to an ADO recordset

The procedure for creating a new record is much the same as that for updating an existing record. To update an existing record you move to that record, add the new field values, and then call the recordset's *Update* method. To create a new record you call the recordset's *AddNew* method, move in the new field values, and then call the recordset's *Update* method.

To illustrate this process, the next example modifies the counter1.asp page so that if no *hitcount* record exists for a given URL, the page creates one. Recall that the counter1.asp page contained this code:

```
If rsHits.EOF Then
    Response.Write "<p>No hit counter defined.</p>"
Else
    curCount = rsHits("hitcnt") + 1
    rsHits("hitcnt") = curCount
     rsHits("lasthit") = Now()
    rsHits.Update
    Response.Write "<p>Hits so far for this page: " & curCount & _
      "</p>"
End If
```

This code handles the no record condition by displaying the message, "No hit counter defined." To make it create a new record instead, make the code read as follows:

```
If rsHits.EOF Then
    rsHits.AddNew
    rsHits("url") = thisURL
    curCount = 1
```

```
Else
    curCount = rsHits("hitcnt") + 1
End If
rsHits("hitcnt") = curCount
rsHits("lasthit") = Now()
rsHits.Update
Response.Write "<p>Hits so far for this page: " & curCount
```

If no *hitcount* record already exists, this code calls the Recordset object's *AddNew* command, loads the *url* field with the URL of the current page, and sets the current hit count to 1.

If a matching *hitcount* record does exist, the code sets the current hit count to the previous hit count plus one.

In both cases, the code finishes by storing the new hit count and the new last hit date into the database record, calling the recordset's *Update* method to commit the change, and then displaying the new hit count for the Web visitor.

Here's how the example looks when integrated into a complete Web page. You can find this page located within the sample files as ch04\counter2.asp. When run, it produces essentially the same visual results you saw in Figure 4-4.

```
<html>
<head>
<title>Hit Counter</title>
<!-- #include file="../adovbs.inc" -->
</head>
<body>
<%
thisURL = Request.ServerVariables("PATH_INFO")
Response.Write "<p>This page's URL is: " & thisURL & _
  "</p>" & vbCrLf

Set cnn1 = Server.CreateObject("ADODB.Connection")
openStr = "driver={Microsoft Access Driver (*.mdb)};" & _
          "dbq=" & Server.MapPath("coinclub.mdb")
cnn1.Open openStr,"",""

sql = "SELECT url, hitcnt, lasthit" & _
      "FROM hitcounts " & _
      "WHERE url = '" & thisURL & "';"
Set rsHits = Server.CreateObject("ADODB.Recordset")
rsHits.Open sql, cnn1, adOpenDynamic, adLockPessimistic, adCmdText

If rsHits.EOF Then
    rsHits.AddNew
    rsHits("url") = thisURL
    curCount = 1
Else
    curCount = rsHits("hitcnt") + 1
End If
rsHits("hitcnt") = curCount
```

(continued)

```
rsHits("lasthit") = Now()rsHits.Update
Response.Write "<p>Hits so far for this page: " & curCount & _
  "</p>"
rsHits.Close
Set rsHits = Nothing
cnn1.Close
Set cnn1 = Nothing
%>
</body>
</html>
```

Whenever you attempt to add a record, the data provider will of course force an error if it detects that some requirement isn't met. For example, you might supply an unacceptable value in some field, or forget to supply a value for a required field. The code shown above contains no error handling statements, so if the ADO method fails, the script fails and the Web visitor will get an obscure message from the data provider. Later in this chapter, "Using the ADO Error Object" explains how to provide more customized error handling.

The problem of supplying all required fields can be a vexing one, especially if there are required fields that your recordset doesn't contain. Here are two examples of this problem.

- Suppose that the *hitcnt* table also contains a field named *owner*, and this field is marked within the database as a required field. This means the database will reject any attempt to add a record with a blank or missing *owner* field. If you try to add a *hitcnt* record through a recordset that doesn't contain the *owner* field, the addition can't possibly succeed.

- Suppose that you used a JOIN statement to combine the *hitcnt* table with an employee table based on the hypothetical *owner* field, and then tried to add a new record. Should the database system add a new *hitcnt* record, add a new employee record, or both? And what if the employee record had required fields not projected into your recordset?

To avoid such problems, many experienced programmers prefer updating recordsets that include all fields in the table and that don't involve any join operations.

Delete a record in an ADO recordset

The procedure for deleting a record is even simpler than those for adding or modifying records. Simply position to the desired (or more correctly, the no-longer-desired) record, and then call the recordset's *Delete* method.

The following example reports and then deletes any record in the *hitcounts* table with a *lasthit* date more than 180 days old. To search for such records, the example constructs a SQL statement that looks something like this:

```
SELECT * FROM hitcounts WHERE lasthit < #10/17/1999#
```

This statement selects all fields from all records in the *hitcounts* table that have a *lasthit* value prior to a specified date. Note the pound signs surrounding the date literal. Because *lasthit* is a date field, you must compare it to a date literal—a valid date, time, or both surrounded by pound signs. The code to generate this SQL statement looks like this:

```
sql = "SELECT * " & _
      "FROM hitcounts " & _
      "WHERE lasthit < #" & _
      FormatDateTime(Now()-180) & _
      "#;"
```

The *FormatDateTime* function used in the fourth line is a VBScript built-in function that converts date values to text. The *Now* function always returns the current date. Subtracting 180 from the current date produces the cutoff value.

Note The date values used by the *FormatDateTime* function in VBScript are double precision floating point values denoting days since December 30, 1899. Values to the left of the decimal represent the date and values to the right of the decimal represent time. To add 30 days to a date, add 30. To subtract six hours, subtract 0.25. Dates prior to December 30, 1899, will be negative.

The loop to report and delete any records found by this SQL statement looks like this:

```
Do While Not rsHits.EOF
  Response.Write _
    "<tr>" & vbCrLf & _
    "  <td>" & rsHits("url") & "</td>" & vbCrLf & _
    "  <td>" & rsHits("hitcnt") & "</td>" & vbCrLf & _
    "  <td>" & rsHits("lasthit") & "</td>" & vbCrLf & _
    "</tr>" & vbCrLf
  rsHits.Delete
  rsHits.MoveFirst
Loop
```

The first time this loop executes, the *rsHits* recordset will be at the beginning because you just opened it. Then

- The *Response.Write* statement reports the current record.

- The *rsHits.Delete* statement deletes the current record.

- The *rsHits.MoveFirst* statement positions the recordset to the beginning.

- The *Loop* statement repeats the loop.

Because the last statement before the end of the loop positions to the beginning of the recordset, the *rsHits.EOF* property won't become *True* until the recordset is empty. The loop reports the first record in the recordset, then deletes it, then positions to the new first record, then deletes that one, and so on.

You can find the complete Web page that follows among the sample files at the folder location \webdbdev\ch04\countdel.asp.

```
<html>
<head>
<title>Hit Counter</title>
<!-- #include file="../adovbs.inc" -->
</head>
<body>
<%
' Open connection to data provider.
Set cnn1 = Server.CreateObject("ADODB.Connection")
openStr = "driver={Microsoft Access Driver (*.mdb)};" & _
          "dbq=" & Server.MapPath("coinclub.mdb")
cnn1.open openStr,"",""


' Construct SQL statement to return all
' hit counters not used for 180 days.
sql = "SELECT * " & _
      "FROM hitcounts " & _
      "WHERE lasthit < #" & _
      FormatDateTime(now()-180) & _
      "#;"
' Open recordset.
Set rsHits = Server.CreateObject("ADODB.Recordset")
rsHits.Open sql, cnn1, adOpenDynamic, adLockPessimistic, adCmdText
' If there are no such records, just display a message.
If rsHits.EOF Then
  Response.Write "<p>No old hit counters.</p>"
' If there are some matching records, begin
' emitting table HTML and headings.
Else
  Response.Write "<table border=1>" & vbCrLf
  Response.Write "<caption>Deleted Hit Counters" & _
    "</caption>" & vbCrLf
  Response.Write _
    "<tr>" & vbCrLf & _
    "  <th>URL</th>" & vbCrLf & _
    "  <th>Count</th>" & vbCrLf & _
    "  <th>Last Hit</th>" & vbCrLf & _
    "</tr>" & vbCrLf
' Report first record, delete it, position to new
' first record, and repeat until no records remain.
Do While Not rsHits.EOF
  Response.Write _
    "<tr>" & vbCrLf & _
    "  <td>" & rsHits("url") & "</td>" & vbCrLf & _
    "  <td>" & rsHits("hitcnt") & "</td>" & vbCrLf & _
    "  <td>" & rsHits("lasthit") & "</td>" & vbCrLf & _
    "</tr>" & vbCrLf
  rsHits.Delete
  rsHits.MoveFirst
Loop
```

```
   ' Terminate HTML table.
     Response.Write "</table>" & vbCrLf
End If
' Close and release Recordset and Connection objects.
rsHits.Close
Set rsHits = Nothing
cnn1.Close
Set cnn1 = Nothing
%>
</body>
</html>
```

Figure 4-5 shows typical output from this Web page. The ASP code has deleted all the listed hit count records from the database.

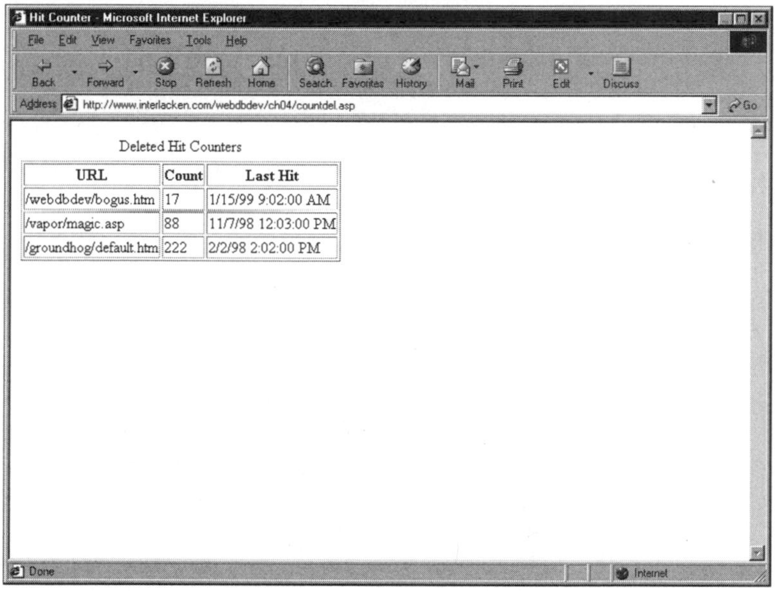

Figure 4-5 *Running the countdel.asp page reports and deletes old records in the hitcnt table.*

Close an ADO Recordset object

Several times in the preceding examples you've already seen how to close a Recordset object—you simply call its *Close* method. Then, unless you plan to reuse the object in some way, you should release its memory by setting it to *Nothing*. Here's some typical code:

```
rsMbrs.Close
set rsMbrs = Nothing
```

If you forget to close or release a Recordset (or any other) object, ASP will usually do it for you when it's done processing your Web page. However, the surest way to clean up memory from objects you no longer need is to do it yourself.

Using ADO Commands

The ADO *Command* object holds a database command suitable for use in opening a recordset. To understand how this works, first recall the following code. (The members1.asp page used this code to open its database connection.)

```
Set cnn1 = Server.CreateObject("ADODB.Connection")
openStr = "driver={Microsoft Access Driver (*.mdb)};" & _
          "dbq=" & Server.MapPath("coinclub.mdb")
cnn1.Open openStr,"",""
```

The following code then created and opened a recordset named *rsMbrs*:

```
sql = "SELECT * FROM members;"
Set rsMbrs = Server.CreateObject("ADODB.Recordset")
rsMbrs.Open sql, cnn1, adOpenForwardOnly, adLockReadOnly, adCmdText
```

Opening the same recordset by using a Command object requires a two-step process: first you must create and initialize the Command object, and then you must create and open the Recordset object. Here's the code to create and initialize the Command object:

```
sql = "SELECT * FROM members;"
Set cmdQuery = Server.CreateObject("ADODB.Command")
Set cmdQuery.ActiveConnection = cnn1
cmdQuery.CommandText = sql
cmdQuery.CommandType = adCmdText
```

The first line stores a SQL statement in a variable for later use. The second line creates an ADO Command object named *cmdQuery*. The third line associates the *cmdQuery* Command object with the ADO connection *cnn1*. The fourth line stores the SQL statement from line 1 in the Command object. The fifth line specifies that the text supplied in line 4 is a database command (that is, for this provider—a SQL statement.)

As this point, the Command object's *Execute* method is capable of creating the desired recordset. However, the earlier example specified the *adOpenForwardOnly* and *adLockReadOnly* options, which the *Execute* method can't accept. To set these options and then open the recordset requires these statements:

```
Set rsMbrs = Server.CreateObject("ADODB.Recordset")
rsMbrs.CursorType = adOpenForwardOnly
rsMbrs.LockType = adLockReadOnly
Set rsMbrs = cmdQuery.Execute()
```

The first line creates an ADO Recordset object named *rsMbrs*. The second line sets the recordset's *CursorType* property to *adOpenForwardOnly*. The third line sets the recordset's *LockType* property to *adLockReadOnly*. The last line calls the Command object's *Execute* method to open the Recordset object.

In this example, opening a Recordset object directly requires three statements, while opening a Recordset object using a Command object requires nine. For this reason alone, most developers prefer not to use Command objects for ordinary queries. Nevertheless, Command objects are quite useful in at least two situations:

- When the command doesn't produce a result set. This would include any SQL command other than SELECT.

- When the command is a parameter query. The next section discusses parameters.

Note   If you don't need to override any default recordset properties, you don't need to explicitly create the Recordset object before using the Command object's *Execute* method. The *Execute* method will create the recordset for you.

Using ADO Parameters

In all the examples you've seen so far, the script code within the Web page has built SQL statements that request services from the data provider. This has the advantage of keeping all the code for a given Web page in one place, but it also has three disadvantages:

- It often means repeating the same SQL code in many different pages.

- If you need to change a database or a table, locating and correcting all the affected SQL statements can be difficult.

- In large organizations, it requires giving SQL experts access to program code, and programming experts access to SQL code. This might be in conflict with job descriptions.

To address these issues, many data providers support stored queries, stored procedures, or both. A *stored query* is a SQL statement that resides within the database system and that applications invoke by name. A *stored procedure* is some other piece of code—usually coded in a language such as Transact*SQL or Visual Basic for Applications—that meets the same criteria.

Stored queries and stored procedures frequently accept *parameters*: named values that the database system will substitute into the stored code. Imagine a stored query that looks up specific coin club members, for example. It wouldn't make sense to store a different stored query for looking up each different coin club member, but it would make sense to store a query that accepted *memberid* as a parameter.

Chapter 2, "Understanding Database Concepts and Terms," showed you how to do exactly that in Microsoft Access; if you've forgotten, review "Create a Parameter Query" in that chapter.

Using a parameter query in a Web page involves five steps:

1. Open an ADO connection to the desired provider.

2. Create an ADO Command object to invoke the stored query.

3. Create an ADO Parameter object to hold each parameter's name and value.

4. Attach the Parameter object or objects to the Command object.

5. Create a Recordset object by using the Command object's *Execute* method.

Open an ADO connection to the desired provider

In practice, this isn't as complicated as it sounds. The first step—opening a connection—follows the pattern of previous examples:

```
Set cnn1 = Server.CreateObject("ADODB.Connection")
openstr = "driver={Microsoft Access Driver (*.mdb)};" & _
          "dbq=" & Server.MapPath("coinclub.mdb")
cnn1.Open openstr,"",""
```

Create an ADO Command object to invoke the stored query

The section "Using ADO Commands," earlier in the chapter, described how to create an ADO Command object. The following code should therefore be familiar:

```
Set cmdQuery = Server.CreateObject("ADODB.Command")
Set cmdQuery.ActiveConnection = cnn1
cmdQuery.CommandText = "qmemname"
cmdQuery.CommandType = adCmdStoredProc
```

Create an ADO Parameter object to hold each parameter's name and value

Here's the code to create and initialize a Parameter object. To keep the example simple, it always searches for the surname "Davolio". The example would be more realistic if it searched for a value specified in a URL or an HTML form, but that involves complexities not explained until Chapter 6, "Organizing Your Web Environment."

```
surname = "Davolio"
Set parQsname = Server.CreateObject("ADODB.Parameter")
parQsname.Name = "qsname"
parQsname.Direction = adParamInput
parQsname.Type = adVarChar
parQsname.Size = Len(surname)
parQsname.Value = surname
```

Line one stores the search value "Davolio" in the variable *surname*. Line two creates an ADO Parameter object named *parQsname*. Line three stores the parameter name "*qsname*" in the Parameter object's *Name* property. Line four states that this object supplies an input parameter. (A Parameter object can also receive output parameters from a stored procedure.) Line five states that the parameter value is a string. Line six specifies the length of the parameter value. The *Len* function is built into VBScript; it returns the length of its argument. Line seven, at long last, specifies the parameter's value.

Attach the Parameter object to the Command object

The next step in running a parameter query is to append each Parameter object to the intended Command object. The following statement will append the Parameter object just created—*parQsname*—to the Command object *cmdQuery* created previously.

```
cmdQuery.Parameters.Append parQsname
```

Create a recordset by using the Command object's Execute method

The last step is to create a recordset by executing the query. Unlike the example in the section "Using ADO Commands," earlier in the chapter, this code accepts all default recordset properties and therefore doesn't need to create the Recordset object explicitly.

```
Set rsQmem = cmdQuery.Execute()
```

The rest of this Web page is very much like the members1.asp page discussed earlier in the chapter. You'll find this code on the companion CD-ROM. Open the sample file \webdbdev\ch04\qsname.asp. Figure 4-6 shows the results of running the ASP page.

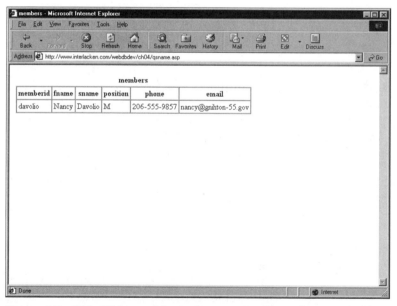

Figure 4-6 *This Web page shows the same results as the query in Figure 2-13. It should; it uses the same stored parameter query!*

The primary advantage of using stored queries is that they aren't stored throughout the script code of multiple Web pages, but centrally, in the same database they query. However, as the following code illustrates, there are certainly easier ways of merging search values into SQL statements.

```
surname = "Davolio"
sql = "SELECT memberid, fname, sname, " & _
            "position, phone, email " & _
        "FROM members " & _
        "WHERE (sname='" & surname & "'); "
```

Using the ADO Error Object

The examples discussed so far haven't included any code for handling serious errors. If any component in these Web database pages reports a serious error, processing stops and the Web visitor receives a relatively obscure error message. There are at least three reasons to avoid this behavior:

- You might consider some errors normal—that is, they reflect conditions you expect to occur and know how to handle.

- You might wish to word your own error messages rather than accept the system error messages.

- Web visitors generally form a poor opinion of sites that send only half a Web page and then a cryptic message indicating that something has clearly bombed.

To allow your own code to detect and handle errors, you must first tell VBScript to let your code keep executing after an error occurs. The following statement performs this function:

```
On Error Resume Next
```

This tells VBScript that when an error occurs, it should resume execution with the next statement following the one that created the error. This behavior continues until you exit the *Sub* or *Function* that contains the "On Error Resume Next" statement, or until you execute this statement:

```
On Error GoTo 0
```

When "On Error Resume Next" is in effect, your code must check for and respond to errors after each statement that might create one. The VBScript Err object supports this by exposing the properties listed in Table 4-15 for the last statement executed. *Err.Number* will be zero if the statement completed without errors, and nonzero if something went wrong.

Table 4-15   VBScript Error Object Properties

Property	Description
Number	A numeric value that identifies an error
Description	A text string that describes an error in words
Source	The name of the object or application that generated an error
HelpFile	The fully qualified path to a Windows Help file that explains an error
HelpContext	A pointer to a specific topic within a Windows Help file

Here's a typical coding example:

```
On Error Resume Next
cnn1.Open ConnectStr, "", ""
If Err.Number <> 0 Then
    Response.Write "<p>Cannot connect to database.</p>"
End If
```

Quite often you'll see the third statement in this code abbreviated as shown below. This form is equivalent because *Number* is the Err object's default property and because VBScript evaluates all nonzero values as *True*.

```
On Error Resume Next
cnn1.Open ConnectStr, "", ""
If Err Then
    Response.Write "<p>Cannot connect to database.</p>"
End If
```

For most Web database applications, the Err object will provide all the error information you need (with perhaps even a bit left over). However, ADO does include an Error object that provides two kinds of additional information. First, the ADO Error object reports the two additional properties listed in Table 4-16. Second, the ADO Error object belongs to an Errors collection within each Connection object. The Errors collection can thus report multiple errors that occurred while handling a single ADO call.

Table 4-16 Additional ADO Error Object Properties

Property	Description
NativeError	The numeric value a data provider uses to identify a specific error
SQLState	A five-character string value used by a data provider to report errors that occur while processing a SQL statement

The code below intentionally creates and then reports an error. Figure 4-7 shows the results.

```
Set cnn1 = Server.CreateObject("ADODB.Connection")
' Turn off default VBScript error handling.
On Error Resume Next
' Intentionally trigger an error.
cnn1.Open "nothing"
' Determine whether an error has occurred.
If Err Then
    ' Report properties of VBScript Err object.
    Response.Write "<p><b>VBScript Err Object:</b><br>" & _
        "Number: "      & Err.Number      & "<br>" & _
        "Description: " & Err.Description & "<br>" & _
        "Source: "      & Err.Source      & "<br>" & _
        "HelpFile: "    & Err.HelpFile    & "<br>" & _
        "HelpContext: " & Err.HelpContext & "</p>"
    ' Start looping through all objects in cnn1's Errors collection.
    For i = 0 To cnn1.Errors.Count - 1
```

(continued)

```
                        ' Report properties of ADO Error object.
                        Response.Write  "<p><b>ADO Error Object:</b><br>" & vbCrLf & _
                          "Number: "       & cnn1.Errors(i).Number      & "<br>" & vbCrLf & _
                          "Description: " & cnn1.Errors(i).Description & "<br>" & vbCrLf & _
                          "Source: "       & cnn1.Errors(i).Source      & "<br>" & vbCrLf & _
                          "HelpFile: "     & cnn1.Errors(i).HelpFile     & "<br>" & vbCrLf &
                          "HelpContext: " & cnn1.Errors(i).HelpContext & "<br>" & vbCrLf & _
                          "SQL State: "   & cnn1.Errors(i).SQLState    & "<br>" & vbCrLf & _
                          "NativeError: " & cnn1.Errors(i).NativeError & _
                          "</p>" & vbCrLf
                    ' End the range of the loop through all Error objects.
                    Next
                End If
            On Error GoTo 0
```

Figure 4-7 *This ASP page generates and reports an ADO error.*

ADO resets a connection's Errors collection every time you call an ADO method that uses that connection. Thus, at any given time, the Errors collection contains only those errors that occurred during the most recent call. To determine the success of a particular call, you must check the connection's Errors collection before making another ADO call.

Chapter Summary

This chapter primarily discussed the ADO Recordset object, which provides access to the tables, records, and fields in a database. It also discussed the Command and Parameter objects, which run parameter queries, and the Error object, which provides more information about database errors than VBScript's Err object.

The next chapter will explain the Web server environment needed for Web database pages to run.

Chapter 5

Customizing Web Content with Server-Side Scripting

In this chapter, you'll learn

- How to integrate server-side VBScript code with an ASP page.

- How VBScript differs from other forms of Visual Basic.

- How your code can use built-in Web server objects to receive requests from Web visitors, to access resources on the server, and to create outgoing responses.

For many Web developers, their entry into database development is also their entry into server-side programming. Instead of sending fixed content (Web pages) to the browser and then programming the browser to customize the display, Web database applications program the Web server to customize content before sending it to the browser. The customization can be as simple as inserting values from a query or as complex as generating a unique page for each combination of Web visitor and inquiry.

Developing scripts—short blocks of high-level programming code—that run on a Web server is quite a bit different from developing scripts that run on a browser.

- The predominant language for browser-side scripts is JavaScript. For server-side scripts, it's VBScript for Microsoft Web servers; for most of the other servers, it's Perl, C, or Java.

- Most browser-side scripts address issues of visual presentation. They have no access to any part of the Web visitor's system except for the display. Server-side scripts can access any and all resources on the server itself and on the server's network (provided, of course, that the server's administrator has granted such access). This includes files, databases, mail systems, printers, and fax servers, to name just a few.

- Running server-side scripts consumes more server resources and presents greater security risks than delivering simple Web pages. For these reasons, obtaining server-side script resources from your service provider or IT department is usually more difficult, more expensive, or more restrictive—or all three—than obtaining nonscripted Web space.

- If your Web pages consist of HTML and browser scripts only, you can test them by opening disk files with your browser. To test a server-side script, you must have a Web server to run it on. If you have no other test facility, you might need to install a Web server on your own PC.

This chapter will explain the basics of server-side scripting and how it interfaces with the delivery of Web requests, server resources, and Web responses.

Structuring ASP Applications and Pages

Programmers have been writing server-side scripts since the early days of the Web. Even before browser-side scripts were available, a specification called Common Gateway Interface (CGI) supported server-side processing.

A CGI program executes once every time a Web visitor requests its URL. The run-time environment is somewhat like MS-DOS: CGI programs receive data from standard input or from environment variables, and write outgoing HTML as if to standard output. The Web server handles the details of transmitting the outgoing HTML to the Web visitor who submitted the request.

CGI programs are relatively inefficient because every time a Web visitor requests the URL, the Web server has to allocate memory, create a process, launch the CGI program, run it, terminate the process, and then discard the memory. This usually isn't terribly efficient—overhead time often exceeds application-processing time by a large margin—but it works.

Like everything else on the Web, server-side programs usually demand rapid development. The Web operates on development schedules based in hours or days—not in weeks, months, or years. This explains why both browser-side and server-side scripts tend to be written in slapdash, high-level, interpreted languages such as JavaScript, VBScript, and Perl. And use of these languages explains why people call both browser-side and server-side programs *scripts*.

Microsoft Web servers provide a way to run server-side scripts that's much more efficient than CGI. Server-side scripts on Microsoft Web servers usually run as Internet Server Application Programming Interface (ISAPI) programs. ISAPI programs run in the Web server's memory space, avoiding the overhead of creating and destroying a memory space for each CGI request. Furthermore, because they're actually DLLs, a single copy of an ISAPI program can service multiple requests at the same time and even remain in memory between requests.

One such ISAPI program is the ASP interpreter asp.dll. Microsoft Web servers run this DLL whenever three conditions occur:

- A Web visitor requests a URL that has a .asp filename extension.

- A page with the given filename and extension (.asp) exists at the designated location in the server's file system.

- That page resides in a folder marked *executable*.

Locating a suitable Web server and getting a folder marked executable are usually the toughest parts of getting an ASP page to run. UNIX-based servers won't run ASP pages, for example, because there's no asp.dll for UNIX. If your existing ISP or Web server isn't running Microsoft Windows 2000 or Microsoft Windows NT, you'll probably have to switch. If you want an executable folder, you might have to provide extra justification or sign up for more expensive service. The added expense is due to the additional resource consumption and security risks that server-side scripts entail.

The next chapter will explain the process of marking Web folders executable (assuming you're the server administrator). This chapter covers the ASP pages themselves.

Note To locate an ISP that provides Windows 2000 Web servers, browse *http://www.microsoftwpp.com/wppsearch/.*

Add ASP code to a Web page

Structurally, ASP pages resemble ordinary HTML pages with one or more blocks of server-side script code added. The most common way to mark a block of script code is with <% and %> tags, like this:

```
<html>
<head>
</head>
<body>
<%
Response.Write "<p>This is some paragraph text.</p>" & vbCrLf
%>
</body>
</html>
```

The ampersand (&) is the VBScript operator for string concatenation. You can also join strings with the plus sign (+), but VBScript might end up performing arithmetic when you don't want it to. For example, 2 + 3 equals 5, but 2 & 3 equals 23.

Almost every example in this book uses the *Response.Write* statement because that's how ASP code sends customized HTML to the Web visitor. The ASP processor doesn't send the code between the <% and %> tags to the Web visitor's browser, but it does send the surrounding HTML code and the output of any *Response.Write* statements. After processing the ASP page listed above, for example, the ASP interpreter would send this HTML to the Web visitor:

```
<head>
</head>
<body>
<p>This is some paragraph text.</p>
</body>
</html>
```

The expression vbCrLf is a constant built into VBScript. It represents a carriage return character followed by a linefeed character.

The entire ASP page executes as one program, even if it contains multiple script blocks. For example, consider the following page, which contains three blocks of script code.

```
<html>
<head>
<%
Sub WriteParagraph(argText)
    Response.Write "<p>" & argText & "</p>" & vbCrLf
End Sub
%>
</head>
<body>
<%
cnt = 1
WriteParagraph "This is paragraph " & cnt & "."
%>
<hr>
<%
cnt = cnt + 1
WriteParagraph "This is paragraph " & cnt & "."
%>
<hr>
</body>
</html>
```

The first block of ASP code defines a subroutine named *WriteParagraph*. This subroutine accepts any text string, surrounds it with <p> and </p> tags, appends carriage return and line feed characters, and then writes the result into the outgoing HTML. The second block stores the value 1 in a variable named *cnt*, constructs a text string containing the value of *cnt*, and calls the *WriteParagraph* subroutine with that string as an argument. The last block adds 1 to the value of *cnt*, constructs another text string containing the value of *cnt*, and once again calls *WriteParagraph*.

Running this code produces the results shown below. Note that the value of *cnt* persists from script block two to script block three. Note also that while the *WriteParagraph* subroutine resides in the ASP page's <head> section, its *Response.Write* output appears in place of the script block that called the *WriteParagraph* subroutine.

```
<html>
<head>
</head>
<body>
<p>This is paragraph 1.</p>
<hr>
<p>This is paragraph 2.</p>
<hr>
</body>
</html>
```

If you put the start and the end of a loop in different script blocks, the intervening HTML will appear in the outgoing Web page once per iteration of the loop. Consider this ASP page:

```
<html>
<head>
</head>
<body>
<%
For cnt = 1 To 5
%>
<p>One-line paragraph.</p>
<%
Next
%>
</body>
</html>
```

This page will write the string *<p>One-line paragraph.</p>* into the outgoing Web page five times. In other words, it produces this:

```
<html>
<head>
</head>
<body>
<p>One-line paragraph.</p>
<p>One-line paragraph.</p>
<p>One-line paragraph.</p>
<p>One-line paragraph.</p>
<p>One-line paragraph.</p>
</body>
</html>
```

If you need to create a script block that contains only one statement, and if that statement is a *Response.Write*, the following syntax can save both space and typing:

<% = expression %>

Here's an example:

```
<% = "<p>The current date and time is " & Now() & "</p>" %>
```

The opening <% tag, the equal sign, the expression, and the closing %> tag must all be on the same line. This is exactly equivalent to the following statements:

```
<%
Response.Write "<p>The current date and time is " & Now() & "</p>"
%>
```

The following block of code is *almost* equivalent to the previous two, but not quite.

```
<script runat=server language=VBScript>
Response.Write "<p>The current date and time is " & Now() & "</p>"
</script>
```

The <script runat=server> tag is roughly equivalent to an opening <% tag, and the </script> tag to a closing %>. This form has the advantage of letting you specify languages other than VBScript, but it suffers a serious quirk. ASP internally stores any script code it finds within <script runat=server> and </script> tags and then runs it at the very end of your Web page. This is hardly ever what you want, and it's a very good reason to use <% and %> tags for all your work.

Introducing VBScript

This book clearly doesn't have space for a complete description of the VBScript programming language. Fortunately, as the next section describes, the complete reference manual is available from a variety of online sources. You could even have a copy on your own computer and not know it! If you need a printed tutorial, you can choose from dozens of books.

Locating VBScript Documentation

The VBScript Language Reference on Microsoft's Web site lists all VBScript functions and features, and provides explanations and sample code for each one. You can find this the documentation through the MSDN library or directly through the Microsoft Windows Script Technologies Web site. Browse to *http://msdn.microsoft.com/scripting* and then, at the left of the display, navigate through the topics VBScript, Documentation, and Language Reference. Figure 5-1 shows this operation in progress.

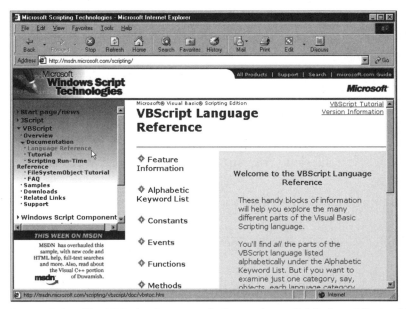

Figure 5-1 *The VBScript Language Reference is available from Microsoft's Web site.*

Installing Microsoft Personal Web server on a Windows 95 or Windows 98 computer also installs a copy of the VBScript documentation. To access this version, try this URL:

http://localhost/iishelp/pws/misc/default.asp

You can see the results in Figure 5-2. If you're looking for the same page on a networked Windows 95 or Windows 98 machine, replace the string *localhost* with the Web server's DNS name or IP address.

If your Web server runs on Windows NT Server, the URL is slightly different: *http://localhost/iishelp/iis/misc/default.asp*. This URL also exists on a Windows 2000 Web server, but in at least some versions it simply points to the documentation on Microsoft's Web site.

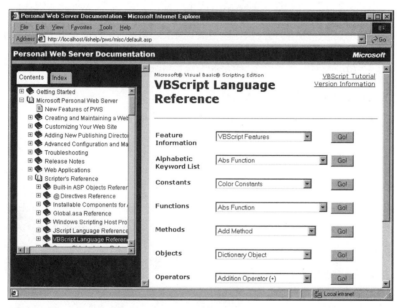

Figure 5-2 *An online copy of the VBScript Language Reference comes with every copy of Microsoft Personal Web Server.*

Differences Between VBScript and Other Forms of Visual Basic

If you've used other forms of Microsoft Visual Basic—such as Visual Basic for Applications or the full Visual Basic product—most of what you know will carry over to VBScript. Nevertheless, there are differences between VBScript and those other forms:

- Lack of visual aspect

- Implicit definition of variables

- Weakly typed variables

- Objects unique to VBScript

- Scope of variables

- Formatting functions

- Additional string functions

Lack of Visual Aspect

Remember Fuzzy Wuzzy, the bear who wasn't fuzzy? Well Visual Basic Scripting Edition isn't visual. It can't display windows or dialog boxes and, when running within an ASP page, it doesn't even support *MsgBox* or *InputBox* functions. The reason for this is quite simple: because ASP scripts run on the Web server, any dialog boxes a script displayed would appear on the server's console, inaccessible to anyone. Of course, the script can write the HTML to create visual displays of any type on the Web visitor's browser.

A common misconception is that lack of a visual interface prevents VBScript from using ActiveX objects. VBScript *can* use ActiveX objects, and in fact does so extensively. All ADO objects are ActiveX objects, for example. However, ActiveX objects designed for server use have no visual aspect—they're just software modules that provide methods and properties to any programs that use them.

Implicit Definition of Variables

Ordinary variables require no explicit definition in VBScript. To create a new variable, just start using it! Many experienced programmers consider it good practice to declare all variables with the *Dim* statement, but this isn't a requirement of VBScript.

Arrays present an exception to this rule. If you try to use an array without declaring it, VBScript will create an ordinary variable. Trying to use a subscript will then produce a Type Mismatch error. Declare arrays by using the *Dim* statement as follows:

Dim *arrayname(index)*

VBScript's implicit variable names mean that misspelling a variable name doesn't produce any kind of compile error; it just produces a new variable with the misspelled name. Be careful with spelling, and keep this in mind when debugging.

To require *Dim* statements for all variables, code the following statement before any other VBScript or HTML statements in an ASP page. This creates an error if you forget to declare a variable, but it detects an error if you misspell a variable name elsewhere in the code.

```
<% Option Explicit %>
```

Weakly Typed Variables

VBScript supports only two variable types: objects and variants. Objects are fairly easy to recognize—you create them with a statement of this form:

Set *object* = Server.CreateObject("*class*")

All other variables are variants, which means they automatically assume the data characteristics of any value you store in them. For example, the following statements cause *myValue* to be an integer, a string, and a date, respectively.

```
myValue = 6
myValue = "Jim"
myValue = #06/01/2000 3:34 PM#
```

To force a variable to be a certain type, use one of the type conversion functions listed in Table 5-1. For example, both of the following statements force the variable *rslt* to store the assigned value as a double-precision floating-point number.

```
rslt = CDbl(5)
rslt = 5E00
```

Table 5-1   VBScript Type Conversion Functions

Function	Description
CBool	Any zero argument returns *False*. Any nonzero numeric argument returns *True*. A non-numeric argument generates a run-time error.
CByte	Returns a one-byte integer. If the argument isn't a number in the range 0-255, a run-time error occurs.
CCur	Converts a numeric argument to a currency value. If the argument isn't numeric, a run-time error occurs.
CDate	Converts any valid date or time expression to a VBScript date or time.
CDbl	Converts any numeric argument to a double-precision floating-point number.
CInt	Converts any numeric argument to an integer.
CLng	Converts any numeric argument to a long integer.
CSng	Converts any numeric argument to a single-precision floating-point number.
CStr	Converts any argument to a string. Boolean values become the word *True* or *False*, and date values appear in the local system's short date format. A null argument generates a run-time error.

For the most part, VBScript's weak typing means you can use any variable anywhere, and VBScript will automatically perform any necessary type conversions. It's seldom necessary for code to determine a variable's type, but if you do need this information, you can get it from the *VarType* function. The expression *VarType(variable)* indicates the internal format of its argument by returning one of the values listed in Table 5-2.

Table 5-2   VBScript Variant Types

Constant	Value	Description
vbEmpty	0	empty (uninitialized)
vbNull	1	null (no valid data)
vbInteger	2	integer
vbLong	3	long integer
vbSingle	4	single-precision floating-point number
vbDouble	5	double-precision floating-point number
vbCurrency	6	currency
vbDate	7	date
vbString	8	string
vbObject	9	automation object
vbError	10	error
vbBoolean	11	Boolean
vbVariant	12	variant (used only with arrays of variants)
vbDataObject	13	a data-access object
vbByte	17	byte
vbArray	8192	array

The functions listed in Table 5-3 are similar to—but also different from—the *VarType* function. Two of those functions, *IsDate* and *IsNumeric*, predict whether converting a variable to their respective formats will be successful. The *IsDate* function can determine whether VBScript can convert a string value received from a Web visitor into a date value in a database, for example:

- *VarType("06/11/2000")* would return *vbString*, which is 8.

- *IsDate("06/11/2000")* would return *True*.

Table 5-3   VBScript Type Determination Functions

Function	Description
IsArray	Returns *True* if the argument is an array.
IsDate	Returns *True* if the argument is (or is convertible to) a date or time. Examples: *IsDate("4:40 PM")* returns *True*. *IsDate("12/12/1999")* returns *True*. *IsDate("13/13/1999")* returns *False*.
IsEmpty	Returns *True* if the argument is uninitialized or is explicitly set to Empty.
IsNull	Returns *True* if the argument contains no valid data.
IsNumeric	Returns *True* if the argument is (or is convertible to) a number. Example: *IsNumeric("2" & "3")* returns *True*.
IsObject	Returns *True* if the argument is an automation object (such as an ActiveX object).

The remaining functions in Table 5-3—*IsArray*, *IsEmpty*, *IsNull*, and *IsObject*—provide the same information as using the *VarType* function and comparing to the appropriate constant from Table 5-2.

Objects Unique to VBScript

VBScript provides several objects not included in Visual Basic or in Visual Basic for Applications As you can see in Table 5-4, most of these objects pertain to file access and replace traditional commands such as *Open*, *Line Input*, *Print*, *Close*, *Dir$*, *FileAttr*, and *FileDateTime*.

Table 5-4   Objects Unique to VBScript

Category	Object	Type	Description
Array	Dictionary	Object	Stores an array of values, each identified by a unique alphanumeric key. Essentially, this is an array that uses alphanumeric subscripts.
File	Drive	Object	Provides access to the properties of a particular disk drive or network share.
	Drives	Collection	Provides a read-only list of the drives on the local computer.
	Err	Object	Contains information about run-time errors.
	File	Object	Provides access to all the properties of a file (for example, to the file's Last Changed date).
	Files	Collection	Provides a read-only list of files in a given directory on the local computer.
	FileSystem-Object	Object	Provides information about and access to a computer's file system; provides file-oriented methods as *Open*, *Create*, *Delete*, *Move*, *Copy*, and *IfExists*.
	Folder	Object	Provides access to the properties of a folder.
	Folders	Collection	Provides a read-only list of all Folder objects contained within another Folder object.
	TextStream	Object	Provides sequential access to a file on the local computer; provides file access methods such as *Open*, *Read*, *ReadLine*, *Write*, *WriteLine*, and *Close*.

Use the Dictionary object

The Dictionary object has nothing to do with files; instead, it provides an array of elements identified by alphanumeric keys rather than by numbers. Dictionary objects in VBScript are similar to associative arrays in Perl. The following statement creates a Dictionary object named *person*:

```
Set person = Server.CreateObject("Scripting.Dictionary")
```

Once created, a Dictionary object has the methods listed in Table 5-5 and the properties listed in Table 5-6. Statements such as the following use the *Add* method to populate the array with data. The first argument is the key, which subsequently identifies each element in the array. The second argument, of course, becomes the item's value.

```
person.Add "fname", "Jim"
person.Add "sname", "Buyens"
person.Add "city", "Phoenix"
person.Add "state", "Arizona"
```

The following statements accomplish the same results. When you specify an existing key, you replace its corresponding item value. When you specify a new key, the Dictionary object adds both the new key and the new item value to the array.

```
person.Item("fname") = "Jim"
person.Item("sname") = "Buyens"
person.Item("city") = "Phoenix"
person.Item("state") = "Arizona"
```

Because *Item* is the default property for any Dictionary object, the four statements below are a third alternative to the forms shown above.

```
person("fname") = "Jim"
person("sname") = "Buyens"
person("city") = "Phoenix"
person("state") = "Arizona"
```

Tip   If you try to read a key that doesn't exist in a Dictionary object, the object will create that key and give it a null value.

Table 5-5   Dictionary Object Methods

Method	Arguments	Description
Add	key, data	Adds a key and its associated item value to the array
Exists	key	Returns *True* if a specified key exists and *False* if it doesn't
Items	(none)	Returns an array that contains all the item values in the array

Method	Arguments	Description
Keys	(none)	Returns an array that contains all the key values in the array
Remove	key	Removes a key and its associated item value from the array
RemoveAll	(none)	Removes all key and item pairs from the array

Once a Dictionary object contains items, you can access them with expressions such as the following. Once again, these statements are equivalent because *Item* is the default property for any Dictionary object.

```
person.Item("sname")
person("sname")
```

Table 5-6   Dictionary Object Properties

Property	Description
CompareMode	Controls and reports the comparison mode for key strings. This property is read-only unless the array is empty.
Count	Returns the number of items in the array.
Item	Sets or returns the item value for a specified key in the array. This is the default property.
Key	Renames a key in the array. To modify this property, code a statement with the following syntax:
	object.Key(*key*) = *newkey*

Table 5-7 shows the values for the *CompareMode* property. As the table shows, a Dictionary object's key lookups can be case-sensitive or not.

Table 5-7   *CompareMode* Values

Constant	Value	Description
vbBinaryCompare	0	Performs a binary (case-sensitive) comparison.
vbTextCompare	1	Performs a textual (case-insensitive) comparison. This is the default.

The *For Each* loop is usually the easiest way to iterate through all the keys in a Dictionary object. Here's an example:

```
For Each kn In person
    Response.Write "<p>" & kn & "=" & person(kn) & "</p>" & vbCrLf
Next
```

VBScript will run this loop once for each key-and-item pair in the *person* Dictionary object (that is, it will run it *person.Count* times). During each iteration, VBScript will supply (in the variable *kn*) a different key value from the array.

Dictionary objects are very handy for storing temporary copies of database records. Take a look at the following code:

```
Set holdRec = Server.CreateObject("Scripting.Dictionary")
For Each fld In rsMbrs.Fields
  holdRec(fld.Name) = fld.Value
Ncxt
For Each ky In holdRec
  Response.Write "<p>" & ky & "=" & holdRec(ky) & "</p>" & vbCrLF
Next
```

This code

- Creates a Dictionary object named *holdRec*.

- Loads the *holdRec* object with key names and item values that correspond to each field name and field value in a database record.

- Displays the contents of the *holdRec* object as HTML.

Note that during the first loop, the *fld* variable successively points to each object in the *rsMbrs.Fields* collection. The objects in a Fields collection are, of course, Field objects. This explains how the *fld* variable can access the current *name* and *value* properties of each field in the *rsMbrs* object. The *fld* variable successively becomes an alias for each Field object in the *rsMbrs.Fields* collection.

The sample files from the companion CD-ROM contain a file named \webdbdev\ch05\dictdb.asp that illustrates this technique.

Use the file system objects

To access the local computer's file system, VBScript abandons the familiar commands of Visual Basic and Visual Basic for Applications. For example, the *Open*, *Line Input*, *Print*, *Close*, *Dir$*, *FileAttr*, and *FileDateTime* commands are all missing. In their place, VBScript provides the file objects that are listed in Table 5-4 (on page 113).

To gain a cursory understanding of how file system objects work, consider the Web page shown in Figure 5-3. It's a simple menu page—visually bankrupt, some might say—but it does have one interesting feature: it tells the Web visitor the date someone updated each listed page. This information is always up-to-date because the Web page obtains it automatically.

You can find the code for this Web page among the sample files at \webdbdev\ch05\revolts.asp, but here it is in print:

```
<html>
<head>
<title>The Alternative News</title>
<%
```

```
' Create global FileSystemObject for use elsewhere
Set fs = Server.CreateObject("Scripting.FileSystemObject")

' Define a function to get the file date of a URL.
Function GetFileDate(argURL)
' Translate the argument URL to a physical location in the
' server's file system, and then create an associated file object.
  Set fileObj = fs.GetFile(Server.MapPath(argURL))
' Specify the file's Date Last Modified as
' the function's return value.
  GetFileDate = fileObj.DateLastModified
' Destroy the file object.
  Set fileObj = Nothing
End Function
%>
</head>
<body>
<h1>The Alternative News</h1>
<table border="0" cellpadding="0" cellspacing="5">
  <tr>
    <th>Topic</th>
    <th>Last Updated</th>
  </tr>
  <tr>
    <td><a href="revoltfr.htm">News of the French Revolution</a></td>
<!--Get and display the revoltfr.htm file's Date Last Modified. -->
    <td><%=GetFileDate("revoltfr.htm")%></td>
  </tr>
  <tr>
    <td><a href="revoltam.htm">News of the American Revolution</a></td>
<!--Get and display the revoltam.htm file's Date Last Modified. -->
    <td><%=GetFileDate("revoltam.htm")%></td>
  </tr>
  <tr>
    <td><a href="revoltgg.htm">News of the Revolting Grunge
Groups</a></td>
<!--Get and display the revoltgg.htm file's Date Last Modified. -->
    <td><%=GetFileDate("revoltgg.htm")%></td>
  </tr>
</table>
</body>
</html>
```

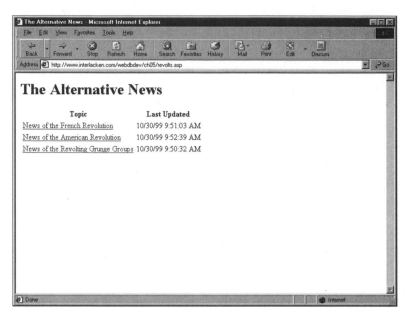

Figure 5-3 *The Last Updated column on this menu page automatically reports the file system date of each target page.*

Most of this page is ordinary HTML, but the interesting parts are the blocks of VBScript code:

- The following statement, located in the Web page's <head> section, creates a VBScript *FileSystemObject* object named *fs*.

```
Set fs = Server.CreateObject("Scripting.FileSystemObject")
```

- The next five statements define a VBScript function that accepts a URL on the local Web server and returns its *DateLastModified* property as indicated in the server's file system.

```
Function GetFileDate(argURL)
   Set fileObj = fs.GetFile(Server.MapPath(argURL))
   GetFileDate = fileObj.DateLastModified
   Set fileObj = Nothing
End Function
```

   The first statement names the function *GetFileDate* and makes provisions to receive one argument named *argURL*.

   The second statement uses the file system object created previously as *fs* to create a File object named *fileObj*. This File object contains information about the file whose physical location corresponds to the argument *argURL*. (Recall that the *Server.MapPath* method converts a local URL to a local physical file location.)

   The third statement retrieves the *fileObj* object's *DateLastModified* property and makes it the function's return value. The fourth and fifth statements release the *fileObj* object and mark the end of the function, respectively.

- Within the HTML that lists each menu item, code such as the following looks up and displays the corresponding file date.

```
<%=GetFileDate("revoltam.htm")%>
```

This statement gets and displays the file date corresponding to the URL *revoltam.htm*. This is the same URL referenced in the corresponding menu item's hyperlink.

For more information about VBScript file system objects, refer to "Locating VBScript Documentation" earlier in the chapter.

Most file system objects work in the same manner. First you create a *Scripting.FileSystemObject* object (one per Web page will suffice) and then, using that object, you create the object you actually need. Finally, you manipulate the object's properties and methods to get the results you want.

Scope of Variables

Unlike other forms of Visual Basic, VBScript doesn't support the concept of multiple code modules. And with no visual aspect, of course it doesn't support form modules at all. Instead, it treats all server-side scripting in the same Web page as a single module. This means there's no distinction between a variable or constant being global or local, and VBScript therefore lacks support for these declarations.

Variables created within subroutines and functions are available only within those structures, and within any subroutines or functions they call. To make a variable or constant available to all the server-side script code in a Web page, define it outside of any function or subroutine.

Formatting Functions

Most other versions of Visual Basic use *Format* to format numbers, percentages, and dates for display. VBScript replaces this command with the six commands listed in Table 5-8, each more specific in usage than the original *Format*.

Table 5-8   VBScript Formatting Functions

Function	Syntax	Description
FormatCurrency	FormatCurrency(*expression* [, *numDigitsAfterDecimal* [, *includeLeadingDigit* [, *useParensForNegativeNumbers* [, *groupDigits*]]]])	Returns an expression formatted as a currency value, using the currency symbol defined in the computer's Regional settings
FormatDateTime	FormatDateTime(*date* [, *namedFormat*])	Returns an expression formatted as a date or a time
FormatNumber	FormatNumber(*expression* [, *numDigitsAfterDecimal* [, *includeLeadingDigit* [, *useParensForNegativeNumbers* [, *groupDigits*]]]])	Returns an expression formatted as a number

(continued)

Table 5-8 *continued*

Function	Syntax	Description
FormatPercent	FormatPercent(*expression* [, *numDigitsAfterDecimal* [, *includeLeadingDigit* [, *useParensForNegativeNumbers* [, *groupDigits*]]]])	Returns an expression formatted as a percentage (multiplied by 100 with a trailing % character)
MonthName	MonthName(*month* [, *abbreviate*])	Returns a string indicating the specified month
WeekdayName	WeekdayName(*weekday* [, *abbreviate*[, *firstDayOfWeek*]])	Returns a string indicating the specified day of the week

Table 5-8 also shows the syntax of each command. Arguments enclosed in square brackets are optional. Don't be confused by the nesting of square brackets—this simply means that the specified number of commas must precede each argument. For example, suppose you want to display a currency value and suppress digit grouping. You would use the following statements:

```
amt = 1004.95
Response.Write FormatCurrency(amt,,,,False)
```

If you omit any of the four commas preceding the argument *False*, the *FormatCurrency* function will apply that value to its first, second, or third argument rather than to the fourth argument, *GroupDigits*. Therefore, you must code the correct number of commas before each argument, even if you don't supply values between them. Trailing commas, of course, are unnecessary. If you didn't want to suppress digit grouping, you could just code

```
Response.Write FormatCurrency(amt)
```

Table 5-9 explains the permissible values for all the special argument values that Table 5-8 mentions.

Note   The style of digit grouping varies from country to country. For example, the United States places commas every three digits, starting from the decimal point. Many other countries, however, use spaces or periods. The decimal-point character also varies—some countries use periods and others use commas. Of course, the grouping character and the decimal-point character must always be different!

Table 5-9   VBScript Formatting Arguments from Table 5-8

Argument	Usage
abbreviate	*True* or *False*. If this argument is zero or absent, the function returns a fully spelled out name. If the argument is present and nonzero, the function returns an abbreviated name.
firstDayOfWeek	Indicates which day number (1 through 7) is the first day of the week. (See Table 5-10 for more details.)

Argument	Usage
groupDigits	Tristate value that indicates whether to group digits using the delimiter specified in the computer's regional settings. (See Table 5-11 for values.)
includeLeadingDigit	Tristate value that indicates whether to display a leading zero for values between +1 and −1. (See Table 5-11 for values.)
namedFormat	Indicates the date/time format to use. The default is *vbGeneralDate*. (See Table 5-12 for details.)
numDigits-AfterDecimal	Indicates how many places to display at the right of the decimal. The default is −1, which applies the computer's regional settings.
useParensFor-NegativeNumbers	Tristate value that indicates whether to surround negative values with parentheses. (See Table 5-11 for values.)

Use the values in Table 5-10 for the *WeekdayName* function's *firstDayOfWeek* argument.

Table 5-10   *firstDayOfWeek* Argument Values

Constant	Value	Description
vbUseSystem	0	Use National Language Support (NLS) API setting
vbSunday	1	Sunday (default)
vbMonday	2	Monday
vbTuesday	3	Tuesday
vbWednesday	4	Wednesday
vbThursday	5	Thursday
vbFriday	6	Friday
vbSaturday	7	Saturday

Table 5-11 details the Tristate values used for a number of the arguments to the VBScript formatting functions. These argument values are represented by tristate constants.

Table 5-11   Tristate Argument Values

Constant	Value	Description
tristateTrue	−1	True
tristateFalse	0	False
tristateUseDefault	−2	Use the setting from the computer's Regional settings

Table 5-12 details the possible settings of the *FormatDateTime* function's *namedFormat* argument.

Table 5-12   *namedFormat* Argument Settings

Constant	Value	Description
vbGeneralDate	0	Display the date part, if present, as a short date; display the time part, if present, as a long time
vbLongDate	1	Display only the date part and use the long date format specified in the computer's Regional settings
vbShortDate	2	Display only the date part and use the short date format specified in the computer's Regional settings
vbLongTime	3	Display only the time part and use the time format specified in the computer's Regional settings
vbShortTime	4	Display only the time part and use the 24-hour format (hh:mm)

Several arguments mention defaults taken from the computer's Regional settings. To display these settings, click Start, Settings, Control Panel, and then double-click Regional Options. The Numbers, Currency, Time, and Date tabs in the resulting dialog box contain the Regional settings in question.

The Number, Currency, Time, Long Date, and Short Date formats that apply to your ASP script will be those specified in the Web server's Control Panel. If you use different servers for development and production, these defaults might be different depending on the server currently in use. The risk of different defaults is even more likely if you deploy the same script on multiple servers in different countries.

Additional String Functions

VBScript includes a number of string functions not present in other forms of Visual Basic. Like the Dictionary object, most of these string functions resemble functions previously available only in Perl. Table 5-13 lists the new functions (providing enhanced string-handling and array-handling features), and Table 5-14 describes their arguments.

Table 5-13   String Functions Unique to VBScript

Function	Syntax	Description
Filter	Filter(*inputStrings, value* [, *include* [, *compareMode*]])	Returns an array containing all elements of another array that contain (or don't contain) a specified substring.
InstrRev	InStrRev(*string1, string2* [, *start* [, *compareMode*]])	Returns the position of one string within another, searching right to left.
Join	Join(*list* [, *delimiter*])	Copies all elements of an array into one string, optionally delimiting each array value with a specified character.

Function	Syntax	Description
Replace	Replace(*expression, find, replaceWith* [, *start* [, *count* [, *compareMode*]]])	Given a string expression, replaces occurrences of one substring with another and then returns the result.
Split	Split(*expression* [, *delimiter* [, *count* [, *compareMode*]]])	Copies a delimited string to a one-dimensional array. Whenever *Split* finds the delimiter character, it begins copying to a new array element.
StrReverse	StrReverse(*string*)	Reverses the order of characters in a string and returns the result— for example, *StrReverse("abc")* returns *"cba"*.

Table 5-14   VBScript String Function Arguments

Argument	Description
compareMode	Indicates the kind of string comparison to use. (See Table 5-7 for values.)
count	Number of substrings to process. If omitted, the default value is −1, which means process all substrings.
delimiter	A character that separates the substrings in a longer string. If omitted, the space character—Chr(32)—is used. If you specify an empty delimiter, the input or output string will have no delimiters.
find	Substring being searched for.
include	If *include* is *True*, the *Filter* function returns array elements that contain *value* as a substring. If *include* is *False*, the *Filter* function returns array elements that don't contain *value* as a substring.
replaceWith	Replacement substring.
start	The position within an expression where substring searching should begin. If omitted, searching begins at the start or end of the string, depending on the search direction.
value	String operated on.

The *Split*, *Join*, and *Filter* functions deal with arrays as well as strings. The *Split* function copies a string into an array, advancing to a new array element every time it finds a character you specify as a delimiter. The following statement creates a four-element array named *status* containing the values *richer*, *poorer*, *better*, and *worse*.

```
status = Split("richer,poorer,better,worse", ",")
```

The *Join* function does the reverse: it copies all the data in an array into one long string, optionally placing a specified delimiter between the data from each cell. The following statement reverses the previous one:

```
csvStat = Join(status, ",")
```

The *Filter* function creates a new array containing selected elements from an existing array. The function can select elements based on either the presence or the absence of a specified string. For example, the statement below selects all elements in the *status* array that contain the string *er* and places them in the *notWorse* array. The *notworse* array would contain *richer*, *poorer* and *better*, but not *worse*.

```
notWorse = Filter(status,"er")
```

The *InStrRev*, *Replace*, and *StrReverse* functions have nothing to do with arrays. The *InStrRev* function works very much like the *InStr* function that's been in Visual Basic since the beginning, except that *InStrRev* works backward. The *InStr* function searches left to right for one string within another and returns the position of the first match. *InStrRev* does the same thing, searching right to left and returning the position of the rightmost match. The first statement below returns 3, while the second returns 9.

```
InStr("--xy----xy--", "xy")
InStrRev("--xy----xy--", "xy")
```

The *Replace* function searches for one string within another, replaces one or more occurrences with another string, and returns the result. The following expression returns *motorcycle*:

```
Replace("bicycle", "bi", "motor")
```

Of course, VBScript also supports time-honored Visual Basic string functions such as *Mid*, *Left*, *Right*, *UCase*, *LCase*, and *Trim*. You can find descriptions of these in almost any Visual Basic language reference.

Loop and Logic Control

VBScript supports most of the same looping and logic constructs that Visual Basic has supported for years. Table 5-15 itemizes these constructs. The *GoTo* and *GoSub* statements are notable omissions.

Table 5-15   Visual Basic Loop Constructs

Syntax	Description
Do [{While | Until} *condition*] [Exit Do] Loop	Executes a loop while or until the condition is *True*. Depending on *condition*, the loop might not execute at all.
Do [Exit Do] Loop [{While | Until} *condition*]	Executes a loop while or until the condition is *True*. The loop will execute at least once.

Syntax	Description
For *counter* = *start* To *end* [Step *step*] [Exit For] Next	Executes a loop once for each value in a series that begins with *start*, ends with *end*, and increments by *step*.
For Each *element* In *group* [Exit For] Next	Executes a loop once for each element in a collection or array. During each iteration, the *element* variable points to a different element.
While *expression* Wend	Executes a loop while the condition is *True*. The *Do While...Loop* structure is equivalent.
If *expression* Then Else End If	If *expression* is *True*, processes any statements between *Then* and *Else*. Otherwise, processes any statements between *Else* and *End If*.
Select Case *testExpression* Case *expressionList* Case Else End Select	If *testExpression* matches any *Case expressionList* clause, any statements following that *Case* clause (and preceding the next *Case* or *End Select* statement) will execute.

VBScript supports the same subroutine and function features as other forms of Visual Basic. For your reference, the required syntaxes appear here:

```
Sub name [(argument, ...)]
    [statements]
    [Exit Sub]
    [statements]
End Sub

Function name [(argument, ...)]
    [statements]
    [Exit Function]
    [statements]
    name = expression
End Function
```

The main difference between a subroutine and a function is that a function supplies a return value. The code within the function specifies the return value by assigning it to the function's name. Because it returns a value, you can invoke a function within an expression. Here's an example:

```
Response.Write = "The result is: " & MyFunction(argument, fact)
```

In addition, you can invoke both subs and functions using either syntax illustrated below. However, if you invoke a function this way, Visual Basic discards its return value.

```
Call MySub(argument, fact)
Call MyFunction(argument, fact)
MySub argument, fact
MyFunction argument, fact
```

VBScript supports recursive subroutine and function calls, meaning that a subroutine or function can call itself any number of times. However, deeply nesting such calls can lead to stack or memory overflow. Don't call a subroutine or a function recursively more than a few times without exiting.

Introducing ASP Objects

Back in Chapter 3, "Accessing Databases with ADO and ODBC," Figure 3-1 showed the relationships among incoming Web requests, Active Server Pages, database software, and outgoing Web pages. Chapter 3 and Chapter 4, "Accessing Tables and Records with ADO," explained the database software, and the first half of this chapter introduced VBScript, the language most programmers use within ASP.

Those prior discussions leave only one major topic left to describe—the interfaces between ASP and the surrounding Web environment, including incoming requests, outgoing Web pages, and the Web server itself. The rest of this chapter will describe those interfaces.

When a Web visitor clicks a hyperlink or a Submit button, the browser connects to the server named in the URL and transmits several lines of text. The first of these lines contains the word *GET* or *POST* followed by a directory path and possibly a filename. If the server can find that path and filename (or that path and a default filename, if no filename is present) in its file system, it transmits that file to the user's browser. This explanation excludes a number of important details, but it describes the essence of Hypertext Transfer Protocol (HTTP). That is, it describes how Web visitors request—and Web servers deliver—most ordinary kinds of Web content: HTML files, GIF and JPEG pictures, and so on.

A deviation from this process occurs if the Web visitor requests an *executable* file. This is a file that satisfies two criteria:

- It has a filename extension that indicates the file is some kind of executable program: .exe, .dll, .pl, and .asp are common examples.

- It resides in an *executable folder*. For a folder to become executable, an administrator must tell the Web server that it's OK to run programs from that location.

Server-side programs written in a compiled language such as C++ execute directly on the Web server. Interpreted languages such as VBScript, JavaScript, and Perl run indirectly—they require the Web server to load an interpreter that compiles and then runs any supplied source statements. The Web server selects the mode of execution and, if necessary, the proper interpreter based on the requested file's filename extension.

If the filename extension is .asp, the Web server loads an interpreter named asp.dll. This interpreter initializes certain built-in objects and then reads through the ASP file itself. If it encounters any blocks of server-side script code, it loads the proper script interpreter to compile and run the code.

The asp.dll file provides the six built-in objects listed below. These objects provide the interfaces for ASP to receive information from the Web visitor, to request services from the Web server, and finally to respond to the Web visitor.

- The *Request* object contains information received from or about the Web visitor's request.

- The *Response* object receives the output from processing an ASP page and sends it to the Web visitor.

- The *Server* object provides utility functions for creating objects, encoding strings, and translating URLs to physical locations.

- The *Application* object provides a common storage area for all ASP pages in the same application. It can also contain subroutines that run whenever the application starts and stops.

- The *Session* object provides persistent storage for a series of interactions with the same Web visitor. It can also contain subroutines that run whenever a series of interactions starts and stops

- The *ObjectContext* object either commits or aborts a transaction managed by Microsoft Transaction Server. Use of this object exceeds the scope of this book.

Locating Active Server Pages Documentation

If you were successful in locating the VBScript online documentation, you're bound to be successful in locating the corresponding documentation on Active Server Pages. Browse *http://msdn.Microsoft.com/library*, and then open Tools and Technologies, Active Server Pages.

Using the Request Object

The Request object contains information about the request that triggered the ASP page. In a sense, it answers the questions, "Why am I here?" and "What am I supposed to do?" Table 5-16 lists the collections, property, and method that the Request object provides.

Table 5-16 The Request Object's Collections, Property, and Method

Category	Name	Description
Collections	ClientCertificate	Field values stored in a client certificate that arrived with an HTTP request
	Cookies	The values of any cookies received with an HTTP request

(continued)

Table 5-16 *continued*

Category	Name	Description
Collections, *continued*	Form	Any form elements values that arrived with an HTTP request
	QueryString	Any HTTP query string values that arrived with an HTTP request
	ServerVariables	The values of defined environment variable
Property	*TotalBytes*	The total number of bytes the client sent in the body of a request (read-only)
Method	*BinaryRead*	The exact data the client sent to the server as part of a POST request

Use the Request.ClientCertificate collection

The Request.ClientCertificate collection will be empty unless the Web visitor's browser submits a digital certificate along with a normal Web request. If the browser submits a digital certificate, the collection will contain an entry for each field in the certificate. For more information, see the sidebar, "Digital Certificates."

Use the Request.Cookies collection

The Request.Cookies collection contains one entry for each cookie value you sent to a Web visitor as part of an earlier response. This is one solution to the problem of Web transactions being *stateless*. (Refer to the sidebar, "HTTP and Stateless Transactions.") The following statements send cookies to the browser that requested the current Web page.

```
Response.Cookies("greeting") = "howdy"
Response.Cookies("woes")("death") = "permanent"
```

Digital Certificates

A digital certificate is a scrap of data that contains one or several named fields, and is encrypted (or checksummed and the checksum encrypted) with a private key belonging to the Web visitor. (A *checksum* is a number calculated from the numeric values of each byte in a string or document. Most checksum formulas are designed so that the chances of two documents producing the same result are small.)

Data encrypted with a private key can only be decrypted with the corresponding public key. Thus, if a Web visitor claims a certain identity and submits a digital certificate as proof, the Web server can verify that identity by getting the certificate's public key from an independent and trusted source, and then attempting to decrypt the certificate or checksum. If the decryption works, the sender must be holding the identity's private key and therefore must be genuine.

```
Response.Cookies("woes")("illness") = "curable"
```

A subsequent execution of the same page, requested by the same browser, could retrieve these values by using the following statements. Note the use of a Dictionary object in the second group of statements to hold an array of alpha-numeric-keyed values.

```
greet = Request.Cookies("greeting")
Set woes = Server.CreateObject("Scripting.Dictionary")
For Each hardship In Request.Cookies("woes")
    woes(hardship) = Request.Cookies("woes")(hardship)
Next
```

The properties shown in the following code modify the expiration date of the cookie, the range of URLs that will receive the cookie, and the need to securely encrypt the cookie.

```
Response.Cookies("greeting") = "trick or treat"
Response.Cookies("greeting").Expires = "October 31, 2000"
Response.Cookies("greeting").Domain = "interlacken.com"
Response.Cookies("greeting").Path = "/webdbdev/ch05/"
Response.Cookies("greeting").Secure = True
```

A complication arises because the Web server transmits cookies as part of the HTTP headers, and it transmits the headers before any part of the Web page itself. Using a script located within the HTML to store cookie values can therefore generate a run-time error. There are two solutions to this problem: you can store

HTTP and Stateless Transactions

The Web's original designers created HTTP as a *stateless* protocol. That is, they specified that a Web server should handle every request from the same starting point and remember nothing about any request after responding to the Web visitor. This created a problem for applications, such as order entry and online shopping, that require the Web server to accumulate data from multiple submissions.

Solving this problem requires including—with every response—either all the data accumulated so far or a key to a holding area for all the accumulated data. You can include such data fairly easily by using either hidden form fields or data appended to the URL, but both methods suffer the same deficiency: if the Web visitor browses some other site and then returns to yours, all the accumulated data is lost.

Cookies solve this problem by storing data at the browser in a more persistent way. A cookie is a named value that you can send to the browser and that the browser will then send back to you. The browser remembers the origin of each cookie by server; by server and path; or by server, path, and filename; and it only returns a given cookie to its origin.

To send a cookie, add it to the Response.Cookies collection. To check for an incoming cookie, look in the Request.Cookies collection.

the cookie within script code located before the <html> statement, or you can tell the Web server to *buffer* the outgoing page. Buffering the page retains every part of it on the server until you're done processing it and thus allows modification of the headers from within the body. The following statement, located anywhere before the <html> statement, invokes buffering.

```
Response.Buffer = True
```

Use the Request.Form collection

The Request.Form collection contains any values the browser transmitted from an HTML form using the *POST* method. An HTML form is any part of a Web page enclosed by <form> and </form> tags. Most HTML forms contain one or more Submit buttons plus an assortment of text boxes, selection lists, check boxes, and radio buttons. Each of these form elements has a name and a value. When the Web visitor clicks the Submit button, the browser sends all the form element names and values to a URL specified in the <form> statement's *action* attribute.

If an HTML form's *action* attribute specifies an ASP page, and if the form also specifies the *POST* method, all the named form element values appear in the Request.Form collection. For example, consider the following Web page:

```
<html>
<head>
<title>Form Post Example</title>
</head>
<body>
<form method="POST" action="formpost.asp">
  <p><input type="text" name="box1" size="20"
            value="<%=UCase(Request.Form("box1"))%>">
    <input type="Submit" value="Submit" name="button1"></p>
</form>
</body>
</html>
```

As you can see, the <form> tag specifies both the *POST* method and an *action* attribute that specifies an ASP page. In fact, that ASP page is the one shown. Whenever the Web visitor clicks the Submit button, the browser will send two form field values to the server: the value of the text box named *box1* and the value of the Submit button named *button1*. Script code within the ASP page can access these values using the following expressions:

```
Request.Form("box1")
Request.Form("button1")
```

Note that in the example, the text box's default value is whatever the Web visitor submitted in the text box, converted to upper case.

You can find and run this file—named \webdbdev\ch05\formpost.asp—in the sample files on the CD.

Use the Request.QueryString collection

The Request.QueryString collection works a lot like the Request.Form collection, but under different circumstances. The Request.QueryString collection receives named values in two cases:

- The Web visitor submits an HTML form, and the <form> tag specifies *method= GET.*

- The Web visitor submits a URL containing a *query string.* This is a series of *name=value* pairs, introduced by a question mark and separated by ampersands. This URL contains a query string: *http://www.interlacken.com/ webdbdev/ch05/showquery.asp?fn=Jim&sn=Buyens*

Here's a simple loop that displays any values an ASP page receives in the Request.QueryString collection:

```
For Each name In Request.QueryString
   Response.Write "<tr>" & vbCrLf
   Response.Write "  <td>" & name & "</td>" & vbCrLf
   Response.Write "  <td>" & Request.QueryString(name) & _
     "</td>" & vbCrLf
   Response.Write "</tr>" & vbCrLf
Next
```

Even when you specify it in a <form> tag, using the *GET* method to transmit named fields increases the length of the URL. If the URL exceeds the capacity of either the browser or the Web server, this can lead to loss of data. This makes the *POST* method preferable for any forms you create. Code *method= POST* within the <form> tag, and then, in whatever page the action property specifies, look for submitted data in the Request.Form collection.

The *GET* method and the Request.Query collection are still useful in another context, however. Suppose, for example, that an ASP page creates the following output:

```
<table>
<tr>
   <th>Member Name</th>
</tr><tr>
   <td>Steven Buchanan</td>
</tr><tr>
   <td>Nancy Davolio</td>
</tr>
</table>
```

Suppose further that whenever a Web visitor clicks on a member name, you want to run an ASP page named minfo.asp that displays more information about that member. You can do this rather easily by modifying the first ASP page to produce this output instead, as shown on the next page.

```
<table>
<tr>
  <th>Member Name</th>
</tr><tr>
  <td><a href="minfo.asp?id=buchanan">Steven Buchanan</a></td>
</tr><tr>
  <td><a href="minfo.asp?id=davolio">Nancy Davolio</a></td>
</tr>
</table>
```

Now, the minfo.asp page just needs to look in *Request.QueryString("id")*, query the database for that *memberid*, and display the output.

Remembering whether to look in the Request.Form collection or the Request.QueryString collection can be a nuisance, as can the desire to have the same ASP page respond to either kind of input. The solution in both cases is to skip coding any collection name at all! For example, you could just code

```
Request("id")
```

When you don't specify a collection, the ASP processor searches the following collections in the order shown below. If there were no value named "id" in the Request.QueryString collection, the interpreter would search the Form collection, the Cookies collection, and so on for a value with that name.

1. QueryString

2. Form

3. Cookies

4. ClientCertificate

5. ServerVariables

Note You should consider two precautions when you don't specify a Request collection. First, searching up to five collections demands more resources from the Web server than searching one collection. Second, if the name you want exists in more than one collection, the one you get might not be the one you want.

Use the Request.ServerVariables collection

For information about the Web visitor, the visitor's browser, the Web server, and other details of a particular transaction, look in the Request.ServerVariables collection. The exact items available will vary somewhat depending on the circumstances, but you can display this collection quite easily by coding the following loop:

```
For Each key In Request.ServerVariables
  val = Request.ServerVariables(key)
  Response.Write _
    "<tr>" & vbCrLF & _
    "  <td valign=top>" & key & "</td>" & vbCrLf & _
```

```
"   <td valign=top>" & val & " </td>" & vbCrLf & _
"</tr>" & vbCrLF
Next
```

The file \webdbdev\ch05\request.asp contains exactly this loop. You can see part of its display in Figure 5-4, but to get the whole picture you should run it on your own Web server.

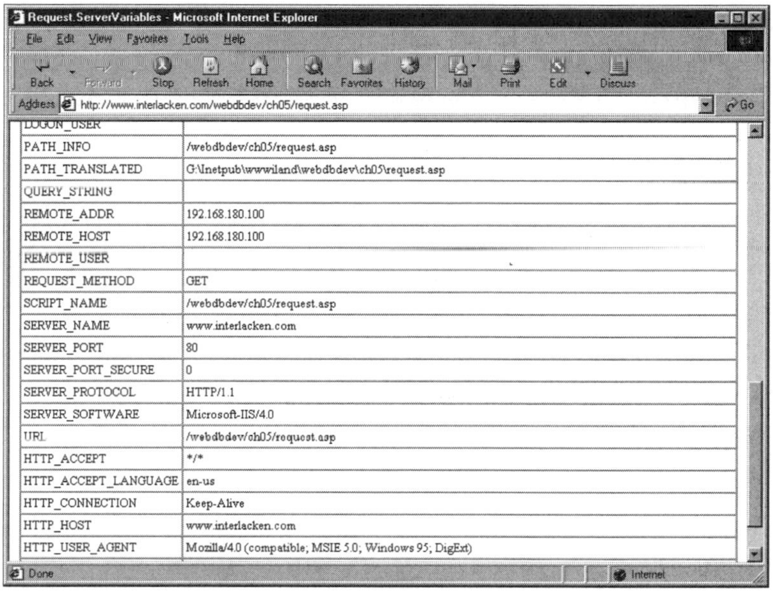

Figure 5-4 *The Request.ServerVariables collection provides a wealth of information about an incoming request.*

Determining Browser Capabilities

One of the more interesting items in the Request object is the value *Request.ServerVariables("HTTP_USER_AGENT")*. This contains a string that identifies the user's browser, operating system, and other facts. A typical *HTTP_USER_AGENT* string looks like this:

```
Mozilla/4.0 (compatible; MSIE 5.0; Windows 95; DigExt)
```

Microsoft Web servers provide an object that analyzes these strings and returns properties that indicate the features of the submitting browser. You can use this information to customize the Web page the visitor receives:

Set *variable* = Server.CreateObject("MSWC.BrowserType")

The properties available depend on a file named browscap.ini. To stay up-to-date with the latest browser versions, the server administrator can download this file from time to time from Microsoft's Web site. New versions of the browscap.ini file might contain new properties, but the ones pictured in Figure 5-5 are well established.

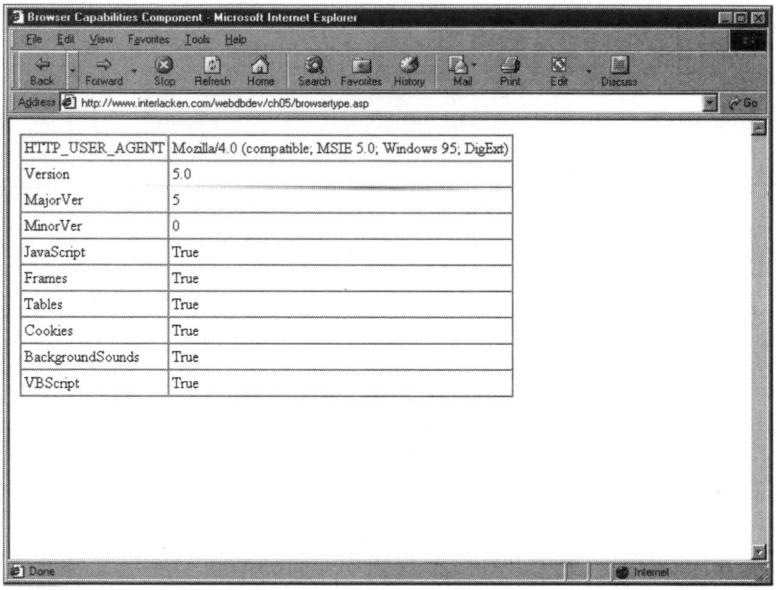

Figure 5-5   *The first row in this Web page displays the* Request.ServerVariables ("HTTP_USER_AGENT") *value, and the remaining rows show what capabilities the MSWC.BrowserType object infers from that value.*

One caution: although the MSWC.BrowserType object can tell you a browser's capabilities, it can't tell you whether the Web visitor has turned them off.

Using the Response Object

The most complex of ASP's built-in objects is the Response object, which transmits an ASP page's output to the Web visitor who submitted a request. Most of its many features are seldom used, however, and only deserve minimal coverage in this section. For a list of all Response object collections, properties, and methods, consult Table 5-17. For more information, refer to "Introducing Active Server Page Objects," earlier in this chapter and consult the online documentation.

Table 5-17   The Response Object's Collections, Properties, and Methods

Category	Name	Description
Collection	Cookies	Contains any cookie values received from the client, or that you want to send to the client.
Properties	*Buffer*	Indicates whether to buffer page output.
	CacheControl	Determines whether proxy servers should cache the output generated by ASP.
	Charset	Adds a character set name to the content-type header.

Category	Name	Description
	ContentType	Specifies the outgoing HTTP content type. (Changing this property tells the browser you're sending something other than HTML.)
	Expires	The number of minutes a browser can cache this page.
	ExpiresAbsolute	The date and time when a browser must discard any cached copies of this page.
	IsClientConnected	Indicates whether the client has disconnected from the server.
	Pics	Adds the value of a PICS label to the *pics-label* field of the response header. (PICS is a system for rating Web page content.)
	Status	The value of the status line returned by the server.
Methods	*AddHeader*	Adds or overrides an outgoing HTML header.
	AppendToLog	Adds a string to the end of the Web server log entry for this request.
	BinaryWrite	Writes the given information to the current HTTP output without any character-set conversion.
	Clear	Erases any buffered HTML output.
	End	Stops processing the ASP file and transmits any output created so far.
	Flush	Immediately sends any buffered output to the Web visitor.
	Redirect	Sends a message to the browser that tells it to connect to a different URL.
	Write	Writes an expression to the current HTTP output as character data.

See "Use the Request.Cookies collection," earlier in this chapter, for more information on how to send and receive cookies.

The *Response.Buffer* property is a True/False switch that tells the Web server whether to delay transmitting the outgoing Web page until it's complete. This requires certain resources from the Web server, but if code in the middle of an ASP page modifies headers or other information at the beginning, buffering is the only option. The *Response.Clear* method erases the buffer and the *Response.Flush* method transmits whatever you've written so far. However, using either method is rare.

Note Experience has shown that buffering outgoing ASP pages actually consumes fewer server resources than not buffering them. This is because the Web server can transmit buffered pages in larger, more efficient TCP/IP packets than unbuffered pages. Buffering is therefore the default in Windows 2000 but not in Windows NT 4.0.

To turn on buffering for a single page, insert the following statement before the opening <html> tag.

```
<%
Response.Buffer = True
%>
```

The *ContentType* property controls a header field that tells the browser what kind of output you're sending. The default, of course, is text/html. If your ASP code is generating something other than HTML—plain text or Extensible Markup Language (XML), for example—you'll need to modify this property to text/plain or text/xml. For detailed information about XML, see Part 5, "Exchanging Data With XML."

Because the *ContentType* property modifies a header field, you must either change it before the opening <html> tag or, as just described, turn on buffering.

To control how long a Web visitor's browser can cache a page, modify the page's *Response.Expires* or *Response.ExpiresAbsolute* property. *Response.Expires* specifies a number of minutes, while *Response.ExpiresAbsolute* specifies a date and time. Setting *Response.Expires* to zero tells the browser it should request a fresh copy of the page every time the Web visitor views it. This is another HTTP header field and requires the same precautions as the *ContentType* property.

Response.Status specifies a three-digit status code followed by one space and then a brief text message. The default value is "200 OK" but you can modify this to values such as "401 Unauthorized" or "301 Moved Permanently". A 401 status code tells the browser to prompt the Web visitor for a user name and password and then resubmit the request. Combined with a *Response.Redirect* value (described below), a 301 status code tells the browser to automatically redirect all future requests. This is another header field and requires the usual precautions (that is, buffering or placement before the first HTML or *Response.Write* statement).

Note   For a list of HTTP status codes, either browse *http://msdn.microsoft.com/ workshop/networking/wininet/reference/constants/statuscodes.asp* or browse *http:// msdn.microsoft.com/search* and search for the words, "HTTP status codes."

The *Response.AddHeader* method adds any header information you want to the outgoing Web page. Headers consist of a text identification string, a colon, a space, and then a value. Obviously, the browser must understand any header you send; otherwise, the browser ignores it. And of course, the usual precautions regarding the timing of headers apply.

The *Response.End* method tells the Web server to stop processing the ASP page immediately. The Web server will send the Web visitor any output you created prior to invoking the *Response.End* method.

The *Response.Redirect* method sends the Web visitor to another URL that you specify as an argument. For example, coding

If your data might contain characters that look like HTML to the browser, you should run it through the Server.HTMLEncode method before transmitting it.

```
Response.Redirect "/default.htm"
```

sends the Web visitor to the server's home page. If you specify a URL on the same Web server as the ASP page, the server simply abandons the current request and delivers the redirect page instead. If you specify a URL on a different server, the current server sends the browser a message that tells it to contact the other server. The usual precautions for modifying header fields apply.

Last but not least, the *Response.Write* statement sends the Web visitor any string you specify as an argument. The characters sent can be HTML, data, JavaScript, or anything else the browser understands. This book has already shown you many examples of the *Response.Write* statement and will show you many more.

If you develop an ASP page that codes data into a URL (probably as a query string), you should definitely run it through the Server.URLEncode method unless you're absolutely sure it will never contain anything but letters, numbers, and hyphens.

Using the Server Object

Compared to the Response object, the Server object is refreshingly simple. It supports the one property and four methods listed in Table 5-18.

Table 5-18　The Server Object's Property and Methods

Category	Name	Description
Property	ScriptTimeout	The amount of time a script can run before timing out.
Methods	CreateObject	Creates an instance of a server component.
	HTMLEncode	Applies HTML encoding to a string.
	MapPath	Maps a virtual path into a physical path. The virtual path can be an absolute path on the current server or a path relative to the current page.
	URLEncode	Applies URL encoding rules, including escape characters, to a string.

The Server object's one property is *Server.ScriptTimeout*, which specifies how many seconds a script can execute before the server terminates it. An administrator configures the default *ScriptTimeout* value at the server level, but it's usually 90 seconds. ASP code can lengthen (but not shorten) this interval.

The *Server.CreateObject* method creates any non-built-in objects your ASP page requires. Its syntax appears below. Examples of the *Server.CreateObject* method appear throughout this book.

Set *variable* = Server.CreateObject(*"ObjectName"*)

The *Server.HTMLEncode* method examines a string argument, replaces any special characters with their HTML mnemonic equivalents, and returns the result. For example, any ampersands in the argument appear as *&amp*; any quotation marks as *&quot*; and so on.

The *Server.URLEncode* method performs a different kind of conversion: it converts any argument you give it to a string suitable within a URL. The rules appear at the top of the following page.

- Letters, numbers, and hyphens remain unchanged.

- Spaces change to plus signs.

- All other characters change to a percent sign followed by the character's two-digit hex code.

Using the Application Object

As you've seen mentioned several times in this book, ASP files must reside in an executable folder in order to execute. And for a folder to be executable, an administrator must configure it to be so. Once a folder is executable, all its subfolders are, by default, executable as well.

No ASP file can belong to two applications. If the administrator marks some folder executable and then explicitly marks one of its subfolders executable, the files in that subfolder belong only to the subfolder's application.

In ASP parlance, an *application* consists of all the ASP files that exist within a single executable folder tree. The Application object provides an area where all these pages can exchange data among themselves, and a means by which you can schedule code to run whenever the application starts or stops. Table 5-19 lists the Application object's collections, methods, and events.

Table 5-19 The Application Object's Collections, Methods, and Events

Category	Name	Description
Collections	Contents	Contains all items that script commands have added to the Application object
	StaticObjects	Contains all objects that <object> tags have added to the application
Methods	*Lock*	Prevents other clients from modifying Application object properties
	Unlock	Allows other clients to modify Application object properties
Events	*Application_OnStart*	If a subroutine with this name exists in the global.asa file, it will run whenever the application starts
	Application_OnEnd	If a subroutine with this name exists in the global.asa file, it will run whenever the application terminates

The server automatically processes the global.asa file the first time a Web visitor requests any ASP file in an application.

The Application.Contents collection contains any variables that ASP pages or the global.asa file have added. You can store items in the Application.Contents collection by using statements like the following:

```
Application.Contents("todaysspecial") = "Meatballs"
Application("todaysdessert") = "Avocado Sorbet"
```

The Application.StaticObjects collection contains any objects loaded because of <object> tags in the global.asa file. As a beginning developer, you're extremely unlikely to use this facility. If you do, the circumstances will probably involve packaged software and you should consult the supplier's documentation.

The *Lock* and *Unlock* methods gain and relinquish exclusive control of the Application.Contents collection. This is necessary to prevent two ASP pages (or the same ASP page servicing different Web visitors) from trying to update the same data at the same time. To lock out other users for the duration of your update, surround it with *Lock* and *Unlock* commands as shown here:

```
Application.Lock
Application("hits") = Application("hits") + 1
Application.Unlock
```

The global.asa file must reside in the starting folder of the application—the folder the administrator originally marked executable. Within this file you can optionally code two special subroutines as shown here:

```
<script language=scriptlanguage runat=server>
Sub Application_OnStart
'    Your statements go here.
End Sub

Sub Application_OnEnd
'    Your statements go here.
End Sub
</script>
```

The ASP environment automatically runs any code in the *Application_OnStart* subroutine whenever the application starts; that is, whenever the first Web visitor requests any of the application's ASP pages. This code could, for example, load the Application.Contents collection with constants you don't want to code within each ASP page.

Similarly, the ASP environment automatically runs the *Application_OnEnd* subroutine whenever the application ends. This will usually be when an administrator or server operator stops the Web service. The *Application_OnEnd* routine would perform any tasks necessary to properly shut down the application, such as terminating other processes or writing out statistics. Be aware, however, that the *Application_OnEnd* routine probably won't execute if the server terminates suddenly (in other words, crashes).

Using the Session Object

The first time a Web visitor enters an application (requests one of its ASP pages) the Web server creates a Session object for that visitor. These Session objects are persistent, meaning that they remain in existence until there's no activity from the Web visitor for a specified interval (usually 20 minutes). As long as the object exists, it provides a storage area for data passed from one page execution to the next, or from one page to another.

A *SessionID* uniquely identifies each Session object. The Web server transmits the *SessionID* to the browser as a cookie, and tells the browser to return the *SessionID* cookie with any requests it makes to the same application. The Web server uses the *SessionID* cookie to associate the same Session object with all submissions by the same visitor.

If the visitor fails to submit a request within a timeout period, the Web server discards the Session object. If the visitor later returns, the server creates a new (empty) Session object.

Table 5-20 lists the Session object's collections, properties, methods, and events. The Contents and StaticObjects collections work exactly like the corresponding collections in the Application object, but of course with a scope that includes one Web visitor rather than the entire application. In other words, the Session object provides persistent resources pertaining to one Web visitor's repeated visits.

Table 5-20 The Session Object's Collections, Properties, Methods, and Events

Category	Name	Description
Collections	Contents	Contains all items that script commands have added to the Session object.
	StaticObjects	Contains all objects that <object> tags have added to the session with session scope.
Properties	*CodePage*	The code page (character set) used for symbol mapping.
	LCID	The locale identifier.
	SessionID	The session identification for this user.
	Timeout	The timeout period for the sessions within the current application, stated in minutes.
Methods	*Abandon*	Destroys a Session object and releases its resources.
Events	*Session_OnStart*	If a subroutine with this name exists in the global.asa file, it will run whenever a session begins.
	Session_OnEnd	If a subroutine with this name exists in the global.asa file, it will run whenever a session terminates.

The *Session.CodePage* and *Session.LCID* properties apply to natural language character sets and conventions. For a table of code page values, browse *http://search.microsoft.com/search* and search for article number Q165478. For a table of *LCID* values, browse the same location and search for the keyword kbLocaleID or the article number Q224804.

The *Session.SessionID* property contains the *SessionID* assigned to the current Web visitor. The timeout property controls how long the Session object persists in the absence of incoming requests.

The *Session.Abandon* method destroys the current session object.

The *Session_OnStart* and *Session_OnEnd* events work similarly to the *Application_OnStart* and *Application_OnEnd* methods described earlier in the chapter. If you include a subroutine with one of these names in the global.asa file, that subroutine will execute whenever a session begins or ends.

Using ASP Directives

The ASP interpreter accepts five directives that control how it processes a given page. It's seldom necessary to use any of these directives but, should the need arise, Table 5-21 describes them.

To use a directive, code it within <% and %> tags and make it the first and only statement on its line. For example, to make JScript rather than VBScript the default script language, code

```
<%@ LANGUAGE=JScript %>
```

Table 5-21   Active Server Page Directives

Directive	Description
@CODEPAGE	Determines the code page used to display dynamic content. A code page is roughly equivalent to a character set, such as US English, German, or Japanese.
@ENABLESESSIONSTATE	Turns session tracking on (True) or off (False).
@LANGUAGE	Sets the default language that interprets the commands in a script: the language that applies within <% and %> tags. IIS ships with two script engines, VBScript and JScript.
@LCID	Determines the location identifier used to display dynamic content.
@TRANSACTION	Indicates whether Microsoft Transaction Server will create a transaction to coordinate any updates the script makes.

Chapter Summary

This chapter described how to integrate server-side VBScript code into ASP, and also how VBScript differs from other forms of Visual Basic. It then explained how your code can access the Request object to get information about the Web visitor's request, the Server object to access built-in Web server methods, and the Response object to transmit HTML to the Web visitor. Finally, it explained how the Application and Session objects store data beyond the duration of processing a single Web page.

Chapter 6, "Organizing Your Web Environment," will explain how to configure a Web server for running Web database pages.

Organizing Your Web Environment

Chapter Objectives	Estimated Time: 35 minutes

In this chapter, you'll learn

- How to obtain and configure a Microsoft Web Server for use in developing Web database pages.

- What capabilities to look for when selecting a Web Presence Provider.

- What kinds of Web database capabilities various Microsoft products provide.

Developing Web database pages requires a variety of software. Previous chapters have discussed ADO, Microsoft Visual Basic, Scripting Edition, and the IIS server objects. What those chapters didn't discuss is how and where to install these tools and how to configure them. The first part of this chapter addresses those issues.

In many cases, of course, you won't operate your own Web server. Instead, you'll obtain Web server space and services from your information technology department, a public Internet service provider (ISP), or a public Web hosting provider. In any of these cases, you'll need to know what services to request. This is the second topic addressed in this chapter.

The last part of this chapter introduces three software products applicable to producing Web database pages: Microsoft Access, Microsoft FrontPage, and Microsoft Visual InterDev.

Setting Up a Development Environment on Your Own PC

If your Web pages up to now have been simple HTML pages, you've probably needed only one Web server: the one your Web visitors access. You probably developed these pages on your own PC and tested them by opening the disk files with your browser. When you decided a page was ready for prime time, you put it on the Web server using file sharing, FTP, or a Web publishing system such as Microsoft FrontPage.

Such an arrangement is usually sufficient for developing simple HTML pages, but developing Web database pages usually requires two Web servers: one for you to use while developing and another for Web visitors to use when accessing the finished application. There are four reasons for this.

Note: Within this book, a Web database page is an ASP page that accesses a database.

- You can't run a Web database page by loading it directly off your disk and into your browser. As earlier chapters have illustrated, Web database pages orchestrate a variety of software resources that only exist in a true Web server environment.

- You probably don't want Web visitors running your Web database pages until you think those pages are ready. This is especially true when you're modifying an existing page; your visitors could end up seeing a page that isn't exactly the old version, isn't exactly the new version, and isn't exactly working.

- If you have limited bandwidth to your production Web server, the speed, reliability, and cost of that connection can prohibit extensive development directly on that server.

- To interactively debug an ASP page—to watch each statement execute, pause at breakpoints, and examine variables and objects during execution—you must be sitting at the Web server's console. And installing Web server software on your own PC is usually simpler than getting access to a production Web server console.

Chapter 16, "Debugging" explains how to debug ASP pages interactively.

Active Server Pages, ActiveX Data Objects, and Visual Basic Scripting Edition are all Microsoft products that come with Microsoft Web servers. Microsoft's flagship Web server—and the only one suited for production Web sites—is part of Internet Information Services. IIS runs on Microsoft Windows 2000 and, as shown in Table 6-1, is currently at version 5.0.

Table 6-1   Internet Information Server Versions

Version	Released With
1.0	Post release feature for Microsoft Windows NT Server 3.51
2.0	Windows NT Server 4.0
3.0	Post release feature for Windows NT Server 4.0
4.0	Windows NT 4.0 Option Pack
5.0	Windows 2000

As you can see, new versions of IIS tend to appear more frequently than new versions of Windows NT Server (now Windows 2000 Server). New releases of ADO appear even more frequently than those of IIS, and usually coincide with new releases of Microsoft Access or Microsoft SQL Server. However, some ADO releases are strictly for bug fixes or other interim maintenance. There's no set schedule to new releases of VBScript. And just to make life interesting, some Windows NT Service Packs have included fixes and enhancements for IIS as well as for Windows NT itself.

Note   Fortunately, the software interfaces used by Web database developers have been very stable since IIS version 4.0. Microsoft has no desire for millions of existing ASP pages to fail because of a new release. It's likely that the development techniques shown in this book will continue to work for many years, despite occasional upgrades to the underlying software base.

IIS also runs on Windows NT Workstation, Windows 98, and Windows 95. On those operating systems, however, it's called Microsoft Personal Web Server (PWS) and a few features are scaled back or removed completely. PWS only supports one Web server per computer, for example, and the Windows 95 and Windows 98 versions have limited security features.

Don't install the version of IIS that comes with Windows NT 4.0 or an earlier CD because this version of IIS doesn't support the technologies used in this book.

Obtaining a Microsoft Web Server

If you're running Windows 2000, you can install IIS either initially, when you install the operating system, or later, from Control Panel. Microsoft Personal Web Server is included with Windows 98, and you can install it from the Windows 98 CD.

If you're running Windows NT 4 or Windows 95, you should obtain the Windows NT Server 4.0 Option Pack (or its successor, if there is one) from the downloads option at *http://www.microsoft.com/ntserver*.

Even if you have Windows 2000 or Windows 98, you should check Microsoft's Web site for newer versions, patches, or updates.

Note   For clarity, the Components list boxes in Figures 6-1, 6-2, 6-3, 6-4, and 6-6 are artificially lengthened.

Install Web services on Windows 2000

Installation of IIS on Windows 2000 begins with the dialog box shown in Figure 6-1. This dialog box appears during initial setup and whenever you follow these steps:

1. Open Control Panel.

2. Double-click Add/Remove Programs.

3. Click Add/Remove Windows Components.

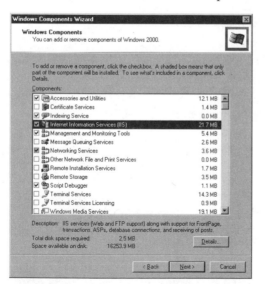

Figure 6-1   *To install a Web server on Windows 2000, check Internet Information Services (IIS) within this dialog box.*

The list of components will vary depending on whether you run Windows 2000 Server or Windows 2000 Professional. Figure 6-1 shows the options for Windows 2000 Server. The following options relate to Web database development:

Chapter 11, "Performing Text Queries," will explain how to create Web pages that use Indexing Service.

- **Indexing Service** is a full-text search engine that can index the pages in a Web site. You should install this option if your Web site (or any other application on the server) would benefit from full-text searching.

- **Internet Information Services (IIS)** comprise the Web server itself. You should definitely choose this option if you want the server to deliver Web pages of any sort to Web visitors.

Chapter 16 explains how to use the Script Debugger.

- **Script Debugger** provides an interactive debugging facility for Web pages, complete with step-by-step execution, breakpoints, and run-time access to variables. You should select this option on any machine you plan to use for ASP development.

IIS includes subcomponents you can install or exclude as necessary. To view the list of subcomponents and make selections, select Internet Information Services (IIS) and then click the Details button. You'll see the dialog box shown in Figure 6-2.

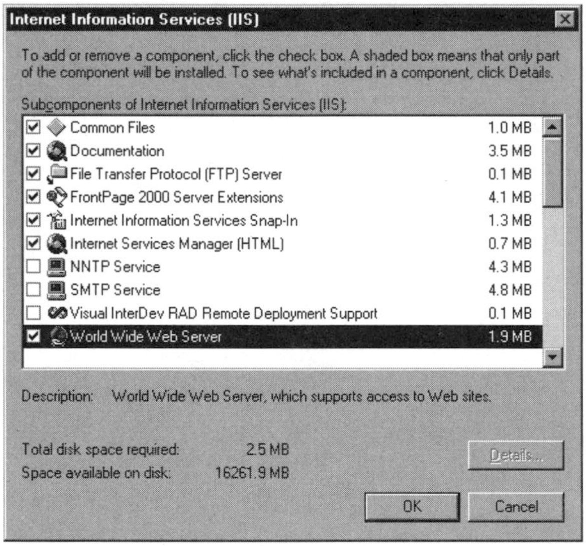

Figure 6-2 *This dialog box lists installable components for Internet Information Services.*

Installable components for IIS include the following:

- **Common Files** refers to various files used by one or more other subcomponents. If you specify any other subcomponents, you'll probably need to specify this one, too.

- **Documentation** includes information about administering and programming the other subcomponents. Check this option.

- **File Transfer Protocol (FTP) Server** accepts incoming connections from remote users using FTP client software. Install this subcomponent only if you want to support such connections.

- **FrontPage 2000 Server Extensions** provide enhanced Web publishing capability for all versions of FrontPage, all versions of Visual InterDev, and the Web Folders feature in Office 2000. The extensions also provide server-side programs that some FrontPage features need to work. Choose this option only if you need to support FrontPage, Visual InterDev, or the Office 2000 Web Folders facility.

- **Internet Information Services Snap-In** provides software for administering the Web server through Microsoft Management Console (MMC). Always check this option.

- **Internet Services Manager (HTML)** provides a series of Web pages for administering the Web server remotely. Check this option only if you anticipate administering the Web server from locations having only HTTP connectivity.

- **NNTP Service** accepts and forwards Internet newsgroup feeds. It also supports connections from individual users running newsgroup clients (newsreaders). Check this option only if you expect to send and receive Internet news feeds or if you want to set up your own news server. This option isn't available on Windows 2000 Professional.

- **SMTP Service** accepts incoming electronic mail messages and periodically tries to forward them to another server. It stores such messages only until forwarding is successful and then deletes them. There's no support for client e-mail software to receive messages. Servers with reliable access to another SMTP server seldom need this subcomponent.

- **Visual InterDev RAD Remote Deployment Support** adds more functions to the FrontPage Server Extensions. These functions register server-side components and set up Microsoft Transaction Server packages at the request of developers using Visual InterDev remotely. Install this option only if developers using Visual InterDev need such support.

- **World Wide Web Server** provides Web visitors with access to ordinary Web pages, ASP pages, and other server-side programs via HTTP. For Web database development, always install this option.

Install Web services on Windows NT 4.0

To install IIS on a Windows NT 4.0 server or workstation, download the Windows NT Server 4.0 Option Pack from *http://www.microsoft.com/ntserver*, and then run the setup program. Respond to the usual startup prompts, choose Custom Installation, and then wait for the Option Pack setup to display the dialog box shown in Figure 6-3.

For Web database development you should install these three options:

- **Internet Information Server (IIS)** is the component that includes the Web server software. This option is mandatory if you want to test or deliver ASP applications on the local computer. In Windows NT Workstation, an option called Personal Web Server replaces this option.

- **Microsoft Script Debugger** provides an interactive debugging facility for Web pages. You should select this option on any machine you plan to use for ASP development.

- **NT Option Pack Common Files** installs various files used by other components. If you specify any other components, you'll probably need to specify this one as well.

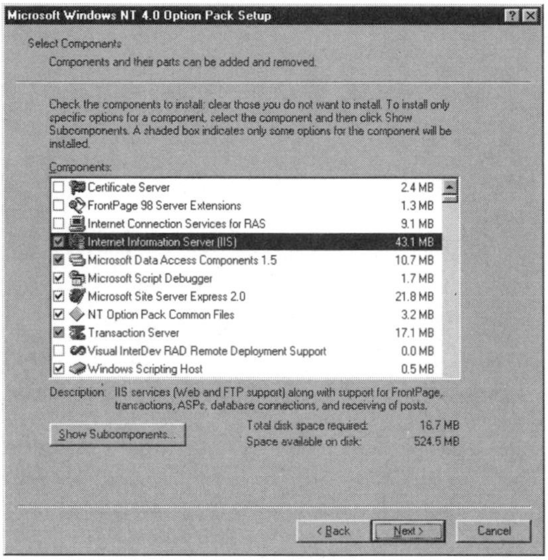

Figure 6-3 *This dialog box lists optional components of the Windows NT 4.0 Option Pack.*

The following components are outdated. Even if you choose to install the versions that come with the Option Pack, you should still download and install the latest versions from Microsoft's Web site.

Chapter 16 explains how to debug ASP page with Microsoft Script Debugger.

- **FrontPage 98 Server Extensions** provide enhanced Web publishing capability for all versions of FrontPage, all versions of Visual InterDev, and the Web Folders feature in Office 2000. However, if you need these features, you should install a current version of the FrontPage 2000 Server Extensions. There are at least three ways to do this:

  - Run Setup from disc 1 of the Office 2000 Premium CD set, selecting the following choices under Microsoft FrontPage for Windows: Server Extensions Resource Kit and—if you want to administer the extensions via your browser—Server Extension Admin Forms.

  - Insert disc 3 of the Office 2000 Premium CD set and then choose Install Microsoft Office Server Extensions from the splash screen. This installs not only the FrontPage 2000 Server Extensions but also some additional features that work with Microsoft Office. However, you can install the Office Server Extensions only on a Windows 2000 system or a Windows NT server.

- Download the latest version of the FrontPage 2000 Server Extensions from Microsoft's Web site at *http://msdn.microsoft.com/workshop/ languages/fp/2000/winfpse.asp* and follow the instructions provided. Even if you install the extensions from the Office CDs, it's a good idea to check this site for updates and fixes.

- **Microsoft Data Access Components 1.5** provides an early version of ActiveX Data Objects. Whether you install this component or not, you should still download and install the latest version of the Microsoft Data Access Pack. See "Obtaining and Installing ADO" in Chapter 3 ("Access ing Databases with ADO and ODBC") for a description of how to do this.

Once you've selected these options, highlight Internet Information Server (IIS), click the Show Subcomponents button, and verify the resulting list. Figure 6-4 provides an example. For an explanation of each subcomponent, refer to "Install Web services on Windows 2000" earlier in this chapter. You can ignore minor differences in subcomponent names.

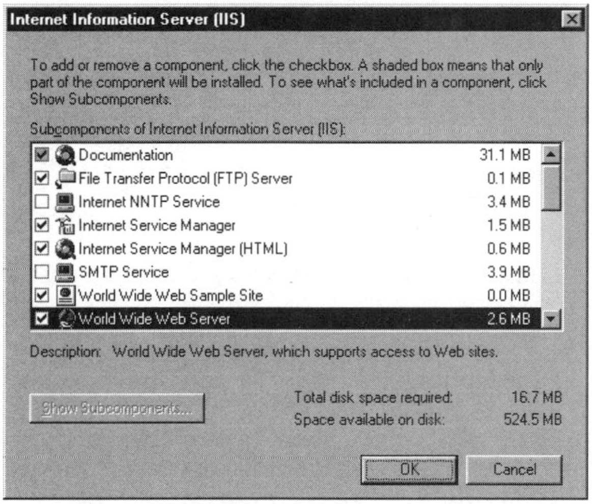

Figure 6-4 *This dialog box lists subcomponents for Internet Information Server 4.0.*

The option pack subcomponent named Internet Service Manager installs two items: a copy of Microsoft Management Console and the Internet Information Server Snap-In. Windows 2000 installs MMC natively and doesn't need to do it again when installing IIS.

The NNTP and SMTP services aren't available when you install the option pack on Windows NT Workstation.

Install Web services on Windows 95 and Windows 98

If you're running Windows 98, you can install Personal Web Server from the Windows 98 CD. You can get a pointer to the PWS installation files on the CD by choosing Internet Tools in the Add/Remove Programs Properties dialog box available from Control Panel. Figure 6-5 shows the Internet Tools dialog box. Check the Personal Web Server option, and click OK.

Figure 6-5 *Personal Web Server is one of the Internet Tools available with Windows 98 SE.*

Strange as it might seem, to install Microsoft Personal Web Server on Windows 95 you must install the Windows NT 4.0 Option Pack. When you start the Option Pack's setup program, it detects the computer's operating system and installs the proper software. Figure 6-6 shows the components available when you choose Custom setup on Windows 95.

The choices you should make on Windows 95 are essentially those you should make on Windows NT Workstation. In other words, you must install at least Common Program Files and Personal Web Server.

You'll also need to install Microsoft Data Access Components, but you should download the latest version from Microsoft's Web site and install it after the

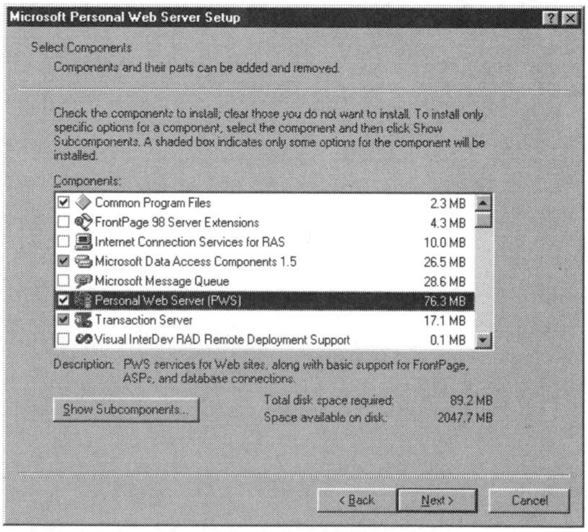

Figure 6-6 *Installing the Windows NT 4.0 Option Pack on Windows 95 offers these components.*

option pack setup completes. If you need the FrontPage Server Extensions, install the FrontPage 2000 version from the Office 2000 Premium CD or from Microsoft's Web site.

Creating Executable Folders

Every Web server associates a specific folder with the URL "/". This folder is the *HTTP root*. When a Web visitor requests a URL, the Web server looks for the requested path and filename relative to the HTTP root. Table 6-2 shows some examples of this concept in action. Assume that the HTTP root is the folder C:\InetPub\wwwroot.

Table 6-2   Resolving URLs Relative to an HTTP Root Location

Requested URL	File Delivered
http://<server>/default.htm	C:\InetPub\wwwroot\default.htm
http://<server>/xyz/info.htm	C:\InetPub\wwwroot\xyz\info.htm
http://<server>/images/logo.gif	C:\InetPub\wwwroot\images\logo.gif

Because this Web server's HTTP root is C:\InetPub\wwwroot\, it normally resolves URLs relative to that location. This is a simple and elegant scheme, but not a flexible one. Sooner or later, every Web administrator needs a URL path and the corresponding physical path to be different.

Suppose, for example, that installing a software product named Flakey Bits installs Web-based documentation files at E:\Program Files\FlakeyBits\docs\. You could copy this documentation to a new folder named C:\InetPub\wwwroot\FlakeyDocs, but it would be far more direct to somehow associate the URL *http://<server>/FlakeyDocs* with the physical location E:\Program Files\FlakeyBits\docs\. Most Web servers, including those from Microsoft, support such requirements with a facility called *virtual directories*. A virtual directory associates a URL path with a physical path that isn't necessarily within the HTTP root.

Over time, Web servers have adapted the virtual directory concept to control much more than path translations. Any folder setting or property that pertains to Web server use—and not to ordinary file use—tends to reside in a virtual directory entry. This is true even if the virtual path and the physical path are the same.

One such setting pertains to a folder's *executable* property. This property tells the Web server whether it's OK to run ASP pages and other executable objects located within a given folder. If you put an ASP page in a folder that isn't executable, the Web server won't run it.

The following procedures guide you through the process of creating a virtual directory and marking it executable. If you're the Web server's administrator (perhaps because you're configuring a Web server on your own PC), you can do these things yourself. Otherwise, you'll need to get the server's administrator to do them for you.

Create an executable directory on Windows 2000

The following steps explain how to create an executable virtual directory on Windows 2000:

1. From the Start button, choose Programs, Administrative Tools, and Internet Services Manager. (Any configuration of Microsoft Management Console that includes the Internet Information Services Snap-In will work as well.)

2. If the computer that will contain the executable virtual directory isn't listed under Internet Information Services, right-click Internet Information Services, choose Connect, enter the computer name, and click OK.

3. If the computer that will contain the executable virtual directory is preceded by a plus sign, click the plus sign to show the next level of detail.

4. Right-click the Web server that will contain the executable virtual directory, choose New from the pop-up menu, and then choose Virtual Directory. Figure 6-7 illustrates this operation in progress.

If your Windows 2000 Start menu doesn't display an Administrative Tools menu, right-click the taskbar, choose Properties, click the Advanced tab, and under Start Menu Settings check Display Administrative Tools.

Figure 6-7 *To create a virtual directory, choose New from the Web server's MMC pop-up menu.*

5. When the Virtual Directory Creation Wizard appears, click the Next button to bypass the opening screen, and then enter the Virtual Directory Alias you have in mind. This is the path that Web visitors will see in their URLs. Figure 6-8 shows this panel and the next.

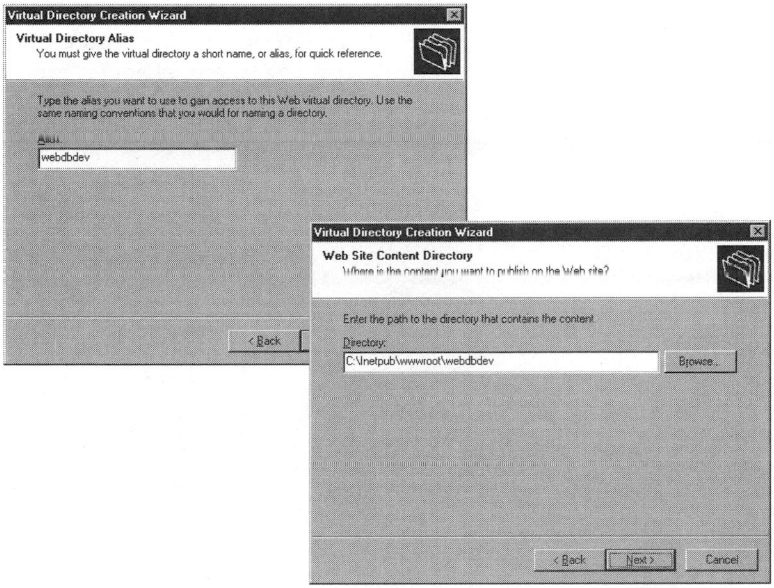

Figure 6-8   *Specify the virtual directory's alias (URL path) and its physical location on these two panels.*

6. Click the Next button and then, on the wizard's third panel, enter the Web Site Content Directory. This can be any directory that physically exists on the server, or a file-sharing location specified in Universal Naming Convention (UNC) format.

7. Click the Next button again to display the screen shown in Figure 6-9, which offers these security options for the new virtual directory:

   A UNC file-sharing location has the format \\<server>\ <sharename>\ <path>\<file>.

   - **Read** specifies that the Web server can respond to ordinary GET requests for files in the virtual directory. That is, it can deliver HTML, GIF, JPEG, and other such files in the usual way.

   - **Run Scripts** specifies that the Web server can respond to GET and POST requests that specify a location within the virtual directory and that cause a script interpreter to run Web pages containing server-side scripts. For Active Server Pages to work properly, you *must* check this option.

   - **Execute** specifies that the Web server can execute any program files (such as .exe and .dll files) that are within the virtual directory and specified as part of a URL.

   - **Write** specifies that the Web server can receive files from Web visitors and create or overwrite corresponding files in the virtual directory. This is a rarely used option except when Web designers use certain HTML editors.

- **Browse** specifies that when a Web visitor submits a URL with no file-name, and when the specified path doesn't contain a default Web page, the Web server will respond with a clickable directory listing of files in that directory.

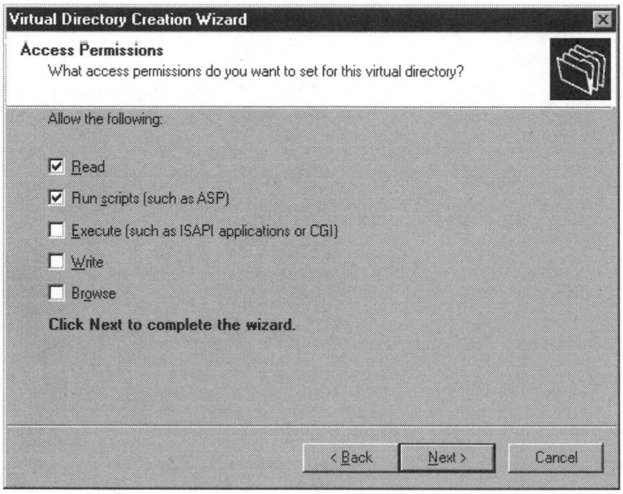

Figure 6-9 *Specify virtual directory security settings by using this screen. The defaults shown here permit ASP to run.*

8. Click Next once more to get the wizard's closing screen, and then click Finish. The new virtual directory should appear beneath the Web server's entry in MMC.

9. To review or modify your results, right-click the new virtual directory in MMC and then choose Properties from the pop-up menu. This will display the dialog box shown on the left in Figure 6-10. Clicking the Configuration button displays the dialog box at the right, where the first option on the App Debugging tab enables or disables interactive script debugging.

   The Read, Write, and Directory Browsing options along the left edge correspond to the Read, Write, and Browse options in the wizard. The options in the Execute Permissions drop-down list box correspond to the wizard's Run Scripts and Execute options.

10. The Virtual Directory Properties dialog box shown on the left in Figure 6-10 obviously contains a myriad of options that the Virtual Directory Creation Wizard doesn't configure. Fortunately, the default settings are perfectly acceptable for most work. If not, you can get additional guidance by clicking the Help button or by consulting a book about IIS. One setting, however, deserves particular mention. Clicking the Configuration button—which is partially hidden in Figure 6-10—and then choosing the App Debugging tab reveals the following option:

- **Enable ASP Server-Side Script Debugging** must be turned on if you want to interactively debug your ASP applications as described in Chapter 16.

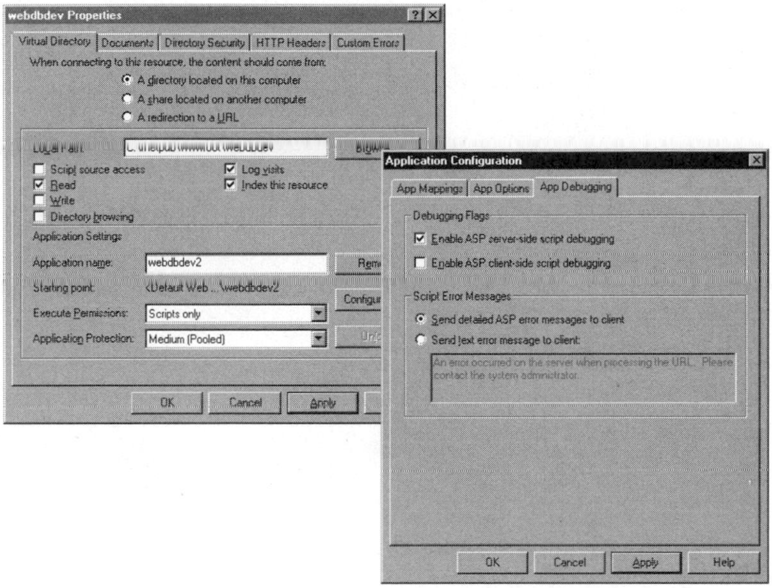

Figure 6-10 *The IIS Snap-In uses the dialog box at the left to display the properties of an existing virtual directory.*

Create an executable directory on Windows NT 4.0

With the exception of minor visual changes, the procedure for setting up a virtual directory on Windows NT 4.0 is the same as that on Windows 2000. Start the process by clicking the Start button, Programs, Windows NT 4.0 Option Pack, Microsoft Internet Information Server, and finally Internet Service Manager. (As usual, look for Personal Web Server instead of Internet Information Server on Windows NT 4.0 Workstation.)

Create an executable directory on Windows 95 or Windows 98

The following steps create an executable virtual directory on Microsoft Personal Web Server running on Windows 95 or Windows 98:

1. Start Personal Web Manager with either of the following methods:

   • Double-click the Personal Web Server icon in the system tray.

   • Click the Start button, Programs, Microsoft Personal Web Server, and then Personal Web Manager.

2. When the Personal Web Manager dialog box appears, click the icon bar choice titled Advanced. The dialog box should then resemble the large one shown at the left of Figure 6-11.

3. Click the Add button to display the Add Directory dialog box shown at the right of Figure 6-11.

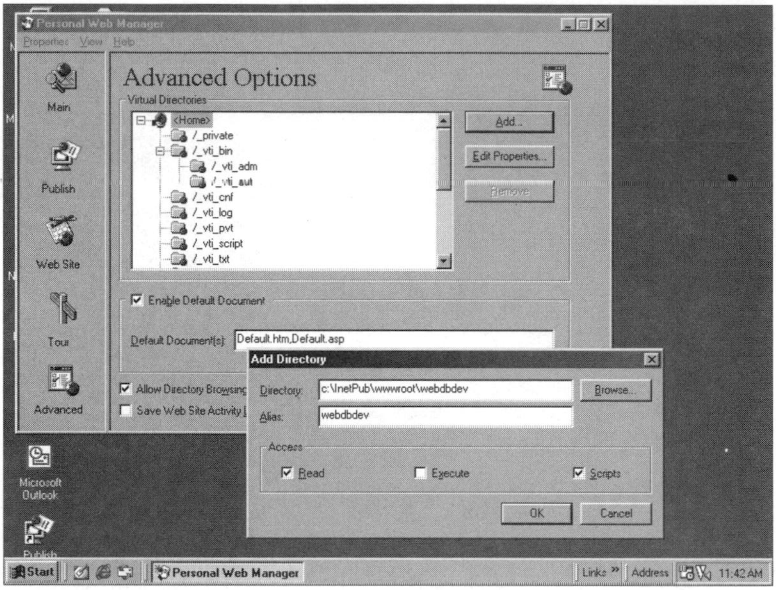

Figure 6-11 *On Windows 95 and Windows 98, these dialog boxes offer options to create virtual directories on Microsoft Personal Web Server.*

4. Specify the following options:

- **Directory**   Enter the physical path to the content you want Web visitors to perceive as residing in the virtual directory.

- **Alias**   Enter the URL path you want Web visitors to specify to access this content.

- **Access: Read**   Check this option if the Web server should honor requests for ordinary file types such as HTML, GIF, and JPEG located within the virtual directory.

- **Access: Execute**   Check this option if the Web server should execute programs that reside in the virtual directory and have filename extensions such as .exe and .dll.

- **Access: Scripts**   Check this option if the Web server should honor requests that specify a location within the virtual directory and that cause a script interpreter to run Web pages containing server-side scripts. For Active Server Pages to work properly, you *must* check this option.

5. Click OK to create the virtual directory.

To view or modify an existing virtual directory, select it in the Virtual Directories list box shown in Figure 6-11 and then click the Edit Properties button. To remove an existing virtual directory, select it the same way but click the Remove button.

Create an executable directory with Microsoft FrontPage

You can organize the Web pages you create with FrontPage in three ways:

• As individual HTML or ASP files.

• As a group of files on your disk. FrontPage calls this a *disk-based Web*.

• As a group of files on a Web server. FrontPage calls this a *server-based Web*.

As a Web database developer who needs to test ASP pages on a Web server, you should choose a server-based Web. By a stroke of luck (or could it be planning?), FrontPage makes sure that the root of every server-based FrontPage Web is also a virtual directory. Using a server-based Web means you never have to worry about creating virtual directories—FrontPage creates them for you.

If you have permission to administer a server-based Web, you can view and modify its essential virtual directory properties. To do this,

1. Open the server-based Web in FrontPage.

2. Right-click the Web's root folder.

3. Choose Properties from the pop-up menu. This will display the dialog box shown in Figure 6-12, which controls the Web's virtual directory settings through the following three settings:

  • **Allow Programs To Be Run** tells the Web server that if an incoming URL specifies an .exe or .dll program residing in the current Web, the server should run that program.

  • **Allow Scripts To Be Run** tells the Web server that if an incoming URL specifies a file type that's processed by a server-side script interpreter, the server should accept and process the request. You *must* check this option for Active Server Pages to work properly.

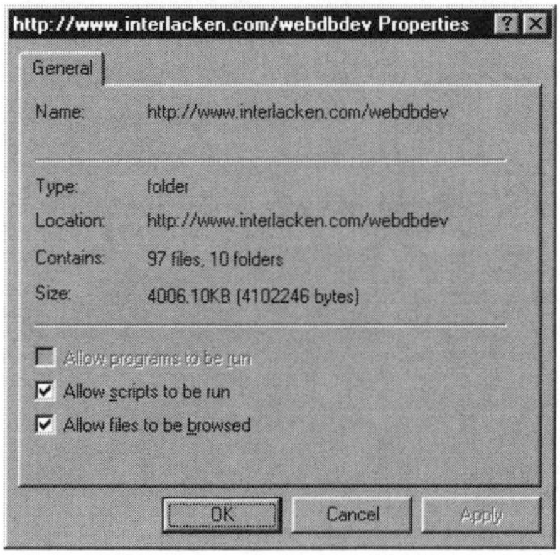

Figure 6-12 *FrontPage provides this dialog box to control a Web's virtual directory settings.*

  • **Allow Files To Be Browsed** tells the Web server to provide read-only access to simple file types such as HTML, GIF, or JPEG. Note that the Browse option in FrontPage controls whether Web visitors can retrieve specific files via HTTP; it has no effect on directory browsing.

The Browse option in FrontPage corresponds to the Read option in the Web server configuration programs. FrontPage has no option that corresponds to the Browse option in the Web server configuration programs.

Assign an interpreter to a filename extension

Whenever a Web visitor requests content from an executable directory, Microsoft Web servers look up the requested filename extension in a table of *application mappings*. This table assigns, or maps, a script interpreter to each filename extension in the table.

On Windows 2000 and Windows NT you can display and modify the application mapping table. Follow these steps to view this table on a Windows 2000 computer:

1. Start Internet Services Manager (or any other instance of Microsoft Management Console that includes the Internet Information Services Snap-In).

2. Under the Internet Information Server heading, right-click the computer you want to administer, and then choose Properties from the pop-up menu.

3. Make sure the Internet Information Services tab is selected.

4. Ensure that the Master Properties selection list specifies WWW Service, and then click the Master Properties Edit button.

5. When the WWW Service Master Properties dialog box appears, select the Home Directory tab. Figure 6-13 shows the process at this stage.

6. Click the Configuration button to display the dialog box shown in Figure 6-14. The very first tab—App Mappings—lists the associations between filename extensions and script interpreters currently in effect. The figure shows, for example, that C:\WINNT\System32\inetsrv\asp.dll will process any requested files having the filename extension .asp.

7. Use the buttons beneath the Application Mappings list to add, modify, or remove mappings. (This should seldom, if ever, be necessary.)

The procedure on a Windows NT computer is almost identical, except for one small difference in the App Mappings tab. The Windows 2000 table shown in Figure 6-14 includes a Verbs column that specifies which HTTP commands are valid for a given application mapping. As you can see in Figure 6-15, the corresponding Windows NT 4.0 table has an Exclusions column that specifies which HTTP commands are *not* valid for a given mapping.

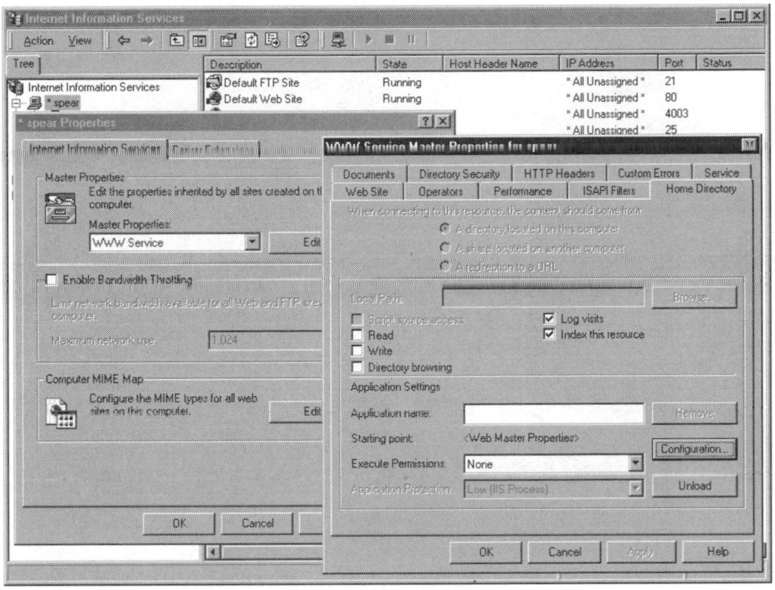

Figure 6-13   *The WWW Service Master Properties dialog box configures default properties for all Microsoft Web servers on a Windows NT or Windows 2000 computer.*

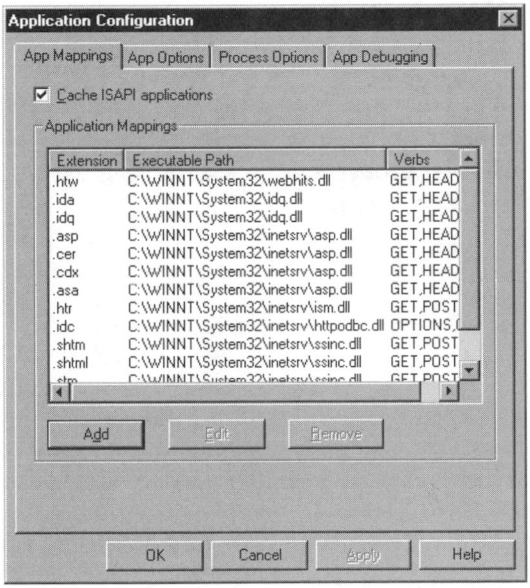

Figure 6-14   *The Application Mappings list assigns script processors to filename extensions.*

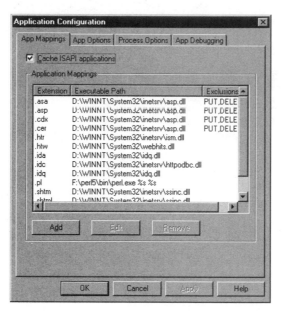

Figure 6-15 *The Windows NT Application Mappings list Exclusions column specifies prohibited HTTP commands. The corresponding Windows 2000 list includes permissible ones.*

You can download the latest version of Perl for Windows NT from http://www.active state.com.

You might also notice that the table in Figure 6-15 includes an entry for the .pl filename extension. This isn't a default entry for either Windows NT 4.0 or Windows 2000, but it's one you'll need if you have any Perl programs to run.

The Home Directory tabs for each Web server and the Directory tab for each virtual directory also contain Configuration buttons that display App Mappings tabs. These override the master properties App Mappings table at the Web server and the virtual directory levels, respectively.

Assign MIME types

Web servers provide literally hundreds of configuration options, far too many for a book such as this to cover comprehensively. However, one more setting relates directly to Web database development.

When a Web server responds to an incoming request, it transmits one or more *header records* before it transmits the actual content. These header records contain status codes, server identifications, file dates to control caching, cookies, and other information required for the Web server and the visitor's browser to communicate intelligently. The actual data stream consists of one or more headers, a blank line, and then the actual content.

One of these headers—the *Content-Type* header—identifies the type of content a Web response contains. Table 6-3 shows some typical Content-Type headers.

The browser uses this information to determine how to handle the file: whether to display it as HTML in the browser window, whether to display it as an image, whether to play it as a sound, and so on. You might think that file-name extensions would control such decisions, but some operating systems don't use filename extensions. Macintosh is one of these. The Web's early inventors therefore chose to describe responses with an existing standard called Multipurpose Internet Mail Extensions (MIME). Codes such as text/html are *MIME types*.

Table 6-3 Typical HTTP Content-Type Headers

Type of Response	Content-Type Header
GIF	image/gif
HTML	text/html
JPEG	image/jpeg
WAV	audio/x-wav

Most Windows-based Web servers assign MIME types based on filename extensions. This implies that the Web server has a table somewhere whose key is filename extension, and which specifies a corresponding MIME type. Follow the following steps to display this table:

1. Follow steps 1 through 3 under "Assign an interpreter to a filename extension" on page 158.

2. Click the Edit button in the Computer MIME Map frame. (On Windows NT 4.0, this button is titled File Types.)

3. The File Types dialog box shown in Figure 6-16 will appear next. To examine entries, scroll up and down the Registered File Types list. To add, remove, and modify entries, use the New Type, Remove, and Edit buttons.

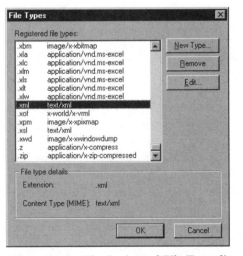

Figure 6-16 *The Registered File Types list shows what MIME type the Web server will specify when transmitting content with a given filename extension.*

Notice that Figure 6-16 includes entries for the filename extensions .xml and .xsl. These entries aren't present in default installations on Windows NT 4.0; if you want to use these extensions on that operating system, you'll have to add the entries yourself.

Like the application mapping list, the MIME type list appears again at the Web server and virtual directory levels. However, at these lower levels, the list is blank except for any overrides in effect.

ASP files can override the standard MIME type mapping by specifying a value in the *Response.ContentType* property. For example, if you write an ASP page that creates XML rather than HTML, the page should begin with the following code:

```
<%
Response.ContentType = "text/xml"
%>
```

When browsers mishandle content, the cause is often a missing or incorrect MIME type assigned on the Web server. However, it's also possible the browser is configured incorrectly (or not configured) to handle a valid MIME type. For Microsoft Internet Explorer, these settings are integrated with the operating system's file-type list. Perform the following steps to view this list on a client computer running Windows 2000:

1. Double-click My Computer, and choose Folder Options from the Tools menu.

2. Click the File Types tab.

To view this list on a client computer running Windows 95, Windows 98, or Windows NT 4.0:

1. Choose Options from the View menu in Windows Explorer.

2. Click the File Types tab.

Managing Windows 2000 and Windows NT Security for Web Pages

Successfully delivering an ASP page from a Windows 2000 or Windows NT Web server requires not only correct virtual directory settings but also correct NTFS file system security as well. And just to keep things simple (or complicated, depending on your perspective), virtual directory security and NTFS security are completely independent—changing one has no effect on the other.

All Microsoft's Windows 2000 and Windows NT Web servers initially use an *anonymous user account* to satisfy Web requests. This account is usually named IUSR_<computername>. Whenever an unidentified Web visitor requests a file, the Web server tries to access that file using the anonymous account. If the access fails, the Web server sends the browser a Not Authorized message. The Web visitor can then try to enter a username and password that *does* have NTFS permission to the given page.

Figure 6-17 shows typical NTFS access control settings that provide anonymous access to a Web page (or Web folder) on a Windows 2000 Server named SPEAR. To display this dialog box, right-click the desired file or folder in Windows Explorer, choose Properties, click the Security tab, and then click the Advanced button.

> **Caution** Never use the built-in account Everyone in NTFS access control lists. Any permissions you grant the Everyone account are available to anyone in the world, with no authentication whatsoever.

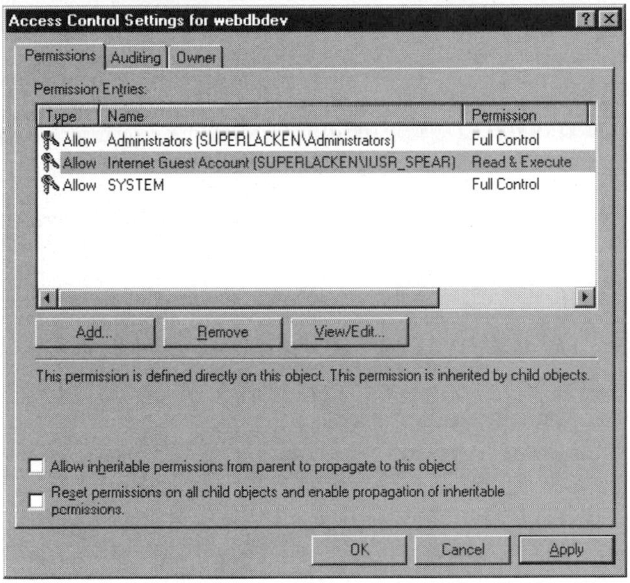

Figure 6-17   *Granting Read or Read & Execute permissions to a Web server's anonymous user account makes that page openly available to Web visitors.*

If the anonymous user account has NTFS permission to read an ASP page, the page might still generate an Access Denied message. This occurs when the anonymous account can't access some piece of software or some other file the ASP page uses. The ASP script interpreter, the ADO software, and the database must all be accessible to whatever account—anonymous or not—the Web visitor uses. This is an excellent reason to understand all the software components your pages use.

When it comes to Access databases, you'll often need to give the anonymous user account Change permission, even for Web pages that only read the database. This is because—depending on how you open the database—the Microsoft Access driver might need to update the database with record-locking information.

The need to provide different security on an Access database (Change) and any related ASP pages (Read-Only) is an excellent reason to keep these files in different folders. In addition, locating an Access database anywhere within a Web server's content space means that anyone who can guess the database's URL can download it. Suppose, for example, that you located a database as coded in the following connection string:

```
cnstCC = "driver={Microsoft Access Driver (*.mdb)};" & _
         "dbq=" & Server.MapPath("../ch03/coinclub.mdb")
```

This database has the URL *../ch03/coinclub.mdb* relative to the current Web page. If the Web server provides Read access to that URL, a Web visitor can download the database. To prevent this, configure the Web server (but not NTFS) to deny access to the folder that contains the database. Alternately, put the database somewhere outside the Web server's HTTP root, and hard-code its file location within a connection string or an ODBC system data source name. The connection string in the following code uses a hard-coded file location:

```
cnstCC = "driver={Microsoft Access Driver (*.mdb)};" & _
         "dbq="E:\WebDbs\CoinClub\coinclub.mdb")
```

Note that defining a virtual directory that points to the E:\WebDbs\ CoinClub\ folder would defeat the purpose of moving the database outside the HTTP root.

Finding a Suitable Web Presence Provider

A Web presence provider (WPP) is someone who operates Web servers for other people to use. In an organizational setting, this might be an information technology department. On the Internet, it might be an independent company that provides Web servers for a monthly or annual fee. Some companies also provide connectivity services, such as dial-up or leased lines. Web server capabilities vary from provider to provider and, of course, according to what you're willing to pay for. The first step in selecting a provider is therefore to understand what capabilities you need.

To run the type of Web database pages described in this book, your production Web server should contain the following software:

- Windows 2000 Server or Windows NT Server 4.0.

- Internet Information Server Release 4 or 5.

- Active Server Pages.

- Microsoft Data Access Components 2.5 or later. (Earlier versions will work with Access 97 databases but not with Access 2000 databases.)

In addition, the following components might be either useful or required, depending on the situation:

- If your database is either large or heavily used, you might need to run it on Microsoft SQL Server. Access 2000 has an Upsizing Wizard that converts Access databases to SQL Server databases, including both the schema and the data.

- If you plan to use either FrontPage or Visual InterDev as a development tool, your production server should have the FrontPage 2000 Server Extensions installed.

If your current service provider or IT department can't provide the required software, you'll probably have to search elsewhere. One place to start looking is the Registered Web Presence Providers page at *http://www.microsoftwpp.com/ wppsearch/*.

Choosing Development Software
for Web Database Applications

For many years, developers have used simple text editors to create Web pages of almost unlimited complexity. There's a certain logic to this—HTML, VBScript, JavaScript, and other Web languages consist entirely of plain text. Editing this text directly offers a maximum of flexibility and control.

Be that as it may, it's hard to think of Notepad as the ultimate Web page development tool. Some tasks benefit from editors with more built in intelligence, and others from development tools with full GUI interfaces. Microsoft has developed a number of products applicable to Web database development, and this section will briefly describe each one. For more information on any Microsoft product, consult its documentation or a more specialized Microsoft Press book.

Regardless of any personal preference you may have, none of these products provides a complete and feature-rich development environment for Web database applications. Given the number of possible applications and unique requirements, no single product can anticipate and automate development of everything you need. At some point, you still have to analyze the requirements and lay the code. That's why the rest of this book explains how to develop Web database pages that *don't* use any of the techniques described below.

Microsoft Access

Chapter 2, "Understanding Database Concepts and Terms," described how to use Microsoft Access for implementing database designs and developing queries. These are useful functions, but what about using Access to develop whole applications? Access has two useful capabilities in this regard, although both have limitations. These capabilities are

- Exporting ASP files

- Data access pages

Exporting ASP files

Access can export any table, query, form, or report as an ASP page. Access puts the ASP file on your local disk or file server. Running the page requires only copying it to an executable directory on your Web server, providing an ODBC system DSN that points to the database, and submitting the URL to the Web server.

Unfortunately, this facility is less fully featured than you might suspect. When you export a table or a query, you get a simple ASP page that displays all the matching columns and rows in an HTML table. When you export a form or report, you get the same thing: an HTML table that displays all the rows and columns. Specifically:

- Exporting an Access report doesn't produce a Web page with all the headings, footings, and control breaks you see in Access. Instead, it produces a simple listing—with no totals or control breaks—formatted as an HTML table.

- Exporting an Access form doesn't produce an HTML version of the same form, complete with text boxes, drop-down menus, push buttons, and any other elements you included. Instead, it once again produces a simple tabular listing of whatever table or query the Access form processes.

Export an Access table, query, form, or report

Perform the following steps to create an ASP page that displays the data in various Access objects:

1. Open the database in Access.

2. Select the object whose data you want to display in an ASP page.

3. Choose Export from the File menu.

4. When the Export Data To dialog box appears, set Save As Type to Microsoft Active Server Pages (*.asp). Override the default filename if you want, and choose a folder where you want the new ASP page to reside.

5. Click the Save button and wait for the dialog box shown in Figure 6-18 to appear. When it does, locate the field titled Data Source Name and enter the name of an ODBC system DSN that will exist on the Web server and point to the database you want to query.

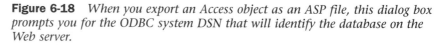

Figure 6-18 *When you export an Access object as an ASP file, this dialog box prompts you for the ODBC system DSN that will identify the database on the Web server.*

6. Click OK.

7. Transfer the ASP file from the location you specified in step 4 to an executable folder on your Web server.

8. If the Web server doesn't have a copy of the database, upload one.

9. If the ODBC System Data Source Name doesn't yet exist, create it.

10. Submit the ASP file's URL to the Web server. You should get results similar to those in Figure 6-19.

If necessary, consult "Defining an ODBC Data Source Name" in Chapter 3.

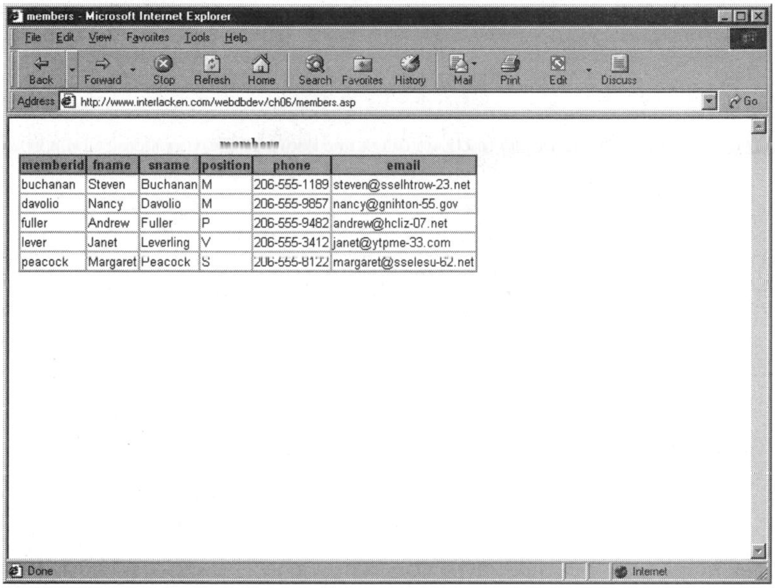

Figure 6-19 *When you export a Microsoft Access table, query, form, or report, you get an ASP page that presents data in this format.*

The visual appearance of ASP pages created by exporting Access objects is crude at best; you'll almost certainly want to enhance any pages you create this way. Any HTML editor—or even Notepad—should be sufficient for this task. To modify the page so it doesn't require an ODBC System Data Source Name, locate and modify the connection string amongst the VBScript code. The necessary line of code looks like this:

```
conn.Open "coinclub","",""
```

To change this statement so it opens a copy of the coinclub.mdb database in the same folder as the ASP page, and so it doesn't require an ODBC System Data Source Name, make it look like this:

```
conn.Open "driver={Microsoft Access Driver (*.mdb)};" & _
          "dbq=" & Server.MapPath("coinclub.mdb")
```

For more information about connection strings, refer to "Open an ADO Connection object" in Chapter 3.

Creating Data Access Pages

Within Access 2000, Microsoft has provided a feature-rich environment for developing Web database pages. Access calls these pages *data access pages*. Unfortunately, data access pages have a couple of characteristics that limit their general-purpose use on the Internet:

- The resulting Web page only works in Internet Explorer version 5 and later running on Windows 95 or above.

- The Web page can only process databases that reside on the Web visitor's computer, or on a file server the Web visitor has connectivity and permission to access.

The reason for these restrictions lies in the very nature of data access pages. A data access page is essentially an ordinary HTML page that contains specifications to load and display a special ActiveX control. Based on these specifications, the ActiveX control displays any formatted text, option boxes, text boxes, pull-down lists, buttons, and other standard elements the developer specified. The ActiveX control and other software installed with Internet Explorer 5 then opens the database using the same mechanism as any other Access application running on the visitor's computer: that is, it opens the .mdb file. The need for Internet Explorer 5 running on Windows and a file-sharing connection to the database generally limits data access pages to well-controlled intranet use.

Create a data access page

Here's how to create a simple data access page that updates the *coinclub* members table:

1. Use Access 2000 to open the database that contains the data you want to process. For this example, open the coinclub.mdb database.

2. Click the Pages icon located in the Objects bar, and then double-click Create Data Access Page By Using Wizard.

3. When the first screen in the Page Wizard appears, expand the Tables/Queries list and select Tables: Members.

4. Click the >> button to select all available fields, and click Next.

5. When asked about grouping levels, just click Next.

6. When asked about sorting, select one to four fields using the drop-down list boxes provided. The accompanying buttons indicate ascending when titled AZ↓ and descending when titled ZA↓. When finished, click Next.

7. When prompted for a title, enter any descriptive text you want, then click Finish.

8. After a few moments, Access will display the data access page shown in Figure 6-20. From this point, you can use the Toolbox window, commands on the Access menu bar, and right-click context menus to modify the wizard's output.

9. Access will save the page to a file location on your disk. To run the data access page, you can either load it into your browser from disk or copy it to a Web page and load it from there.

Do the following to display the file path the data access page will use to open the database:

1. Open the page in Access.

2. Open the Field List window by clicking the Field List button in the toolbar.

3. Choose the Database tab.

4. Right-click the database name.

5. Choose the Connection tab.

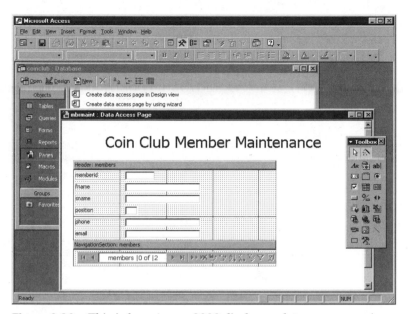

Figure 6-20   *This is how Access 2000 displays a data access page in Design view.*

This specifies the file location every Web visitor using this data access page will try to open. To change this location, you'll need to close the database (but not Access itself), open the data access page by choosing Open from the File menu, and then display the Field List menu.

Figure 6-21 shows how the data access page appears in Internet Explorer. Take note of the filename extension in the URL: .htm. This proves that data access

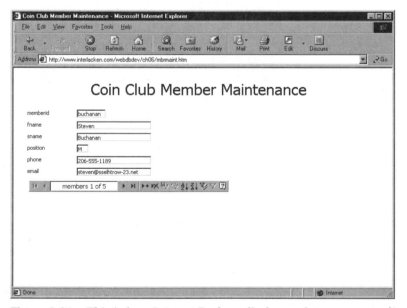

Figure 6-21   *This is how Internet Explorer displays a data access page in use.*

pages involve no server-side processing at all. They depend entirely on ActiveX controls that execute on the browser and that open databases available on the Web visitor's local disk or through file-sharing connections.

The data access page on the companion CD-ROM specifies the database \\Spike\dbfunweb\ch06\coinclub.mdb. This is a location in the author's lab network, and almost certainly not a location you can access. In fact, there is no reliable location accessible to all readers of this book, and that's one of the major limitations of data access pages.

Microsoft FrontPage

Most Web developers who use FrontPage do so because of its site management features and its What You See Is What You Get (WYSIWYG) HTML editing. Nevertheless, FrontPage provides two kinds of features useful to Web database development:

- It provides two different ways to edit HTML directly, namely FrontPage HTML View and Microsoft Script Editor. Script Editor has the added feature of interactive debugging for Active Server Pages.

- It creates two kinds of Web database pages based on information you supply using dialog boxes. The first of these, Save Results to Database, adds a record to a database table every time a Web visitor submits an HTML form. The second, Database Results, displays database information in tabular format.

FrontPage HTML View

Although FrontPage is best known for its WYSIWYG Web page editor, it also provides access to the underlying HTML. To start working with the code, simply click the HTML tab at the bottom of the editing window.

The HTML view editor neither tries nor succeeds in being the world's greatest HTML editor, but it does provide basic editing features such as find, replace, and color-coding of source code. The fact that you can rapidly switch between normal (WYSIWYG) view and HTML view makes it easy to use the best view for each aspect of design.

Past versions of FrontPage encountered some criticism because they automatically reformatted HTML code. FrontPage 2000 addresses these complaints in two ways:

- FrontPage 2000 contains an option called Preserve Existing HTML that remembers exactly how your code was formatted on input, and that formats the code identically on output. In addition, it attempts to use the same formatting conventions for any HTML it creates, even in normal editing mode.

- FrontPage can keep your code formatted any way you want. After you tell FrontPage which tags should always begin on a new line, which tags should cause indentation, and so on, FrontPage will always format code that way.

To reach the dialog box that controls these settings, choose Page Options from the Tools menu and then choose the HTML Source tab. Figure 6-22 shows this tab, with HTML View in the background.

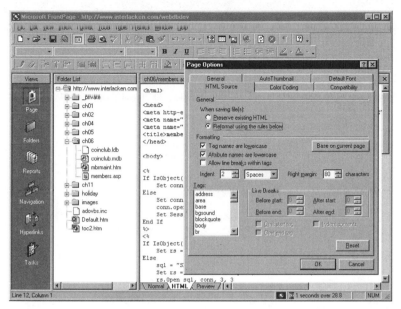

Figure 6-22 *FrontPage 2000 can edit HTML code directly, either preserving the code's original format or applying specific preferences.*

Start Microsoft Script Editor

FrontPage also includes Microsoft Script Editor, which you can invoke using the following procedure:

1. Start FrontPage.

2. Open the Web page you want to edit.

3. Choose Macro from the Tools menu, and then choose Microsoft Script Editor. (Alternatively, press Shift+Alt+F11.)

This will open a window like the one shown in Figure 6-23. The code appears in the central child window. The Toolbox child window at the left provides a collection of common objects you can drag into the code. The Properties list at the right provides menu-driven access to the HTML element that currently, in the code window, contains the cursor.

The Script Editor menu bar contains further commands that insert and modify HTML elements. For example, you can insert hyperlinks, pictures, tables, and forms.

Script Editor also provides an interactive debugging facility. This is always available for debugging browser side scripts, but there are two preconditions for debugging Active Server Pages. First, Script Editor must be installed on a

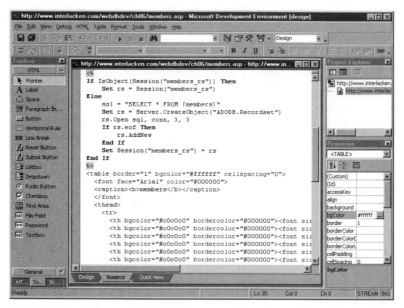

Figure 6-23 *Microsoft Script Editor provides advanced capabilities for editing and debugging Web page code.*

Windows 2000 or Windows NT 4.0 system. Second, the script must run on either IIS or PWS installed on the same system.

With two notable exceptions, Script Editor provides a large subset of the capabilities found in Visual InterDev. First, you can't run Script Editor as a standalone program; you can only run it as a subtask of FrontPage, on Web pages that the application has already opened. Second, the Design tab, which in Visual InterDev provides WYSIWYG editing, is disabled in Script Editor. To revert to WYSIWYG view, you must return to FrontPage.

Create FrontPage database connections

FrontPage has its own way of connecting to databases, which it calls, unsurprisingly, *connections*. Follow these steps to establish a database connection that other FrontPage features can use:

1. Choose Web Settings from the Tools menu.

2. Choose the Database tab on the resulting dialog box.

3. Click the Add button to display the New Database Connection dialog box. Except for the title, this looks exactly like the Database Connection properties dialog box shown in Figure 6-24.

4. Use the Name field to give the connection a meaningful name. The file-name base is usually a good choice for Access databases. If you're connecting to an ODBC System Data Source Name, repeat that name.

5. Choose the type of connection. This can be a file-oriented database such as Microsoft Access, an ODBC System Data Source Name, a networked database server (such as Microsoft SQL Server), or a custom definition contained in an ODBC File Data Source Name.

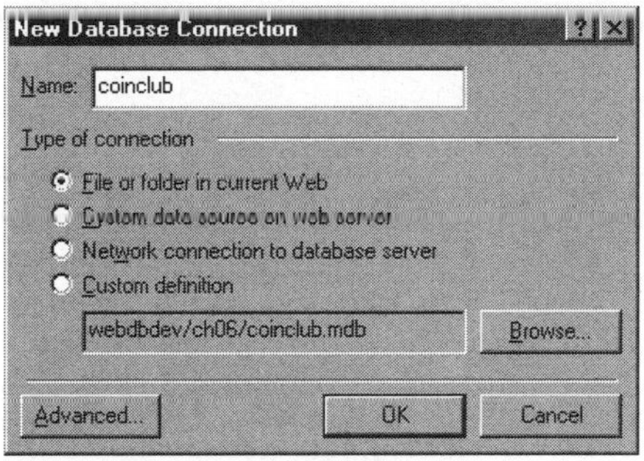

Figure 6-24   *FrontPage database connections define settings used by other FrontPage database features.*

6. Click the Browse button to locate the specific data source. The resulting dialog box will vary, depending on your choice in step 5.

7. Click the Advanced button if you need to specify any settings that appear in the Advanced Connection Properties dialog box shown in Figure 6-24.

8. Click OK to apply, and close each dialog box you've opened.

There's nothing magical or secret about FrontPage database connections; they're simply groups of settings that FrontPage stores as code in the global.asa file. The first time after a restart that a Web visitor requests any ASP page in the FrontPage Web (that is, whenever the application starts), that code stores the connection settings as properties in the Application object. Any Web database page FrontPage generates then accesses the Application object to build the connection strings for opening ADO database connections.

The important thing to remember is that when FrontPage generates a Web database page, it uses the same ADO methods and properties that you would use if you coded the page manually. It's only the method for storing connection string settings that's different.

Save results to a database

The FrontPage Save Results component collects information from an HTML form and sends it as e-mail, appends it to an ordinary file, or saves it as a new record in a database table. Of course, saving information to a database is the method of interest here. The Save Results component creates an ASP page that does its database processing on the Web server. This makes Save Results pages suitable for use over the Internet by a wide variety of browsers.

Figure 6-25 shows the Save Results component in action. A Web visitor has filled out the HTML form in the background and clicked Submit. The FrontPage Server Extensions added the information to the coinclub.mdb database and displayed the foreground Web page as confirmation to the visitor.

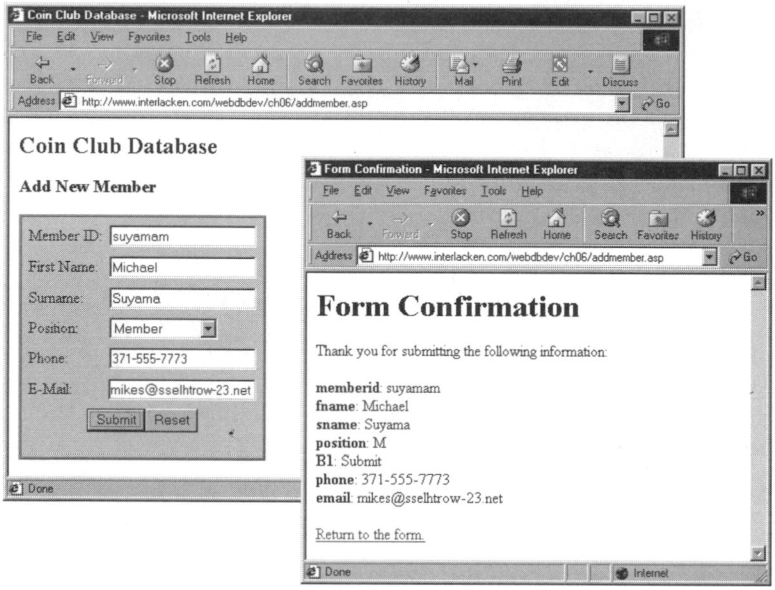

Figure 6-25   *FrontPage can create database data entry screens like this with no coding on your part.*

Figure 6-26 shows the same Web page open in FrontPage.

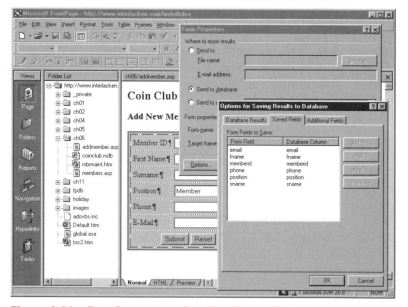

Figure 6-26   *FrontPage creates Save Results applications completely from dialog boxes: no coding required.*

The Web developer performed the following steps:

1. Created the HTML form using menu bar and toolbar commands.
2. Displayed the Form Properties dialog box by right-clicking the form and then choosing Properties.
3. Chose the Send To Database option, and then clicked the Options button.
4. Used the Database Results tab to specify the data storage location: the *members* table of the coinclub.mdb table.
5. Used the Saved Fields tab—the one shown in Figure 6-26—to assign HTML for fields to database fields. In this case, the developer named the form fields the same as their corresponding database fields. This provides a certain consistency but isn't a necessity.

Unfortunately, FrontPage provides no way to modify or delete existing records. To provide those functions, you must create the Web database code yourself.

Database Results

As you've just seen, the Save Results component saves the result of submitting an HTML form. The Database Results component, despite its similar name, does just the opposite: it displays the result of querying a database. Figure 6-27 provides a simple example of what the Database Results component can do.

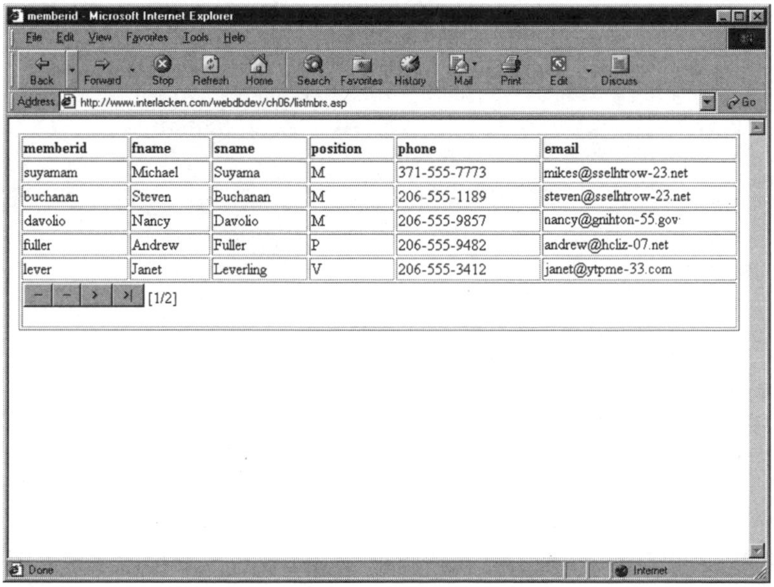
memberid - Microsoft Internet Explorer
File Edit View Favorites Tools Help
Back Forward Stop Refresh Home Search Favorites History Mail Print Edit Discuss
Address http://www.interlacken.com/webdbdev/ch06/listmbrs.asp
Go
memberid fname sname position phone email
suyamam Michael Suyama M 371-555-7773 mikes@sselhtrow-23.net
buchanan Steven Buchanan M 206-555-1189 steven@sselhtrow-23.net
davolio Nancy Davolio M 206-555-9857 nancy@gnihton-55.gov
fuller Andrew Fuller P 206-555-9482 andrew@hcliz-07.net
lever Janet Leverling V 206-555-3412 janet@ytpme-33.com
[1/2]
Done
Internet

Figure 6-27 *The FrontPage Database Results component provides tabular displays of database data. Optionally, it can also create HTML forms that specify selection criteria.*

The following steps create the Database Results page shown in Figure 6-28:

1. Open a server-based FrontPage Web and create a new, blank Web page.

2. Choose Database from the Insert menu, and then choose Results.

3. When the first wizard screen shown in Figure 6-28 appears, choose the database that contains the data you want to display. If the FrontPage Web doesn't already have a connection to that database, choose the option Use A New Database Connection to create one.

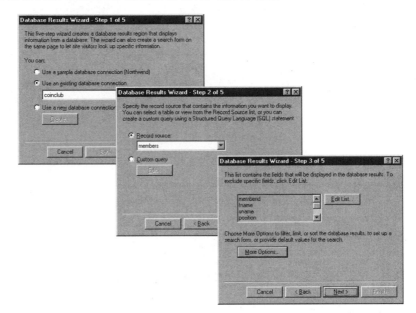

Figure 6-28 *These are the first three screens in the FrontPage Database Results Wizard. This wizard creates Web pages that display database information in tabular form.*

4. Click Next to display the second screen shown in Figure 6-28, and then choose the table or query that contains the data you want to display. To create your own query, use the Custom Query option.

5. Click Next to display the third wizard screen. Review the list of fields offered for display, and click the Edit List button if you need to modify it.

6. Click the More Options button if you need to specify any of the following settings: record selection criteria, record sequence, default form field values, or the maximum number of records to display.

7. Click Next to display the fourth wizard screen, which is the first one shown in Figure 6-29. This screen controls the appearance of the displayed output.

8. Click Next to display the fifth and final screen. Here you can specify whether to display records a certain number at a time or all together on one Web page. If in step 6 you specified any selection criteria that should come from an HTML form, checking the Add Search Form option will create such a form at the top of the Web page.

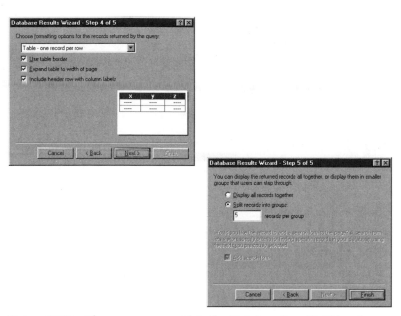

Figure 6-29   *These screens complete the Database Results Wizard.*

9. Click Finish to create the Database Results component and terminate the wizard.

You can rerun the wizard as often as you like simply by right-clicking anywhere in the Database Results region and choosing Database Results Properties. Once you have the page working properly, you can use standard FrontPage editing commands to improve its appearance and surround it with other content.

Microsoft Visual InterDev

If the user interface in Microsoft Script Editor seemed familiar, you probably own one or more Visual Studio applications: Microsoft Visual Basic, Microsoft Visual C++, Microsoft Visual J++, and so on. Visual InterDev provides a Web development environment that operates within the same framework. A full description of Visual InterDev would require a book in itself, so the material presented here is just an overview.

Visual InterDev provides most of the same WYSIWYG editing tools as FrontPage, but arranged much differently. Also, Visual InterDev uses *design-time controls* (DTCs) rather than FrontPage components. A DTC is an ActiveX control that you add to a project from the Toolbox and that runs in the Visual InterDev editor. When you edit an area controlled by a DTC, it displays dialog boxes that prompt for settings. When you save a Web page that contains a DTC, the DTC writes HTML in accordance with your specifications.

Figure 6-30 shows Visual InterDev in Source View, editing a page that contains DTCs. The Design tab at the bottom of that figure displays the Web page in WYSIWYG editing mode, and the Quick View tab displays it as Internet Explorer would (but without performing any server-side scripting).

People who use Visual InterDev are usually advanced developers who are familiar with other Visual Studio applications.

Recordset DTC

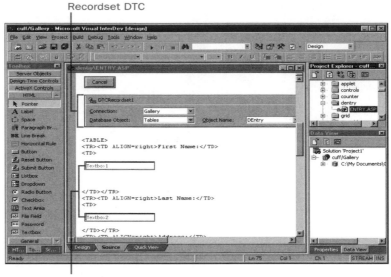

Form field DTCs

Figure 6-30 *Visual InterDev shares its user interface with other Visual Studio tools. The graphic elements mixed in with the code are design-time controls.*

You can use Visual InterDev to enter and debug ASP code and thus create Web database pages as discussed throughout the rest of this book. However, Visual InterDev provides another method using DTCs:

1. Create a connection to the database you want to access.

2. Add a Recordset DTC to the Web page. This type of DTC opens a database table or query but displays nothing to the Web visitor.

3. Configure the Recordset DTC to access the table or query you want.

4. Create a form field DTC for each database field you want to display. This type of DTC displays a text box, drop-down list, push button, or other form element to the Web visitor.

5. Bind each form field DTC you created in step 3 to the Recordset DTC you added in step 1. To begin, first right-click the form field DTC and choose Properties. In the resulting dialog box, set Recordset to the name of the appropriate Recordset DTC and Field to the name of the desired table or query field.

Figure 6-31 shows an example of this technique in use. The large gray box titled *Recordset1* is a Recordset DTC that connects (via the *coinclub* connection) to the *members* table in the coinclub database. The three text boxes are Textbox DTCs, and the object with four push buttons is a RecordsetNavBar DTC.

Right-clicking the TextBox DTC named *txtMbrId* and choosing Properties displays the Textbox Properties dialog box shown. Note the Data frame just below the middle of this dialog box, which *binds* the *txtMbrId* text box to the *memberid* field in the Recordset DTC named *Recordset1*. This binding ties the contents of the *txtMbrId* DTC to that of the *memberid* field in the *Recordset1* DTC.

When you save this Web page, the DTCs will write HTML and ASP code to access the database, display the form fields, and respond to any button clicks. Figure 6-32 shows this Web page in use. The browser is Netscape Navigator 4.03, proving there are no ActiveX controls or other proprietary elements in the Web page delivered to the visitor.

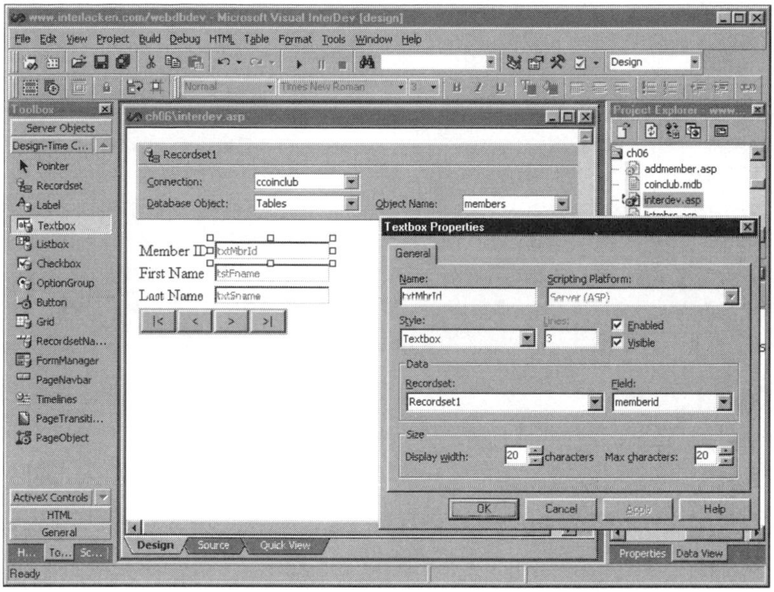

Figure 6-31 *The Recordset and Field properties in the Textbox Properties dialog box associate the* txtMbrId *text box with the* memberid *field in the Recordset control named* Recordset1.

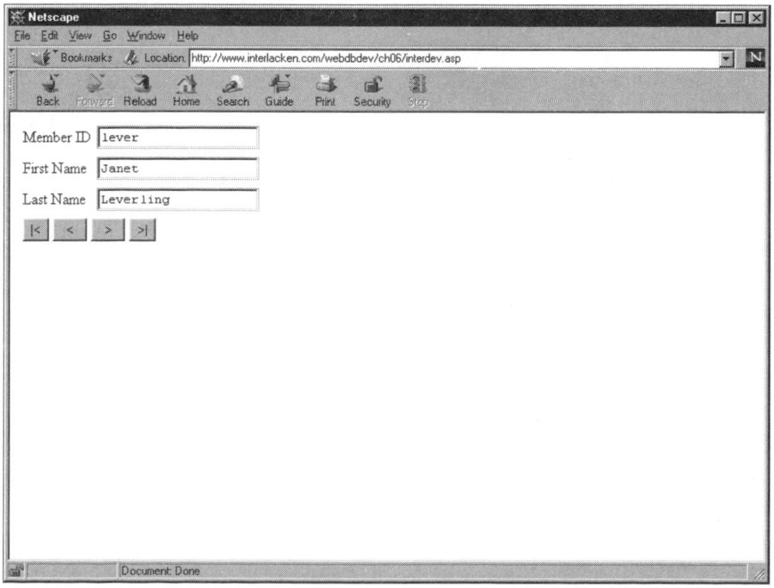

Figure 6-32 *In this figure, Netscape Navigator 4.03 displays a Web page created using Visual Interdev DTCs, proving the page delivered to the Web visitor contains no proprietary elements.*

Visual InterDev's DTCs can help you create a wide variety of applications without requiring you to write any code. Of course, there's a definite learning curve to all this, and you don't generally have access to the HTML or script code that a DTC creates. If you can't manipulate the DTC into working the way you want, you might have to code the application by hand anyway.

Chapter Summary

Part 2 of this book, "Key Concepts," introduced the fundamental technologies you need to create Web database applications that run on Microsoft Web servers. These technologies include database theory and design, database implementation with Microsoft Access, database access using ActiveX Data Objects, server-side scripting with Active Server Pages, and Web servers running Microsoft Internet Information Server or Microsoft Personal Web Server. It also reviewed the Web database capabilities of various Microsoft products.

The next part of the book, "Developing Applications," will present and explain a variety of typical Web database applications.

Developing Applications

Parts 1 and 2 described—as briefly and concisely as possible—the basic technologies you need to construct a Web database page. This is valuable and necessary information, but so are practical examples that show how those technologies fit together in a useful way. The primary goal of Part 3 is to provide and explain a number of such examples.

Chapter 7

Running and Displaying Queries

Chapter Objectives	Estimated Time: 40 minutes

In this chapter, you'll learn how to

- Create a menu page based on items in a database.

- Create a frameset that receives values from a calling URL and passes them to pages in its frames.

- Create a Web page that occupies one frame and displays a title and an icon based on values given to the frameset.

- Create a Web page that occupies another frame and displays a menu choice for each database record matching criteria given to the frameset.

- Create a Web page that occupies a third frame and displays detailed information about any choice clicked.

The most common type of Web database page is one that simply retrieves information from a database and transmits it for display in a Web visitor's browser. You've already seen a number of simple queries in previous chapters. This chapter will show you more—some simple and some not so obvious.

This chapter also introduces an application that will appear repeatedly in the next few chapters: the Holiday Photo Catalog. Your application might or might not consist of showing photographs, but the techniques in this example are generic to collections of all types—that is, to almost any sort of database you want to present.

Understanding the Holiday Application

Displaying catalogs is one of the most common Web database applications. A catalog, in this sense, is any collection of items you want Web visitors to browse. Catalogs usually provide a way for customers (Web visitors, in this case) to find items of interest and then view each matching item. It matters little whether the catalog items are antiques, rare seeds, zoo animals, cars for sale, talent acts, tropical fish, or vacation photos—the application structure remains the same.

The catalog items in this example happen to be vacation photos. I have several reasons for this choice: first, I don't deal in any of those other items. Second, I do take vacations. Third, vacations are a subject everyone understands.

The data for this application resides in a Microsoft Access database named holiday.mdb. This database contains two tables named *categories* and *items*.

The *categories* table contains one record for each group of items. Each category in the example corresponds to one destination visited, but the categories in your application could just as easily be furniture types, animal taxonomies, makes of cars, or anything else.

Figure 7-1 shows the *categories* table open in Access. The primary key is a field called *catnr*. To comply with good database design, the table's other fields all contain data having one and only one value per category number.

The *items* table contains one record for each item in the catalog. Each item in the example corresponds to one vacation photo, but your items could just as easily be plants, animals, buildings, campgrounds, orchestras, employees, trains, planes, or automobiles.

The *items* table, implemented in Access, appears in Figure 7-2. Its primary key consists of two fields: category number and sequence number. As with the *categories* table, each field has one and only one value per primary key value. Note, however, that multiple sequence numbers can exist within each category. That's why *items* and *categories* need to be different tables.

This is obviously a very simple database structure, which has the advantage of keeping the example relatively simple as well. A real application would undoubtedly have more tables, each having more fields. To provide lookup by family member, for example, you'd have to add a table keyed by picture name and family member name, and containing a record for each person in each picture.

For more details about database design, refer to "Designing a Database" (beginning on page 20) in Chapter 2, "Understanding Database Concepts and Terms."

For an example of keyword searching, refer to Chapter 10, "Performing Keyword Searches."

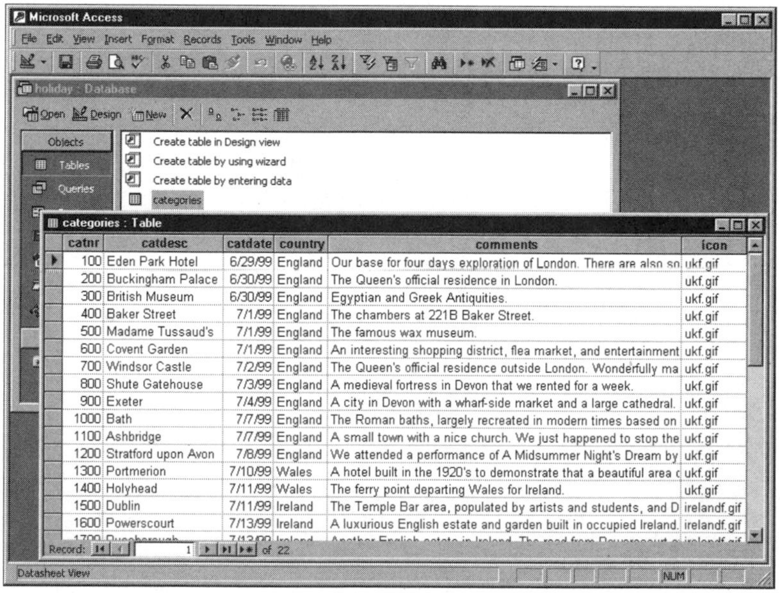

Figure 7-1 *The* categories *table contains one record for each group of items. Fields in this table pertain to the category as a whole rather than to individual items.*

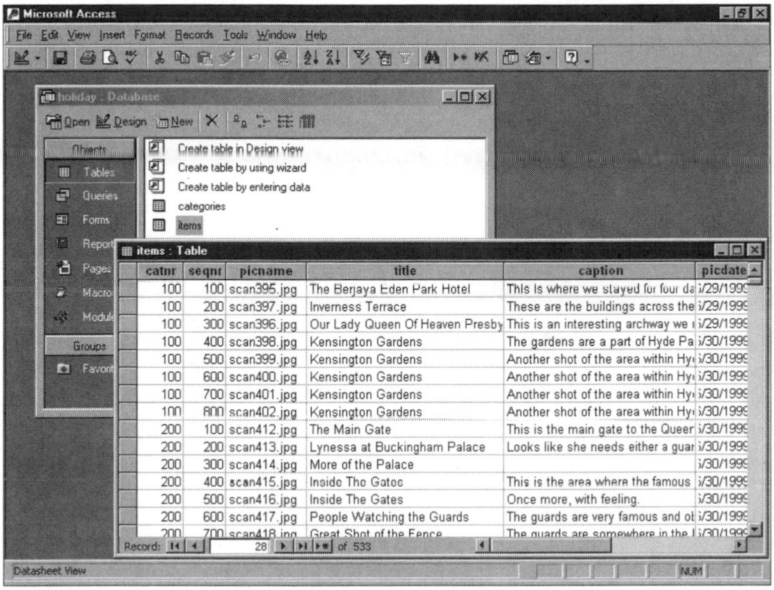

Figure 7-2 *The* items *table contains fields having unique values for each item in the catalog.*

You can find the Web pages for this chapter in the sample files installed from the companion CD; they're in a folder named \webdbdev\ch07. The database and other shared application files, however, are located within a holiday folder as described in Table 7-1.

Table 7-1   Locations for Holiday Photo Catalog

Description	Path
database and shared files	\webdbdev\holiday
full-size pictures	\webdbdev\holiday\images
thumbnail pictures	\webdbdev\holiday\images\thumb

Building the Main Menu Page

Figure 7-3 shows the application's main menu page. Notice the .asp filename extension in the URL and the similarity of content with the *categories* table in Figure 7-1. In fact, this menu page actually displays database query results.

The title graphics, title text, and column heading consist of ordinary HTML. You can view this HTML in the complete listing at the end of this section, or in the sample files at \webdbdev\ch07\default.htm. The only technique even slightly unusual is the following statement, located in the <head> section, which tells the browser to apply an external style sheet having the relative URL ../ *holiday/holiday.css*. The style sheet overrides the normal fonts and colors for various HTML elements.

```
<link rel="stylesheet" type="text/css"
    href="../holiday/holiday.css">
```

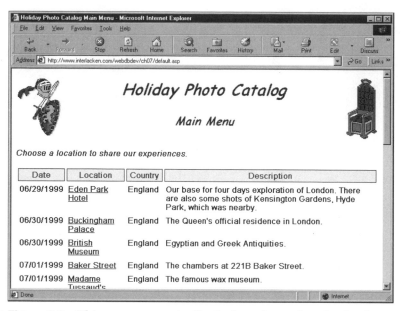

Figure 7-3 *This menu page actually displays the results of a database query. Its content is as current as the database at the time of the request.*

For purposes of page layout, each menu choice occupies one row in an HTML table. The following listing shows the HTML necessary to display one such row. Blue type indicates information that should come from the database.

```
<tr>
<td valign="top">6/29/99</td>
<td valign="top"><a href="catalog.asp?qcatnr=100">Eden Park Hotel</a></td>
<td valign="top">England</td>
<td valign="top">Our base for four days exploration of London. There are
also some shots of Kensington Gardens, Hyde Park, which was nearby.</td>
</tr>
```

Note that the hyperlink in line three specifies a URL that contains a query string. The query string is the part that reads *?qcatnr=100*. If the Web visitor clicks

Cascading Style Sheets

Cascading Style Sheets (CSS) is a technology that provides far more typographical control than ordinary HTML can. You can specify CSS styles within individual HTML tags, within <style> and </style> tags at the top of a Web page, or in a separate file. Having several Web pages reference the same CSS file ensures they'll share a common appearance.

For more information about CSS, browse *http://msdn.microsoft.com/ workshop/author/default.asp?* (Microsoft) and *http://www.w3.org/Style/* (World Wide Web Consortium).

Cascading style sheets modify only the appearance of a Web page and not its underlying function. Their use is therefore optional.

this hyperlink, the catalog.asp page will receive the query string information, query the *items* table for the given category number, and display a list of matching items.

Create the starting menu page

Your initial challenge is to produce the starting menu page. Here's how to code the ASP statements that query the category table, loop through all the matching records, and write the HTML for each catalog choice:

1. Create a new, blank ASP page. Populate it with the basic structural tags, as shown below. Save the file as default.asp.

```
<html>
<head>
<title></title>
</head>
<body>
</body>
</html>
```

2. To define the standard ADO named constants, add the following statement to the <head> section of the default.asp Web page.

```
<!-- #include file="../adovbs.inc" -->
```

Adjust the relative URL *"../adovbs.inc"* if this file doesn't reside in the parent of the folder where the Web page will reside. Then insert this:

```
<link rel="stylesheet" type="text/css"
     href="../holiday/holiday.css">
```

To get a copy of the adovbs.inc file, follow the instructions in "Using ADO Named Constants" (beginning on page 51) in Chapter 3, "Accessing Databases with ADO and ODBC."

3. Within the <body> section begin a table with these column headings:

```
<table>
  <tr>
    <th>Date</th>
    <th>Location</th>
    <th>Country</th>
    <th>Description</th>
  </tr>
<!--  Code to display detail rows will go here -->
</table>
```

4. Create and open an ADO Connection object for the holiday.mdb database. The following code fulfills this requirement, assuming the database resides in a folder whose Web location, relative to the current page, is *../holiday*. This code also closes the connection and destroys the Connection object after all processing is completed.

```
<%
Set cnHol = Server.CreateObject("ADODB.Connection")
cnStHol = "driver={Microsoft Access Driver (*.mdb)};" & _
          "dbq=" & Server.MapPath("../holiday/holiday.mdb")
```

(continued)

```
cnHol.Open cnStHol,"",""
' Code that uses the connection will go here.
cnHol.Close
Set cnHol = Nothing
%>
```

Recall that the *Server.MapPath* method translates a URL location to a physical location in the Web server's file system.

5. Create and open an ADO Recordset object that contains all records in the *categories* table, ordered by category number. This code should replace the comment shown in step 4.

```
Set rsCat = Server.CreateObject("ADODB.Recordset")
sql = "SELECT * FROM categories ORDER BY catnr ; "
rsCat.Open sql, cnHol, adOpenStatic, adLockReadOnly
' Code that uses the recordset will go here.
rsCat.Close
Set rsCat = Nothing
```

Note that the *rsCat.Open* statement opens the recordset in static, read-only mode. Static mode means that if another process changes the database while the recordset is open, the recordset won't reflect those changes. This is hardly an issue during the brief moment it takes to process the ASP page. Read-only mode assures the database software that the Web page won't be updating the recordset, and that the database software needn't lock records to prevent other processes from updating the same records at the same time. Both of these settings minimize the overhead of processing the database.

6. Code a loop that reads through all the records in the *rsCat* recordset—that is, that continually moves to the next record until no more records remain.

```
Do While Not rsCat.EOF
' Code that processes each record will go here.
  rsCat.MoveNext
Loop
```

This code should appear in place of the comment in step 5.

7. Replace the comment in step 6 with code that creates the HTML for one menu choice: in other words, for one row of the HTML table. You can use any combination of ordinary HTML and ASP code to do this—just be sure to add a %> tag whenever you switch to HTML and a <% tag whenever you switch back to ASP script code. The following uses both techniques:

```
%>
<tr>
  <td valign="top"><%=rsCat("catdate")%></td>
  <td valign="top"><%
    Response.Write "<a href=" & _
      Chr(34) & _
      "catalog.asp?" & _
      "qcatnr=" & rsCat("catnr") & _
      Chr(34) & ">" & _
```

```
      rsCat("catdesc") & "</a>"
    %></td>
  <td valign="top"><%=rsCat("country")%></td>
  <td valign="top"><%=rsCat("comments")%></td>
</tr>
<%
```

Notice that all the structural tags—tags such as <tr> and <td>—appear as ordinary HTML. This saves a bit of *Response.Write* coding and facilitates the use of an HTML editor to control the page's visual aspects.

Expressions such as *rsCat("catdate")* return field values from the current record in the *rsCat* recordset. The expression within parentheses specifies the field name or number. Expressions such as *rsCat.Fields("catdate").Value* would be equivalent because the Fields collection is the default property of any Recordset object, and because *Value* is the default property of any Field object.

The ASP code to display the values of the *catdate*, *country*, and *comments* fields uses shortcut notation: an equal sign means *Response.Write*. This notation requires that the <% and %>, the equal sign, and a single expression all appear within the same line.

Because the code for the *catdesc* field and its associated hyperlink is long, coding it all in one line would be awkward (unless, of course, you edit your code on the world's widest computer monitor). This makes the <%= %> notation inappropriate. A full *Response.Write* statement, which permits breaking and continuing lines, therefore creates the HTML for this field and its surrounding hyperlink. Recall that the ampersand (&) is the VBScript operator for joining strings, that the underscore indicates continuation to the next line, and that the *Chr* function returns the ASCII character that corresponds to a given decimal number. The expression *Chr(34)* returns a quotation mark.

This completes the server-side code necessary to query the *categories* table and to display the Web page shown in Figure 7-3. The complete ASP listing for default.asp appears here and also in the sample files at \webdbdev\ch07\. You can open this file with Notepad or any other plain text editor.

```
<html>
<head>
<title>Holiday Photo Catalog Main Menu</title>
<!-- #include file="../adovbs.inc" -->
<link rel="stylesheet" type="text/css"
     href="../holiday/holiday.css">
</head>
<body>
<table align="center"border="0" width="100%"
     cellpadding="3" cellspacing="0">
  <tr>
    <td align="left" rowspan="2">
      <img src="../images/armor.gif" border="0"
         width="88" height="121">
    </td>
```

(continued)

```
        <td align="center">
          <h1>Holiday Photo Catalog</h1>
        </td>
        <td align="right" rowspan="2">
          <img src="../images/throne.gif" border="0"
               width="64" height="125"></td>
    </tr>
    <tr>
        <td align="center">
        <h2>Main Menu</h2>
        </td>
    </tr>
</table>
<p><i>Choose a location to share our experiences.</i></p>
<table border="0" cellpadding="3" cellspacing="4">
    <tr>
        <th>Date</th>
        <th>Location</th>
        <th>Country</th>
        <th>Description</th>
    </tr>
    <%
' Create and open ADO Connection object.
Set cnHol = Server.CreateObject("ADODB.Connection")
cnStHol = "driver={Microsoft Access Driver (*.mdb)};" & _
          "dbq=" & Server.MapPath("../holiday/holiday.mdb")
cnHol.Open cnStHol,"",""
' Create and open ADO Recordset object.
Set rsCat = Server.CreateObject("ADODB.Recordset")
sql = "SELECT * FROM categories ORDER BY catnr ; "
rsCat.Open sql, cnHol, adOpenStatic, adLockReadOnly
' Loop through the Recordset object displaying each record.
Do While Not rsCat.EOF
    %>
    <tr>
        <td valign="top"><%=rsCat("catdate")%></td>
        <td valign="top"><%
          Response.Write "<a href=" & _
            Chr(34) & _
            "catalog.asp?" & _
            "qcatnr=" & rsCat("catnr") & _
            Chr(34) & ">" & _
            rsCat("catdesc") & "</a>"
          %></td>
        <td valign="top"><%=rsCat("country")%></td>
        <td valign="top"><%=rsCat("comments")%></td>
    </tr>
```

```
<%
rsCat.MoveNext
Loop
' Close and destroy the Recordset and Connection objects.
rsCat.Close
Set rsCat = Nothing
cnHol.Close
Set cnHol = Nothing
%>
</table>
</body>
</html>
```

Understanding the Item Display Page

The previous section described how each choice on the Holiday Catalog's main menu links to the same Web page: catalog.asp. It also described how the menu page specified—by means of a query string—which category number to display. The next step, of course, is to create a catalog.asp page that displays proper results given this input. Figure 7-4 shows exactly such a page. Its name is catalog.asp.

Figure 7-4 *This is the main display page for the Holiday Photo Catalog application.*

*For basic instruc-
tions on how to
create framesets,
browse* http://
www.getting
started.net/
basics/frames/
index.html.

The Web page in this figure is a *frameset*—that is, a special type of Web page that provides no content of its own. Instead, it divides its display window into one or more *frames* that display other Web pages. The catalog.asp frameset, for example, has four frames named and used as follows:

- The *control* frame displays an ordinary Web page named control.htm. This page contains the home-page link visible in the top left corner of Figure 7-4.

- The *title* frame occupies the rest of the frameset's top edge and displays an ASP page named title title.asp. This page looks up and displays the name of the current category and its corresponding icon.

- The *piclist* frame occupies the rest of the frameset's left edge. This frame displays a page named piclist.asp that in turn displays a list of thumbnail images. It derives this list by querying the *items* table in the holiday.mdb database for records having a specified category code.

- The *detail* frame occupies the main body of the frameset. The frameset initially loads this frame with a blank page named blank.htm, but this page remains on display for only a few seconds. As soon as the piclist.asp page loads, it tells the browser to reload the detail frame with a page named picshow.asp. This page displays the full-size picture and associated database information corresponding to the first thumbnail picture.

Creating Thumbnail Images

Creating miniature versions for a large set of pictures can be a tedious chore if you use a picture editor to open, resize, and save each one individually. Utilities such as Thumbnailer from Smaller Animals Software, Inc., automate this task quite conveniently. Figure 7-5 shows Thumbnailer in action.

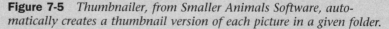

Figure 7-5 *Thumbnailer, from Smaller Animals Software, auto-matically creates a thumbnail version of each picture in a given folder.*

To obtain a shareware copy of Thumbnailer or to register an existing copy, browse Smaller Animals' Web site at *http://www.smaller-animals.com.*

Here's a quick review of the way the main menu page and catalog.asp frameset work together:

- The main menu page (default.asp) sends a category number to the catalog frameset page (catalog.asp).

- The catalog frameset page forwards this category number to title.asp (which it loads in the title frame) and to piclist.asp (which it loads in the piclist frame).

- The piclist.asp page loads the detail frame with a page called picshow.asp, sending it the same category number and the first sequence number within that category.

- The picshow.asp page displays title, picture, caption, and other information corresponding to the given category and sequence numbers.

Once the frameset is completely displayed, clicking any thumbnail in the piclist frame displays the corresponding full-size picture (and its associated information) in the detail frame. This happens because the hyperlinks surrounding each thumbnail specify, as shown in the following code, the picshow.asp page plus a query string that includes the category and sequence number to display.

```
picshow.asp?qcatnr=100&qseqnr=100
```

Building the Item Display Frameset (catalog.asp)

The catalog.asp page defines a fairly ordinary frameset with only three small fragments of ASP code, appearing in blue in the following code:

```
<html>
<head>
<title>Holiday Photo Catalog</title>
<%
catnr = Request("qcatnr")
If catnr = "" Then catnr = 100
If Not IsNumeric(catnr) Then catnr = 100
%>
</head>
<frameset rows="65,*">
  <frameset cols="115,99%">
    <frame name="control"
           src="control.htm"
           target="_self" noresize scrolling="no"
           marginwidth="0" marginheight="0">
    <frame name="title"
           src="title.asp?qcatnr=<%=catnr%>"
           marginwidth="0" marginheight="0">
  </frameset>
```

(continued)

```
<frameset cols="115,99%">
  <frame name="piclist"
         src="piclist.asp?qcatnr=<%=catnr%>"
         scrolling="auto" noresize
         marginwidth="0" marginheight="0">
  <frame name="detail"
         src="blank.htm"
         scrolling="auto" target="_self"
         marginwidth="0" marginheight="0">
</frameset>
<noframes>
<body>
<p>This page uses frames, but your browser doesn't support them.
</p>
</body>
</noframes>
</frameset>
</html>
```

For more information about the Request object, refer to the section titled "Using the Request Object" in Chapter 5, "Customizing Web Content with Server-Side Scripting."

The first block of ASP code verifies that the incoming request contains a valid category number. This value should appear in the expression *Request("qcatnr")*, which searches the following Request collections (in the order given) for a value named *qcatnr*:

1. QueryString   2. Form   3. Cookies

4. ClientCertificate   5. ServerVariables

If the script finds such a value and the value is numeric, the script uses the value as is. Otherwise, it substitutes the default category 100. Whatever the resulting value, the script stores it in a variable named *catnr*.

The other two blocks of ASP code insert the verified *catnr* value into the URLs (or more correctly, the query string portion of the URLs) that load title.asp and piclist.asp into the title and piclist frames. This correctly propagates the *qcatnr* value received from the main menu page to the necessary content pages.

As promised, the detail frame loads a blank page called blank.htm. The section later in this chapter that describes the piclist.asp page will also describe how more interesting content appears in this frame.

Building the Control Page (control.htm)

The control page is by far the simplest page in the catalog frameset. It exists solely to provide a link back to the application's home page. This is a valuable feature, however, because after the Web visitor has viewed 20 or 30 items, returning to the home page would require clicking the browser's Back button 20 or 30 times! This is always something to consider when designing applications that use framesets. Here's the complete HTML listing for the control.htm page:

```
<html>
<head>
<title>Holiday Photo Catalog</title>
```

```
<link rel="stylesheet" type="text/css" href="../holiday/holiday.css">
<base target="_self">
</head>
<body>
<p align="center"><a href="default.asp" target="_top">Home<br>
Page</a></p>
</body>
</html>
```

The <link> tag references the same style sheet used by all other pages in the application and thus preserves a common appearance. The hyperlink attribute *target="_top"* tells the browser to replace the entire frameset—not just the current frame—with the default.asp file.

Building the Title Page (title.asp)

The ASP code to display the current category name is simple; in fact, it's almost a miniature replica of the code in the default.asp page. The following ASP code goes into the body of a page named title.asp:

```
<%
' Check for presence of valid category number;
' take default if missing or invalid.
catnr = Request("qcatnr")
If catnr = "" Then catnr = 100
If Not IsNumeric(catnr) Then catnr = 100

' Create and open an ADO connection to the holiday.mdb database.
Set cnHol = Server.CreateObject("ADODB.Connection")
cnStHol = "driver={Microsoft Access Driver (*.mdb)};" & _
          "dbq=" & Server.MapPath("../holiday/holiday.mdb")
cnHol.Open cnStHol,"",""

' Create an ADO Recordset object, and use it to query
' the categories table for the specified category code.
Set rsCat = Server.CreateObject("ADODB.Recordset")
sql = "SELECT * FROM categories WHERE (catnr=" & catnr & ")  "
rsCat.Open sql, cnHol, adOpenStatic, adLockReadOnly

' If there's no category record, supply a default title.
' If there is such a record, save its catdesc field.
If rsCat.EOF Then
  CatTitle = "Holiday"
Else
  CatTitle = rsCat("catdesc")
' If the category has an icon assigned, store the HTML
' code that displays it in a variable named catIcon.
' Otherwise, store a null string in that variable.
  If IsNull(RsCat("icon")) Then
    catIcon = ""
```

(continued)

```
      Else
        If rsCat("icon") = "" Then
          catIcon = ""
        Else
          catIcon = "<img src=" & chr(34) & _
                    "../images/" & rsCat("icon") & _
                    Chr(34) & " border=0 >" & vbCrLf
        End If
      End If
End If


' Close and destroy the Recordset and Connection objects.
rsCat.Close
Set rsCat = Nothing
cnHol.Close
Set cnHol = Nothing
%>
```

Unlike the code in default.asp, this code includes a specific category number in its SELECT statement. Because it expects to receive only a single database record, it doesn't bother looping through the result set. And finally, instead of writing out the title immediately, it stores it in a variable named *CatTitle*. Another portion of the Web page can then use the expression <%=CatTitle%> to display the title. Similarly, when the category's icon field specifies a filename, the ASP code creates an <img> tag and stores it in a variable named *catIcon*. Code later in the page can then display the icon by using the expression <%=catIcon%>.

To view the code for this page, open the complete page located within the sample files at \webdbdev\ch07\title.asp.

Building the Thumbnail Page (piclist.asp)

By now you should recognize a pattern in all these query pages. Open the Connection and Recordset objects, write a loop that reads through any record retrieved, and inside that loop write out the HTML that displays each record. The piclist.asp page certainly follows this pattern, but it has the following specific requirements:

- It needs to obtain a list of all pictures recorded in the *items* table as belonging to a given category. The *items* table contains only the filenames of these pictures—not the pictures themselves.

- It needs to display a thumbnail version of each picture, arranged in a vertical list. The list will consist of a one-column HTML table having a separate row for each picture. The thumbnail pictures reside in a folder whose Web location, relative to the piclist.asp page, is *../holiday/images/thumb*. Displaying this picture requires creating an appropriate <img> tag within each table cell.

- Clicking any thumbnail should display, in the detail frame, a Web page containing the corresponding full-size picture plus selected fields from the *items* table. This requires an anchor tag that looks like this:

```
<a href=picshow.asp?qcatnr=200&qseqnr=300 target=detail>
```

   Of course, the category and sequence numbers will be different for each picture. This anchor tag—plus the closing </a> tag—will surround each <img> tag. The attribute *target=detail* tells the browser to display the resulting Web page in the detail frame, even though the anchor tag appears in the piclist frame.

- To warn Web visitors with slow connections, the size of each full-size picture should appear below the corresponding thumbnail picture. Because this information isn't recorded in the *items* table, the piclist.asp page will query the Web server's file system for it. The full-size pictures reside in a folder whose Web location, relative to the piclist.asp page, is *../holiday/images/*.

- When the piclist.asp page initially loads, it needs to replace the blank.htm file in the detail frame. That is, it needs to simulate the Web visitor clicking the first thumbnail.

   This presents a problem. An ASP page can modify itself at will, but it can't modify framesets, pages, or other elements already displayed on the Web visitor's browser. The piclist.asp page therefore takes the indirect approach: using the same technique it uses for creating HTML, it creates a browser-side script that reloads the detail frame. When the browser receives the resulting Web page, it runs the script and replaces the desired frame.

Create the thumbnail page

Here are the steps required to create the piclist.asp page:

1. Create a .asp file containing the following code:

```
<html>
<head>
<title>Holiday Photo Catalog Picture List</title>
<!-- #include file="../adovbs.inc" -->
<link rel="stylesheet" type="text/css"
      href="../holiday/holiday.css">
</head>
<body>
</body>
</html>
```

   The *#include* file statement makes the standard ADO named constants available to VBScript code. The <link> statement references a shared cascading style sheet.

2. Verify that the page has received an acceptable category number and, if it hasn't, substitute the default category 100—that is, add the statements shown at the top of the next page just before the </head> tag.

```
<%
catnr = Request("qcatnr")
If catnr = "" Then catnr = 100
If Not IsNumeric(catnr) Then catnr = 100
%>
```

3. To prepare for getting file sizes from the Web server's file system, add the following statement just before the closing %> tag you created in step 2.

```
Set fs = Server.CreateObject("Scripting.FileSystemObject")
```

4. To create, open, close, and destroy an ADO Connection object, insert the following code between the <body> and </body> tags:

```
<%
Set cnHol = Server.CreateObject("ADODB.Connection")
cnStHol = "driver={Microsoft Access Driver (*.mdb)};" & _
          "dbq=" & Server.MapPath("../holiday/holiday.mdb")
cnHol.Open cnStHol,"",""
' Statements to create, open, process, close, and destroy a
' recordset containing the requested item records will go here.
cnHol.Close
Set cnHol = Nothing
%>
```

5. To create, open, close, and destroy an ADO Recordset object that contains all records for the requested category, add the following statements in place of the comment in step 4. Note that the SQL statement selects only records having the requested category, and orders the result set by sequence number.

```
Set rsItm = Server.CreateObject("ADODB.Recordset")
sql = "SELECT catnr, seqnr, picname " & _
      "FROM items " & _
      "WHERE (catnr=" & catnr & ") " & _
      "ORDER BY seqnr "
rsItm.Open sql, cnHol, adOpenStatic, adLockReadOnly
' Statements to process the recordset will go here.
rsItm.Close
rsItm = Nothing
```

6. When the *rsItm.Open* statement in step 5 executes, ADO will either point the *rsItm* recordset to the first matching record or, if there are no matching records, it will set the *rsItm.EOF* property to True. This is the perfect spot to create the browser-side script that updates the detail frame. If the *rsItm.EOF* property is true, the required script statements are

```
<script>
parent.frames.detail.location = "blank.htm"
</script>
```

If the *rsItm.EOF* property is false, the script statements should be

```
<script>
parent.frames.detail.location = _
   "picshow.asp?qcatnr=200&qseqnr=300"
</script>
```

The parent object, by the way, refers to the frameset (catalog.asp) that created the frame where the current page (piclist.asp) resides. The frames collection contains all frames within that frameset. The detail object refers to the frame named detail, and the *location* property refers to its URL. Changing this *location* property reloads the specified frame from the given URL.

Use the following statements to write out the <script> and </script> tags, to test the *rsItm.EOF* property, and to modify the browser's *parent.frames.detail.location* property accordingly. They belong immediately after the *rsItm.Open* statement in step 5. Notice that the long *Response.Write* statement beginning on the sixth line creates a query string from values in the first item record.

```
Response.Write "<script>" & vbCrLf
If rsItm.EOF Then
   Response.Write "parent.frames.detail.location = " & _
                  Chr(34) & "blank.htm" & Chr(34) & vbCrLf
Else
   Response.Write "parent.frames.detail.location = " & _
                  Chr(34) & _
                  "picshow.asp" & _
                  "?qcatnr=" & rsItm("catnr") & _
                  "&qseqnr=" & rsItm("seqnr") & _
                  Chr(34) & vbCrLf
End If
Response.Write "</script>" & vbCrLf
```

7. Insert the following statements in place of the comment shown in step 5. These begin and end the HTML table that will organize the thumbnail pictures.

```
Response.Write "<table align=center>" & vbCrLf
' Statements to process the recordset will go here.
Response.Write "</table>" & vbCrLf
```

8. Insert the following statements to read through all the records in the *rsItm* recordset. They should replace the comment in step 7.

```
On Error Resume Next
Do While Not rsItm.EOF
' Statements to process each record will go here.
   rsItm.MoveNext
Loop
```

The *On Error* statement tells VBScript not to terminate the script even if a serious error occurs. Instead, the script simply continues at the next statement. This is necessary because the statement described in step 9 may legitimately fail.

9. Immediately after the *Do While Not* statement in step 8, insert the following statement to get the physical file properties of the picture file named in the current *item* record.

```
Set f = fs.GetFile(Server.MapPath( _
        "../holiday/images/" & rsItm("picname")))
```

To review the use of file system objects, refer to the section titled "Use the file system objects" in Chapter 5.

This statement retrieves the *picname* field from the current *item* record and prefixes it with the required URL path. The *Server.MapPath* method converts the resulting URL to a physical file location, and the *GetFile* method creates a file object pertaining to that physical file. Finally, the variable *f* receives a pointer to that file object. Assuming all goes well, *f* now provides access to a number of properties that describe the given file. In particular, *f.Size* contains its size in bytes.

If the *GetFile* method can't find the specified file, it normally generates a serious error and terminates the script. For this application, it's better to just report a zero file size and continue processing—that's why step 8 included an *On Error Resume Next* statement.

10. The HTML to display each thumbnail picture should follow the model shown below. The variable portions appear in blue.

```
<tr>
  <td class=pic align=center>
    <a href=picshow.asp?qcatnr=100&qseqnr=100 target=detail>
    <img src=../holiday/images/thumb/scan395.jpg border=0>
    </a>
    <br>12.2 KB
  </td>
</tr>
```

The following ASP code will create this HTML, minus spaces, carriage returns, line feeds, and other white space characters.

```
Response.Write "<tr>" & _
  "<td class=pic align=center>" & _
    "<a href=picshow.asp" & _
      "?qcatnr=" & rsItm("catnr") & _
      "&qseqnr=" & rsItm("seqnr") & _
      " target=detail>" & _
    "<img src=../holiday/images/thumb/" & _
      rsItm("picname") & _
      " border=0></a>" & _
    "<br>" & Round(f.Size/1024,1) & " KB" & _
  "</td></tr>" & vbCrLf
```

Notice that the *catnr*, *seqnr*, and *picname* fields come from the current record in the *rsItm* recordset. In the next-to-last line, the expression

Round(f.Size/1024,1) gets the file size *f.Size* retrieved in step 9, divides it by 1 KB, and rounds the quotient to one decimal place.

This completes the coding for the piclist.asp page. The complete listing appears here. If you understood the preceding 10 steps, this listing shouldn't contain any surprises.

```
<html>
<head>
<title>Holiday Photo Catalog Picture List</title>
<!-- #include file="../adovbs.inc" -->
<link rel="stylesheet" type="text/css"
      href="../holiday/holiday.css">
<%
' Check for valid requested category.
' Revert to the default (100) if necessary.
catnr = Request("qcatnr")
If catnr = "" Then catnr = 100
If Not IsNumeric(catnr) Then catnr = 100
' Create a FileSystemObject to use for looking up file sizes.
Set fs = Server.CreateObject("Scripting.FileSystemObject")
%>
</head>
<body>
<%
' Create and open ADO Connection object.
Set cnHol = Server.CreateObject("ADODB.Connection")
cnStHol = "driver={Microsoft Access Driver (*.mdb)};" & _
          "dbq=" & Server.MapPath("../holiday/holiday.mdb")
cnHol.Open cnStHol,"",""
' Create and open ADO Recordset object.
Set rsItm = Server.CreateObject("ADODB.Recordset")
sql = "SELECT catnr, seqnr, picname " & _
      "FROM items " & _
      "WHERE (catnr=" & catnr & ") " & _
      "ORDER BY seqnr "
rsItm.Open sql, cnHol, adOpenStatic, adLockReadOnly
' Write a browser-side script to update another frame (named
' detail) within the same frameset that displays this page.
Response.Write "<script>" & vbCrLf
If rsItm.EOF Then
  Response.Write "parent.frames.detail.location = " & _
                 Chr(34) & "blank.htm" & Chr(34) & vbCrLf
Else
  Response.Write "parent.frames.detail.location = " & _
                 Chr(34) & _
                 "picshow.asp" & _
                 "?qcatnr=" & rsItm("catnr") & _
                 "&qseqnr=" & rsItm("seqnr") & _
                 Chr(34) & vbCrLf
```

(continued)

```
     End If
     Response.Write "</script>" & vbCrLf
     ' Begin an HTML table.
     Response.Write "<table align=center>" & vbCrLf
     ' Loop through all matching item records, creating
     ' an HTML table row for each one.
     On Error Resume Next
     Do While Not rsItm.EOF
       Set f = fs.GetFile(Server.Mappath( _
             "../holiday/images/" & rsItm("picname")))
       Response.Write "<tr>" & _
         "<td class=pic align=center>" & _
           "<a href=picshow.asp" & _
             "?qcatnr=" & rsItm("catnr") & _
             "&qseqnr=" & rsItm("seqnr") & _
             " target=detail>" & _
           "<img src=../holiday/images/thumb/" & _
             rsItm("picname") & _
             " border=0></a>" & _
           "<br>" & Round(f.Size/1024,1) & " KB" & _
         "</td></tr>" & vbCrLf
       rsItm.MoveNext
     Loop
     ' End the HTML table.
     Response.Write "</table>" & vbCrLf
     ' Close and destroy Recordset object.
     rsItm.Close
     Set rsItm = Nothing
     ' Close and destroy Connection object.
     cnHol.Close
     Set cnHol = Nothing
     %>
     </body>
     </html>
```

Building the Detail Page (picshow.asp)

The fourth, final, and largest frame in the catalog.asp frameset is the detail frame. In the Holiday Photo Catalog application, this is the frame that displays the full-size picture and its corresponding information from the *items* table. In your application, the detail frame would display one item from whatever collection the application presents.

Initially, the detail frame contains a blank page, but the piclist.asp page quickly replaces that with a page called picshow.asp. The picshow.asp page receives a category number and a sequence number in its query string, looks up those values in the *items* table, and formats a Web page that displays information from the matching record. In short, it's a fairly typical query page.

To add flexibility, the sequence number is optional. If the picshow.asp page doesn't receive a sequence number, it displays the first sequence number within the given category.

To see how the picshow.asp page should look, refer again to the frame labeled "detail frame" in Figure 7-4. Two HTML tables organize page layout. The first table consists of a single column centered on the page. The picture title, the picture itself, and the picture caption each occupy one row. Because the caption often runs to multiple lines, it's left-justified for easy reading. The picture title and the picture itself, however, are centered to provide symmetry and balance.

The remaining fields—picture date and picture name—occupy a two-column table defined within the last row of the centered one-column table. Existing within a separate table, these two columns can collapse naturally to the left.

The picshow.asp page takes care not to display certain fields if they're empty. If there's no caption, for example, the page doesn't display a blank line where the caption would normally appear.

Create the detail page

Here's the step-by-step procedure for creating the picshow.asp page:

1. Open a new file in your favorite text editor and enter the basic structural elements of a Web page. The following code will suffice:

```
<html>
<head>
<title>Holiday Photo Catalog Detail</title>
<!-- #include file="../adovbs.inc" -->
<link rel="stylesheet" type="text/css"
      href="../holiday/holiday.css">
</head>
<body>
</body>
</html>
```

The adovbs.inc file provides the standard ADO named constants. The <link> statement references a shared style sheet that provides uniform typography throughout the application.

2. Insert an ASP script block just before the </head> tag and insert code to verify that the incoming request specifies a valid category number. If the category number is missing or non-numeric, substitute 100 as a default value. Here's the necessary code:

```
<%
catnr = Request("qcatnr")
If catnr = "" Then catnr = 100
If Not IsNumeric(catnr) Then catnr = 100
%>
```

3. After the <body> tag, insert the following HTML tags to mark the beginning and end of a centered table:

```
<table align="center">
</table>
```

4. Between these tags, insert a block of ASP code that creates, opens, closes, and destroys an ADO Connection object:

```
<%
Set cnHol = Server.CreateObject("ADODB.Connection")
cnStHol = "driver={Microsoft Access Driver (*.mdb)};" & _
          "dbq=" & Server.MapPath("../holiday/holiday.mdb")
cnHol.Open cnStHol, "", ""
' Statements to create, open, process, close, and destroy a
' recordset containing the requested item record will go here.
cnHol.Close
Set cnHol = Nothing
%>
```

5. In place of the comments in step 4, insert the following code to create a recordset containing the specified record, open it, close it, and destroy it.

```
Set rsItm = Server.CreateObject("ADODB.Recordset")
seqnr = Request("qseqnr")
If Not IsNumeric(seqnr) Then
  seqnr = ""
End If
If seqnr = "" Then
  seqwhere = ""
Else
  seqwhere = " AND (seqnr=" & seqnr & ") "
End If
sql = "SELECT * " & _
      "FROM items " & _
      "WHERE (catnr=" & catnr & ") " & seqwhere & _
  "ORDER BY seqnr "
rsItm.Open sql, cnHol, adOpenStatic, adLockReadOnly
' Code to display requested record will go here.
rsItm.Close
Set rsItm = Nothing
```

The second line in this code fragment retrieves the desired sequence number from the incoming request. The next three lines erase this value if it isn't numeric. The next five lines construct a fragment of SQL code named *seqwhere* that's either empty (if no sequence number is available) or that specifies the given sequence number.

The next four lines construct the SQL statement that queries the *item* table. The third of these lines includes the *seqwhere* variable explained in the previous paragraph. The ORDER BY clause is extraneous but harmless if *seqwhere* specifies a sequence number, because in that case the result set will contain at most one record. (The combination of category number and sequence number are the item table's primary key, and primary keys are always unique.) If *seqwhere* is empty, however, the ORDER BY clause ensures that the first record in the result set is the one with the lowest sequence number.

The remaining lines open, close, and destroy the required recordset. These should be quite familiar by now; if not, review the earlier examples in this book.

6. Replace the comment in step 5 with the following *If* statement, which determines whether any matching records are available.

```
If Not rsItm.EOF Then
' Code to display one record will go here.
End If
```

7. The next four steps replace the comment line in step 6 with code that displays each desired field from the *items* table, provided the field isn't null or empty. The first such field is the item title.

```
If Not IsNull(rsItm("title")) Then
  If rsItm("title") <> "" Then
    Response.Write "<tr><td align=center class=titl>" & _
      rsItm("title") & _
      "</td></tr>" & vbCrLf
  End If
End If
```

Determining whether the *title* field contains a value is a two-step process. The first step uses the VBScript *IsNull* function to determine if the value is null. If it isn't, the second step determines if the value is

Dealing with Null Values

You might occasionally find database fields that are *null*, which means they contain no value at all, not even an empty string or a zero. Comparing a null value with an empty string produces a VBScript run-time error and immediately terminates ASP processing. This is a nuisance with only three solutions:

- Use the *IsNull* function before referencing any field that might be null. This is the choice illustrated.

- Keep all null values out of the database. This might be a viable choice if you can code the database system to enforce it.

- Surround the statement with *On Error Resume Next* and on *Error GoTo 0* statements. However, in the case of an *If Then Else* structure, this results in neither the *If* nor the *Else* code executing.

empty. If a record field is null, that means it contains no value at all—not even an empty string value or a zero.

If the *title* field does contain a value, the code writes it out surrounded by <tr>, <td>, </td>, and </tr> tags. The <td> tag specifies *align=center* so that the caption appears centered within the HTML table (which, in turn, is centered on the Web page).

8. Next insert the following lines after the two *End If* statements to display the full-size picture named in the current *item* record:

```
Response.Write "<tr><td align=center>" & _
  "<img src=../holiday/images/" & _
  rsItm("picname") & ">" & _
  "</td></tr>" & vbCrLf
```

This code writes an ordinary <img> tag, again surrounded by <tr>, <td>, </td>, and </tr> tags. The string *"../holiday/images/"* specifies the path to the application's full-size pictures relative to the picshow.asp page.

9. Insert the following lines immediately after those in step 8 to test for the presence of a caption value and display it if available:

```
If Not Isnull(rsItm("caption")) Then
  If rsItm("caption") <> "" Then
    Response.Write "<tr><td class=capt>" & _
      rsItm("caption") & _
      "</td></tr>" & vbCrLf
  End If
End If
```

Except for minor formatting differences, this duplicates the code explained in step 5.

10. Insert the following lines to define a new table inside one cell of the existing table:

```
Response.Write "<tr><td><table>" & vbCrLf
'   Display additional field names and values here.
Response.Write "</table></td></tr>" & vbCrLf
```

11. To display the picture date from the current *items* record, replace the comment line in step 10 with this code:

```
If Not IsNull(rsItm("picdate")) Then
  If rsItm("picdate") <> "" Then
    Response.Write _
      "  <tr>" & vbCrLf & _
      "    <td>Date:</td>" & vbCrLf & _
      "    <td>" & rsItm("picdate") & "</td>" & vbCrLf & _
      "  </tr>" & vbCrLf
  End If
End If
```

These statements basically repeat the techniques of step 7 except that they create two table cells instead of one. The first cell displays the field's name; the second cell displays its value.

12. To display the picture's filename, insert the following statements after those in step 11. Because *picname* is a required field, there's no need to test it for a null or empty value.

```
Response.Write _
   "  <tr>" & vbCrLf & _
   "     <td>Picture:</td>" & vbCrLf & _
   "     <td>" & rsItm("picname") & "</td>" & vbCrLf & _
   "  </tr>" & vbCrLf
```

This completes the coding for the picshow.asp page, and in fact for all the pages in the catalog.asp frameset. A complete and annotated listing of the picshow.asp page appears here:

```
<html>
<head>
<title>Holiday Photo Catalog Detail</title>
<!-- #include file="../adovbs.inc" -->
<link rel="stylesheet" type="text/css"
      href="../holiday/holiday.css">
<%
' Check for valid requested category.
' Revert to the default (100) if necessary.
catnr = Request("qcatnr")
If catnr = "" Then catnr = 100
If Not IsNumeric(catnr) Then catnr = 100
%>
</head>
<body>
<table align="center">
<%
' Create and open ADO Connection object.
Set cnHol = Server.CreateObject("ADODB.Connection")
cnStHol = "driver={Microsoft Access Driver (*.mdb)};" & _
          "dbq=" & Server.Mappath("../holiday/holiday.mdb")
cnHol.Open cnStHol, "", ""
' Create and open ADO Recordset object.
' If the request specified a sequence number, query for it.
' Otherwise, retrieve all records within the requested
' category and display the first one.
Set rsItm = Server.CreateObject("ADODB.Recordset")
seqnr = Request("qseqnr")
If Not IsNumeric(seqnr) Then
  seqnr = ""
```

(continued)

```
          End If
          If seqnr = "" Then
            seqwhere = ""
          Else
            seqwhere = " AND (seqnr=" & seqnr & ") "
          End If
          sql = "SELECT * " & _
                "FROM items " & _
                "WHERE (catnr=" & catnr & ") " & seqwhere & _
                "ORDER BY seqnr "
          rsItm.Open sql, cnHol, adOpenStatic, adLockReadOnly
          ' If the query found any matching records, display the first one.
          If Not rsItm.EOF Then
          ' Display the title field, if present.
            If Not IsNull(rsItm("title")) Then
              If rsItm("title") <> "" Then
                Response.Write "<tr><td align=center class=titl>" & _
                  rsItm("title") & _
                  "</td></tr>" & vbCrLf
              End If
            End If
          ' Display the full-size picture.
            Response.Write "<tr><td align=center>" & _
              "<img src=../holiday/images/" & _
              rsItm("picname") & ">" & _
              "</td></tr>" & vbCrLf
          ' Display the caption field, if present.
            If Not IsNull(rsItm("caption")) Then
              If rsItm("caption") <> "" Then
                Response.Write "<tr><td class=capt>" & _
                  rsItm("caption") & _
                  "</td></tr>" & vbCrLf
              End If
            End If
          ' Create a table within a table, to display named fields.
            Response.Write "<tr><td><table>" & vbCrLf
          ' Display the picture date field, if present.
            If Not IsNull(rsItm("picdate")) Then
              If rsItm("picdate") <> "" Then
                Response.Write _
                  "  <tr>" & vbCrLf & _
                  "    <td>Date:</td>" & vbCrLf & _
                  "    <td>" & rsItm("picdate") & "</td>" & vbCrLf & _
                  "  </tr>" & vbCrLf
              End If
```

```
    End If
' Display the picture name field.
    Response.Write _
        "  <tr>" & vbCrLf & _
        "    <td>Picture:</td>" & vbCrLf & _
        "    <td>" & rsItm("picname") & "</td>" & vbCrLf & _
        "  </tr>" & vbCrLf
' End the table within a table.
    Response.Write "</table></td></tr>" & vbCrLf
End If
' Close and destroy the Recordset object.
rsItm.Close
Set rsItm = Nothing
' Close and destroy the Connection object.
cnHol.Close
Set cnHol = Nothing
%>
</table>
</body>
</html>
```

In total, the Holiday Photo Catalog provides lookup and display of more than 500 photographs. Doing this with seven Web pages is certainly easier than doing it with 500. In fact, the entire application contains less than 400 lines of code, including HTML, VBScript, CSS—everything. Learning to program Web database pages is certainly worth the effort.

Chapter Summary

This chapter explained how to create a typical catalog browsing application using content from a simple database. This involved five ASP pages, four of which performed database queries: a main menu page, a page that displayed a category title within one frame of a frameset, a page that displayed a list of thumbnails in another frame, and a page that displayed a full-size picture and some corresponding database information. The techniques used in this example apply—with minor changes—to a wide range of catalog applications.

Chapter 8, "Updating Tables," will explain how to update catalog information from a Web page.

Updating Tables from a General Purpose Form

Chapter Objectives   Estimated Time: 45 minutes

In this chapter, you'll learn how to

- Create an HTML form that finds and updates records in a database table.

- Add, delete, and modify database records.

For some Web database applications, read-only database access is all that's required. An offline process updates the database, and Web visitors only view it. For many other applications, however, Web pages that update the database are an integral part of the system. Chapter 4, "Accessing Tables and Records with ADO," described a few simple Web pages that updated a database, but it didn't address the complexities of building a fully functional maintenance transaction. That's what this chapter will do.

Maintaining Holiday Items

The number of reasons for Web pages to update databases is almost limitless, as is the number of ways to go about such a task. The example presented here is a relatively straightforward Web database page that queries, adds, modifies, and deletes item records in the *items* table of the Holiday Photo Catalog database, holiday.mdb. This type of page has two advantages as an example. First, it provides a useful function that's easy to understand. Second, it illustrates all the common database update commands.

The name of this page is "Holiday Item Maintenance," and it appears in Figure 8-1. The group of form objects titled *query controls* specifies the record that's displayed on the page. You can choose to display a specific item record, the record just before the current record, or the one following the current record. The Web visitor (probably the site administrator) must display a record before changing or deleting it.

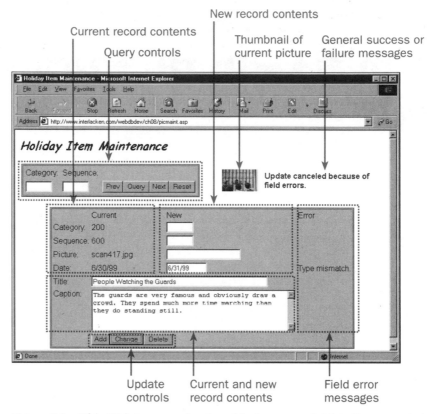

Figure 8-1 *This Web page can locate, add, change, and delete item records in the Holiday Photo Catalog application.*

The current record, in this sense, is the record last displayed. The Web visitor can specify a different starting location by entering values in the *query controls* Category and Sequence boxes. If, for example, the visitor entered 500 in the Category box and then clicked the Next button, the Web page would display the first record in category 500.

The Holiday Item Maintenance page displays an item record by showing the value of each field under the Current heading. This heading is in the large box that occupies most of the page. The *category*, *sequence*, *picname*, and *picdate* values appear as ordinary text, while the *title* and *caption* values appear in text boxes. A thumbnail version of the current picture appears to the right of the query controls box.

Change Holiday Item Maintenance records

Once the correct record is on display, the visitor can enter new values for the *category*, *sequence*, *picname*, and *picdate* fields by typing them into the text boxes below the New heading. To change the title and caption fields, the visitor modifies the existing values. To apply the change, the visitor clicks the Change button.

If the ASP page succeeds in changing the *items* record, it displays the message, "Record changed." In the Current column it displays the resulting record, and in the New column it displays empty text boxes.

The ASP page can encounter two types of errors while trying to update the requested record—those pertaining to individual fields and those pertaining to the record update:

- If an error occurs while updating an individual field, the page displays the ADO error message under the Error label and to the right of the field name. The Error label is displayed only when an error occurs. The message "Type mismatch," in Figure 8-1, for example, pertains to the *picdate* field. If any field errors occur, the Web page cancels the update in progress and displays the message "Update canceled because of field errors."

- If an error occurs while the ASP page is opening the database connection, opening an *items* recordset, or using the recordset's *Update* method, the Web page displays the ADO error message and again cancels the update.

After encountering either type of error, the ASP page redisplays the Web page exactly as the visitor submitted it (except, of course, for adding the error messages). That is, it displays the original, unchanged record in the Current column and the visitor's previous text box entries in the New column.

Delete Holiday Item Maintenance records

The procedure for deleting an *items* record is much the same as for changing one; first display the record you want to delete, and then click the Delete button. No field entries are required.

If the deletion succeeds, the ASP page displays a "Record deleted" message. The Current column will be empty because the record previously displayed no longer exists. The ASP page does, however, display the former contents of the deleted record in the New column. This makes it easy to add the record back into the database if the visitor deleted it by mistake.

If the deletion fails, the page redisplays both the Current and New columns as it received them.

Add Holiday Item Maintenance records

The procedure for adding an *items* record is similar, except that there's no reason to display an existing record. Simply enter a category number, a sequence number, and a picture name, and then click the Add button. The Date, Title, and Caption fields are optional.

If the addition succeeds, the Holiday Item Maintenance page displays the new record in the Current column and empties the fields in the New column. If the addition fails, the page displays both columns as it received them.

Note that the *Add* function doesn't upload the picture file—or, for that matter, its thumbnail equivalent—to the Web site. Whoever maintains the Web site will still have to upload those files the same way they upload Web pages and other content.

Additional Processing Notes

The picmaint.asp page allows changes to the *catnr* and *seqnr* fields, which together form the primary key of the *items* table. This feature is convenient but not without ramifications. The page is fully capable of creating an *items* record having no matching records in the *category* table, for example, and of removing all records from an existing category. This example assumes these conditions are acceptable, and it takes no special provision to avoid them. If your application is less tolerant, you might have to add code to your programs, define referential integrity rules in your database, or prohibit key changes.

Adds, changes, and deletions in this Web page are an all-or-nothing proposition. An error updating any field cancels the entire update. This is the easiest type of operation for Web visitors to understand, but some other applications might demand another approach. If an optional field is too long, for example, it may be preferable to just truncate it. Issues like these have no right or wrong answers that apply in every situation; instead, you must consider the needs of each application.

Building the Holiday Item Maintenance Page

The programming logic needed to process two outcomes—success and failure—of six transaction codes—*Prev*, *Query*, *Next*, *Add*, *Change*, and *Delete*—is too complex to run the code and produce the outgoing HTML at the same time. The order of the output fields within the HTML is just too different from the order in which the code derives them. Therefore, almost all the ASP code resides in the Web page's <head> section. The <body> section contains static HTML—arranged spatially with HTML tables—to display the field headings and contents.

The two gray rectangles are one-celled HTML tables that provide borders and a background color. Additional tables (within the one-celled tables) organize the form elements and titles. Figure 8-2 shows how Microsoft FrontPage displays these tables in visible form.

With two exceptions, everything in the <body> section consists of ordinary HTML or simple ASP field references—that is, <%=expression%> tags. The two exceptions are

- The thumbnail picture. A trivial piece of code writes out an <img> tag if the *picname* field contains characters or writes nothing if the *picname* field is empty.

- The heading for the Error column. Another very simple piece of code emits this title if there were any field errors and suppresses it if not.

The code in the <head> section loads four Dictionary objects with the values that the <body> section will display. Like a VBScript array, a Dictionary object holds a collection of single-valued items. Unlike such an array, a Dictionary object uses an alphanumeric key to identify each item. As you'll see when you examine the code, it's convenient for the items in these Dictionary objects to have the same names as their corresponding database fields. Table 8-1 lists the Dictionary objects in the Holiday Items maintenance page.

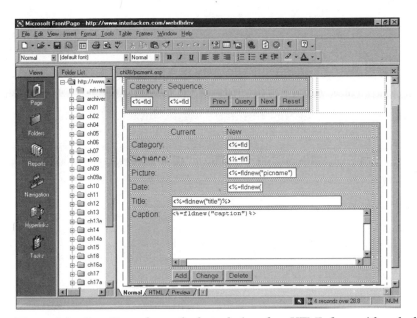

Figure 8-2 *FrontPage shows the boundaries of an HTML form with a dashed line and the borders of table cells with a dotted line.*

Table 8-1   Dictionary Objects in the Holiday Item Maintenance Page

Object Name	Item Keys	Description
fldQry	qcatnr qseqnr	Contains the Category and Sequence fields from the Query Controls area.
fldCur	catnr seqnr picname picdate title caption	Contains the field values that will appear in the Current column. The *fldCur("catnr")* value also appears in a hidden form field named *hcatnr*. The *fldCur("seqnr")* value similarly appears in a hidden field named *hseqnr*. Each execution of the picmaint.asp page uses these hidden fields to identify the current record displayed in the previous execution.
fldNew	catnr seqnr picname picdate title caption	Contains the field values received from (and in the event that an update isn't successful, sent to) the fields in the New column.
fldMsg	catnr seqnr picname picdate title caption	Contains any error messages related to a specific field.

For more information about Dictionary objects, refer to "Use the Dictionary object" beginning on page 116 in Chapter 5, "Customizing Web Content with Server-Side Scripting."

Constructing the ASP code for the Holiday Item Maintenance page involves the following steps. Most of the remainder of this chapter will explain these steps in detail and in the order given here:

1. Code the static HTML.

2. Create the four Dictionary objects.

3. Load and validate input from the Web visitor.

4. Create and open a recordset for the *items* table.

5. Process the *Add* transaction code.

6. Process the *Change* transaction code.

7. Process the *Delete* transaction code.

8. Process the *Prev*, *Query*, and *Next* transaction codes.

9. Clean up and terminate.

10. Write the *CopyRsToCur* subroutine.

11. Write the *CopyNewToRs* subroutine.

12. Write the *GetNextPrevKey* subroutine.

Code the static HTML

The following steps provide general guidance for coding the HTML for the Holiday Photo Catalog Item Maintenance page. There are two reasons for not describing this code in detail: First, this book presumes you already know HTML. Second, the companion CD-ROM contains a copy of the complete Web page, including all the HTML.

1. Using HTML statements, create an ordinary Web page that contains all the form elements shown in Figure 8-2. The starting and ending form tags should be

```
<form method="POST" action="picmaint.asp">
'   Form contents go here.
</form>
```

2. Immediately after the <form> tag, code these two hidden form elements:

```
<input type="hidden" name="hcatnr" value="<%=fldCur("catnr")%>">
<input type="hidden" name="hseqnr" value="<%=fldCur("seqnr")%>">
```

Invisible to the Web visitor, these fields provide each execution of the picmaint.asp page with the key values used by the previous execution.

3. Designate all the push button objects except Reset as Submit buttons; name each one of them *btnSub*. Be sure to give each button the title value shown in the figure. Here's a typical example:

```
<input type="Submit" value="Prev" name="btnSub">
```

4. Name the text boxes in the query box *qcatnr* and *qseqnr*.

5. Name the text boxes in the update box *catnr*, *seqnr*, *picname*, *picdate*, *title*, and *comment*.

Note   When you submit a form, the browser transmits button values only for the button you click. If several buttons have the same name, code running on the server can use a button's value—for example, the value in *Request.Form("btnSub")*—to determine which button the Web visitor clicked.

Create the four Dictionary objects

Just before the </head> tag, insert the following code to create the Dictionary objects that will contain the data values returned to the Web visitor:

```
<%
Set fldQry = Server.CreateObject("Scripting.Dictionary")
Set fldCur = Server.CreateObject("Scripting.Dictionary")
Set fldNew = Server.CreateObject("Scripting.Dictionary")
Set fldMsg = Server.CreateObject("Scripting.Dictionary")
' Additional processing code will go here.
%>
```

Load and validate input from the Web visitor

The code created in this section will analyze the input received from the Web visitor and store it for later processing. It replaces the comment line shown in the procedure just above.

1. Initialize five variables named *fMsg*, *iMsg*, *keyCatNr*, *keySeqNr*, and *fldFail* for later processing:

   ```
   fMsg = ""
   iMsg = ""
   keyCatNr = ""
   keySeqNr = ""
   fldFail = False
   ```

   The variables *fMsg* and *iMsg* will contain fatal and informational messages—the messages that tell the Web visitor whether the transaction worked. The *keyCatNr* and *keySeqNr* variables will contain the category number and sequence number values the transaction will process. To make the same copy of these variables accessible both inside and outside any subroutines or functions, you must create them outside any function or subroutine. The *fldFail* variable indicates whether any errors occurred while moving data into the fields in a new or modified *items* record.

2. Get the current transaction code. Recall the following points:

   - Each transaction code has its own Submit button.
   - All these Submit buttons have the same name: *btnSub*.
   - Each button's title and form field value are by definition the same.
   - The only button that transmits data is the one the Web visitor clicks.

   Because all six buttons are Submit buttons, clicking any of them tells the browser to request the page specified in the <form> tag's *action* property: picmaint.asp. If the Web visitor clicks the Prev button, server-side code in the picmaint.asp page will find that *Request("btnSub")* contains the string *Prev*. When the visitor clicks the Query button, *Request("btnSub")* will contain the string *Query*. The same is true for each remaining button.

When coding, it's usually easier to deal with codes such as *A, C,* and *D* than with words such as *Add, Change,* and *Delete.* Therefore, the following code takes only the first character of the clicked button's title, converts it to upper case, and stores the result in a variable named *trancd.* (In theory, the first character should always be upper case because that's the way it's coded in the HTML. In practice, it costs almost nothing to be sure.)

```
trancd = UCase(Left(Request("btnSub"),1))
```

3. Validate the transaction code. The following code first determines whether the *trancd* variable created in the previous step is empty. If so, the code substitutes the default transaction code *Q*. If not, it determines whether *trancd* contains one of the letters *P, Q, N, A, C,* or *D*. If it doesn't, the code again substitutes the default transaction code *Q*.

```
If trancd = "" Then
  trancd = "Q"
Else
  If InStr("PQNACD", trancd) = 0 Then
    trancd = "Q"
  End If
End If
```

4. Select the key the transaction should process. The key will consist of a category number and a sequence number, because the *catnr* and *seqnr* fields are the primary key for the *items* table.

   - If the transaction code is *A (Add)*, the transaction will add a record with *catnr* and *seqnr* fields taken from the New column.

   - If the transaction code is *C* or *D (Change* or *Delete)*, the transaction will change or delete the record that the previous transaction displayed. Those *catnr* and *seqnr* values are recorded in two hidden form fields named *hcatnr* and *hseqnr*.

   - If the transaction code is *N* or *P (Next* or *Prev)*, the transaction will search the following fields, in order, for a nonempty value: the *qcatnr* field in the query box, the *hcatnr* field recorded by the previous transaction, and the *catnr* field in the New column. If all these fields are empty, the transaction will use a default value of zero for *N* transactions or 2,147,483,647 (the largest possible value) for *P* transactions.

   Once the transaction locates a category number, it uses the sequence number from the same source or—if that value is empty—a default value of 0 for *N* transactions or 2,147,483,647 for *P* transactions.

Because the algorithm for determining these keys is lengthy and repetitious, it resides in a function called *GetNextPrevKey*. The code for this function appears later in this chapter. For now, take it on faith that the function accepts the default value as an argument and updates the *keyCatNr* and *keySeqNr* variables as required.

Note 2,147,483,647 is the default category number for *P* transactions because, in the *items* table, the *seqnr* field is a long (32-bit) integer; 2,147,483,647 is the largest value such an integer can contain. To find the last category in the table, the transaction will search for a category less than or equal to this value. Because the value 2,147,483,647 isn't particularly easy to remember, the code actually uses the expression *CLng(&H7FFFFFFF)*. The literal *&H7FFFFFFF* specifies a hexadecimal value equivalent to one zero bit followed by 31 one bits. The first bit in a long integer is a sign bit, with zero indicating positive. *CLng* is a VBScript built-in function that converts an expression to a long integer.

- If the transaction code is *Q*, the transaction will search for an *items* record whose category and sequence numbers match the *qcatnr* and *qseqnr* fields in the query box.

The following code implements these rules. Note that in the case of transaction code *Q*, this code also saves the input *qcatnr* and *qseqnr* fields in the *fldQry* Dictionary object. Later, *fldQry("qcatnr")* and *fldQry("qseqnr")* will provide output values for the Category and Sequence text boxes in the query box.

```
Select Case trancd
   Case "A"
      keyCatNr = Request("catnr")
      keySeqNr = Request("seqnr")
   Case "C"
      keyCatNr = Request("hcatnr")
      keySeqNr = Request("hseqnr")
   Case "D"
      keyCatNr = Request("hcatnr")
      keySeqNr = Request("hseqnr")
   Case "N"
      GetNextPrevKey (0)
   Case "P"
      GetNextPrevKey (CLng(&h7FFFFFFF))
   Case Else ' Default transaction code is "Q"
      keyCatNr = Request("qcatnr")
      keySeqNr = Request("qseqnr")
      fldQry("qcatnr") = Request("qcatnr")
      fldQry("qseqnr") = Request("qseqnr")
End Select
```

5. If the transaction code is *A*, *C*, or *D*, save the field values specified in the New column in the *fldNew* Dictionary object, as shown on the next page.

```
If trancd < "E" Then
  fldNew("catnr") = Request("catnr")
  fldNew("seqnr") = Request("seqnr")
  fldNew("picname") = Request("picname")
  fldNew("picdate") = Request("picdate")
  fldNew("title") = Request("title")
  fldNew("caption") = Request("caption")
End If
```

6. Ensure that the *keyCatNr* variable is nonempty and numeric. If not, store an error messages in the *fMsg* (fatal message) variable:

```
If keyCatNr = "" Then
  fMsg = "Enter category number."
Else
  If Not IsNumeric(keyCatNr) Then
    fMsg = "Category must be numeric."
  End If
End If
```

7. Ensure that the *keySeqNr* variable is nonempty and numeric. If not, store an error messages in the *fMsg* (fatal message) variable:

```
If fMsg = "" Then
  If keySeqNr= "" Then
    fMsg = "Sequence missing."
  Else
    If Not IsNumeric(keySeqNr) Then
      fMsg = "Sequence must be numeric."
    End If
  End If
End If
```

Create and open a recordset for the items table

At this point, the transaction either has valid keys to work with or a message in the *fMsg* variable. If the *fMsg* variable is empty, the next step is to create and open ADO Connection and Recordset objects to obtain the desired records. Of course, if the *fMsg* variable contains a message, the transaction skips all further processing and just reports the error.

The *A*, *C*, *D*, and *Q* transaction codes all require a SQL statement that retrieves an *items* record with specific *catnr* and *seqnr* values. The *N* transaction code requires a SQL statement that retrieves the first record with key values greater than those specified; the *P* transaction code requires a SQL statement that retrieves the first record with key values less than those specified.

The following steps create the required code:

1. Determine whether a fatal error has already occurred; proceed only if one hasn't.

```
If fMsg = "" Then
```

2. Create and open an ADO Connection object that points to the holiday.mdb database:

```
Set cnHol = Server.CreateObject("ADODB.Connection")
cnStHol = "driver={Microsoft Access Driver (*.mdb)};" & _
          "dbq=" & Server.MapPath("../holiday/holiday.mdb")
cnHol.Open cnStHol,"",""
```

3. Create an ADO Recordset object:

```
Set rsItm = Server.CreateObject("ADODB.Recordset")
```

4. Begin a *Select Case* statement that tests the transaction code:

```
Select Case trancd
```

5. If *trancd* is *N*, build a SQL statement that retrieves all records from the *items* table having either of the following two criteria:

- A category number (*catnr*) equal to *keyCatNr* and a sequence number (*seqnr*) greater than *keySeqNr*

- A category number greater than *keyCatNr*

Present all such records in ascending sequence by *catnr* and *seqnr* so that the first record returned is the lowest one that satisfies the criteria:

```
Case "N"
  sql = "SELECT * FROM items " & _
        "WHERE ((catnr = " & keyCatNr & ") AND " & _
               "(seqnr > " & keySeqNr & ")) " & _
           "OR (catnr > " & keyCatNr & ") " & _
        "ORDER BY catnr, seqnr ; "
```

6. If *trancd* is *P*, build a SQL statement that retrieves all records from the *items* table having either of the following two criteria:

- A category number (*catnr*) equal to *keyCatNr* and a sequence number (*seqnr*) less than *keySeqNr*

- A category number less than *keyCatNr*

Present all such records in descending sequence by *catnr* and *seqnr* so that the first record returned is the highest one that satisfies the criteria:

```
Case "P"
  sql = "SELECT * FROM items " & _
        "WHERE ((catnr = " & keyCatNr & ") AND " & _
               "(seqnr < " & keySeqNr & ")) " & _
           "OR (catnr < " & keyCatNr & ") " & _
        "ORDER BY catnr DESC, seqnr DESC ; "
```

7. For all other transaction codes, build a SQL statement that retrieves all records from the *items* table having the specific category and sequence numbers stored in *keyCatNr* and *keySeqNr*. Because *catnr* and *seqnr* are the table's primary keys, there can be only one such record. The order of presentation is therefore irrelevant.

```
          Case Else
            sql = "SELECT * " & _
                    "FROM items " & _
                    "WHERE (catnr = " & keyCatNr & ") " & _
                    "AND (seqnr = " & keySeqNr & ") ; "
```

8. Terminate the *Select Case* statement:

```
End Select
```

9. Open the recordset:

```
rsItm.Open sql, cnHol, adOpenDynamic, adLockOptimistic
```

Process the Add transaction code

The following steps will process the *Add* transaction code. This code performs the actual work of adding a record to the database. Recall that the previous section opened the necessary recordset and, if a record with the desired key already existed, retrieved it. Recall also that an earlier *If* statement keeps this code from executing if a fatal error has already occurred.

1. Begin a *Select Case* statement that tests the transaction code:

```
Select Case trancd
```

2. Initiate the case for transaction code *A*:

```
Case "A"
```

3. Check to see if the *rsItm* recordset contains a record:

```
If rsItm.EOF Then
```

4. If it doesn't, tell ADO to create a new record and then call the *CopyNewToRs* function:

```
rsItm.AddNew
fMsg = CopyNewToRs
```

Here's what *CopyNewToRs* does:

- It copies all the field values from the *fldNew* Dictionary object to the new record.

- If ADO rejects any field values, the *CopyNewToRs* function cancels the update and returns a fatal error message.

- If ADO doesn't reject any field values, the function tells ADO to complete the update and once again checks for errors. If ADO reports an error, the function returns it as a fatal error. If not, the function returns a null string.

   A procedure later in this section will explain how to create the *CopyNewToRs* function.

5. If no fatal error has occurred, store the informational message "Record Added" in the variable *iMsg*, erase all the data in the *fldNew* Dictionary object, and call the *CopyRsToCur* subroutine to load the *fldCur* Dictionary object with the contents of the new *items* record:

```
If fMsg = "" Then
    iMsg = "Record added."
    fldNew.removeall
    CopyRsToCur
End If
```

Note the effect of erasing the *fldNew* Dictionary object and loading the *fldCur* Dictionary object from the new *items* record: it displays the successfully added record as the new current record and presents a set of blank fields the Web visitor can use for adding another record.

If the attempt to add the new record did produce a fatal error, no further action is required. The *fldNew* Dictionary object already contains the field values the Web visitor entered and can now correct; the *fldCur* Dictionary object needn't contain anything.

6. If step 3 determined that the *items* table already contains a record with the proposed key, the code will skip steps 4 and 5 and execute the code in this step instead. This code records the fatal error message "Record already exists" and, by calling the *CopyRsToCur* subroutine also used in step 5, copies the existing record's contents to the *fldCur* Dictionary object. This shows the Web visitor the contents of the existing, conflicting record in the Current column. Not disturbing the *fldNew* Dictionary object redisplays the visitor's original input in the New column:

```
Else
    fMsg = "Record already exists."
    CopyRsToCur
End If
```

Process the Change transaction code

The code to change an existing record follows much the same pattern as the code to add a new one:

1. Initiate the case for transaction code *C*:

```
Case "C"
```

2. Check to see if the *rsItm* recordset contains a record:

```
If rsItm.EOF Then
```

3. If it doesn't, record a fatal error message and exit:

```
fMsg = "Record not found."
```

4. If it does, call the *CopyNewToRs* function used in step 4 of the *Add* transaction. This copies any nonblank input fields from the *fldNew* Dictionary object to the current record in the *rsItm* recordset, noting any field errors in the *fldMsg* Dictionary object. *CopyNewToRs* then tells ADO to update

the record. If any of these operations create an error, the function returns an error message:

```
Else
    fMsg = CopyNewToRs
```

5. If the process has completed without a fatal error, record the informational message "Record Changed" and erase all the fields in the *fldNew* Dictionary object. (These field values have been stored in the database and therefore are of no further use.)

   Regardless of any fatal error message, if *RsItem* recordset found a current record, call the *CopyRsToCur* subroutine to display it:

```
If fMsg = "" Then
    iMsg = "Record changed."
    fldNew.removeall
End If
CopyRsToCur
End If
```

Process the Delete transaction code

Processing a *Delete* transaction again follows the same basic pattern as processing an add or a change:

1. Initiate the case for transaction code *D*:

```
Case "D"
```

2. Check to see if the *rsItm* recordset contains a record:

```
If rsItm.EOF Then
```

3. If it doesn't, record the fatal error message "Record not found" and terminate the process. There is no record to display in the *fldCur* Dictionary object; the *fldNew* Dictionary object already contains any input fields the Web visitor entered.

```
fMsg = "Record not found."
```

4. If the *rsItm* recordset does contain a record, copy each of its field values to the *fldNew* Dictionary object. This provides a way for the Web visitor to add the record back into the database after deleting it in error.

```
Else
    For Each fld In rsItm.Fields
        fldNew(fld.Name) = fld.Value
    Next
```

   The *For Each* loop runs once for each member of the *rsItm.Fields* collection: that is, once for each field in the recordset. During each iteration, the variable *fld* points to a different Field object. If during a given iteration, the *fld* variable points to the *catnr* field, the following expressions are equivalent:

```
rsItm.Fields.catnr.Name
fld.Name
```

Of course, the value of either expression would be the string *"catnr"*. The following expressions are therefore equivalent:

```
fldNew(fld.Name) = fld.Value
fldNew("catnr") = rsItm.Fields.catnr.Value
fldNew("catnr") = rsItm("catnr")
```

The third statement is equivalent because Fields is the default collection of any Recordset object and *Value* is the default property of any Field object.

It should now be clear that the loop listed above copies each field in the *rsItm* recordset to a similarly named item in the *fldNew* Dictionary object. This cool piece of code concisely illustrates the value of Dictionary objects.

5. Tell VBScript that if a serious error occurs, it should continue with the next statement rather than displaying an error message and terminating the script:

```
On Error Resume Next
```

6. Delete the current record in the *rsItm* recordset:

```
rsItm.Delete
```

7. If the deletion failed, copy the ADO error message into the *fMsg* variable and replace each item in the *fldNew* Dictionary object with the corresponding value from the Request object. This undoes the action of copying the existing record contents into the *fldNew* Dictionary object in step 4.

```
If Err Then
  fMsg = "Delete failed: " & Err.Description
  For Each fld In fldNew
    fldNew(fld) = Request(fld)
  Next
```

Because it's enumerating the keys of a Dictionary object, this *For Each* loop puts ordinary string values (successively containing each key name) into the *fld* variable. If it were enumerating a collection of objects, it would put in successive pointers to those objects.

8. If the deletion succeeded, record the informational message "Record deleted" in the *iMsg* field and erase all entries in the *fldCur* Dictionary object:

```
Else
  iMsg = "Record deleted."
  fldCur.RemoveAll
End If
```

9. Revert to normal error handling and terminate the *If* statement begun in step 2:

```
On Error GoTo 0
End If
```

Process the Prev, Query, and Next transaction codes

The same code processes the *Prev*, *Query*, and *Next* transaction codes. Furthermore, it's refreshingly simple when compared to the code for add, change, and delete.

1. Initiate the case for all other transaction codes:

```
Case Else
```

2. Check to see if the *rsItm* recordset contains a record:

```
If rsItm.EOF Then
```

3. If it doesn't, record the fatal error message "Record not found" in the *fMsg* variable:

```
fMsg = "Record not found."
```

4. If the *rsItm* recordset does contain a record, copy its field values to the *fldCur* Dictionary object by calling the *CopyRsToCur* subroutine. Then clear the input fields on the outgoing form and remove all items from the *fldQry* Dictionary object:

```
Else
   CopyRsToCur
   fldQry.removeall
```

5. Terminate the *If* statement begun in step 2 and the *Select Case* statement begun in step 1 of the procedure for processing the *Add* transaction code:

```
   End If
End Select
```

Clean up and terminate

To complete the processing for any transaction code, follow these steps:

1. Close the Recordset and Connection objects created in the earlier section "Create and open a recordset for the *items* table."

```
rsItm.Close
set rsItm = Nothing
cnHol.Close
set cnHol = Nothing
```

2. Terminate the *If* statement begun in step 1 of the earlier section "Create and open a recordset for the *items* table."

```
End If
```

3. The Web page contains a single text box for both input and output of the *title* field and only one text box for the *caption* field as well. Normally, these two boxes display the *fldNew("title")* and *fldNew("caption")* dictionary items, respectively. This is fine if the *fldNew* Dictionary object contains echoed input values, but useless for displaying current record values. Therefore, the following statements check these two *fldNew* items and, if they're blank, replace them with the corresponding *fldCur* values:

```
If fldNew("title") = "" Then fldNew("title") = fldCur("title")
If fldNew("caption") = "" Then fldNew("caption") = fldCur("caption")
```

Write the CopyRsToCur *subroutine*

The code for transaction codes *A*, *C*, *P*, *Q*, and *N* calls the *CopyRsToCur* subroutine to copy the contents of a current *items* record to the *fldCur* Dictionary object. Here's the code:

```
Sub CopyRsToCur ()
  For Each fld In rsItm.Fields
    fldCur(fld.Name) = fld.Value
  Next
End Sub
```

Write the CopyNewToRs *function*

The *CopyNewToRs* function, used in the *Add* and *Change* transactions, updates each field in the *rsItm* recordset's current record with the corresponding value from the *fldNew* Dictionary object—provided the dictionary value isn't empty. If ADO reports that the recordset can't accept any field, the function stores the ADO error message in the *fldMsg* Dictionary object, cancels the update, and exits returning an error message. If there are no field errors, the function tells ADO to update the record. If this is successful, the function returns an empty string. If it isn't successful, the function returns the ADO error message.

Here are the steps required to code the *CopyNewToRs* function:

1. Declare the function, expecting no arguments:

```
function CopyNewToRs()
```

2. Initialize the *fldFail* variable, and tell VBScript that if a serious error occurs, it should continue with the next statement rather than displaying an error message and terminating the script:

```
fldFail = False
On Error Resume Next
```

3. Code a loop that iterates through each field in the *rsItm* recordset:

```
For Each fld In rsItm.Fields
'   Code to process each field will go here.
  Next
```

4. For each field, determine if the similarly named item in the *fldNew* Dictionary object is empty.

- If so, take no action.

- If the *fldNew* item contains data, copy it into the current recordset field.

- If copying the *fldNew* value into the current recordset field results in an error, take two actions. First, store the ADO error message in a *fldMsg* item whose key equals the current field name. Second, set the *fldFail* variable to True.

The loop now looks like this:

```
For Each fld In rsItm.Fields
  If fldNew(fld.Name) <> "" Then
    fld.Value = fldNew(fld.Name)
    If Err Then
      fldMsg(fld.Name) = Err.Description
      fldFail = True
    End If
  End If
Next
```

5. If the loop completes and the *fldFail* variable is True, tell ADO to cancel the update and set the function's return value to the message "Update canceled because of field errors."

```
If fldFail Then
  rsItm.CancelUpdate
  CopyNewToRs = "Update canceled because of field errors."
Else
```

6. If the loop completes and the *fldFail* variable is still False, tell ADO to update the record. If ADO returns an error code, set the function's return value to the ADO message. If ADO reports success, set the function's return value to an empty string:

```
rsItm.Update
If Err Then
  CopyNewToRs = "Update failed: " & Err.Description
  rsItm.CancelUpdate
Else
  CopyNewToRs = ""
End If
```

7. Terminate the *If* statement begun in step 5, resume normal error handling, and exit the function:

```
  End If
  On Error GoTo 0
End Function
```

Write the GetNextPrevKey subroutine

The *Next* and *Prev* transactions are designed to work with imprecise keys and should therefore return some kind of result no matter what input the Web visitor supplies. Because of this, and because essentially the same code needs to run in two different places, it makes sense to code it as a subroutine.

The *GetNextPrevKey* subroutine stores a starting category number in a variable named *keyCatNr* and a starting sequence number in a variable named *keySeqNr*. Code elsewhere in the Web page defined these fields outside the scope of any subroutine or function, making them globally available to all code in the page. Code elsewhere in the page will locate the record whose key (in the case of the *Next* transaction) is greater than *keyCatNr* and *keySeqNr* or whose key (in the case of the *Prev* transaction) is just less than these values.

The following steps create the code for the *GetNextPrevKey* subroutine:

1. Declare the subroutine, expecting one argument. This argument will supply a default value in case the subroutine can't locate a category number or a sequence number:

```
Sub GetNextPrevKey (argDft)
```

2. Search the following locations, in order, for a nonempty category number:

- The *qcatnr* field in the query box

- The *hcatnr* field recorded by the previous transaction

- The *catnr* field in the New column

    If all of these are empty, assign the default value to the *keyCatNr* and *keySeqNr* variables. If one of them contains data, assign both the *catnr* and *seqnr* values from that location to the *keyCatNr* and *keySeqNr* fields:

```
If Request("qcatnr") = "" Then
  If Request("hcatnr") = "" Then
    If Request("catnr") = "" Then
      keyCatNr = argDft
      keySeqNr = argDft
    Else
      keyCatNr = Request("catnr")
      keySeqNr = Request("seqnr")
    End If
  Else
    keyCatNr = Request("hcatnr")
    keySeqNr = Request("hseqnr")
  End If
Else
  keyCatNr = Request("qcatnr")
  keySeqNr = Request("qseqnr")
End If
```

3. If the keySeqNr field is still empty, assign the default value:

```
If keySeqNr = "" Then
  keySeqNr = argDft
End If
```

4. Terminate the subroutine:

```
End Sub
```

Reviewing the Complete Holiday Item Maintenance Page

In the interest of brevity, a complete copy of this Web page—including both HTML and ASP code—won't appear here. You can find a copy in the companion CD files at \webdbdev\ch08\picmaint.asp; open it and inspect it at your leisure. The section titled "Code the static HTML," earlier in this chapter, explains the salient features of the HTML code.

The complete VBScript code to process all six transaction types follows. All this code belongs in the <head> section of the Web page. When it finishes executing, all that remains is to display its results using <%=expression %> tags.

```
<%
' Define CopyRsToCur subroutine.
Sub CopyRsToCur ()
  For Each fld In rsItm.Fields
    fldCur(fld.Name) = fld.Value
  Next
End Sub
' Define CopyNewToRs function.
Function CopyNewToRs()
  fldFail = False
  On Error Resume Next
' Loop through and update each field in the rsItm recordset.
  For Each fld In rsItm.Fields
    If fldNew(fld.Name) <> "" Then
      fld.Value = fldNew(fld.Name)
      If Err Then
        fldMsg(fld.Name) = Err.Description
        fldFail = True
      End If
    End If
  Next
' Check for field errors; cancel update if found.
  If fldFail Then
    rsItm.CancelUpdate
    CopyNewToRs = "Update canceled because of field errors."
  Else
' Proceed with record update if there were no field errors.
    rsItm.Update
    If Err Then
      CopyNewToRs = "Update failed: " & Err.Description
    Else
      CopyNewToRs = ""
    End If
  End If
  On Error GoTo 0
End Function
' Define GetNextPrevKey subroutine.
```

```
Sub  GetNextPrevKey (argDft)
    If Request("qcatnr") = "" Then
       If Request("hcatnr") = "" Then
          If Request("catnr") = "" Then
             keyCatNr = argDft
             keySeqNr = argDft
          Else
             keyCatNr = Request("catnr")
             keySeqNr = Request("seqnr")
          End If
       Else
          keyCatNr = Request("hcatnr")
          keySeqNr = Request("hseqnr")
       End If
    Else
       keyCatNr = Request("qcatnr")
       keySeqNr = Request("qseqnr")
    End If
    If keySeqNr = "" Then
       keySeqNr = argDft
    End If
End Sub
' Create Dictionary objects.
Set fldQry = Server.CreateObject("Scripting.Dictionary")
Set fldCur = Server.CreateObject("Scripting.Dictionary")
Set fldNew = Server.CreateObject("Scripting.Dictionary")
Set fldMsg = Server.CreateObject("Scripting.Dictionary")
' Initialize global variables.
fMsg = ""
iMsg = ""
keyCatNr = ""
keySeqNr = ""
fldFail = False
' Determine and validate specified transaction code.
trancd = UCase(Left(Request("btnSub"),1))
If trancd = "" Then
  trancd = "Q"
Else
  If instr("PQNACD", trancd) = 0 Then
    trancd = "Q"
  End If
End If
' Determine what key fields to use depending on transaction code.
Select Case trancd
  Case "A"
    keyCatNr = Request("catnr")
    keySeqNr = Request("seqnr")
```

(continued)

```
      Case "C"
        keyCatNr = Request("hcatnr")
        keySeqNr = Request("hseqnr")
      Case "D"
        keyCatNr = Request("hcatnr")
        keySeqNr = Request("hseqnr")
      Case "N"
        GetNextPrevKey (0)
      Case "P"
        GetNextPrevKey (clng(&h7FFFFFFF))
      Case Else ' Default transaction code is "Q"
        keyCatNr = Request("qcatnr")
        keySeqNr = Request("qseqnr")
        fldQry("qcatnr") = Request("qcatnr")
        fldQry("qseqnr") = Request("qseqnr")
    End Select
    ' Save input fields for transaction codes A, C, and D.
    If trancd < "E" Then
      fldNew("catnr") = Request("catnr")
      fldNew("seqnr") = Request("seqnr")
      fldNew("picname") = Request("picname")
      fldNew("picdate") = Request("picdate")
      fldNew("title") = Request("title")
      fldNew("caption") = Request("caption")
    End If
    ' Check for missing or invalid key values.
    If keyCatNr = "" Then
      fMsg = "Enter category number."
    Else
      If Not IsNumeric(keyCatNr) Then
        fMsg = "Category must be numeric."
      End If
    End If
    If fMsg = "" Then
      If keySeqNr = "" Then
        fMsg = "Enter sequence number."
      Else
        If Not IsNumeric(keySeqNr) Then
          fMsg = "Sequence must be numeric."
        End If
      End If
    End If
    ' Process transaction if no fatal errors have yet been noted.
    If fMsg = "" Then
    ' Create and open ADO Connection object.
      Set cnHol = Server.CreateObject("ADODB.Connection")
      cnStHol = "driver={Microsoft Access Driver (*.mdb)};" & _
                "dbq=" & Server.MapPath("../holiday/holiday.mdb")
      cnHol.Open cnStHol,"",""
```

```
' Create and open ADO Recordset object.
' Transaction codes N and P require different WHERE clauses
' than transaction codes A, C, D, and Q.
  Set rsItm = Server.CreateObject("ADODB.Recordset")
  Select Case trancd
    Case "N"
      sql = "SELECT * FROM items " & _
            "WHERE ((catnr = " & keyCatNr & ") AND " & _
                "(seqnr > " & keySeqNr & ")) " & _
              "OR (catnr > " & keyCatNr & ") " & _
            "ORDER BY catnr, seqnr ; "
    Case "P"
      sql = "SELECT * FROM items " & _
            "WHERE ((catnr = " & keyCatNr & ") AND " & _
                "(seqnr < " & keySeqNr & ")) " & _
              "OR (catnr < " & keyCatNr & ") " & _
            "ORDER BY catnr DESC, seqnr DESC ; "
    Case Else
      sql = "SELECT * " & _
              "FROM items " & _
              "WHERE (catnr = " & keyCatNr & ") " & _
              "AND (seqnr = " & keySeqNr & ") ; "
  End Select
  rsItm.Open sql, cnHol, adOpenDynamic, adLockOptimistic
' Process each transaction code.
  Select Case trancd
' Process Add transaction.
    Case "A"
      If rsItm.EOF Then
        rsItm.AddNew
        fMsg = CopyNewToRs
        If fMsg = "" Then
          iMsg = "Record added."
          fldNew.RemoveAll
          CopyRsToCur
        End If
      Else
        fMsg = "Record already exists."
        CopyRsToCur
      End If
' Process Change transaction.
    Case "C"
      If rsItm.EOF Then
        fMsg = "Record not found."
      Else
        fMsg = CopyNewToRs
        If fMsg = "" Then
          iMsg = "Record changed."
          fldNew.RemoveAll
```

(continued)

```
                End If
                CopyRsToCur
             End If
' Process Delete transaction.
          Case "D"
             If rsItm.EOF Then
                fMsg - "Record not found."
             Else
                For Each fld In rsItm.Fields
                   fldNew(fld.Name) = fld.Value
                Next
                On Error Resume Next
                rsItm.Delete
                If Err Then
                   fMsg = "Delete failed: " & Err.Description
                   For Each fld In fldNew
                      fldNew(fld) = Request(fld)
                   Next
                Else
                   iMsg = "Record deleted."
                   fldCur.RemoveAll
                End If
                On Error GoTo 0
             End If
' Process Prev, Query, and Next transactions.
          Case Else
             If rsItm.EOF Then
                fMsg = "Record not found."
             Else
                CopyRsToCur
                fldQry.RemoveAll
             End If
       End Select
' Close ADO Recordset and Connection objects.
       rsItm.Close
       set rsItm = Nothing
       cnHol.Close
       set cnHol = Nothing
    End If
' Make sure the current record values for Title and Caption
' get displayed whenever possible (that is, whenever the
' relevant items in the fldNew Dictionary object don't already
' contain values).
If fldNew("title") = "" Then fldNew("title") = fldCur("title")
If fldNew("caption") = "" Then fldNew("caption") = fldCur("caption")
%>
```

Chapter Summary

This chapter explained how to write a single Web database page that adds, changes, and deletes records in the Holiday Photo Catalog *items* table. The same Web page can query the items table for specific keys, and move forward and backward one record at a time. The query and movement functions are designed to locate records for updating or deletion. This is easily the most complex Web database page presented so far, but also the most powerful.

Chapter 9, "Updating Tables via Multiple Web Pages," will present another method to accomplish the same objective—one involving more (but simpler) Web pages.

Updating Tables via Multiple Web Pages

| **Chapter Objectives** | Estimated Time: 35 minutes |

In this chapter, you'll learn how to

- Create a frameset that finds and updates records in a database table.

- Control interaction among frames in the same frameset.

The Holiday Item Maintenance page in Chapter 8, "Updating Tables from a General Purpose Form," illustrates a common approach to updating tables: a single screen provides all the maintenance functions for all the fields in a table. By changing the numbers and names of the input fields, you can modify this approach to update almost any table you choose.

Although highly general, this approach doesn't fully integrate with the rest of the Holiday Photo Catalog application. To see the effect of changes, you must either leave the item maintenance page and display the photo catalog main menu or keep two browser windows open: one for maintenance and one for viewing.

This chapter demonstrates a second solution to the problem addressed in Chapter 8. This solution differs from the previous one by navigating through the database for maintenance in the same way as the viewing application presented in Chapter 7, "Running and Displaying Queries." In fact, the solution will add viewing as an integral part of the maintenance function.

Introducing the Holiday Photo Update Application

The initial Web page for this second approach to maintenance appears in Figure 9-1. If this page seems remarkably familiar, you undoubtedly recall the Holiday Photo Catalog main menu shown back in Figure 7-3 on page 186. In fact, there are only two differences:

- The heading text and page title are "Holiday Photo Update" rather than "Holiday Photo Catalog."

- Clicking the link for any category requests a frameset page called itmmaint.asp rather than the catalog.asp frameset page described in Chapter 7.

As Figure 9-2 reveals, the itmmaint.asp frameset is quite similar to its cousin from Chapter 7.

Figure 9-1   *The hyperlinks in this main menu differ from those in the Holiday Photo Catalog main menu only by specifying a different frameset.*

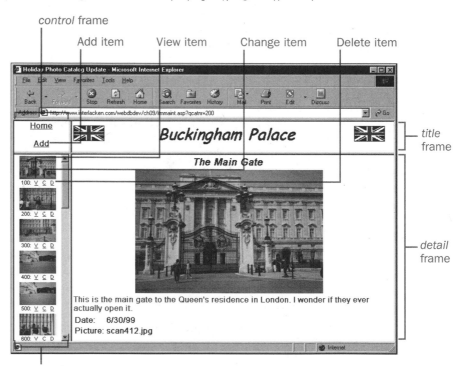

Figure 9-2   *All the hyperlinks on the Holiday Photo Catalog Update main menu link to this page, which not only displays photos in that category but also provides hyperlinks for adding, viewing, changing, and deleting records in the* items *table.*

However, there are several important differences:

- The control frame, at the top left corner, displays not only a link to the home page, but also a link for adding new records. Clicking the Add link displays the HTML form shown in the bottom-right frame in Figure 9-3. The Web page that displays this form is itmadd.asp.

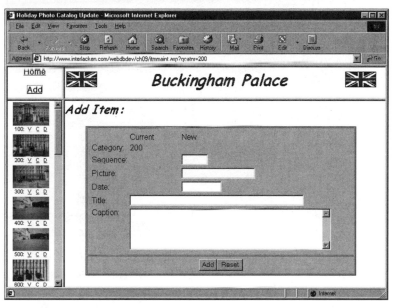

Figure 9-3 *This Web page displays an HTML form that adds records to the* items *table.*

For simplicity, the itmadd.asp page can add records within the current category number only. As a result, the itmadd.asp page has no text box for the category number field; instead, it gets this information from the requesting hyperlink (for example, *<a href="itmadd.asp?qcatnr=200">*). To customize this hyperlink, the itmmaint.asp frame-set loads the control frame with a page named control.asp, passing it the category number as a query string. The control.asp page then incorporates this value when it builds the hyperlink that requests itmadd.asp.

- Located directly beneath the *control* frame is the *itmlist* frame, which displays a Web page named itmlist.asp. Unlike the piclist.asp page that occupied this position in Chapter 7 and displayed each picture's download size, the itmlist.asp page displays each picture's sequence number and the following three hyperlinks:

  - *V* loads a page that displays the full-size image corresponding to the thumbnail. It does so by loading the *detail* frame (the large frame at the bottom right corner of the window) with the picshow.asp page developed in Chapter 7.

- *C* displays an HTML form that can update the *items* record that corresponds to the thumbnail. Figure 9-4 shows this form. The Web page that displays this form is named itmchange.asp.

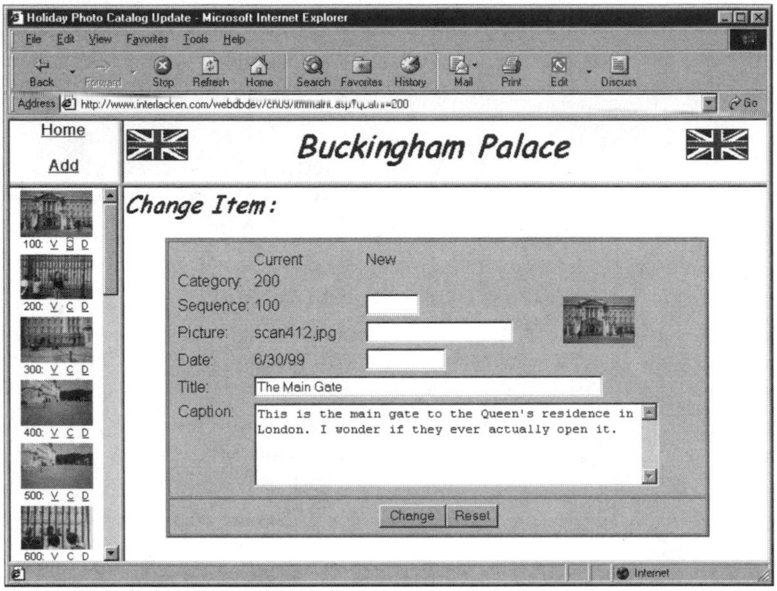

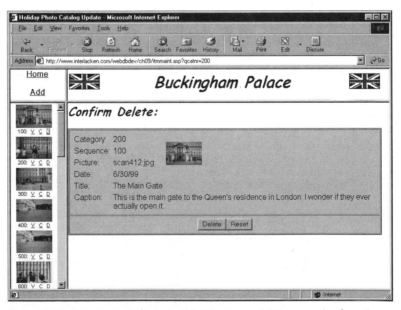

Figure 9-4 *This Web page displays an HTML form that changes records in the* items *table.*

- *D* displays a form that can delete the *items* record for the current thumbnail. A Web page named itmdelete.asp displays this form, with results shown in Figure 9-5.

Figure 9-5 *The HTML form in this Web page deletes records from the* items *table.*

- The *title* frame in the top right corner displays the title.asp page precisely as developed in Chapter 7.

- The *detail* frame in the bottom right corner initially displays the picshow.asp page. This page is unchanged from Chapter 7, but the method of loading it is different. In Chapter 7, the frameset initially displayed a page called blank.htm and then, when the server generated the piclist.asp page, the ASP code created a browser-side script that replaced blank.htm with picshow.asp. The browser-side script also told that page (via the query string) which category and sequence numbers it should display.

  In this chapter, the itmmaint.asp frameset loads the picshow.asp page directly, specifying (via the query string) the category number but not the sequence number. The picshow.asp page responds by displaying the first sequence number within the given category, which—initially—is always the correct one.

  Following its initial load, the *detail* frame displays any of the following four pages, depending on which hyperlinks the Web visitor clicks in the *control* or *itmlist* frames: picshow.asp, itmadd.asp, itmchange.asp, or itmdelete.asp. In every case except itmadd.asp, these pages display the record with the category number and sequence number associated with the hyperlink that loads them. The itmadd.asp page initially displays only the category number.

Adding, changing, or deleting any record in the *items* table makes the thumbnail listing in the *itmlist* frame out of date. Therefore, whenever one of these operations succeeds, the corresponding Web response contains not only a message to the Web visitor, but also a script that tells the browser to reload itmlist.asp.

Reloading the itmlist.asp page solves the problem of the *itmlist* frame being out of date but has the unfortunate side effect of positioning the list to the top. To position the refreshed list so that the item just maintained is visible, a couple of things need to happen:

- As the itmlist.asp page creates the anchor tag surrounding each thumbnail picture, it assigns an anchor name consisting of the letter *s* followed by the sequence number. For example, here's the anchor tag that itmlist.asp would create for category 200, sequence number 500. The code that defines the anchor name appears in blue.

```
<a name=s500
   href=../ch07/picshow.asp?qcatnr=200&qseqnr=500
   target=detail>
<img src=../holiday/images/thumb/scan416.jpg
     border=0
     alt="Inside The Gates">
</a>
```

- Whenever an itmadd.asp or itmchange.asp page updates the *items* table and reloads the *itmlist* frame, the page also updates that frame's target location to include an anchor name that points to the record just added or changed.

If, for example, the itmchange.asp page updated the *items* record for category 200, sequence number 500, it would change the target location of the *itmlist* frame to the following location. The code that positions to the correct anchor name appears in blue.

```
itmlist.asp?qcatnr=200#s500
```

This URL tells the browser to request the itmlist.asp page from the server, and to send that page the value *qcatnr=200* as a query string. It also tells the browser that when the Web server responds, the browser should position the page to the anchor name *s500*.

Because updating the *detail* frame can make the *itmtlist* frame reload, updating the *itmlist* frame shouldn't make the *detail* frame reload. This would replace the *detail* frame before the Web visitor could read any messages it displayed. That's why, on initial load, the frameset loads picshow.asp directly into the *detail* frame rather than (as in Chapter 7) loading a blank page into the *detail* frame and having the thumbnail page replace it.

There are two more questions to consider before examining the code for each Web page in the itmmaint.asp frameset. Both involve maintenance to category numbers:

• Should the Add and Delete transactions allow Web visitors to add or delete records in categories not currently on display?

• Should the Change transaction allow Web visitors to move records in and out of the category currently on display?

The answer is no in both cases. This simplifies the example and ensures that the Web visitor receives full visual feedback on the effect of all changes.

Building the Item Update Frameset

This section is the first of several that will describe each Web page new to the Holiday Photo Update application. For descriptions of the default.asp menu page, the title.asp title page, and the picshow.asp detail page, refer back to Chapter 7.

The itmmaint.asp frameset consists almost entirely of ordinary HTML. There are only two instances of ASP code. The first uses the following statements to verify the presence of a correct category number. If the correct number isn't present, the code substitutes the default category 100.

```
catnr = Request("qcatnr")
If catnr = "" Then catnr = 100
If Not IsNumeric(catnr) Then catnr = 100
```

The second use of ASP code inserts the *catnr* value developed above into the query string portion of the URLs that load the *title, control, itmlist,* and *detail* frames. This accounts for the four blue <%=*catnr*%> expressions in the complete HTML listing shown here:

```
<html>
<head>
<title>Holiday Photo Catalog</title>
<%
catnr = Request("qcatnr")
If catnr = "" Then catnr = 100
If Not IsNumeric(catnr) Then catnr = 100
%>
</head>
<frameset rows="65,*">
  <frameset cols="115,99%">
    <frame name="control"
           src="control.asp?qcatnr=<%=catnr%>"
           target="_self"
           noresize scrolling="no"
           marginwidth="0" marginheight="0">
    <frame name="title"
           src="../ch07/title.asp?qcatnr=<%=catnr%>"
           marginwidth="0" marginheight="0">
  </frameset>
  <frameset cols="115,99%">
    <frame name="itmlist"
           src="itmlist.asp?qcatnr=<%=catnr%>"
           scrolling="auto" noresize
           marginwidth="0" marginheight="0">
    <frame name="detail"
           src="../ch07/picshow.asp?qcatnr=<%=catnr%>"
           scrolling="auto" target="_self"
           marginwidth="0" marginheight="0">
  </frameset>
  <noframes>
  <body>
  <p>This page uses frames, but your browser doesn't support
     them.</p>
  </body>
  </noframes>
</frameset>
</html>
```

Building the Control Page

The control page is even simpler than the Item Update frameset. Its content consists solely of two hyperlinks, one of which links to the home page in a perfectly ordinary way. The other hyperlink loads the itmadd.asp page into the *detail* frame, specifying a query string of *?qcatnr=<%=request("qcatnr")%>*. This ensures that whatever *qcatnr* value the control.asp page receives, itmadd.asp will also receive that value.

```
<html>
<head>
<title>Holiday Photo Catalog</title>
<link rel="stylesheet" type="text/css"
      href="../holiday/holiday.css">
</head>
<body>
<p align="center">
  <a href="default.asp" target="_top">Home</a></p>
<p align="center">
  <a href="itmadd.asp?qcatnr=<%=request("qcatnr")%>"
      target="detail">Add</a></p>
</body>
</html>
```

Building the Item List Page

The itmlist.asp page greatly resembles the piclist.asp page in Chapter 7. First it queries the *items* table for all records in a given category. For each record found, it then displays the corresponding thumbnail image and some hyperlinks in one row of an HTML table.

Here's the HTML for a typical row in the table created by itmlist.asp. Characters in blue will vary based on the current *items* record. The Web page needs to repeat this code once for each record in the given category.

```
<tr><td>
' Hyperlink and image tag for thumbnail picture.
<a name=s100
    href=../ch07/picshow.asp?qcatnr=200&qseqnr=100
    target=detail>
<img src=../holiday/images/thumb/scan412.jpg
    border=0 alt="The Main Gate">
</a>
' Caption for thumbnail picture.
<br>100:  
' Hyperlink for code V (View).
<a href=../ch07/picshow.asp?qcatnr=200&qseqnr=100
    target=detail>V</a>
  
' Hyperlink for code C (Change).
<a href=itmchange.asp?qcatnr=200&qseqnr=100 target=detail>C</a>
  
' Hyperlink for code D (Delete).
<a href=itmdelete.asp?qcatnr=200&qseqnr=100 target=detail>D</a>
</td></tr>
```

Create the item list page

If you understood the HTML code in the previous section and you understood the piclist.asp page from Chapter 7, you might already have all the explanation you need. If not, take a look at the following steps for coding this page.

1. Starting with an empty Web page, enter the basic HTML tags, an *include* statement for the adovbs.inc file, and any style sheet information you want. The following code is used for itmlist.asp.

```
<html>
<head>
<title>Holiday Photo Update List</title>
<!-- #include file="../adovbs.inc" -->
<link rel="stylesheet" type="text/css"
      href="../holiday/holiday.css">
</head>
<body>
</body>
</html>
```

2. Verify that the page has received an acceptable category number. If it hasn't, substitute the default category 100. To do this, add the following statements just before the </head> tag.

```
<%
catnr = Request("qcatnr")
If catnr = "" Then catnr = 100
If Not IsNumeric(catnr) Then catnr = 100
%>
```

3. Insert the following code between the <body> and </body> tags. This code creates, opens, closes, and destroys an ADO Connection object.

```
<%
Set cnHol = Server.CreateObject("ADODB.Connection")
cnStHol = "driver={Microsoft Access Driver (*.mdb)};" & _
          "dbq=" & Server.MapPath("../holiday/holiday.mdb")
cnHol.Open cnStHol,"",""
' Statements to create, open, process, close, and destroy a
' recordset containing the requested item records will go here.
cnHol.Close
Set cnHol = Nothing
%>
```

4. Replace the comments in step 3 with the following code. This code creates, opens, closes, and destroys an ADO Recordset object containing all *items* records for the requested category in sequence number order.

```
Set rsItm = Server.CreateObject("ADODB.Recordset")
sql = "SELECT * " & _
      "FROM items " & _
```

(continued)

```
                    "WHERE (catnr=" & catnr & ") " & _
                    "ORDER BY seqnr "
        rsItm.Open sql, cnHol, adOpenStatic, adLockReadOnly
        ' Statements to process the recordset will go here.
        rsItm.Close
        rsItm = Nothing
```

5. Replace the comment in step 4 with the following statements. These statements delimit the HTML table that will organize the thumbnail pictures and hyperlinks.

```
        Response.Write "<table align=center>" & vbCrLf
        ' Statements to process the recordset will go here.
        Response.Write "</table>" & vbCrLf
```

6. Replace the comment in step 5 with the following code. This code reads through all the records in the *rsItm* recordset.

```
        Do While Not rsItm.EOF
        '    Statements to process each record will go here.
          rsItm.MoveNext
        Loop
```

7. The HTML to display each thumbnail picture should follow the model shown at the beginning of this section. To create this HTML for the current items record, replace the comment in step 6 with the following code.

```
        ' Construct the query string for the picshow.asp,
        ' itmadd.asp, and itmdelete.asp pages.
          qstring = "?qcatnr=" & rsItm("catnr") & _
                    "&qseqnr=" & rsItm("seqnr")
        ' Select the tooltip text.
          tip = rsItm("title")
          If tip = "" Then
            tip = rsItm("picname")
          End If
        ' Begin a new table row and cell.
          Response.Write "<tr><td class=pic align=center>" & vbCrLf
        ' Write the hyperlink and image tab for the thumbnail picture.
          Response.Write _
              "<a name=s" & rsItm("seqnr") & _
                " href=../ch07/picshow.asp" & qstring & _
                " target=detail>" & _
            "<img src=../holiday/images/thumb/" & _
                rsItm("picname") & _
                " border=0" & _
                " alt=" & Chr(34) & tip & Chr(34) & _
                "></a>"
        ' Start a new line beneath the thumbnail picture.
          Response.Write "<br>" & vbCrLf
```

```
' Display the sequence number and some white space.
   Response.Write rsItm("seqnr") & ":  "
' Display the V(iew) hyperlink.
   Response.Write _
      "<a href=../ch07/picshow.asp" & qstring & _
      " target=detail>V</a>  " & vbCrLf
' Display the C(hange) hyperlink.
   Response.Write _
      "<a href=itmchange.asp" & qstring & _
      " target=detail>C</a>  " & vbCrLf
' Display the D(elete) hyperlink.
   Response.Write _
      "<a href=itmdelete.asp" & qstring & _
      " target=detail>D</a> " & vbCrLf
' End the table row and cell.
   Response.Write "</td></tr>" & vbCrLf
```

Notice that the *catnr*, *seqnr*, *title*, and *picname* fields come from the current record in the *rsItm* recordset.

The *alt* attribute in the thumbnail picture's <img> tag will contain either the picture's title or, if that's blank, the picture's file name. If the Web visitor's browser doesn't display pictures, it will display this text instead. If the browser does display pictures, it will display this text whenever the Web visitor holds the mouse pointer over the picture.

This completes the coding for the itmlist.asp page. The complete HTML listing is shown here. If you understood the preceding seven steps, this listing shouldn't contain any surprises.

```
</html>
<html>
<head>
<title>Holiday Photo Update List</title>
<!-- #include file="../adovbs.inc" -->
<link rel="stylesheet" type="text/css"
      href="../holiday/holiday.css">
<%
' Check for valid requested category.
' Revert to the default (100) if necessary.
catnr = Request("qcatnr")
If catnr = "" Then catnr = 100
If Not IsNumeric(catnr) Then catnr = 100
%>
</head>
<body>
<%
```

(continued)

```
' Create and open ADO Connection object.
Set cnHol = Server.CreateObject("ADODB.Connection")
cnStHol = "driver={Microsoft Access Driver (*.mdb)};" & _
          "dbq=" & Server.MapPath("../holiday/holiday.mdb")
cnHol.Open cnStHol,"",""
' Create and open the ADO Recordset object.
Set rsItm = Server.CreateObject("ADODB.Recordset")
sql = "SELECT * " & _
        "FROM items " & _
        "WHERE (catnr=" & catnr & ") " & _
        "ORDER BY seqnr "
rsItm.Open sql, cnHol, adOpenStatic, adLockReadOnly
' Begin HTML table.
Response.Write "<table align=center>" & vbCrLf
' Loop through all matching item records, creating
' an HTML table row for each one.
Do While Not rsItm.EOF
' Construct the query string for the picshow.asp,
' itmadd.asp, and itmdelete.asp pages.
  qstring = "?qcatnr=" & rsItm("catnr") & _
              "&qseqnr=" & rsItm("seqnr")
' Select the tooltip text.
  tip = rsItm("title")
  If tip = "" Then
    tip = rsItm("picname")
  End If
' Begin a new table row and cell.
  Response.Write "<tr><td class=pic align=center>" & vbCrLf
' Write the hyperlink and image tab for the thumbnail picture.
  Response.Write _
    "<a name=s" & rsItm("seqnr") & _
      " href=../ch07/picshow.asp" & qstring & _
      " target=detail>" & _
    "<img src=../holiday/images/thumb/" & _
      rsItm("picname") & _
      " border=0" & _
      " alt=" & Chr(34) & tip & Chr(34) & _
      "></a>"
' Start a new line beneath the thumbnail picture.
Response.Write "<br>" & vbCrLf
' Display the sequence number and some white space.
  Response.Write rsItm("seqnr") & ":  "
' Display the V(iew) hyperlink.
  Response.Write _
    "<a href=../ch07/picshow.asp" & qstring & _
      " target=detail>V</a>  " & vbCrLf
' Display the C(hange) hyperlink.
  Response.Write _
    "<a href=itmchange.asp" & qstring & _
      " target=detail>C</a>  " & vbCrLf
```

```
' Display the D(elete) hyperlink.
  Response.Write _
    "<a href=itmdelete.asp" & qstring & _
    " target=detail>D</a> " & vbCrLf
' End the table row and cell.
  Response.Write "</td></tr>" & vbCrLf
  rsItm.MoveNext
Loop
' End HTML table.
Response.Write "</table>" & vbCrLf
' Close and destroy Recordset object.
rsItm.Close
Set rsItm = Nothing
' Close and destroy Connection object.
cnHol.Close
Set cnHol = Nothing
%>
</body>
</html>
```

Building the Holiday Item Add Page

When initially displayed, the Item Add page—itmadd.asp—shows an HTML form with a row of display fields for each field in the *items* table. The first column of this display contains field names. The second column, Current, displays the content of a current *items* record. The third column, New, contains a text box where the Web visitor can enter new values for each field except category number. The last column, Error, is displayed only when an error occurs. This column displays any error messages that pertain to a particular field. The Item Add page appeared in Figure 9-3.

When first displayed, the Current column shows only the category number (if any) specified in the hyperlink that requested the page. All the other fields and columns are blank. The Web visitor fills in the remaining fields and then clicks the Add button.

At this point, the Item Add page builds a new *items* record containing the preset category number and the visitor-specified sequence number, picture name, picture date, title, and caption. If this process succeeds, the values in the new record appear in the Current column and the text boxes in the New column turn blank (in preparation for adding another record). If the addition fails, the Current and New columns simply retain their values so that the Web visitor can correct them.

As you might suspect from its appearance, this page borrows heavily from the *Add* function in the Holiday Item Maintenance page (picmaint.asp) discussed in Chapter 8. However, several requirements are different as described on the following page.

- The itmadd.asp page requires no support for the following transaction codes: Prev, Next, Change, and Delete.

- The itmadd.asp page should only perform database operations when the Web visitor submits the HTML form (that is, only when the Web visitor clicks the Add button). When the Web visitor requests the page in some other way—such as clicking the Add hyperlink in the control.asp page—it should only display a blank form ready for input.

- The itmadd.asp page has no Query button. Instead, it automatically performs a query whenever category and sequence number fields contain nonempty numeric values.

- After successfully adding a record, the itmadd.asp page must refresh the contents of the *itmlist* frame.

Like the picmaint.asp page discussed in Chapter 8, the itmadd.asp page makes extensive use of Dictionary objects. Specifically, itmadd.asp uses the *fldCur*, *fldNew*, and *fldMsg* Dictionary objects described in Table 8-1 (on page 215). It does not, however, use the *fldQry* object described in that table.

Create the item add page

The HTML code for this page is quite conventional and thus warrants no special explanation. You can examine it by using any text editor to open the sample file ch09\itmadd.asp on the companion CD. All the Web database code resides in the <head> section; that's what the following steps describe.

1. Using any HTML or text editor, create a new Web page and lay out the HTML form shown in Figure 9-3. You must also make the following changes:

   - Under the Current column, display the ASP variables *keyCatNr*, *fldCur("seqnr")*, *fldCur("picname")*, and *fldCur("picdate")*.

   - Under the New column, display the ASP variables *fldNew("catnr")*, *fldNew("seqnr")*, *fldNew("picname")*, *fldNew("picdate")*, *fldNew("title")*, and *fldNew("caption")*.

   - Under the Error column, display the ASP variables *fldMsg("catnr")*, *fldMsg("seqnr")*, *fldMsg("picname")*, *fldMsg("picdate")*, *fldMsg("title")*, and *fldMsg("caption")*.

   - Name the Add button btnSub.

   - Define a hidden form field named *hcatnr* with a value equal to the ASP variable *keyCatNr*

   - Define a hidden form field named *add* that always contains the value *Y* Note that the itmadd.asp page will receive this value only when a Web visitor requests the page by submitting its HTML form. If the visitor requests the page some other way—perhaps by clicking an ordinary hyperlink—*request("add")* will be empty.

- Make sure an HTML form encloses all these fields listed above, and that the form's *action* property specifies the itmadd.asp page.

- In the top right corner, display the ASP variables *fMsg* and *iMsg*.

- To display the Error title only when an error occurs, code it as follows:

```
<% If fldError Then Response.Write "Error" %>
```

2. Insert the following lines anywhere in the <head> section (just before the </head> tag is a good place).

```
<%
Set fldCur = Server.CreateObject("Scripting.Dictionary")
Set fldNew = Server.CreateObject("Scripting.Dictionary")
Set fldMsg = Server.CreateObject("Scripting.Dictionary")
' Additional code will go here.
%>
```

This code creates three Dictionary objects named *fldCur*, *fldNew*, and *fldMsg*. Recall that Dictionary objects store collections of items (that is, values), each identified by an alphanumeric key.

3. Insert the following code just after the three *Set* statements in step 2. These statements initialize a variable for fatal error messages, a variable for informational messages, a variable that indicates an error has occurred while copying a value into the *items* table, and a variable that indicates whether this execution of the itmadd.asp page has successfully added a record.

```
fMsg = ""
iMsg = ""
fldError =   False
recAdded =   False
```

4. Step 1 defined two hidden form fields: *add* and *hcatnr*. The *add* field always contains *Y*, but this value will only appear in the Request collection when the Web visitor submits the form. In this case, the expression *Request.Form("add")* will equal *Y*.

   If the visitor requests the itmadd.asp page some other way, such as clicking the Add hyperlink in the control frame, *Request.Form("add")* will contain an empty value.

   If *Request.Form("add")* equals *Y*, the Web visitor has clicked the Add button and itmadd.asp should try to add an *items* record. To provide this behavior, the code below performs these actions:

- It saves the current category number (previously saved in the hidden form field *hcatnr*) and the desired sequence number (specified by the Web visitor in the text box named *seqnr*) in two variables named *keyCatNr* and *keySeqNr*.

- It executes a subroutine called *AddItemsRecord* that opens the database and adds a new record.

If *Request.Form("add")* doesn't contain *Y*, the Web visitor didn't press the Add button and *itmadd.asp* should simply display the form for input. Therefore, in this case, the code loads *keyCatNr* and *keySeqNr* from fields in the query string, loads those values into the *fldCur* Dictionary object for display, and exits.

```
addRec = UCase(Left(Request.Form("add"),1))
If addRec = "Y" Then
  keyCatNr = Request("hcatnr")
  keySeqNr = Request("seqnr")
  AddItemsRecord
Else
  keyCatNr = Request("qcatnr")
  keySeqNr = Request("qseqnr")
  fldCur("catnr") = keyCatNr
  fldNew("seqnr") = keySeqNr
End If
```

5. Begin coding the *AddItemsRecord* subroutine by inserting the following statements immediately after the statements you added in step 4.

```
Sub AddItemsRecord()
' Code to add items record goes here.
End Sub
```

6. The first step in adding an *items* record is to verify the existence of valid key values. Specifically, neither the category number nor the sequence number can be empty, and both fields must be numeric. The following statements check for these conditions and, upon finding one, place an appropriate error message in the *fMsg* variable. They should replace the comment in step 5.

```
If keyCatNr = "" Then
  fMsg = "Category number missing."
ElseIf keySeqNr = "" Then
  fMsg = "Sequence number missing."
ElseIf Not IsNumeric(keyCatNr) Then
  fMsg = "Catagory number invalid."
ElseIf Not IsNumeric(keySeqNr) Then
  fMsg = "Sequence number invalid."
End If
```

7. Next use the following statements to copy each value received in the Request.Form collection to a like-named value in the *fldNew* Dictionary object and to copy the saved *keyCatNr* value into that *Dictionary* object as well.

```
For Each fld in Request.Form
  fldNew(fld) = Request.Form(fld)
Next
fldNew("catnr") = keyCatNr
```

The *fldNew* object will provide all the field values for the new record. In addition, if adding that record fails, the *fldNew* object will return the values to the Web visitor for correction.

Note To iterate through a collection of Request values, you must iterate through a specific collection such as Request.QueryString or Request.Form. A For Each statement based on the Request object would sequentially return its five collections (ClientCertificate, Cookies, Form, QueryString, and ServerVariables) rather than the contents of those collections.

---

8. The following statements check to see whether the code run so far has detected a fatal error. If so, the *Exit Sub* statement exits the subroutine before attempting any database activity. Insert these statements immediately after the code added in step 7.

```
If fMsg <> "" Then
   Exit Sub
End If
```

9. Insert the following statements to open the database and query the *items* table for a record with the category number and sequence number the Web visitor wants to add.

```
cnStHol = "driver={Microsoft Access Driver (*.mdb)};" & _
          "dbq=" & Server.MapPath("../holiday/holiday.mdb")
Set rsItm = Server.CreateObject("ADODB.Recordset")
sql = "SELECT * " & _
        "FROM items " & _
        "WHERE (catnr = " & keyCatNr & ") " & _
        "AND (seqnr = " & keySeqNr & ") ; "
rsItm.Open sql, cnStHol, adOpenDynamic, adLockOptimistic
' Code to check for existing record (and, if none
' is found, to add a new one) goes here.
rsItm.Close
Set rsItm = Nothing
```

The *rsItm.Open* statement takes the shortcut of specifying a connection string rather than a connection object in the *Open* method's second argument. This saves a line of code but increases—slightly—the overhead of opening two or more recordsets. When a Web page opens only a single recordset, the additional overhead is nil.

10. The next step determines whether a record with the given category and sequence number already exists. This requires merely checking the recordset's *EOF* property. If the *EOF* property is *False*, the code should record a fatal error message and copy the existing record's contents into the *fldCur* Dictionary object for display to the Web visitor. If the recordset's *EOF* property is *True,* there's no existing record and the code can proceed to create one.

To implement this logic, insert the following statements in place of the two-line comment in step 9:

```
If Not rsItm.EOF Then
  fMsg = "Record already exists."
  For Each fld in rsItm.Fields
    fldCur(fld.Name) = fld.Value
  Next
Else
' Code to add a record goes here.
End If
```

11. To start creating the new record, first turn off normal error checking for a range of statements. Then, within that range, tell the *rsItm* recordset to create a buffer for the new record. The following statements, which replace the comment in step 10, accomplish this.

```
On Error Resume Next
rsItm.AddNew
'   Code to continue adding a record goes here.
On Error GoTo 0
```

12. Use a *For Each* loop to load each field in the new record buffer with the value from the *fldNew* Dictionary object, if one is present. If doing this for any field results in an error, first store the error message in the *fldMsg* Dictionary object, using the current field name as a key; and then record the fact that a field error has occurred by setting the *fldError* variable to *True*.

The following code, which replaces the comment in step 11, fulfills these requirements.

```
For Each fld in rsItm.Fields
  If fldNew(fld.Name) <> "" Then
    fld.Value = fldNew(fld.Name)
    If Err Then
      fldMsg(fld.Name) = Err.Description
      fldError = True
    End If
  End If
Next
'   Code to continue adding a record goes here.
```

Note that this code iterates through the *rsItm.Fields* collection and not through the items in the *fldNew* Dictionary object. This is because the *rsItm.Fields* collection is guaranteed to contain a correct set of field names, while the *fldNew* object isn't.

Some common errors that occur when adding field data are: values out of range (such as too large, too small, too short, or too long) and values that don't conform to the field's type (such as non-numeric values for a number field or nondate values for a date field).

If step 11 hadn't turned off error checking, attempting to store an invalid field value would have immediately terminated script processing for the ASP page. Instead, the script now performs its own error handling.

13. After the attempt to load the new *items* record with data, the next step determines whether any field errors occurred. The *fldError* variable provides this information. If *fldError* is *True*, the script needs to record a fatal error message and discard the new record in progress.

```
If fldError Then
  fMsg = "Addition cancelled because of field errors."
  rsItm.CancelUpdate
Else
'   Code to complete addition goes here.
End If
```

This code replaces the comment in step 12.

14. If no field errors occurred, there's nothing left to do but add the new record to the database. The recordset's *Update* method, coded in the first statement below, takes this action:

```
rsItm.Update
If Err Then
  fMsg = "Addition failed:" & Err.Description
  rsItm.CancelUpdate
Else
  iMsg = "Record added."
  recAdded = True
  For Each fld in rsItm.Fields
    fldCur(fld.Name) = fld.Value
  Next
  fldNew.RemoveAll
End If
```

Of course, any number of conditions could cause the *Update* method to fail. The new record could be missing a required field, for example. If the code detects such an error, it records a fatal error message and tells the recordset to discard the new, failed record.

If no errors occurred, the code records an informational message and sets the *recAdded* variable to *True*. Next, a *For Each* loop copies all the fields from the new record to the *fldCur* Dictionary object for display. Finally, the *fldNew.RemoveAll* statement erases all items in the *fldNew* Dictionary object, indirectly clearing all the HTML form's input fields so that the Web visitor can add another record.

15. At this point, all database processing is complete and the last two statements in step 9 can execute. However, two matters are left to consider. The first involves the *title* and *caption* fields.

Because of their length, these fields don't have separate form fields for a current value and a new value; there's only a *New* field. Therefore, if the value in the *fldNew* object (destined for the New column) is blank and the value in the *fldCur* object (which never gets displayed) isn't, the following statements copy the current values to the new values (that is, to the *fldNew* object):

```
If fldNew("title") = "" Then fldNew("title") = fldCur("title")
If fldNew("caption") = "" Then fldNew("caption") = fldCur("caption")
```

This code should appear after the code for all steps described above.

16. The second matter to consider applies only if the Web page succeeded in adding a record to the items table—that is, only if step 14 set the *recAdded* variable to *True*. In that case, the itmadd.asp page needs to contain a script that performs the following actions when it arrives at the browser:

- It updates the Web location displayed in the *itmlist* frame.

- It forces the *itmlist* frame to reload.

Here's a typical two-line script that performs these actions. Blue indicates the variable portions: *200* is the category to display and *50* is the sequence number for positioning the list.

```
<script>
parent.frames.itmlist.location = "itmlist.asp?qcatnr=200#s50"
parent.frames.itmlist.location.reload(true)
</script>
```

The following code creates these statements—provided the *recAdded* variable is *True*. This code should appear immediately after the code developed in step 15.

```
If recAdded Then
  Response.Write "<script>" & vbCrLf
  Response.Write "parent.frames.itmlist.location = " & _
    Chr(34) & _
    "itmlist.asp" & _
    "?qcatnr=" & keyCatNr & _
    "#s" & keySeqNr & _
    Chr(34) & vbCrLf
  Response.Write "parent.frames.itmlist.location.reload(true)" & vbCrLf
  Response.Write "</script>" & vbCrLf
End If
```

You've now completed the ASP code required in the itmadd.asp page. Here's the complete listing, with everything merged into the right place:

```
<%
' Create Dictionary objects.
Set fldCur = Server.CreateObject("Scripting.Dictionary")
Set fldNew = Server.CreateObject("Scripting.Dictionary")
Set fldMsg = Server.CreateObject("Scripting.Dictionary")
' Initialize global variables.
fMsg = ""
```

```
iMsg = ""
fldError = False
recAdded = False
' Determine whether request came from this page's HTML form.
addRec = UCase(Left(Request.Form("add"),1))
If addRec = "Y" Then
' If so, save appropriate keys and attempt database update.
  keyCatNr = Request("hcatnr")
  keySeqNr = Request("seqnr")
  AddItemsRecord
' If not, save alternate keys and just display form.
Else
  keyCatNr = Request("qcatnr")
  keySeqNr = Request("qseqnr")
  fldCur("catnr") = keyCatNr
  fldNew("seqnr") = keySeqNr
End If
Sub AddItemsRecord()
' Subroutine to add an items record.
' Validate key syntax; record error message if faulty.
  If keyCatNr = "" Then
    fMsg = "Category number missing."
  ElseIf keySeqNr = "" Then
    fMsg = "Sequence number missing."
  ElseIf Not IsNumeric(keyCatNr) Then
    fMsg = "Catagory number invalid."
  ElseIf Not IsNumeric(keySeqNr) Then
    fMsg = "Sequence number invalid."
  End If
' Copy form fields to fldNew Dictionary object.
  For Each fld in Request.Form
    fldNew(fld) = Request.Form(fld)
  Next
  fldNew("catnr") = keyCatNr
' Exit subroutine if a fatal error has occurred.
  If fMsg <> "" Then
    Exit Sub
  End If
' Build ADO connection string.
  cnStHol = "driver={Microsoft Access Driver (*.mdb)};" & _
            "dbq=" & Server.MapPath("../holiday/holiday.mdb")
' Create and open an ADO Recordset object.
  Set rsItm = Server.CreateObject("ADODB.Recordset")
  sql = "SELECT * " & _
        "FROM items " & _
        "WHERE (catnr = " & keyCatNr & ") " & _
          "AND (seqnr = " & keySeqNr & ") ; "
```

(continued)

```
        rsItm.Open sql, cnStHol, adOpenDynamic, adLockOptimistic
' If a matching record already exists, record an error
' message, copy the existing record to the curflds object
' for display, and exit.
    If Not rsItm.EOF Then
       fMsg = "Record already exists."
       For Each fld in rsItm.Fields
          fldCur(fld.Name) = fld.Value
       Next
    Else
' Turn off normal error checking. The script will detect
' and handle its own errors.
       On Error Resume Next
' If no matching record exists, initialize a new record
' and load its fields from the fldNew Dictionary object.
       rsItm.addnew
       For Each fld in rsItm.Fields
          If fldNew(fld.Name) <> "" Then
             fld.Value = fldNew(fld.Name)
' If a field error occurred, store it in the fldMsg
' Dictionary object for later display and set the
' fldError variable to True.
          If Err Then
             fldMsg(fld.Name) = Err.Description
             fldError = True
          End If
       End If
    Next
' If a field error occurred, record a fatal error message
' and cancel the update.
    If fldError Then
       fMsg = "Addition cancelled because of field errors."
       rsItm.CancelUpdate
' If no field error occurred, add the record to the database.
    Else
       rsItm.Update
' If the record can't be added, record a fatal error message
' and cancel the update.
       If Err Then
          fMsg = "Addition failed:" & Err.Description
          rsItm.CancelUpdate
' If the record addition succeeded, record an informational
' message, copy the new record to the fldCur Dictionary object,
' and clear all entries in the fldNew Dictionary object.
       Else
          iMsg = "Record added."
          recAdded = True
          For Each fld in rsItm.Fields
```

```
            fldCur(fld.Name) = fld.Value
         Next
         fldNew.RemoveAll
      End If
   End If
' Resume normal error checking.
   On Error GoTo 0
   End If
' Close and destroy the Recordset object.
   rsItm.Close
   Set rsItm = Nothing
' Make sure the current record values for Title and Caption
' get displayed whenever possible (that is, whenever the
' relevant items in the fldNew Dictionary object don't already
' contain values).
   If fldNew("title") = "" Then fldNew("title") = fldCur("title")
   If fldNew("caption") = "" Then fldNew("caption") = fldCur("caption")
' If the record addition succeeded, emit a browser-side script
' that reloads and repositions the itmlist frame.
   If recAdded Then
      Response.Write "<script>" & vbCrLf
      Response.Write "parent.frames.itmlist.location = " & _
         Chr(34) & _
         "itmlist.asp" & _
         "?qcatnr=" & keyCatNr & _
         "#s" & keySeqNr & _
         Chr(34) & vbCrLf
      Response.Write "parent.frames.itmlist.location.reload(true)" & vbCrLf
      Response.Write "</script>" & vbCrLf
   End If
End Sub
%>
```

Building the Holiday Item Change Page

The ASP code in the itmchange.asp page strongly resembles that in the itmadd.asp page and therefore doesn't warrant a detailed, step-by-step explanation. If you understand how one of these pages works, you understand how the other works as well. The primary differences occur in the following areas:

- The word *change* replaces the word *add* in all error messages and comments.

- When the itmadd.asp page first loads, it requires only that a category number be present in the query string. It then displays a blank form for that category and doesn't access the database. When the itmchange.asp page first loads, it requires that both a category number and a sequence number be present in the query string. It uses these values to search for and display existing record values the Web visitor can replace.

- The effect of finding an existing record with the specified key is reversed. When adding records, finding an existing record with the same key is an error. When changing records, not finding such a record is an error.

- Because the *catnr* and *seqnr* fields form the *items* table's primary key, the itmadd.asp page always copies values into these fields. Because the Web visitor can't change the *catnr* field, the itmchange.asp page never copies values into that field. Because changing the *seqnr* field is optional, itmchange.asp only copies nonempty values into that field.

An annotated listing of the ASP code in the itmchange.asp page follows. As you read through it, you should notice both the similarities to itmadd.asp and the differences just described. To view the complete listing, including both ASP and HTML code, view the sample file \webdbdev\ch09\itmchange.asp on the companion CD.

```
<%
' Create Dictionary objects.
Set fldCur = Server.CreateObject("Scripting.Dictionary")
Set fldNew = Server.CreateObject("Scripting.Dictionary")
Set fldMsg = Server.CreateObject("Scripting.Dictionary")
' Initialize global variables.
fMsg = ""
iMsg = ""
fldError =  False
recchanged =  False
' Determine whether request came from this page's HTML form.
cngRec = UCase(Left(Request.Form("change"),1))
If cngRec = "Y" Then
' If so, save the previously displayed keys.
  keyCatNr = Request("hcatnr")
  keySeqNr = Request("hseqnr")
Else
' If not, save any keys found in the query string.
  keyCatNr = Request("qcatnr")
  keySeqNr = Request("qseqnr")
End If
' Attempt database update.
ChangeItemsRecord
Sub ChangeItemsRecord()
' Subroutine to change an items record.
' Validate key syntax; record error message if faulty.
  If keyCatNr = "" Then
    fMsg = "Category number missing."
  ElseIf keySeqNr = "" Then
    fMsg = "Sequence number missing."
  ElseIf Not IsNumeric(keyCatNr) Then
    fMsg = "Catagory number invalid."
```

```
      ElseIf Not IsNumeric(keySeqNr) Then
        fMsg = "Sequence number invalid."
      End If
' Copy form fields to fldNew Dictionary object.
      For Each fld in Request.Form
        fldNew(fld) = Request.Form(fld)
      Next
' Exit subroutine if a fatal error has occurred.
      If fMsg <> "" Then
        Exit Sub
      End If
' Build ADO connection string.
      cnStHol = "driver={Microsoft Access Driver (*.mdb)};" & _
              "dbq=" & Server.MapPath("../holiday/holiday.mdb")
' Create and open ADO Recordset object.
      Set rsItmrsItm = Server.CreateObject("ADODB.Recordset")
      sql = "SELECT * " & _
            "FROM items " & _
          "WHERE (catnr = " & keyCatNr & ") " & _
            "AND (seqnr = " & keySeqNr & ") ; "
      rsItm.Open sql, cnStHol, adOpenDynamic, adLockOptimistic
' If no matching record already exists, record a fatal
' error message.
      If rsItm.EOF Then
        fMsg = "Record not found."
' If a matching record does exist and if this page is running
' because the Web visitor clicked the Change button, replace
' the record values with any nonblank values in the fldNew
' Dictionary object.
      Else
        If cngRec = "Y" Then
' Turn off normal error checking. The script will detect
' and handle its own errors.
          On Error Resume Next
          For Each fld in rsItm.Fields
            If (fld.Name <> "catnr") and (fldNew(fld.Name) <> "") Then
              fld.Value = fldNew(fld.Name)
' If a field error occurred, store it in the fldMsg
' Dictionary object for later display and set the
' fldError variable to True.
              If Err Then
                fldMsg(fld.Name) = Err.Description
                fldError = True
              End If
            End If
          Next
' If a field error occurred, record a fatal error
' message and cancel the update.
```

(continued)

```
            If fldError Then
                fMsg = "Update cancelled because of field errors."
                rsItm.CancelUpdate
' If no field error occurred, replace the database record.
            Else
                rsItm.Update
' If the record update failed, record a fatal error message.
                If Err Then
                    fMsg = "Update failed:" & Err.Description
' If the record update succeeded, record an informational
' message and clear all entries in the fldNew Dictionary object.
                Else
                    iMsg = "Record changed."
                    recChanged = True
                    fldNew.RemoveAll
                End If
' Resume normal error checking.
                On Error GoTo 0
            End If
' Copy the existing (possibly revised) record
' to the fldCur Dictionary object.
            For Each fld in rsItm.Fields
                fldCur(fld.Name) = fld.Value
            Next
        End If
' Close and destroy the Recordset object.
        rsItm.Close
        Set rsItmrsItm = Nothing
' Make sure the current record values for Title and Caption
' get displayed whenever possible (whenever the
' relevant items in the fldNew Dictionary object don't already
' contain values).
        If fldNew("title") = "" Then fldNew("title") = fldCur("title")
        If fldNew("caption") = "" Then fldNew("caption") = fldCur("caption")
' If the record addition succeeded, emit a browser-side script
' that reloads and repositions the itmlist frame.
        If recChanged Then
            Response.Write "<script>" & vbCrLf
            Response.Write "parent.frames.itmlist.location = " & _
                Chr(34) & _
                "itmlist.asp" & _
                "?qcatnr=" & keyCatNr & _
                "#s" & fldCur("seqnr") & _
                Chr(34) & vbCrLf
            Response.Write "parent.frames.itmlist.location.reload(true)" & vbCrLf
            Response.Write "</script>" & vbCrLf
        End If
End sub
%>
```

Building the Holiday Item Delete Page

The itmdelete.asp page is yet another variation on the theme established by the itmadd.asp and itmchange.asp pages. Like the Item Change page, the Item Delete page expects the hyperlink that loads it to specify both a category number and a sequence number in its query string. The Item Delete page also requires that the *items* table contain an existing record with keys matching these values. The following requirements, however, are unique to the Item Delete page:

- The Item Delete page has no input fields. When first loaded, it verifies that a record with the specified keys exists, and if so displays its contents. If the Web visitor clicks the Delete button, the page deletes that record.

- Because there are no input fields, there's no need for a *fldNew* Dictionary object to provide values for them.

- Because no values are ever moved into the database, no field errors can occur and no *fldMsg* Dictionary object is required.

Given these requirements, the Item Delete page basically becomes a stripped down version of the Item Change page, with all field-by-field processing removed and the *rsItm.Delete* method replacing *rsItm.Update*. You should be able to identify these differences in the following ASP code listing. To view a complete listing of the itmdelete.asp page, examine the sample file \webdbdev\ch09\itmdelete.asp on the companion CD.

```
<%
' Create Dictionary object.
Set fldCur = Server.CreateObject("Scripting.Dictionary")
' Initialize global variables.
fMsg = ""
iMsg = ""
recDeleted =  False
' Determine whether request came from this page's HTML form.
dltRec = UCase(Left(Request.Form("delete"),1))
If dltRec = "Y" Then
' If so, save the previously displayed keys.
  keyCatNr = Request("hcatnr")
  keySeqNr = Request("hseqnr")
Else
' If not, save any keys found in the query string.
  keyCatNr = Request("qcatnr")
  keySeqNr = Request("qseqnr")
End If
' Validate key syntax; record error message if faulty.
If keyCatNr = "" Then
  fMsg = "Category number missing."
ElseIf keySeqNr = "" Then
  fMsg = "Sequence number missing."
ElseIf Not IsNumeric(keyCatNr) Then
  fMsg = "Catagory number invalid."
```

(continued)

```
        ElseIf Not IsNumeric(keySeqNr) Then
          fMsg = "Sequence number invalid."
        End If
      ' Execute remaining code only if there are no fatal errors
      ' so far.
      If fMsg = "" Then
      ' Build ADO connection string.
        cnStHol = "driver={Microsoft Access Driver (*.mdb)};" & _
                  "dbq=" & Server.MapPath("../holiday/holiday.mdb")
      ' Create and open ADO Recordset object.
        Set rsItm = Server.CreateObject("ADODB.Recordset")
        sql = "SELECT * " & _
              "FROM items " & _
              "WHERE (catnr = " & keyCatNr & ") " & _
              "AND (seqnr = " & keySeqNr & ") ; "
        rsItm.Open sql, cnStHol, adOpenDynamic, adLockOptimistic
      ' If no matching record already exists, record a fatal
      ' error message.
        If rsItm.EOF Then
          fMsg = "Item record not found."
          fldCur("catnr") = keyCatNr
          fldCur("seqnr") = keySeqNr
        Else
      ' If a matching record does exist, copy its field values to
      ' the fldCur Dictionary object.
          For Each fld in rsItm.Fields
            fldCur(fld.Name) = fld.Value
          Next
      ' If this page is running because the Web visitor clicked the
      ' Delete button, delete the record.
          If dltRec = "Y" Then
      ' Turn off normal error checking. The script will detect
      ' and handle its own errors.
            On Error Resume Next
      ' Attempt to delete the current record.
            rsItm.Delete
      ' If the deletion fails, record a fatal error message.
            If Err Then
              fMsg = "Deletion failed: " & Err.Description
      ' If the deletion succeeds, record an informational message
      ' and set the recdeleted indicator to True.
            Else
              iMsg = "Record deleted."
              recDeleted = True
            End If
      ' Resume normal error checking.
            On Error GoTo 0
          End If
        End If
```

```
' Close and destroy the Recordset object.
   rsItm.Close
   Set rsItm = nothing
End If
' If the record deletion succeeded, emit a browser-side script
' that reloads the itmlist frame.
If recDeleted Then
    Response.Write "<script>" & vbCrLf
    Response.Write "parent.frames.itmlist.location = " & _
                   Chr(34) & _
                   "itmlist.asp" & _
                   "?qcatnr=" & keyCatNr & _
                   "#s" & keySeqNr & _
                   Chr(34) & vbCrLf
    Response.Write "parent.frames.itmlist.location.reload(true)" _
                   & vbCrLf
    Response.Write "</script>" & vbCrLf
End If
%>
```

Chapter Summary

This chapter presented a second way to develop Web database pages that update tables. Instead of using a single page with multiple transaction codes, this example used multiple pages, each supporting a single transaction code. A frameset—similar to the one ordinary Web visitors would use for viewing—integrated these multiple pages into a cohesive application. Because of its resemblance to the viewing frameset, the update frameset also provided increased visual feedback regarding the effect of changes.

Chapter 10, "Performing Keyword Searches," will illustrate two applications: one that assigns keywords to photos in the *items* table, and another that searches for items with given keywords and values.

Performing Keyword Searches

Chapter Objectives	Estimated Time: 60 minutes

In this chapter, you'll learn

- How to provide Web visitors with a keyword search facility.

- How to integrate HTML form elements and database values.

The examples in the previous two chapters illustrated a variety of database update techniques. Except for some complexities associated with framesets, however, the user interfaces were simplistic. Text boxes, although easy to program, require the Web visitor to know which values are acceptable, which values are required, and which are neither. Elements such as drop-down list boxes and radio buttons provide the visitor with much better guidance. This chapter will present and explain some HTML forms that use these elements and that populate list choices from values in the database.

Designing such forms is rather pointless, of course, without an application to develop. This chapter's example illustrates a feature that's both practical and popular within almost any database system: searching. To use this application, Web visitors will fill out an HTML form to specify search criteria, click a Submit button, and then view a frameset with search results listed at the left and details about any clicked item at the right. This presumes, of course, that someone has assigned keywords to the items. The application therefore includes another Web page that performs keyword maintenance. Finally, the Holiday database needs two new tables: one to hold a list of valid keywords and another to hold the keywords assigned to each item.

Introducing the Keyword Search Pages

The finished search form, search.asp, appears in Figure 10-1. The Web visitor can search for items matching any category, matching any country, occurring before, on, or after any date, and having up to four preassigned keywords.

Drop-down lists itemize the valid choices for category, country, and the four keyword choices. This guarantees that any choice the Web visitor makes is valid, at least from an application point of view. (No data entry form can keep a Web visitor from selecting a different list item from the one he or she intended.)

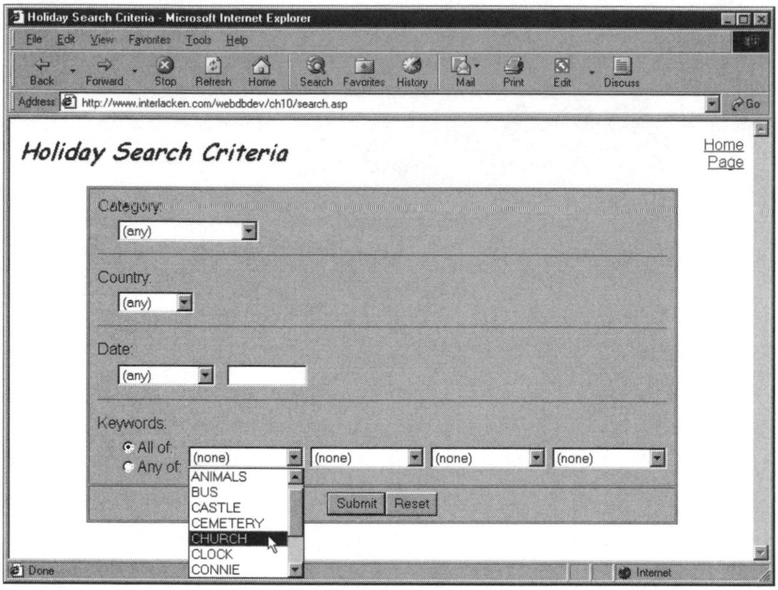

Figure 10-1 *Web visitors can use the HTML form in this Web page to search the Holiday Photo items table.*

The drop-down list for the date field offers six choices:

- (any)
- On
- Before
- On or Before
- After
- On or After

If the Web visitor chooses (any), the search will retrieve items regardless of date. Otherwise, the search will retrieve items related as specified to whatever date the visitor enters in the Date text box. For simplicity, if the visitor enters an invalid date, the search will retrieve items regardless of date.

The Keywords section of the form has two radio buttons titled All Of and Any Of. If the Web visitor chooses All Of, matching records must be coded with every keyword the Web visitor specifies. If the visitor chooses Any Of, any record coded with one or more specified keywords will match.

Clicking the Submit button in Figure 10-1 displays the Web page shown in Figure 10-2. This page, results.asp, is a frameset with three frames:

- The *title* frame occupies the top portion of the window. It identifies the page and provides a link for starting a new search.

- The *itmfind* frame is the workhorse of the frameset. It receives the search criteria the Web visitor entered on the search.asp page, searches the database for matching items, lists any items found and—on initial load—it reloads the detail frame with the first found item.

- The *detail* frame occupies the bottom right portion of the window. As in Chapter 7, "Running and Displaying Queries," this frame displays the blank.htm page at first. If, however, the itmfind.asp page locates any items matching the Web visitor's search criteria, the page replaces blank.htm with the now familiar (and potentially world-famous) picshow.asp page developed in Chapter 7.

Subsequently, whenever the visitor clicks an item thumbnail in the *itmfind* frame, a hyperlink will use the picshow.asp page to display full information for that item in the *detail* frame.

Search functions of this type are welcome additions to almost any site, but especially to sites featuring a wide variety of items. Whatever kind of items your site contains, you can almost certainly code them by color, size, style, material, manufacturer, artist, species, flavor, product line, age, planet, solar system, or any other useful property. This helps your Web visitors find items of interest quickly and accurately. Saving and analyzing a history of queries can also provide valuable feedback on which kinds of items your Web visitors find most and least interesting.

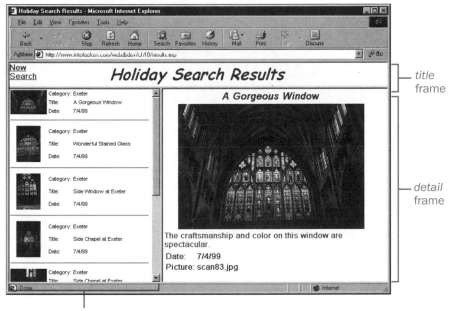

itmfind frame

Figure 10-2 *A Web visitor who submits search criteria using the Web page in Figure 10-1 will receive this frameset of matching items.*

Keyword searching can only be successful, of course, if you also have (and use!) a method of keyword assignment. The Web page kwdmaint.asp shown in Figure 10-3 provides exactly this sort of facility.

The kwdmaint.asp page updates two new tables in the holiday.mdb database: a *pickwd* table that contains the keywords associated with each picture, and a *keywords* table that contains a list of valid keywords.

The gray box in the top left corner provides navigation through the *items* table. The Prev, Query, and Next buttons work much like those in the picmaint.asp page from Chapter 8 ("Updating Tables from a General Purpose Form"), except they traverse the *items* table in *picname* sequence rather than *catnr* and *seqnr*. The current picture appears at the top of the Web page.

The gray boxes at the bottom of the page contain a list of keywords already associated with the current picture, a list of valid keywords, and a text box for

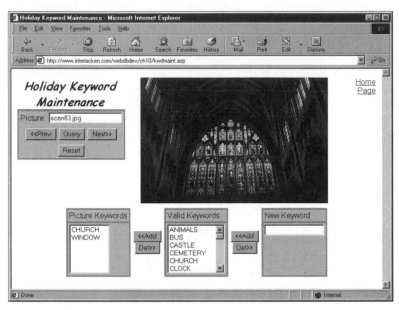

Figure 10-3   *This Web page updates two tables: one that contains a list of valid keywords and one that contains keywords associated with a given picture.*

adding new keywords to the valid list. The Add and Del buttons between the first two boxes assign and remove keywords associated with the current picture. The Add and Del buttons between the second and third boxes add and remove keywords from the valid list.

There are two reasons for creating a new *pickwd* table rather than adding keyword fields to the *items* table:

- To belong in the *items* table, a field must depend on its primary keys: the *catnr* and *seqnr* fields. The keywords in this application relate to pictures, not to categories and sequence numbers.

- Keywords have a zero-to-many relationship with the *picname* field and thus constitute a repeating group. This requires a separate table containing one record for each assignment of a keyword to a picture name.

You can see the definition of the *pickwd* table in Figure 10-4. There are only two fields, *picname* and *keyword*. Both form the table's primary key. You could certainly add more fields to this table—a date-last-changed field, for example—but the two fields listed are sufficient for this exercise.

The *keywords* table has two uses. For maintenance, it encourages consistency by guiding the maintainer toward a list of terms already in use and away from new terms that duplicate the meanings of old ones. It also eliminates spelling errors. For searching, it populates the drop-down list boxes in Figure 10-1 and thereby helps the Web visitor choose keywords that produce useful results.

Adding these two tables to the holiday.mdb database should present no problems. Just follow the steps under "Create a new table" in Chapter 2 ("Understanding Database Concepts and Terms").The data type for both the *picname* and *keyword* fields is Text, with a field size of 50 characters, the default.

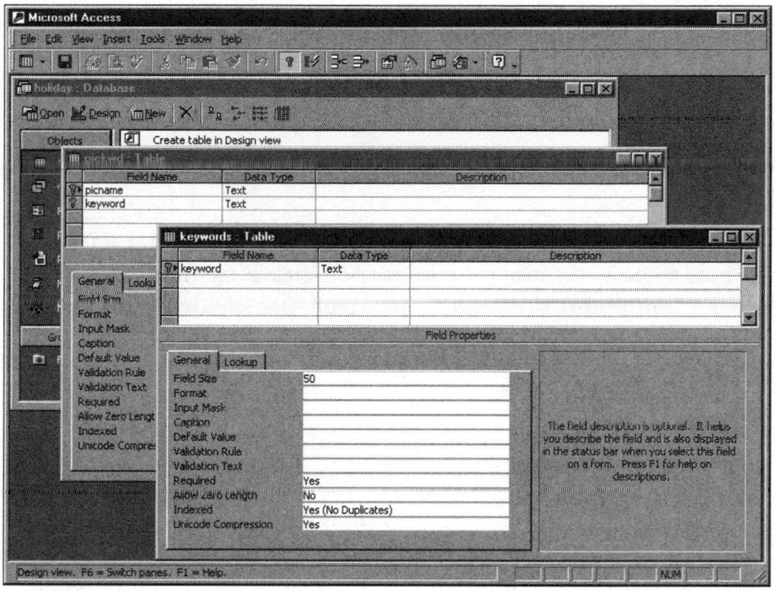

Figure 10-4   *The* pickwd *and* keywords *tables consist of primary key values only.*

Subsequent sections will describe the Holiday Keyword Maintenance page, the Holiday Search Criteria page, and the results frameset, in that order.

Building the Holiday Keyword Maintenance Page

This section will walk you through the four main tasks required to create the kwdmaint.asp page:

- Initializing the page
- Responding to the navigation buttons
- Responding to the Add and Del buttons
- Showing database values in the HTML form

Initialize the Holiday Keyword Maintenance page

This procedure lays out the HTML form and performs any processing required, no matter what button the Web visitor clicks.

1. Open your favorite HTML editor and create a new .asp page. It should contain the usual structural tags plus an ASP *Option Explicit* statement before the <html> tag, an include statement for the adovbs.inc file and, if you want one, a style sheet link.

```
<% Option Explicit %>
<html>
<head>
<!-- #include file="../adovbs.inc" -->
```

(continued)

```
<link rel="stylesheet" type="text/css"
      href="../holiday/holiform.css">
<title>Holiday Keyword Maintenance</title>
</head>
<body>
</body>
</html>
```

This example makes use of the *Option Explicit* statement primarily because there's too much code to spell-check by hand. For more information about this statement, refer to the sidebar on the next page.

2. Lay out the Web page in accordance with Figure 10-3 and the following instructions:

- Enclose the entire contents of the *<body>* section within an HTML form that specifies *method="POST"* and *action="kwdmaint.asp"*.

- Name the Picture text box *picname*.

- Code the Prev, Query, and Next buttons as *type=submit*, and name them *btnPrev*, *btnQuery*, and *btnNext*.

- Name the drop-down menu in the Picture Keywords box *pickwd*. Don't worry about providing values for this list just yet.

- Code the Add and Del buttons near the Picture Keywords box as *type=submit*, and name them *btnPicAdd* and *btnPicDel*.

- Name the drop-down menu in the Valid Keywords box *valkwd*. Again, don't worry about providing a list of values.

- Code the Add and Del buttons near the Picture Keywords box as *type=submit*, and name them *btnKwdAdd* and *btnKwdDel*.

- Name the text box in the New Keyword box *newkwd*.

3. Insert a pair of <% and %> tags just before the </head> tag, and then insert the following code between them. This code declares all the variables used within the Web page's ASP code.

```
CONST KW_NONE = "(none)"
Dim cnHol, cnStHol
Dim rsKwd, rsItm, rsPkw
Dim sql
Dim fld
Dim trancd
Dim curPic
Dim curKwd
Dim oldKwd
Dim fMsg
Dim optCnt
```

4. Insert the following code immediately after the code you added in step 3. This code creates an ADO Connection object and three ADO Recordset objects. Later code will use these Recordset objects to open the *keyword*, *items*, and *pickwd* tables in the holiday.mdb database.

```
Set cnHol = Server.CreateObject("ADODB.Connection")
Set rsKwd = Server.CreateObject("ADODB.Recordset")
Set rsItm = Server.CreateObject("ADODB.Recordset")
Set rsPkw = Server.CreateObject("ADODB.Recordset")
```

5. The next step opens the *cnHol* Connection object and points it to the holiday.mdb database. As before, this requires you to first create a connection string and then supply that string as an argument to the Connection object's *Open* method. To do this, insert the following code immediately after the code you inserted in step 4.

```
cnStHol = "driver={Microsoft Access Driver (*.mdb)};" & _
          "dbq=" & Server.MapPath("../holiday/holiday.mdb")
cnHol.Open cnStHol,"",""
```

6. No matter what else happens, the kwdmaint.asp page always displays a current list of valid keywords. This always requires opening the *keywords* table, so insert the following statements next in line:

```
sql = "SELECT * FROM keywords ORDER BY keyword ; "
rsKwd.Open sql, cnHol, adOpenDynamic, adLockOptimistic
```

You've completed the code that must execute no matter which function the Web visitor chose—in other words, no matter which button the visitor clicked. Now it's time to figure out which button that was.

The picmaint.asp page in Chapter 8 featured six buttons with the same name—*btnSub*—differentiated based on their caption values. That approach doesn't work for this example because there are two Add buttons and two Del buttons. That's why step 1 assigned each button a different name.

The *Option Explicit* Statement

The *Option Explicit* statement tells VBScript that it shouldn't create variable names on the fly; instead, it should only create variables you define explicitly through a *Dim* statement. This has the advantage that if you misspell a variable name, VBScript will report an error instead of just creating a new variable with the misspelled name. Of course, it also has the disadvantage of forcing you to declare all your variables with *Dim* statements. Experienced programmers usually prefer to declare their variables and get errors when they misspell something, but the choice is yours.

If you decide to use the *Option Explicit* statement, it must appear before any other VBScript or HTML code.

The seven button names in the kwdmaint.asp page all begin with *btn*; no other form elements begin with that prefix. The browser transmits only the name and caption value of the button the Web visitor pressed. Thus, the Request.Form collection will only contain one entry with a name that begins *btn*; the rest of that name will identify the button the Web visitor clicked.

All that remains is to loop through all the elements in the Request.Form collection. Upon finding an element name that begins with *btn*, the code copies the fourth through the last characters of the name into a variable named *trancd*, and then exits the loop. This code immediately follows the code you added in step 6.

```
For Each fld in Request.Form
  If LCase(Left(fld,3)) = "btn" Then
    trancd = Mid(fld,4)
    Exit For
  End If
Next
```

Note that if the Web visitor didn't click a button, *trancd* will be empty. This occurs when an ordinary URL requests the page.

Responding to the Navigation Buttons

By design decision, keywords apply to a specific picture and not to a specific combination of category and item numbers. The keyword maintenance page therefore navigates the *items* table in *picname* sequence. The Next button should move to the next picture name and the Prev button should move to the previous picture name. The Query button should retrieve a specific picture name.

These movements assume, of course, that there's a current *picname* value to move forward or backward from, or to query. If there's not such a value, the Next and Query buttons should return the first picture in the table, and the Prev button should return the last. Table 10-1 summarizes the navigation requirements, listing which items are available from the *items* table when a particular button is chosen and in what order the items are traversed.

Table 10-1   Holiday Keyword Maintenance Navigation Requirements

Button	*picname* Text Box	*items* Table Records	Order
Prev	Empty	All items available	Descending
Prev	Value	All items with picture names less than the *picname* value	Descending
Next	Empty	All items available	Ascending
Next	Value	All items with picture names greater than the *picname* value	Ascending
Query	Empty	All items available	Ascending
Query	Value	Specific record with picture name equal to *picname*	Irrelevant

The following code creates one of six SQL statements corresponding, in order, to the six cases listed in Table 10-1. In each case, the desired record will be the first one in the result set. Insert this code immediately after the code described in step 7 of the previous section.

```
sql = ""
Select Case trancd
  Case "Prev"
    If Request("picname") = "" Then
      sql = "SELECT * FROM items " & _
          "ORDER BY picname DESC ; "
    Else
      sql = "SELECT * FROM items " & _
              "WHERE picname < '" & Request("picname") & "' " & _
          "ORDER BY picname DESC ; "
    End If
  Case "Next"
    If Request("picname") = "" Then
      sql = "SELECT * FROM items " & _
          "ORDER BY picname ; "
    Else
      sql = "SELECT * FROM items " & _
              "WHERE picname > '" & Request("picname") & "' " & _
          "ORDER BY picname ; "
    End If
  Case "Query"
    If Request("picname") = "" Then
      sql = "SELECT * FROM items " & _
          "ORDER BY picname ; "
    Else
      sql = "SELECT * FROM items " & _
              "WHERE picname = '" & Request("picname") & "' ; "
    End If
End Select
```

If this code fails to produce a SQL statement, the Web visitor must not have clicked the Prev, Query, or Next button. Any further processing will therefore use the picture name value from the *picname* text box. The code below the next paragraph stores this value in a variable named *curPic*.

If the code above does produce a SQL statement, the *Else* condition within the following code uses it to open the *rsItm* recordset. If this recordset is empty (that is, if its *eof* or its *BOF* property is *True*), the code again stores the value from the *picname* text box into the *curPic* variable. If the recordset isn't empty, the code saves the *picname* value from the first record in the *curPic* variable.

```
If sql = "" Then
  curPic = Request("picname")
Else
  rsItm.Open sql, cnHol , adOpenDynamic, adLockOptimistic
  If rsItm.EOF or rsItm.BOF Then
    curPic = Request("picname")
```

continued

```
    Else
      curPic = rsItm("picname")
    End If
    rsItm.Close
  End If
```

The rest of the Web page doesn't use the *rsItm* recordset. It therefore makes sense to close it here and now. The *rsItm.Close* statement in the preceding code does exactly that.

If executing the code described so far produces a nonempty *curPic* value, the next step is to query the *pickwd* table for keywords assigned to that picture. To do this, insert the following code next in sequence:

```
IF curPic <> "" Then
  sql = "SELECT * FROM pickwd " & _
        "WHERE picname = '" & curPic & "' " & _
     "ORDER BY keyword ; "
  rsPkw.Open sql, cnHol , adOpenDynamic, adLockOptimistic
End If
```

Note that code elsewhere in the page can determine whether the *rsPkw* recordset is open by inspecting its *state* property. If *rsPkw.state* equals *adStateOpen*, the recordset is open.

Responding to the Add and Del Buttons

The kwdmaint.asp page now knows what picture the Web visitor wants to work with. The next task is to process the remaining button clicks: adding or deleting keywords for the picture, or adding or deleting keywords from the valid list.

Step 2 in the previous section established *valkwd* as the name of the list box that displays all currently valid keywords. Whenever the Web visitor clicks any of the seven Submit buttons, the browser transmits the keyword currently selected in this box, and the ASP code receives it in *Request.Form("valkwd")*. The first statement in the following code saves this value in a variable named *curKwd* for use in processing button clicks. The *curKwd* variable also controls which item is initially selected in the valid keyword list sent back to the Web visitor.

The remaining statements invoke functions that process each of the remaining button clicks. Each function returns an empty string if the function succeeded or a fatal error message if it encountered a serious error.

```
curKwd = UCase(Request.Form("valkwd"))
Select Case trancd
  Case "PicAdd"
    fMsg = PictureAdd()
  Case "PicDel"
    fMsg = PictureDel()
  Case "KwdAdd"
    fMsg = KeywordAdd()
  Case "KwdDel"
    fMsg = KeywordDel()
End Select
```

The following sections will describe each of these functions.

Add a keyword to a picture

The *PictureAdd* function assigns a valid keyword to a given picture. *PictureAdd* is coded as a separate function to segregate the code for future maintenance, and to facilitate an early exit should anything run amok. If the function completes normally, it returns an empty string. If it encounters a failure, it returns an error message. The following steps explain how to code this function.

1. Mark the beginning and end of the function with *Function* and *End Function* statements, and name the function *PictureAdd*. Insert these statements after the code described in previous sections and before the %> and </head> tags.

```
Function PictureAdd()
  '  Procedural statements will go here.
End Function
```

2. When you assign a keyword to a picture, both the current keyword value and the current picture name are required values. Therefore, the following statements exit with an error message if either the *curKwd* or the *curPic* variable is empty. Insert these statements in place of the comment in step 1.

```
If curKwd = "" Then
  PictureAdd = "Keyword missing."
  Exit Function
End If
If curPic = "" Then
  PictureAdd = "Picture name missing."
  Exit Function
End If
```

3. Insert the following statement so that if a run-time error occurs, VBScript returns it to the ASP code rather than terminating the script.

```
On Error Resume Next
```

4. Insert the following statements to initialize a new, empty record in the *rsPkw* recordset. If an error occurs, exit the function and return the error message that ADO supplied.

```
rsPkw.AddNew
If Err Then
  PictureAdd = Err.Description
  Exit Function
End If
```

5. Copy the *curPic* variable into the *picname* field of the new, blank record. If this results in an error (for example, if the keyword is longer than the field can accommodate), set the function's return value to the ADO error message, cancel the update (that is, discard the new, blank record), and exit the function.

```
rsPkw("picname") = curPic
If Err Then
  PictureAdd = Err.Description
  rsPwk.CancelUpdate
  Exit Function
End If
```

6. Copy the *curKwd* variable into the *keyword* field. In the event of an error, again cancel the update and exit with the ADO error message.

```
rsPkw("keyword") = curKwd
If Err Then
  PictureAdd = Err.Description
  rsPkw.CancelUpdate
  Exit Function
End If
```

7. Add the new (and now complete) record to the *pickwd* table. In the event of an error, cancel the update and exit with the ADO error message.

```
rsPkw.Update
If Err Then
  PictureAdd = Err.Description
  rsPkw.CancelUpdate
  Exit Function
End If
```

8. Resume normal system error handling.

```
On Error GoTo 0
```

9. In general, new records added to a recordset don't appear in sequence. If the kwdmaint.asp page made no further use of the *rsPkw* recordset, there wouldn't be a problem, but in fact this recordset populates the Picture Keywords list box in the outgoing Web page. Having the list items out of sequence would be annoying to the Web visitor, so requery the recordset (that is, get a fresh copy that's fully in sequence).

```
rsPkw.Requery
```

10. Ensure that the function returns an empty string when it exits normally.

```
fMsg = ""
```

Delete a keyword from a picture

You can use ADO to delete records in several ways, not the least of which involves preparing a SQL statement like the following and passing it to a Connection object's *Execute* method:

```
DELETE * FROM pickwd
  WHERE (picname = 'img001.jpg') AND (keyword = 'HEDGEHOGS')
```

In the current case, however, the *rsPkw* recordset is already open and provides a perfect view of the target record. This makes it easier to delete the desired record using the recordset's *Delete* method.

The keyword to delete, by the way, is not the keyword in the *curKwd* variable. The value in the *curKwd* variable came from the Valid Keywords (*valkwd*) list. The keyword to delete comes from the Picture Keywords (*pickwd*) list.

To code the *PictureDel* function, follow these steps.

1. Mark the bounds of the function with *Function* and *End Function* statements. Insert these statements after the *End Function* statement created in the previous section and before the %> and </head> tags.

```
Function PictureDel()
'   Procedural statements will go here.
End Function
```

2. To delete an existing keyword assignment, you need non-empty values for both picture name and keyword. If either of these values is blank, the following statements exit the function with an error message. Insert these statements in place of the comment in step 1.

```
If (Request("pickwd") = "" ) OR (Request("pickwd") = KW_NONE)Then
   PictureDel = "No keyword selected."
   Exit Function
End If
If curPic = "" Then
   PictureDel= "Picture name missing."
   Exit Function
End If
```

In the case of the keyword value, the string *(none)* is equivalent to an empty value. Later code will display this value in the Picture Keyword text box whenever the current picture has no assigned keywords. To ensure that this value is coded exactly the same when assigned later and when tested here, step 3 in the section "Initialize the Holiday Keyword Maintenance page" defined *(none)* as a constant named *KW_NONE*.

3. To delete a record using the *rsPkw.Delete* method, you must first position to that record. This, in turn, requires you to loop through all the records in the *rsPkw* recordset. Because the *WHERE* clause that created this recordset specified a picture name, there should only be a few records to scan. Insert the following code immediately after the code from step 2.

```
Do While Not rsPkw.EOF
'    Code to check for correct record goes here.
   rsPkw.MoveNext
Loop
```

4. Because the *WHERE* clause that created the *rsPkw* recordset restricted its contents to records with the correct picture name, you need to check only for the correct keyword to find the correct record to delete. Thus, you use the following code to identify the correct record. Insert these statements in place of the comment in step 3.

```
If UCase(Request("pickwd")) = UCase(rsPkw("keyword")) Then
'   Code to delete found record goes here.
    Exit Function
End If
```

Notice that the code converts the values of *Request("pickwd")* and *rsPkw("keyword")* to upper case before comparing them. This makes the equality check case-insensitive.

There are two reasons for exiting the function immédiately after finding (and processing) the correct record. First, scanning any remaining records consumes server resources for no practical purpose. Second, if the loop coded in step 3 completes without exiting the function, this drops to a "not found" condition, which you'll see in step 5.

5. When the *If* statement in step 4 detects the correct record, the code should obviously delete it. First, however, it saves the matching keyword in the *curKwd* variable. This ensures that the keyword the Web visitor last worked with is the keyword highlighted in the Valid Keywords list.

    If the *Delete* method fails, the code exits the function with the error message received from ADO. An *On Error Resume Next* statement tells VBScript not to abort processing if this occurs.

    If the *Delete* method succeeds, the code requeries the recordset to assure proper display and then exits with an empty return value.

```
curKwd = UCase(Request("pickwd"))
On Error Resume Next
rsPkw.Delete
If Err Then
    PictureDel = Err.Description
Else
    PictureDel = ""
    rsPkw.Requery
End If
```

    Insert this code in place of the comment in step 4.

6. If the loop created in step 3 finishes without exiting the function, you have a "not found" condition. To inform the Web visitor this has occurred, insert the following statement after the *Loop* statement you added in step 3 and before *End Function*:

```
PictureDel = "Keyword " & Request("pickwd") & "Not found."
```

Add a valid keyword

The *KeywordAdd* function is so similar to the *PictureAdd* function that no excruciating, step-by-step instructions should be necessary—just be aware of these essential differences:

- The *KeywordAdd* function updates the *keywords* table (via the *rsKwd* recordset) rather than the *pickwd* table (via the *rsPkw* recordset).

- Because the *keywords* table doesn't have a picture name field, the *KeywordAdd* function processes only a *keyword* field.

- The keyword to add is the one the Web visitor specified in the New Keyword text box —that is, the one received as *Request("newkwd")*.

- If the addition succeeds, the *KeywordAdd* function resets *curKwd* to the new keyword value just added. This positions the Valid Keywords list to the new value.

The complete code for the *KeywordAdd* function follows. Insert this code after the *End Function* statement that completes the *PictureDel* function and before the %> and </head> tags in the Web page.

```
Function KeywordAdd()
  If (Request("newkwd") = "") Then
    KeywordAdd = "No new keyword specified."
    Exit Function
  End If
  On Error Resume Next
  rsKwd.AddNew
  If Err Then
    KeywordAdd = Err.Description
    Exit Function
  End If
  rsKwd("keyword") = UCase(Request("newkwd"))
  If Err Then
    KeywordAdd = Err.Description
    rsKwd.CancelUpdate
    Exit Function
  End If
  rsKwd.Update
  If Err Then
    KeywordAdd = Err.Description
    rsKwd.CancelUpdate
    Exit Function
  End If
  On Error GoTo 0
  curKwd = UCase(Request("newkwd"))
  rsKwd.Requery
  KeywordAdd = ""
End Function
```

Delete a valid keyword

The *KeywordDel* function is similar to the *PictureDel* function, except for these essential differences:

- The *KeywordDel* function updates the *keywords* table rather than the *pickwd* table.

- The *KeywordDel* function processes only a keyword field.

- The keyword to delete is the one currently selected in the Valid Keywords box (the one stored previously in the *curKwd* variable).

- If the deletion succeeds, the *KeywordDel* function stores the deleted keyword in a variable named *oldKwd*. Later code will put this value in the New Keyword text box so that if the Web visitor deleted the keyword by mistake, the visitor can easily add it back.

The complete code for the *KeywordDel* function follows. Insert this code after the *End Function* statement that completes the *KeywordAdd* function and before the %> and </head> tags in the Web page.

```
Function KeywordDel()
  If (curKwd = "") Then
    KeywordDel = "No keyword specified."
    Exit Function
  End If
  rsKwd.MoveFirst
  Do While Not rsKwd.EOF
    If UCase(rsKwd("keyword")) = curKwd Then
      On Error Resume Next
      rsKwd.Delete
      If Err Then
        KeywordDel = Err.Description
      Else
        On Error GoTo 0
        rsKwd.Requery
        oldKwd = curKwd
        KeywordDel = ""
      End If
      Exit Function
    End If
    rsKwd.MoveNext
  Loop
  KeywordDel = "Keyword " & curKwd & "Not found."
End Function
```

As coded, this function has one glaring omission: it doesn't consider any records in the *pickwd* table that contain the keyword the Web visitor wants to delete from the *keywords* table. You can handle this situation in several ways:

- After deleting a keyword from the *keywords* table, you can execute a SQL statement such as the following to delete all *pickwd* records having that keyword:

```
DELETE * FROM pickwd WHERE keyword = "HEDGEHOGS"
```

- You can set up referential integrity rules so that deletions in the *keywords* table would cascade to the *pickwd* table.

- You can set up referential rules so that deletions in the *keywords* table would fail if any matching records existed in the *pickwd* table.

- You can let the application remain as is and tell its owner to manually synchronize the tables.

Reviewing the <head> Section

To see how all the code fragments you've seen so far fit together, review the following listing. The rest of the Web page is ordinary HTML, except for three elements explained in detail in the next section.

```
<% Option Explicit %>
<html>
<head>
<!-- #include file="../adovbs.inc" -->
<link rel="stylesheet" type="text/css"
      href="../holiday/holiform.css">
<title>Holiday Keyword Maintenance</title>
<%
' Define constants and variables.
CONST KW_NONE = "(none)"
Dim cnHol, cnStHol
Dim rsKwd, rsItm, rsPkw
Dim sql
Dim fld
Dim trancd
Dim curPic
Dim curKwd
Dim oldKwd
Dim fMsg
Dim optCnt
' Create ADO Connection and Recordset objects.
Set cnHol = Server.CreateObject("ADODB.Connection")
Set rsKwd = Server.CreateObject("ADODB.Recordset")
Set rsItm = Server.CreateObject("ADODB.Recordset")
Set rsPkw = Server.CreateObject("ADODB.Recordset")
' Open the ADO Connection object.
cnStHol = "driver={Microsoft Access Driver (*.mdb)};" & _
          "dbq=" & Server.MapPath("../holiday/holiday.mdb")
cnHol.Open cnStHol,"",""
' Open a recordset for the keywords table.
sql = "SELECT * FROM keywords ORDER BY keyword ; "
rsKwd.Open sql, cnHol , adOpenDynamic, adLockOptimistic
' Scan all the form elements received from the Web visitor
' and identify which button the visitor pressed.
For Each fld in Request.Form
  If LCase(Left(fld,3)) = "btn" Then
    trancd = Mid(fld,4)
    Exit For
  End If
```

(continued)

```
Next
' Construct a SQL statement to query the items table. The correct
' format depends on which button the visitor clicked and whether
' the visitor specified a picture name on this or a previous
' execution.
sql = ""
Select Case trancd
  Case "Prev"
    If Request("picname") = "" Then
      sql = "SELECT * FROM items " & _
          "ORDER BY picname DESC ; "
    Else
      sql = "SELECT * FROM items " & _
            "WHERE picname < '" & Request("picname") & "' " & _
          "ORDER BY picname DESC ; "
    End If
  Case "Next"
    If Request("picname") = "" Then
      sql = "SELECT * FROM items " & _
          "ORDER BY picname ; "
    Else
      sql = "SELECT * FROM items " & _
            "WHERE picname > '" & Request("picname") & "' " & _
          "ORDER BY picname ; "
    End If
  Case "Query"
    If Request("picname") = "" Then
      sql = "SELECT * FROM items " & _
          "ORDER BY picname ; "
    Else
      sql = "SELECT * FROM items " & _
            "WHERE picname = '" & Request("picname") & "' ; "
    End If
End Select
' If the Select Case statement above produced a SQL statement,
' use it to open the rsItm recordset. If this returns a record,
' save its picname field in the variable curPic. Otherwise, save
' the value received from the picname text box in that variable.
If sql = "" Then
  curPic = Request("picname")
Else
  rsItm.Open sql, cnHol , adOpenDynamic, adLockOptimistic
  If rsItm.EOF or rsItm.BOF Then
    curPic = Request("picname")
  Else
    curPic = rsItm("picname")
  End If
  rsItm.Close
End If
```

```
' If a nonempty curPic value is now available, use it to
' query the pickwd table for keywords assigned to that picture.
If curPic <> "" Then
  sql = "SELECT * FROM pickwd " & _
          "WHERE picname = '" & curPic & "' " & _
          "ORDER BY keyword ; "
  rsPkw.Open sql, cnHol , adOpenDynamic, adLockOptimistic
End If
' Save the value currently selected in the valkwd list box
' into the variable curKwd.
curKwd = UCase(Request.Form("valkwd"))
' Execute functions to process the PicAdd, PuicDel,
' KwdAdd, and KwdDel button clicks.
Select Case trancd
  Case "PicAdd"
    fMsg = PictureAdd()
  Case "PicDel"
    fMsg = PictureDel()
  Case "KwdAdd"
    fMsg = KeywordAdd()
  Case "KwdDel"
    fMsg = KeywordDel()
End Select


' Define a function to process PicAdd button clicks.
Function PictureAdd()
' Exit function if there's no current keyword value.
  If curKwd = "" Then
    PictureAdd = "Keyword missing."
    Exit Function
  End If
' Exit function if there's no current picture name.
  If curPic = "" Then
    PictureAdd = "Picture name missing."
    Exit Function
  End If
' Turn off default system error handling.
  On Error Resume Next
' Create new, empty record buffer. Exit on failure.
  rsPkw.AddNew
  If Err Then
    PictureAdd = Err.Description
    Exit Function
  End If
' Copy current picture name into new record buffer.
' Exit on failure.
```

(continued)

```
      rsPkw("picname") = curPic
      If Err Then
        PictureAdd = Err.Description
        rsPwk.CancelUpdate
        Exit Function
      End If
  ' Copy current keyword into new record buffer.
  ' Exit on failure.
      rsPkw("keyword") = curKwd
      If Err Then
        PictureAdd = Err.Description
        rsPkw.CancelUpdate
        Exit Function
      End If
  ' Add new record to table. Exit on failure.
      rsPkw.Update
      If Err Then
        PictureAdd = Err.Description
        rsPkw.CancelUpdate
        Exit Function
      End If
  ' Resume normal error checking.
      On Error GoTo 0
  ' Refresh recordset by repeating original query.
      rsPkw.Requery
  ' Set successful return value.
      PictureAdd = ""
  End Function


  ' Define a function to process PicDel button clicks.
  Function PictureDel()
  ' Exit function if there's no picture keyword value.
      If (Request("pickwd") = "" ) OR (Request("pickwd") = KW_NONE)Then
        PictureDel = "No keyword selected."
        Exit Function
      End If
  ' Exit function if there's no current picture value.
      If curPic = "" Then
        PictureDel= "Picture name missing."
        Exit Function
      End If
  ' Start loop to inspect each record.
      rsPkw.MoveFirst
      Do While Not rsPkw.EOF
  '     Check for matching keyword.
        If UCase(Request("pickwd")) = UCase(rsPkw("keyword")) Then
  '       On match, reset current keyword.
          curKwd = UCase(Request("pickwd"))
          On Error Resume Next
  '       Delete matched record.
```

```
            rsPkw.Delete
            If Err Then
'              On failure, set return error message.
               PictureDel = Err.Description
            Else
'              On success, set good return value.
               PictureDel = ""
'              Refresh recordset by repeating original query.
               rsPkw.Requery
            End If
'          Exit function after processing matched keyword.
            Exit Function
         End If
'      Continue looking for matching record.
         rsPkw.MoveNext
      Loop
'  If loop ends without finding match, return error message.
      PictureDel = "Keyword " & Request("pickwd") & "Not found."
End Function


'  Define a function to process KwdAdd button clicks.
Function KeywordAdd()
'  Exit function if there's no new keyword value.
      If (Request("newkwd") = "") Then
         KeywordAdd = "No new keyword specified."
         Exit Function
      End If
'  Reset current keyword.
      curKwd = UCase(Request("newkwd"))
'  Create new, empty record buffer. Exit on failure.
      On Error Resume Next
      rsKwd.AddNew
      If Err Then
         KeywordAdd = Err.Description
         Exit Function
      End If
'  Copy new keyword into new record buffer. Exit on failure.
      rsKwd("keyword") = UCase(Request("newkwd"))
      If Err Then
         KeywordAdd = Err.Description
         rsKwd.CancelUpdate
         Exit Function
      End If
'  Add new record to table. Cancel update and exit on failure.
      rsKwd.Update
      If Err Then
         KeywordAdd = Err.Description
         rsKwd.CancelUpdate
         Exit Function
      End If
```

(continued)

```
    On Error GoTo 0
' Reset current keyword.
    curKwd = UCase(Request("newkwd"))
' Refresh recordset by repeating original query.
    rsKwd.Requery
' Set successful return value.
    KeywordAdd - ""
End Function


' Define a function to process KwdDel button clicks.
Function KeywordDel()
' Exit function if there's no current keyword value.
If (curKwd = "") Then
    KeywordDel = "No keyword specified."
    Exit Function
    End If
' Start loop to find matching record.
    rsKwd.MoveFirst
    Do While Not rsKwd.EOF
'    Check current record for match.
    If UCase(rsKwd("keyword")) = curKwd Then
'       On match, delete current record.
        On Error Resume Next
        rsKwd.Delete
        If Err Then
'          On failure, set return value to ADO message.
           KeywordDel = Err.Description
        Else
'          On success:
'          Refresh recordset by repeating original query.
'          Store deleted keyword for possible add-back.
'          Set good return value.
           On Error GoTo 0
           rsKwd.Requery
           oldKwd = curKwd
           KeywordDel = ""
        End If
'       Exit function on any match, successful or not.
        Exit Function
    End If
'    Continue looking for matching record.
    rsKwd.MoveNext
  Loop
' If loop ends without finding match, return error message.
    KeywordDel = "Keyword " & curKwd & "Not found."
End Function
%>
</head>
```

Showing Database Values in the HTML Form

The Holiday Keyword Maintenance page contains three elements that display database values: the picture that corresponds to the current picture name, the keywords listed in the Picture Keywords box, and the keywords listed in the Valid Keywords box. The following sections describe how to code each of these elements.

Display the current picture

Code described in the earlier section, "Responding to the Navigation Buttons" (beginning on page 274), created a variable named *curPic* that names the picture file the Web visitor last specified or navigated to. This is also the picture the Web page should display.

In some cases, such as when the Web page first loads, the *curPic* variable will be empty. Thus, to display the current picture, you must first check the value of the *curPic* variable and then, if it isn't empty, build an <img> tag that specifies the *curPic* value as its *src* attribute. The following code does just that.

```
<%
If curPic <> "" Then
   Response.Write "<img src=..\holiday\images\" & curPic & "> "
End If
%>
```

Insert this code wherever you want the picture to appear in the Web page—in other words, wherever you would insert an ordinary <img> tag.

Display the keywords for the current picture

In a general sense, displaying database values in a list box requires only that you write an opening <option> tag, a value, and a closing </option> tag for each database value you want displayed. The following steps explain how to do this for the Picture Keywords list box:

1. Define the list box with <select> and </select> tags, such as the following:

   ```
   <select size="6" name="pickwd" ondblclick="btnPicDel.click();">
   ' Code to create <option> tags will go here.
   </select>
   ```
   The *size* attribute specifies the height of the list box in lines. The value *"6"* means that a maximum of six keywords will be visible at once. The *name* attribute specifies the name of the list box (and therefore, the name the selected value will have in the Request.QueryVariables or Request.Form collection). The *ondblclick* attribute is optional; it specifies a line of JavaScript code the browser should execute if the Web visitor double-clicks any listed item. In this case, it tells the browser to react as if the Web visitor had clicked the *btnPicDel* button.

2. For at least two possible reasons, the Picture Keywords text box might have no keywords to display. First, if the Web visitor hasn't specified

(or navigated to) a valid picture name, there are obviously no corresponding keywords. Second, even if the picture name is valid, it might have no assigned keywords. In either case, you should display at least something in the list box. If the Holiday Keyword Maintenance Page has nothing else to display, it displays the string *(none)*.

To accomplish this, the following code initializes a counter named *optCnt* to zero and then later, if nothing has increased that count, it writes out the line *<option>(none)</option>*. For reasons explained in step 2 in the earlier section, "Delete a keyword from a picture," a constant named KW_NONE supplies the string *(none)*.

```
<%
optCnt = 0
'   Code to create an <option> tag for each keyword will go here.
If optCnt < 1 Then
   Response.Write "<option>" & KW_NONE & "</option>" & vbCrLf
End If
%>
```

3. The *rsPkw* recordset might or might not be open, depending on whether there was a picture name to query. The most direct way to test this condition is to inspect the recordset's *State* property. If this property equals the ADO constant *adStateOpen*, the recordset is open. Otherwise, it isn't. The code to implement this logic follows; replace the comment in step 2 with this code.

```
If rsPkw.State = adStateOpen Then
'   Code to create an <option> tag for each keyword will go here.
End If
```

4. If the recordset is open, the code needs to read records until the recordset's *EOF* property becomes *True*, meanwhile writing an <option> tag that corresponds to each record. Furthermore, the application needs to increment the *optCnt* variable by one for each <option> tag written, which it does with the following code:

```
Do While Not rsPkw.EOF
   Response.Write "<option>" & rsPkw("keyword") & _
     "</option>" & vbCrLf
   optCnt = optCnt + 1
   rsPkw.MoveNext
Loop
rsPkw.Close
```

The last line of code closes the *rsPkw* recordset. Because the Web page makes no further use of the *rsPkw* recordset, and because this block of code already knows that the recordset is open, now is as good a time as any to close it.

When fully assembled, the code that displays the Picture Keywords list appears as shown in the following code. Insert this code wherever you want the list box to appear.

```
<select size="6" name="pickwd" ondblclick="btnPicDel.click();">
<%
optCnt = 0
If rsPkw.state = adStateOpen Then
  rsPkw.MoveFirst
  Do While Not rsPkw.EOF
    Response.Write "<option>" & rsPkw("keyword") & _
      "</option>" & vbCrLf
    optCnt = optCnt + 1
    rsPkw.MoveNext
  Loop
  rsPkw.Close
End If
If optCnt < 1 Then
  Response.Write "<option>" & KW_NONE & "</option>" & vbCrLf
End If
%>
</select>
```

Display the list of valid keywords

This task is even easier than displaying the list of picture keywords. For one thing, the *rsKwd* recordset is always open; for another, you can safely assume this recordset will always contain records. There is, however, one wrinkle to this list box. Each time this page appears on the visitor's browser, the keyword selected in this box should be the one stored in the *curKwd* variable.

The HTML to select a particular list item is quite simple: the <option> tag for that item merely needs to contain the *selected* attribute. The following code accomplishes this by writing out the string *<option*, then optionally writing the string *" selected"*, and then finally writing the string *">HEDGEHOGS</option>"* (where *HEDGEHOGS* is a typical keyword from keywords table).

This code should be obvious if you understood the preceding explanation and the previous section. Insert this code wherever you want the Valid Keywords list to appear: that is, wherever you would put a hard-coded list of the same type.

```
<select size="6" name="valkwd" ondblclick="btnPicAdd.click();">
<%
Do While Not rsKwd.EOF
  Response.Write "<option"
  If rsKwd("keyword") = curKwd Then
    Response.Write " selected"
  End If
  Response.Write ">" & rsKwd("keyword") & "</option>" & vbCrLf
  rsKwd.MoveNext
Loop
%>
</select>
```

Building the Holiday Search Criteria Page

Assigning keywords to items is an interesting application, but the payoff comes from using keywords as search criteria. The search.asp page shown in Figure 10-1 provides this capability—almost.

The search.asp page has no search capabilities of its own; it's actually just a data-entry form. Clicking the Submit button submits the Web visitor's criteria to another page—results.asp—that searches the database and presents the results—again, almost.

The results.asp page is really just a frameset—the frameset shown in Figure 10-2. The Web page that actually does the searching is the one that displays search results in the bottom left frame. That frame is the *itmfind* frame, which displays the itmfind.asp Web page.

The next three sections will describe the results.asp frameset, the title.htm page that occupies its top frame, and the itmfind.asp page that occupies its bottom left frame. The detail.asp page from Chapter 7 occupies the lower right frame. The topic of this section, however, is the search.asp page where the process starts.

You can lay out the search.asp page any way you want, as long as you adhere to the following specifications. There's nothing special about these specifications except that they agree with the ASP code discussed later in this chapter.

- Name the Category list box *qcatnr*, and give it only one hard-coded option: *(any)*.

- Name the Country list box *qcountry*, and give it the same, single, hard-coded option: *(any)*.

- Name the Date list box *datecomp*, and give it the options listed in Table 10-2.

- Name the Date text box *dateval*. If the Web visitor chooses to search for items by date, this box supplies the actual date value.

- Name both radio buttons *kwdmode*. Assign the value *AND* to the radio button titled *All of* and the value *OR* to the radio button titled *Any of*.

- Name the four Keywords list boxes *keyword1*, *keyword2*, *keyword3*, and *keyword4*. Give each one a single hard-coded option: *(none)*.

- You must have a Submit button, but you can name it whatever you want. The code presented here names the button *btnSub*.

- Enclose all the form fields named thus far in an HTML form. Code the <form> tag with *method="POST"* and *action="results.asp"*.

Table 10-2   Holiday Search Date Option Titles and Values

Title	Value	Title	Value
(any)	XX	On	EQ
Before	LT	On or Before	LE
After	GT	On or After	GE

You've now completed the basic parts of the HTML form. If you'd rather look at the final code than create it from scratch, open the sample file webdbdev\ch10\search.asp using your favorite HTML editor.

The following code creates the Category drop-down list. This code uses ordinary HTML to define the list itself and the first list option. Then it opens the *categories* table in *catnr* sequence, reads through all the resulting records, and creates another <option> tag for each one. Here's one such <option> tag, with the variable portions indicated in blue.

```
<option value=100>Eden Park Hotel</option>
```

The actual code follows. You can insert this code wherever you want the Category drop-down list box.

```
<select size="1" name="qcatnr">
  <option>(any)</option>
  <%
  Set rsCat = Server.CreateObject("ADODB.Recordset")
  sql = "SELECT * FROM categories ORDER BY catnr "
  rsCat.Open sql, cnHol, adOpenStatic, adLockReadOnly
  Do While Not rsCat.EOF
    Response.Write "<option value=" & _
      rsCat("catnr") & ">" & _
      rsCat("catdesc") & _
      "</option>" & vbCrLf
    rsCat.MoveNext
  Loop
  rsCat.Close
%>
</select>
```

The code that lists the country codes is almost identical, except that it opens a slightly more complex recordset. Specifically, the SQL statement queries the *categories* table for all *country* values, and then uses a GROUP BY clause to consolidate multiple occurrences of the same country value into one.

```
<select size="1" name="qcountry">
  <option>(any)</option>
  <%
  Set rsCtr = Server.CreateObject("ADODB.Recordset")
  sql = "SELECT country " & _
        "FROM categories " & _
     "GROUP BY country " & _
     "ORDER BY country;"
  rsCtr.Open sql, cnHol, adOpenStatic, adLockReadOnly
    Do While Not rsCtr.EOF
    Response.Write "<option>" & rsCtr("country") & _
      "</option>" & vbCrLf
```

(continued)

```
      rsCtr.MoveNext
    Loop
      rsCtr.Close
    %>
</select>
```

The preceding code has one dangling issue: it neither defines nor opens the *cnHol* Connection object referenced in the *rsCtr.Open* statement. To correct this oversight, add the following statement just before the Web page's </head> tag.

```
<%
Set cnHol = Server.CreateObject("ADODB.Connection")
cnStHol = "driver={Microsoft Access Driver (*.mdb)};" & _
          "dbq=" & Server.MapPath("../holiday/holiday.mdb")
cnHol.Open cnStHol,"",""
%>
```

The code that creates the four Category list boxes also resides in the <head> section. It makes no sense to read through the *keywords* table four times to generate four identical keyword lists, so the code in the <head> section reads through the table once, formats all the <option> tags, and saves the entire list in a variable named *kwOpts*. Here's the code, which belongs immediately after the *cnHol.Open* statement and before the closing %> tag.

```
Set rsKwd = Server.CreateObject("ADODB.Recordset")
sql = "SELECT * FROM keywords ORDER BY keyword "
rsKwd.Open sql, cnHol, adOpenStatic, adLockReadOnly
kwOpts = ""
Do While Not rsKwd.EOF
  kwOpts = kwOpts & "<option>" & _
                    rsKwd("keyword") & _
                    "</option>" & vbCrLf
  rsKwd.MoveNext
Loop
rsKwd.Close
```

Once this code executes, the code to display a Keywords drop-down list box consists of the following statements. Insert this code wherever you want one of the Keywords drop-down list boxes to appear. (For this application, remember to vary the last character in the name attribute from "1" to "4" for each particular listbox.)

```
<select size="1" name="keyword1">
  <option>(none)</option>
  <%=kwOpts%>
</select>
```

Building the Holiday Search Results Page (results.asp)

The Holiday Search Results page is actually a frameset that contains a small amount of ASP code. This code receives form field values from the search.asp page and forwards them to the itmfind.asp page.

A complete HTML listing for this page follows. Blue text indicates the following two instances of ASP code:

- The code that begins on line four assembles a query string that repeats every form field name and value received from the search.asp page.

- The *src* attribute in the second <frame> tag appends this query string to the URL that loads the itmfind.asp page.

The rest of the frameset is perfectly ordinary and quite unremarkable.

```
<html>
<head>
<title>Holiday Search Results</title>
<%
qstring = "?qcatnr=" & Request("qcatnr") & _
          "&qcountry=" & Request("qcountry") & _
          "&dateval=" & Request("dateval") & _
          "&datecomp=" & Request("datecomp") & _
          "&keyword1=" & Request("keyword1") & _
          "&keyword2=" & Request("keyword2") & _
          "&keyword3=" & Request("keyword3") & _
          "&keyword4=" & Request("keyword4") & _
          "&kwdmode=" & Request("kwdmode")
%>
</head>
<frameset rows="50,*">
  <frame name="title" src="title.htm"
         target="_top" scrolling="no"
         marginwidth="0" marginheight="0">
  <frameset cols="40%,60%">
    <frame name="itmfind" src="itmfind.asp<%=qstring%>"
           target="detail" scrolling="auto"
           marginwidth="0" marginheight="0">
    <frame name="detail" src="../ch07/blank.htm"
           target="_self" scrolling="auto"
           marginwidth="0" marginheight="0">
    <noframes>
    <body>
    <p>This page uses frames, but your browser doesn't support them.</p>
    </body>
    </noframes>
  </frameset>
</frameset>
</html>
```

Building the Holiday Search
Title Page (title.htm)

The top frame in the results.asp frameset displays a page named title.htm—an ordinary Web page that simply provides title text and a link back to the Holiday Search Criteria page. To view the code for this page, open the sample file \webdbdev\ch10\title.htm in your favorite HTML editor.

Building the Holiday Search Item Find Page

The Holiday Search thumbnail page (itmfind.asp) isn't terribly different from the thumbnail page (piclist.asp) described in Chapter 7. Both pages create a SQL statement based on visitor criteria, query the *items* table, and display the results as a clickable list of thumbnail pictures organized in an HTML table. What's more, both pages display the detail.asp page (from Chapter 7) in the *detail* frame of their respective framesets—initially and whenever the Web visitor clicks a thumbnail.

There are, however, two distinct differences between these Web pages. The less critical difference is the formatting; the itmfind.asp page is wider and displays more data than the piclist.asp page in Chapter 7. The more significant difference is that piclist.asp page accepted a single criterion—category number—and used it to create a simple SQL statement. By contrast, the itmfind.asp page accepts nine criteria values, all optional, and uses them to create highly complex SQL statements. For example, specifying the criteria shown in Figure 10-5 produces the SQL statement that follows.

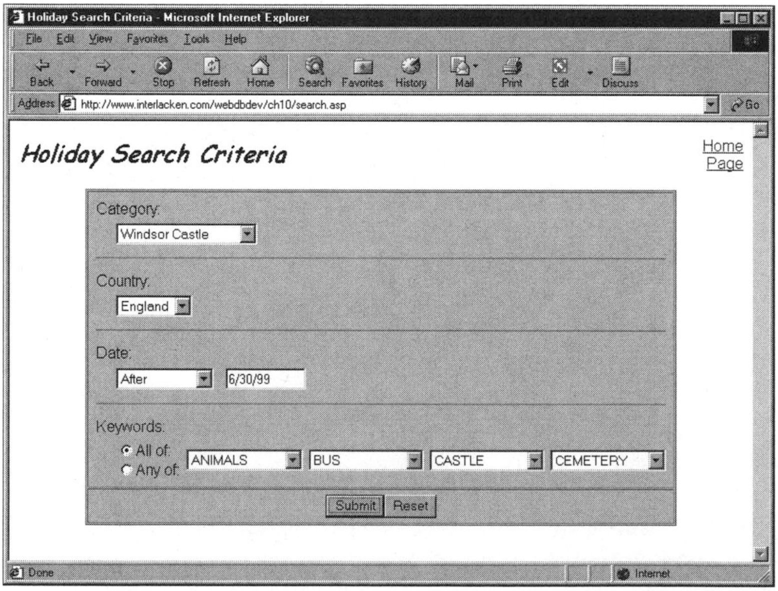

Figure 10-5 *Specifying these criteria activates every SQL option the itmfind.asp page can generate.*

```
SELECT    items.catnr,
          items.seqnr,
          items.picname,
          items.title,
          items.picdate,
          categories.catdesc,
          categories.country,
          Count(pickwd.keyword) AS CountOfkeyword
FROM      (items LEFT JOIN categories
                      ON items.catnr = categories.catnr)
              LEFT JOIN pickwd
                      ON items.picname = pickwd.picname
WHERE     (items.catnr = 700)
    AND (categories.country = 'England')
    AND (picdate > #6/30/99#)
    AND ((pickwd.keyword = 'ANIMALS') OR
         (pickwd.keyword = 'BUS') OR
         (pickwd.keyword = 'CASTLE') OR
         (pickwd.keyword = 'CEMETERY'))
GROUP BY items.catnr,
          items.seqnr,
          items.picname,
          items.title,
          items.picdate,
          categories.catdesc,
          categories.country
HAVING    Count(pickwd.keyword) = 4
ORDER BY items.catnr,
          items.seqnr ;
```

This is quite a SQL statement; fortunately, most of it remains constant. Here's the clause-by-clause explanation:

- The SELECT clause names all the fields that should appear in the result set. This includes fields from the *items*, *categories*, and *pickwd* tables.

  The last field, coded *Count(pickwd.keyword) AS CountOfkeyword*, works together with the GROUP BY clause later in the SQL statement. The GROUP BY clause tell the database software that whenever two or more records in the result set have identical values in a given list of fields, the database software should aggregate these records into one. The expression *Count(pickwd.keyword)* tells the database software to return not a keyword value, but instead the number of keyword values it consolidated into that record.

  Suppose, for example, that because of the GROUP BY clause the database software consolidates a certain three records into one. Suppose also that those records contained the keywords BUS, CASTLE, and CEMETERY. In the aggregated result set, the value of *Count(pickwd.keyword)* would be 3.

In this example, the Web visitor specified four keywords and the *All of* option. The HAVING clause therefore limits returned records to those with *Count(pickwd.keyword)* equal to 4. If the visitor specified *Any of*, the HAVING clause would be omitted.

- The FROM clause specifies how to join the *items*, *categories*, and *pickwd* tables. The following expression means, "For every record in the *items* table that satisfies the WHERE clause (if there is one), find the record in the *categories* table that has the same *catnr* value, and use that *categories* record to supply any *categories* fields named in the SELECT clause. If no matching *categories* record exists, include the information from the *items* table and allow the fields from the *categories* table to be null."

```
(items LEFT JOIN categories ON items.catnr = categories.catnr)
```

Appending the following expression to the preceding one joins the *pickwd* table to the result set obtained by joining the *items* and *categories* tables. Unlike the first join, this one is based on matching *picname* values. Like the first join, this is a LEFT JOIN, and the absence of a matching *pickwd* record doesn't prevent a record from appearing in the result set.

```
LEFT JOIN pickwd ON items.picname = pickwd.picname
```

Figure 10-6 shows the relationship among the *items*, *categories*, and *pickwd* tables when Microsoft Access displays this query.

- The WHERE clause varies depending on which criteria the Web visitor selects. For example, the expression *(items.catnr = 700)* is present because the Web visitor specified a category of Windsor Castle. (Windsor Castle is

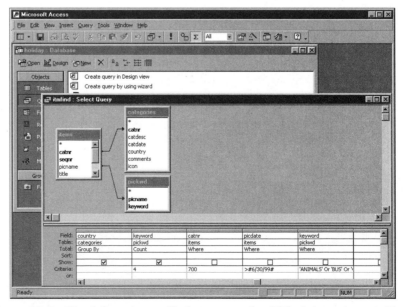

Figure 10-6 *Here's how Access displays a complex SQL statement created by the itmfind.asp page.*

category 700). If the visitor specified a category of *(any)*, this expression would be absent.

The comparison operator > in the expression *(picdate > #6/30/99#)* comes from the Date drop-down list box, where the Web visitor chose *After.* If the visitor chose *(any)* or left the date text box blank, no expression involving the *picdate* field would appear.

Recall that the WHERE clause filters records before any aggregation caused by a GROUP BY clause, while the HAVING clause filters records after any such aggregation.

- The GROUP BY clause, as already mentioned, aggregates all records in the result set having equal values in the listed fields.

- The HAVING clause filters records after aggregation by the GROUP BY clause. If the Web visitor specified one or more keywords and the *All of* option, this clause will be present and require that *Count(pickwd.keyword)* be equal to the number of keywords selected. In any other case, the clause will be absent.

- The ORDER BY clause controls the sequence of any final result set records the database software returns.

Among these clauses, all but the WHERE and HAVING clauses are constant. This simplifies things a bit, but constructing this Web page nevertheless requires the following 10 steps. Each step is described in a subsequent section. If you'd rather review finished results than enter the code from scratch, open the sample file at \webdbdev\ch10\itmfind.asp or check the listing at the end of this chapter.

1. Initialize the Web page.
2. Declare variables.
3. Incorporate category criteria.
4. Incorporate country criteria.
5. Incorporate date criteria.
6. Incorporate keyword criteria.
7. Complete the WHERE and HAVING clauses.
8. Build the SQL statement.
9. Run the query.
10. Display the results.

Initialize the Web page

Using your favorite HTML editor, create a new .asp page. Because this is a complex page with lots of opportunity for misspelling variable names, add an *Option Explicit* statement as the first line in the file. Be sure to include the adovbs.inc file and, if you want, a linked style sheet file.

```
<% Option Explicit %>
<html>
<head>
<!-- #include file="../adovbs.inc" -->
<link rel="stylesheet" type="text/css"
      href="../holiday/holiday.css">
<title>Holiday Photo Search Item Find Page</title>
<base target="detail">
<!-- Code to declare variables and incorporate -->
<!-- search criteria will go here. -->
</head>
<body>
<!-- Code to query database will go here. -->
<!-- Code to display results will go here. -->
</body>
</html>
```

Declare variables

Insert the following code in place of "Code to declare variables and incorporate search criteria will go here." These statements create all the variables used in the ASP code.

```
<%
Dim datecl
Dim sqlWhere
Dim kwdWhere
Dim kwdCnt
Dim sqlHaving
Dim sql
Dim cnHol
Dim cnStHol
Dim rsHit
' Code to incorporate search criteria will go here.
%>
```

Realistically, developers seldom know in advance the names of all the variables they're going to use. Instead, they insert *Dim* statements at the top of the page as needed.

Incorporate category criteria

Honoring the search criteria is largely a matter of coding the correct WHERE clause for a SQL statement. In the case of the Category field this is a fairly simple job. There are only three conditions, and two of them require no action.

The first case requiring no action is when the *qcatnr* field in the Request object is empty. The second is when the *qcatnr* field is non-numeric. Otherwise, the required WHERE clause looks like this (Of course, the actual requested category would replace the number 700, shown in blue.)

```
(items.catnr = 700)
```

If the category code is valid, the following code places this string in a variable named *sqlWhere*. Otherwise, it stores an empty string in that variable. Either way, the WHERE clause is ready for additional criteria, should they exist.

Insert these statements in place of the comment in the previous section.

```
If (Request("qcatnr") = "") Or _
Not IsNumeric(Request("qcatnr")) Then
  sqlWhere = ""
Else
  sqlWhere = "(items.catnr = " & Request("qcatnr") & ")"
End If
```

Incorporate country criteria

If the *qcountry* value received from the search.asp page is empty or contains the default string *(any)*, there's no country criterion and the WHERE clause requires no additional code. If the country value is valid, however, the WHERE clause needs to contain an expression like this:

```
(categories.country = 'Wales')
```

This is very similar to the requirement in the previous section, except for a couple of additional wrinkles:

- *Country* is a string field and thus requires single quotation marks around the comparison value.

- The *sqlWhere* variable might or might not already contain an expression. If it does, the code must append the string *"AND"* to the variable *sqlWhere* before it appends the country expression. If the *sqlWhere* variable is blank, the code can simply append the country expression.

Once you are satisfied that the following code meets these requirements, insert it immediately after the code you inserted in the previous section.

```
If (Request("qcountry") <> "") and _
   (Request("qcountry") <> "(any)") Then
  If sqlWhere <> "" Then
    sqlWhere = sqlWhere & " AND "
  End If
  sqlWhere = sqlWhere & "(categories.country = '" & _
             Request("qcountry") & "')"
End If
```

Incorporate date criteria

A date criteria is valid only if the search.asp page supplies correct values for both the *dateval* and *datecomp* fields. This requirement increases the number of things that can go wrong and makes placing the required code in a subroutine an attractive option. A subroutine has an advantage: whenever anything goes wrong, the code can simply *Exit Sub*.

1. Insert the following code immediately after the code you added in the previous section. The first statement calls the subroutine; the last three lines define it.

```
AppendDateClause
' Code to handle additional criteria will go here.
Sub AppendDateClause()
' Code to check and apply date criteria will go here.
End Sub
```

2. Replace the second comment in step 1 with the following code. This code determines whether the search.asp page supplied an empty *dateval* value, and if so exits the subroutine.

```
If Request("dateval") = "" Then
   Exit Sub
End If
```

3. The following code determines whether the Web visitor entered a valid date in the *dateval* field. If not, the code ignores the criterion by exiting the subroutine.

```
If Not IsDate(Request("dateval")) Then
   Exit Sub
End If
```

Insert this code immediately after the code from step 2.

4. The following code checks the value of the *datecomp* drop-down list box in the search.asp page. The Web visitor uses this list to specify records dated as previously listed in Table 10-2. If the itmfind.asp page receives one of these values, it starts building a WHERE clause in the variable *datecl*. Otherwise, it exits the subroutine. The code belongs immediately after the code you inserted in step 3.

```
Select Case UCase(Request("datecomp"))
  Case "LT"
    datecl = "(picdate < #"
  Case "LE"
    datecl = "(picdate <= #"
  Case "EQ"
    datecl = "(picdate = #"
  Case "GE"
    datecl = "(picdate >= #"
  Case "GT"
    datecl = "(picdate > #"
  Case Else
    Exit Sub
End Select
```

5. If control still resides within the subroutine (that is, if no error conditions have caused an exit), the following code first checks to see if the *sqlWhere* variable already contains criteria. If it does, the code appends the string *" AND "*. Then, in all cases, it appends the *datecl* value, the date received from the *dateval* text box, and a closing pound sign and parenthesis. In other words, it appends a clause like this:

```
AND (picdate > #6/30/99#)
```

To carry out this logic, add the following code immediately after the code you inserted in step 4 and before the *End Sub* statement you created in step 1.

```
If sqlWhere <> "" Then
   sqlWhere = sqlWhere & " AND "
End If
sqlWhere = sqlWhere & datecl & Request("dateval") & "#)"
```

Incorporate keyword criteria

Handling the four keyword criteria fields involves the following considerations:

- To be a valid criterion, a keyword field must not be empty and must not contain the value *(none)*.

- To be a valid criterion, a keyword field must not be equal to any previous keyword field. If the Web visitor selects the keyword ANIMALS twice, it should only count once.

- As shown below, OR operators need to precede the expressions that test for the second and all subsequent keywords.

```
(pickwd.keyword = 'ANIMALS') OR (pickwd.keyword = 'BUS')
```

- The code needs to keep a count of the number of valid keywords. Later, this count will be the basis for determining whether a given item has all the keywords specified.

The following procedure creates the code to handle the four keyword fields. You should insert all the subsequent code in place of the first comment you added in step 1 of the previous section.

1. Initialize the count of keywords found to zero.

```
kwdCnt = 0
```

2. If the first keyword isn't empty and isn't equal to *(none)*, save an expression of the following form in the *kwdWhere* variable, and increment *kwdCnt* by one:

```
(pickwd.keyword = 'ANIMALS')
```

Otherwise, store an empty string in *kwdWhere*.

```
If (Request("keyword1") <> "") and _
   (Request("keyword1") <> "(none)") Then
   kwdWhere = "(pickwd.keyword = '" & Request("keyword1")& "')"
   kwdCnt = kwdCnt + 1
```

(continued)

```
Else
  kwdWhere = ""
End If
```

3. Consider the second keyword valid if it isn't empty, isn't equal to *(none)*, and isn't equal to the first keyword. If the keyword is valid and *kwdWhere* already contains an expression, append the string *" OR "* to *kwdWhere*. Then—whether or not you appended *" OR "*—append an expression of the following form:

```
(pickwd.keyword = 'BUS')
```

The variable *kwdCnt* is then incremented by 1.

```
If (Request("keyword2") <> "") and _
  (Request("keyword2") <> "(none)") and _
  (Request("keyword2") <> (Request("keyword1"))) Then
  If kwdWhere <> "" Then
    kwdWhere = kwdWhere & " OR "
  End If
  kwdWhere = kwdWhere & "(pickwd.keyword = '" & Request("keyword2") & "')"
  kwdCnt = kwdCnt + 1
End If
```

4. Repeat the logic of step 3 for the third keyword. Recall that to be valid, the third keyword can't be null, can't equal *(none)*, and can't equal keywords one or two.

```
If (Request("keyword3") <> "") and _
  (Request("keyword3") <> "(none)") and _
  (Request("keyword3") <> (Request("keyword1"))) and _
  (Request("keyword3") <> (Request("keyword2"))) Then
  If kwdWhere <> "" Then
    kwdWhere = kwdWhere & " OR "
  End If
  kwdWhere = kwdWhere & "(pickwd.keyword = '" & Request("keyword3") & "')"
  kwdCnt = kwdCnt + 1
End If
```

5. Repeat the logic of step 3 again for the fourth keyword. The fourth keyword can't be equal to keywords one, two, or three.

```
If (Request("keyword4") <> "") and _
  (Request("keyword4") <> "(none)") and _
  (Request("keyword4") <> (Request("keyword1"))) and _
  (Request("keyword4") <> (Request("keyword2"))) and _
  (Request("keyword4") <> (Request("keyword3"))) Then
  If kwdWhere <> "" Then
    kwdWhere = kwdWhere & " OR "
  End If
  kwdWhere = kwdWhere & "(pickwd.keyword = '" & Request("keyword4") & "')"
  kwdCnt = kwdCnt + 1
End If
```

6. If the *kwdWhere* variable isn't empty (if steps 1 through 5 have created any expressions), check the *sqlWhere* variable. If it's empty, there are no other criteria; therefore, replace the contents of the *sqlWhere* variable with those of the *kwdWhere* variable. If the *sqlWhere* variable isn't empty, append the values *" AND "*, an opening parentheses, the *kwdWhere* variable, and a closing parentheses.

```
If kwdWhere <> "" Then
  If sqlWhere = "" Then
    sqlWhere = kwdWhere
  Else
    sqlWhere = sqlWhere & " AND (" & kwdWhere & ")"
  End If
End If
```

Complete the WHERE and HAVING clauses

There are just two orders of business to consider before constructing the SQL statement that will search for items matching the visitor's criteria. First, unless the *sqlWhere* variable is empty, you must prefix its value with the SQL reserved word WHERE and suffix its value with a space. This satisfies SQL requirements whether or not *sqlWhere* is empty. This code goes immediately after the code you added in the previous section.

```
If sqlWhere <> "" Then
  sqlWhere = " WHERE " & sqlWhere & " "
End If
```

The second order of business determines whether the SQL statement requires a HAVING clause, and if so constructs it. The HAVING clause, if any, will reside in a variable named *sqlHaving* that the code below initializes to an empty string. The code then determines whether the Web visitor chose *All Of* on the search.asp page and whether the visitor chose any valid keywords. If both of these conditions are *True*, the code constructs a HAVING clause of the following form:

```
HAVING Count(pickwd.keyword) = 4
```

The code replaces the value 4 with the value in *kwdCnt* and places the finished expression, as promised, in the variable *sqlHaving*.

```
sqlHaving = ""
If UCase(Left(Request("kwdmode"),1)) = "A" Then
  If kwdCnt > 0 Then
    sqlHaving = " HAVING Count(pickwd.keyword) = " & kwdCnt
  End If
End If
```

Build the SQL statement

The last block of code in the <head> section creates the SQL statement that will search for and retrieve any records satisfying the Web visitor's criteria. As promised, the entire statement is constant except for inserting the contents of the *sqlWhere* variable in line 12 and the contents of the *sqlHaving* variable in the third line from the bottom. (Both variables are in blue.)

Insert this statement after the code you added in the previous section and before the *Sub AppendDateClause* statement you added earlier, in the section "Incorporate Date Criteria."

```
sql = "SELECT items.catnr, " & _
            "items.seqnr, " & _
            "items.picname, " & _
            "items.title, " & _
            "items.picdate, " & _
            "categories.catdesc, " & _
            "categories.country, " & _
            "Count(pickwd.keyword) AS CountOfkeyword " & _
        "FROM (items " & _
    "LEFT JOIN categories ON items.catnr = categories.catnr) " & _
    "LEFT JOIN pickwd ON items.picname = pickwd.picname " & _
            sqlWhere & _
        "GROUP BY items.catnr, " & _
            "items.seqnr, " & _
            "items.picname, " & _
            "items.title, " & _
            "items.picdate, " & _
            "categories.catdesc, " & _
            "categories.country " & _
            sqlHaving & _
    " ORDER BY items.catnr, items.seqnr ; "
```

Run the query

By now, statements like the following should be quite familiar. To quickly recap: They create an ADO Connection object and an ADO connection string, open the connection, and then create and open an ADO recordset using the SQL statement coded in the previous section. The last two statements close the Recordset and Connection objects after all processing is complete. Insert these statements immediately after the Web page's <body> tag.

```
<%
Set cnHol = Server.CreateObject("ADODB.Connection")
cnStHol = "driver={Microsoft Access Driver (*.mdb)};" & _
          "dbq=" & Server.MapPath("../holiday/holiday.mdb")
cnHol.Open cnStHol,"",""
Set rsHit = Server.CreateObject("ADODB.Recordset")
rsHit.Open sql, cnHol, adOpenStatic, adLockReadOnly
' Code to process recordset will go here.
rsHit.Close
cnHol.Close
%>
```

Display the results

At this point the hard work is done; all that remains is to show the Web visitor whatever the query has found.

1. If no items matched the visitor's criteria, the Web page should display a message to that effect, rather than a blank screen. Therefore, replace the comment in the previous section with these statements:

```
If rsHit.EOF Then
   Response.Write "<P> </p>" & vbCrLf
   Response.Write "<P class=err align=center>" & _
     "No matching items found.</p>" & vbCrLf
Else
' Code to read through recordset and create output will go here.
End If
```

2. If the query did find some records—or at least one—the itmfind.asp page needs to replace the blank.htm page that the result.asp frameset initially loaded into the *detail* frame. The new page should be the picshow.asp page developed in Chapter 7, which requires the key values (category and sequence number) of the record it should display.

   As before, the ASP code in the itmfind.asp page can't reload the *detail* frameset directly. Instead, it uses the following statements to write a browser script into the outgoing Web page. When the browser runs that script, the browser reloads the *detail* frame. Replace the comment in step 1 with these statements:

```
   Response.Write "<script>" & vbCrLf
   Response.Write "parent.frames.detail.location = " & _
     chr(34) & _
     "../ch07/picshow.asp" & _
     "?qcatnr=" & rsHit("catnr") & _
     "&qseqnr=" & rsHit("seqnr") & _
     chr(34) & vbCrLf
   Response.Write "</script>" & vbCrLf
' Code to read through recordset and create output will go here.
```

3. To display the thumbnail and other details for the first detail item, replace the comment in step 2 with the following HTML table. This is a three-column, four-row table where the top three cells in column one merge for the thumbnail picture, and all the cells in the fourth row merge to display a horizontal line. This layout is visible in the following picture.

Because this portion of the code contains much more HTML than ASP code, it's easier to code as plain HTML. Notice, therefore, the closing %>

tag and the opening <% tag before and after the table. The ASP code to display the category name, picture title, and date appears in blue. The next step will add the code that displays the thumbnail picture.

```
%>
<table border="0" cellpadding="2" cellspacing="0">
<!-- Loop to scan all founds items will start here. -->
  <tr>
    <td class="pic" rowspan="3" align="center"><%
'   Thumbnail picture will go here.
       %></td>
    <td class="pic">Category:</td>
    <td class="pic"><%=rsHit("catdesc")%></td>
  </tr>
  <tr>
    <td class="pic">Title:</td>
    <td class="pic"><%=rsHit("title")%></td>
  </tr>
  <tr>
    <td class="pic">Date:</td>
    <td class="pic"><%=rsHit("picdate")%></td>
  </tr>
  <tr>
    <td class="pic" colspan="3">
      <hr>
    </td>
  </tr>
<!-- Loop to scan all founds items will end here. -->
</table>
<%
```

4. Displaying a found item's thumbnail image requires HTML like this:

```
<a href=../ch07/picshow.asp?qcatnr=700&qseqnr=1300
    target=detail>
<img src=../holiday/images/thumb/scan12.jpg border=0>
</a>
```

The only variable portion of the <img> tag is the thumbnail picture's file name, which comes from the *picname* field in the *items* table. The only variable portions in the surrounding <a> and </a> tags are the category and sequence numbers that control which items the picshow.asp page displays. The variable fields appear above in blue. Here's the ASP code to create this HTML for a given found item. Insert this code in place of the comment, "Thumbnail picture will go here." in step 3.

```
<%
Response.Write "<a href=../ch07/picshow.asp" & _
  "?qcatnr=" & rsHit("catnr") & _
  "&qseqnr=" & rsHit("seqnr") & _
```

```
" target=detail>" & _
"<img src=../holiday/images/thumb/" & _
rsHit("picname") & " border=0></a>"
    %>
```

5. To display multiple found items, the ASP code needs to repeat everything between (but not including) the <table> and </table> tags in step 3. To start a loop that performs this repetition, insert the following statements in place of the HTML comment line, "Loop to scan all founds items will start here." in step 3.

```
<%
Do While Not rsHit.EOF
    %>
```

6. To complete the loop started in step 5, replace the HTML comment line, "Loop to scan all founds items will end here." in step 3 with these statements.

```
<%
rsHit.MoveNext
Loop
    %>
```

Review the complete Web page

You've now seen all of the code in the itmfind.asp page. To see how all these code fragments fit together, review the following complete listing:

```
<% Option Explicit %>
<html>
<head>
<!-- #include file="../adovbs.inc" -->
<link rel="stylesheet" type="text/css"
      href="../holiday/holiday.css">
<title>Holiday Photo Search Item Find Page</title>
<base target="detail">
<%
' Declare variables.
Dim datecl
Dim sqlWhere
Dim kwdWhere
Dim kwdCnt
Dim sqlHaving
Dim sql
Dim cnHol
Dim cnStHol
Dim rsHit
' Create a WHERE expression for category number.
If (Request("qcatnr") = "") or _
```

```
    Not IsNumeric(Request("qcatnr")) Then
      sqlWhere = ""
    Else
      sqlWhere = "(items.catnr = " & Request("qcatnr") & ")"
    End If
    ' Create a WHERE expression for country.
    If (Request("qcountry") <> "") and _
       (Request("qcountry") <> "(any)") Then
      If sqlWhere <> "" Then
        sqlWhere = sqlWhere & " AND "
      End If
      sqlWhere = sqlWhere & "(categories.country = '" & _
                 Request("qcountry") & "')"
    End If
    ' Create a WHERE expression for date.
    AppendDateClause
    kwdCnt = 0
    ' Create a WHERE expression for keyword #1.
    If (Request("keyword1") <> "") and _
       (Request("keyword1") <> "(none)") Then
      kwdWhere = "(pickwd.keyword = '" & Request("keyword1")& "')"
      kwdCnt = kwdCnt + 1
    Else
      kwdWhere = ""
    End If
    ' Create a WHERE expression for keyword #2.
    If (Request("keyword2") <> "") and _
       (Request("keyword2") <> "(none)") and _
       (Request("keyword2") <> (Request("keyword1"))) Then
      If kwdWhere <> "" Then
        kwdWhere = kwdWhere & " OR "
      End If
      kwdWhere = kwdWhere & "(pickwd.keyword = '" & Request("keyword2") & "')"
      kwdCnt = kwdCnt + 1
    End If
    ' Create a WHERE expression for keyword #3.
    If (Request("keyword3") <> "") and _
       (Request("keyword3") <> "(none)") and _
       (Request("keyword3") <> (Request("keyword1"))) and _
       (Request("keyword3") <> (Request("keyword2"))) Then
      If kwdWhere <> "" Then
        kwdWhere = kwdWhere & " OR "
      End If
      kwdWhere = kwdWhere & "(pickwd.keyword = '" & Request("keyword3") & "')"
      kwdCnt = kwdCnt + 1
    End If
    ' Create a WHERE expression for keyword #4.
```

```
If (Request("keyword4") <> "") and _
   (Request("keyword4") <> "(none)") and _
   (Request("keyword4") <> (Request("keyword1"))) and _
   (Request("keyword4") <> (Request("keyword2"))) and _
   (Request("keyword4") <> (Request("keyword3"))) Then
  If kwdWhere <> "" Then
    kwdWhere = kwdWhere & " OR "
  End If
  kwdWhere = kwdWhere & "(pickwd.keyword = '" & Request("keyword4") & "')"
  kwdCnt = kwdCnt + 1
End If
' Append expressions for category criteria to WHERE clause.
If kwdWhere <> "" Then
  If sqlWhere = "" Then
    sqlWhere = kwdWhere
  Else
    sqlWhere = sqlWhere & " AND (" & kwdWhere & ")"
  End If
End If
' If there are query criteria, insert the SQL keyword WHERE.
If sqlWhere <> "" Then
  sqlWhere = " WHERE " & sqlWhere & " "
End If
' If the Web visitor demands that all chosen keywords be
' present, create the required HAVING clause.
sqlHaving = ""
If UCase(Left(Request("kwdmode"),1)) = "A" Then
  If kwdCnt > 0 Then
    sqlHaving = " HAVING Count(pickwd.keyword) = " & kwdCnt
  End If
End If
' Build a SQL statement to select all items matching the
' Web visitor's criteria.
sql = "SELECT items.catnr, " & _
             "items.seqnr, " & _
             "items.picname, " & _
             "items.title, " & _
             "items.picdate, " & _
             "categories.catdesc, " & _
             "categories.country, " & _
             "Count(pickwd.keyword) AS CountOfkeyword " & _
        "FROM (items " & _
     "LEFT JOIN categories ON items.catnr = categories.catnr) " & _
     "LEFT JOIN pickwd ON items.picname = pickwd.picname " & _
             sqlWhere & _
         "GROUP BY items.catnr, " & _
             "items.seqnr, " & _
             "items.picname, " & _
             "items.title, " & _
```

(continued)

```
                              "items.picdate, " & _
                              "categories.catdesc, " & _
                              "categories.country " & _
                              sqlHaving & _
                " ORDER BY items.catnr, items.seqnr ; "

        ' Define Subroutine to handle date criteria.
        Sub AppendDateClause()
        ' If the date value is empty, just exit.
          If Request("dateval") = "" Then
            Exit Sub
          End If
        ' If the date value isn't a valid date, just exit.
          If Not IsDate(Request("dateval")) Then
            Exit Sub
          End If
        ' If the date operator is valid, begin building the
        ' WHERE clause. If it isn't, just exit.
          Select Case UCase(Request("datecomp"))
            Case "LT"
              datecl = "(picdate < #"
            Case "LE"
              datecl = "(picdate <= #"
            Case "EQ"
              datecl = "(picdate = #"
            Case "GE"
              datecl = "(picdate >= #"
            Case "GT"
              datecl = "(picdate > #"
            Case Else
              Exit Sub
          End Select
        ' Append date expression to WHERE clause.
          If sqlWhere <> "" Then
            sqlWhere = sqlWhere & " AND "
          End If
          sqlWhere = sqlWhere & datecl & Request("dateval") & "#)"
        End Sub
        %>
        </head>
        <body>
        <%
        ' Create and Open ADO Connection object.
        Set cnHol = Server.CreateObject("ADODB.Connection")
        cnStHol = "driver={Microsoft Access Driver (*.mdb)};" & _
                  "dbq=" & Server.MapPath("../holiday/holiday.mdb")
        cnHol.Open cnStHol,"",""
```

```
' Create and Open ADO Recordset object, using the SQL
' statement created above.
Set rsHit = Server.CreateObject("ADODB.Recordset")
rsHit.Open sql, cnHol, adOpenStatic, adLockReadOnly
' If there are no matching records, display a message.
If rsHit.EOF Then
  Response.Write "<P> </p>" & vbCrLf
  Response.Write "<P class=Err align=center>" & _
    "No matching items found.</p>" & vbCrLf
' If some matching records exist, display them.
Else
'   Write a browser-side script to update another frame (named
'   detail) within the same frameset that displays this page.
  Response.Write "<script>" & vbCrLf
  Response.Write "parent.frames.detail.location =  & _
    chr(34) & _
    "../ch07/picshow.asp" & _
    "?qcatnr=" & rsHit("catnr") & _
    "&qseqnr=" & rsHit("seqnr") & _
    chr(34) & vbCrLf
  Response.Write "</script>" & vbCrLf
'   Big ELSE continues below.
%>
<!-- Arrange the output by using an HTML table. -->
<table border="0" cellpadding="2" cellspacing="0">
  <%
' Start looping through all found records.
Do While Not rsHit.EOF
  %>
  <tr>
    <td class="pic" rowspan="3" align="center"><%
Response.Write "<a href=../ch07/picshow.asp" & _
  "?qcatnr=" & rsHit("catnr") & _
  "&qseqnr=" & rsHit("seqnr") & _
  " target=detail>" & _
  "<img src=../holiday/images/thumb/" & _
  rsHit("picname") & " border=0></a>"
    %></td>
    <td class="pic">Category:</td>
    <td class="pic"><%=rsHit("catdesc")%></td>
  </tr>
  <tr>
    <td class="pic">Title:</td>
    <td class="pic"><%=rsHit("title")%></td>
  </tr>
  <tr>
    <td class="pic">Date:</td>
    <td class="pic"><%=rsHit("picdate")%></td>
  </tr>
```

(continued)

```
  <tr>
    <td class="pic" colspan="3">
      <hr>
    </td>
  </tr>
  <%
' Terminate loop through all found records.
rsHit.MoveNext
Loop
  %>
</table>
<%
' Terminate if rsHit.EOF Then...Else statement.
End If
' Close ADO Recordset and Connection objects.
rsHit.Close
cnHol.Close
%>
</body>
</html>
```

Chapter Summary

In this chapter, you saw several important ways to integrate HTML form elements and database values. You also learned, through some Web database pages of medium complexity, how to provide Web visitors with a keyword search facility.

Part 3, "Developing Applications," put to use, in practical examples, the background material explained in Part 2, "Key Concepts." This included Web pages that perform catalog lookups, that maintain catalog information two different ways, and that maintain and use keyword search terms. While none of these pages are simple, they provide a lot of function for the amount of code required to create them.

Part 4, "Advanced Topics," will explain how to perform full-text document searches and how to manage sessions.

Part 4

Advanced Topics

Chapter 11

Performing Text Queries

Chapter Objectives   Estimated Time: 35 minutes

In this chapter, you'll learn

- How Microsoft Indexing Service builds a database of words contained in a collection of Web pages (or, for that matter, documents of any other type).

- How to open an ADO connection to an Indexing Service catalog.

- How to query an Indexing Service catalog and receive the results as an ADO recordset.

- How to create a Web page that uses these techniques to search for text in a collection of ordinary Web pages.

Keyword searching, the technique illustrated in Chapter 10, "Performing Keyword Searches," is a valuable and useful tool for supporting ad hoc queries against the content of a database. Such queries are ad hoc because neither the database designer, the Web page programmer, or the person who codes the keywords knows what kinds of queries the Web visitors will submit. There are far too many combinations of criteria to plan each one in advance. Nevertheless, the data is well-ordered in a Microsoft Access or Microsoft SQL Server database.

Another type of ad hoc query involves full-text searching of a group of Web pages or other documents. This is quite a different animal. The data in this case doesn't reside neatly in database records; it's scattered through many files and folders on your local disk, file server, or Web server. The information in these documents, expressed in natural language, is imprecise compared to the highly structured and well-defined content of a database. The queries are imprecise as well; the requestor who submits the word *fly* as a search term might expect the words *fly, flew,* and *flown* all to match. The requestor doesn't expect perfect results; he or she expects to see results listed in order by degree of accuracy.

If you think of ADO as just a way to query traditional databases such as Microsoft Access and Microsoft SQL Server, this chapter will probably surprise you. By treating Microsoft Indexing Service as a data source, ADO can submit full-text queries and receive lists of matching documents in almost the same way that it submits queries to and receives results from traditional databases.

Introducing Microsoft Indexing Service

All versions of Microsoft Windows 2000 include a full-text indexing and retrieval search engine called Microsoft Indexing Service. A comparable service is available for Microsoft Windows NT Server 4.0; in that guise, it's called Microsoft Index Server and comes as part of the Windows NT Server 4.0 Option Pack. For purposes of this chapter, consider the Windows 2000 and Windows NT 4.0 versions equivalent. The same ASP code works in either environment.

Every Indexing Service application involves two fundamental entities: a corpus and a catalog. The *corpus* is the collection of documents (files) that the application wants to search. In practice, the corpus is usually a collection of one or more folder trees. Every time someone adds, changes, or deletes a document in the corpus, Indexing Service scans the document and stores its words and properties in a database called the *catalog*. A single copy of Indexing Service can simultaneously maintain several catalogs, and each catalog can index many folder trees.

Applications that use Indexing Service might appear to be searching the corpus, but they're actually searching the catalog. This greatly improves both efficiency and speed.

When you query an Indexing Service catalog via ADO, the result is an ADO recordset containing one record for each matching file in the corpus. If you specify a result set that includes file locations, you can then access those files in the usual way (that is, by using those locations as hyperlink targets).

To scan documents intelligently, Indexing Service uses a collection of filters. The filter for Microsoft Word documents, for example, can extract information that appears in Word's File Properties dialog box. The Microsoft Excel filter can extract information about each worksheet in a workbook; the Microsoft PowerPoint filter can extract information about individual slides, and so on. The Web page filter can extract data enclosed by specific tags such as <title>...</title> and <h1>...</h1>.The fields stored within a given catalog are those available from the file system that contains the corpus, plus those available from any installed filters. Adding a field to the catalog is generally a matter of adding or updating a filter to collect the desired information.

Microsoft provides filters for Office documents and for Web pages. To obtain Indexing Service filters for other document types, contact the software vendor that supports those types.

When configured to work with Internet Information Services, Indexing Service automatically sets up a catalog named *Web* that indexes the default Web server's content tree. To index any additional Web servers running on the same machine, the server's administrator can set up additional catalogs.

Opening an ADO Connection to Indexing Service

An Indexing Service catalog uses proprietary access methods; it's not, for example, an Access or SQL Server database. Even so, ADO can access an Indexing Service catalog in much the same way that it accesses those other databases. For example, the following statements open a connection to an Indexing Service catalog:

```
cnStIx = "provider=msidxs;data source=Interlacken"
Set cnIx = Server.CreateObject("ADODB.Connection")
cnIx.Open cnStIx, "", ""
```

The first statement builds the connection string, and the expression *provider=msidxs* tells ADO you're connecting to Indexing Service. The *data source* attribute specifies an Indexing Service catalog; if the catalog isn't specified, it defaults to the catalog named *Web*.

Tip If your Indexing Service queries seem to be locating documents that belong to the wrong Web server, contact the server's administrator and get the correct catalog name.

The last two statements are unchanged from their syntax in earlier chapters.

Opening an Indexing Service ADO Recordset

As with other databases, querying an Indexing Service catalog requires opening a recordset. First you create a Recordset object and a SQL statement and then, as in the following example, you use the recordset's *Open* method to retrieve any records that match the query.

```
Set rsIx = Server.CreateObject("ADODB.Recordset")
sql = "SELECT Rank, Filename, DocTitle, Path, VPath, Size, Write " & _
        "FROM SCOPE('"/webdbdev"') " & _
      "WHERE (CONTAINS(Contents, '"home"') > 0) " & _
        "AND (VPath NOT LIKE '%[_]vti[_]%') " & _
    "ORDER BY Rank DESC
rsIx.Open sql, cnIx, adOpenForwardOnly
```

Two details in this example should get your attention right away:

- The FROM clause specifies a SCOPE expression rather than a table name or JOIN expression. A *scope* describes what portion of the corpus you want to search. No document can be a match unless it resides within the specified scope.

- The WHERE clause specifies some odd-looking search criteria. The first expression specifies that matching documents must contain the word *home*. The second expression disqualifies any document with a URL that contains the string *_vti_*.

Note The Microsoft FrontPage and Microsoft Office Server Extensions create numerous internal files in directories whose names begin with the characters *_vti_*. Because these aren't legitimate content files, you should exclude them from any search results.

Less obvious but equally important are the field names following the SELECT verb: what data do these fields contain and what others are available? To provide these answers and more, the following section will explain the details of coding SQL statements for use with Indexing Service.

Using SQL to Query Indexing Service

Although the ADO provider for Indexing Service accepts commands coded in SQL, the format of those commands is highly specialized. The following sections will cover how to code the SELECT statement and three allowable clauses: FROM, WHERE, and ORDER BY.

Coding the SELECT Statement

The SELECT statement retrieves records from the Indexing Service catalog. Each of these records represents a document file that meets the SELECT statement's criteria. The general format of an Indexing Service SELECT statement is

SELECT	*<field 1, ... field n>*
FROM	*<scope>*
WHERE	*<criteria>*
ORDER BY	*<field 1, ... field n>*

The SELECT clause specifies the fields of interest. The FROM clause controls the scope (the set of files) for the search. The WHERE clause specifies the search criteria. All these clauses are mandatory.

The ORDER BY clause tells ADO how to sort the result set. This field is optional except that few Web visitors appreciate a randomly ordered list of documents.

Table 11-1 lists the most common fields available in an Indexing Service catalog. If the Query dot is filled in, you can use the corresponding field name in a WHERE clause. If the Retrieve dot is filled in, you can specify the corresponding field after the SELECT statement. To see why this distinction is necessary, consider the *All* field. You can use this field name to search all document properties for a given string, but you can't use it to retrieve all document properties—including the document's contents—jammed into one field for display.

In practice, not all fields are present in all catalogs. To determine which fields are present in a Windows 2000 catalog, take the following steps:

1. Open the Computer Management snap-in for Microsoft Management Console.

2. Open the Services and Applications node.

3. Open the Indexing Service node.

4. Open the catalog you want to query.

5. Highlight the Properties folder for that catalog.

Table 11-1 Indexing Service Catalog Field Names

Name	Type	Description	Query	Retrieve
A_HRef	Text	Corresponds with the Indexing Service property *HtmlHRef* described later in this table	●	○
Access	Date/Time	The date and time anyone last accessed the file	●	●
All	n/a	A combination of every other property	●	○
AllocSize	Number	The number of bytes of disk space allocated to a file	●	●
Attrib	32 bits	Windows file attribute bits (Archive, Read-Only, and so on)	●	●
ClassId	GUID	The class ID of an object; indirectly indicates the associated application	●	●
Characterization	Text	An abstract of the file, as derived by Indexing Service	●	●
Contents	n/a	The main contents of a file	●	○
Created	Date/Time	The date and time someone created the file	●	●
Directory	Text	The physical path to the file, excluding the filename	●	●
DocAppName	Text	The name of the application that created the file	●	●
DocAuthor	Text	The author of the file	●	●
DocByteCount	Number	The number of bytes in a file	●	●
DocCategory	Text	The type of file (such as a memo, a schedule, or a white paper)	●	●
DocCharCount	Number	The number of characters in the file	●	●
DocComments	Text	Comments about the file	●	●
DocCompany	Text	The company that owns the file	●	●
DocCreatedTm	Date/Time	The date and time someone created the file	●	●
DocEditTime	Time	The total time spent editing the file	●	●
DocHiddenCount	Number	The number of hidden slides in a PowerPoint file	●	●
DocKeywords	Text	Any keywords coded within the file	●	●
DocLastAuthor	Text	The user who most recently edited the file	●	●
DocLastPrinted	Date/Time	The date and time someone last printed the file	●	●

(continued)

Table 11-1 *continued*

Name	Type	Description	Query	Retrieve
DocLastSavedTm	Date/Time	The date and time someone last saved the file	●	●
DocLineCount	Number	The number of lines contained in a file	●	●
DocManager	Text	The file author's manager	●	●
DocNoteCount	Number	The number of PowerPoint pages with notes	●	●
DocPageCount	Number	The number of pages in a file	●	●
DocParaCount	Number	The number of paragraphs in a file	●	●
DocPartTitles	Text	The name of file parts (names of worksheets in an Excel workbook, names of slides in a PowerPoint, presentation, or names of files in a Word master file)	●	●
DocPresentationTarget	Text	The target format (35mm, printer, video, and so on) for a PowerPoint presentation	●	●
DocRevNumber	Text	The current version number of a file	●	●
DocSlideCount	Number	The number of slides in a Power-Point file	●	●
DocSubject	Text	The subject of a file	●	●
DocTemplate	Text	The name of a file's template	●	●
DocTitle	Text	The file's title	●	●
DocWordCount	Number	The number of words in a file	●	●
FileIndex	Number	The unique ID of a file	●	●
FileName	Text	The name of a file	●	●
HitCount	Number	The number of matching query words (hits) in file	●	●
HtmlHRef	Text	Text within HTML HREF attributes	●	○
HtmlHeading1	Text	Text within HTML <H1> tags	●	○
HtmlHeading2	Text	Text within HTML <H2> tags	●	○
HtmlHeading3	Text	Text within HTML <H3> tags	●	○
HtmlHeading4	Text	Text within HTML <H4> tags	●	○
HtmlHeading5	Text	Text within HTML <H5> tags	●	○
HtmlHeading6	Text	Text within HTML <H6> tags	●	○
Img_Alt	Text	Text within *alt* attributes of <IMG> tags	●	○
Path	Text	The full physical path to the file, including filename	●	●

Name	Type	Description	Query	Retrieve
Rank	Number	Match ranking (1000 indicates the best match to a query; 0 indicates the worst.)	●	●
RankVector	Number	The ranks of individual components of an array or vector query	●	●
ShortFileName	Text	The short (8.3) filename	●	●
Size	Number	The size of a file, in bytes	●	●
USN	Number	The Update Sequence Number (pertains only to NTFS drives)	●	●
VPath	Text	The full virtual path to the file, including filename (If more than one path will work, Indexing Service chooses one path as best.)	●	●
WorkId	Number	The internal ID for the file (used within Indexing Service)	●	●
Write	Date/Time	The last date and time anyone wrote to a file	●	●

To examine the list of fields available in a Windows NT 4.0 Index Server catalog,

1. Open the Index Server snap-in for Microsoft Management Console.

2. Open the catalog you want to query.

3. Highlight the Properties folder for the catalog of interest.

In either case, the list of fields will appear in the right MMC panel under the Friendly Name column heading. The right pane in Figure 11-1 shows the format of this display.

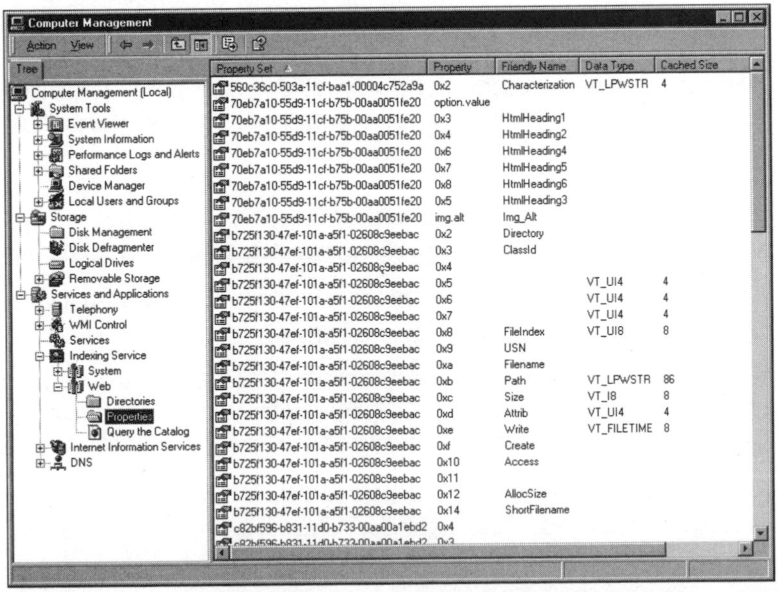

Figure 11-1 *The Friendly Name column shows the field names available in a given Indexing Service catalog.*

Coding the FROM Clause

The FROM clause specifies one or more folders where matching documents can reside. Indexing Service calls each such folder or folder tree a *scope*, and it only searches for documents within the scope or scopes you specify. You can code this clause in two ways:

FROM *<Catalog Name>* SCOPE('*<Scope Arguments>*')
FROM *<Catalog Name>* *<View Name>*

The following bullets explain the variable portions of these statements.

- **Catalog Name** optionally specifies the name of a catalog to search. However, Microsoft recommends specifying the catalog via the *data source* value in an ADO connection string rather than within the FROM clause.

- **SCOPE** specifies one or more folder locations to search for documents. These locations must reside within a path already known to the Indexing Service catalog—that is, within a path listed when you select the catalog's Directories folder, which is visible but not selected in Figure 11-1.

- **Scope Arguments** specify the paths or virtual roots to search and how to traverse them. The general format of a scope argument is

'*<Traversal Type>* "*<Path 1>*" , ..., "*<Path n>*"'

There are two traversal types:

- **DEEP TRAVERSAL OF** searches the specified folder and all folders it contains. This is the default.

- **SHALLOW TRAVERSAL OF** searches the specified folder only.

You must enclose each path—that is, *<Path 1>* through *<Path n>*—in double quotation marks and the entire scope argument in single quotation marks. If you specify multiple paths, separate them with commas.

Each path can be a physical folder, such as *d:\InetPub\wwwroot\webdbdev* or a Web location such as */webdbdev/*. A scope definition can include zero, one, or many physical folder and Web locations. The default scope is the Web location /. To use this default, specify SCOPE with an empty argument list.

If you specify one or more paths that don't exist, Indexing Service ignores them. If none of the paths exist, the result set will be empty.

For more information on view names, consult the Indexing Service documentation.

- **View Name** specifies either a predefined or nonpersistent view defined by a *CREATE VIEW* statement.

Here's a typical FROM clause that includes a SCOPE expression. The default traversal type—DEEP TRAVERSAL OF—will apply. Double quotes enclose the one and only path; single quotes enclose the entire scope argument.

```
FROM SCOPE('"/webdbdev"')
```

Coding the WHERE Clause

The WHERE clause restricts the records that can appear—based on their content—in the result set. In other words, it specifies the search criteria. At a high level, its syntax is

WHERE <*Search Conditions*>

The search conditions consist of one or more expressions (called *predicates*) separated by the operators AND or OR. Use parentheses to control the order of evaluating multiple predicates.

You can precede any expression but the first with the NOT operator. For example, the WHERE clause in the first *SELECT* statement here is illegal. The second SELECT statement, however, is legal.

```
SELECT FileName
  FROM SCOPE()
 WHERE NOT CONTAINS(Contents, 'elephants')>0
   AND CONTAINS(Contents, 'mice')>0

SELECT FileName
  FROM SCOPE()
 WHERE CONTAINS(Contents, 'mice')>0
   AND NOT CONTAINS(Contents, 'elephants')>0
```

The CONTAINS predicate returns a positive value for each catalog record that contains a given string (such as *mice*) anywhere within a given field (such as *Contents*). Comparing the return value to zero produces the required *True/False* value. Table 11-2 lists the relational operators you can use with Indexing Service predicates, including CONTAINS.

Table 11-2   Indexing Service Relational Operators

Operator	Symbol	Operator	Symbol
Equals	=	Not equals	!= or <>
Greater than	>	Greater than or equal to	>=
Less than	<	Less than or equal to	<=

Indexing Service supports a total of six predicates: CONTAINS, FREETEXT, LIKE, MATCHES, ARRAY, and NULL. The following sections describe these predicates.

Code the CONTAINS predicate

The CONTAINS predicate searches for a given value anywhere within a given catalog field. Code this predicate as follows:

CONTAINS (<*Field Name*>, '<*Content Search Conditions*>') > 0

The bullets on the next page describe how to code the variable portions of this predicate.

- **Field Name** specifies the field you want to search. If you don't specify a field name, the default is the *Contents* field. Thus, the following clauses are equivalent:

```
WHERE CONTAINS (Contents, 'antipasto') > 0
WHERE CONTAINS ('antipasto') > 0
```

- **Content Search Conditions** specifies one or more search terms. If you specify two or more search terms, separate them with AND, AND NOT, or OR operators. The symbolic operators & (for AND), | (for OR), and ! (for NOT) are also acceptable.

    If you have any doubt how Indexing Service will evaluate multiple expressions, use parentheses to specify what you want.

- **> 0** causes the expression to produce a Boolean result. This is mandatory.
    The following expression searches for all Web pages that contain either the string *www.microsoft.com* or the string *msdn.microsoft.com* in a hyperlink.

```
CONTAINS (HtmlHRef, 'www.microsoft.com' OR 'msdn.microsoft.com') > 0
```

Code the FREETEXT predicate

The FREETEXT predicate searches for catalog records having content that matches the meaning—rather than the exact wording—of the query. A FREETEXT query resembles the CONTAINS predicate in syntax:

FREETEXT (*<Field Name>*, '*<Free Text String>*') > 0

This predicate requires the following arguments:

- **Field Name** specifies the field name to search. Its data type must be compatible with the format of the free text string specified. Usually, both values must be strings. If you don't specify a field name, the default is the *Contents* field.

- **Free Text String** specifies one or more values to search for. As with the CONTAINS predicate, you must separate these with AND, AND NOT, or OR operators, and you can group them with parentheses.

- **> 0** causes the expression to produce a Boolean result. This is mandatory.

The following expression searches for files with contents that mention travel to Marrakech or empathy with Marketing:

```
WHERE FREETEXT('how can I get to Marrakech') > 0
    OR FREETEXT('how can I get Marketing to understand') > 0
```

Code the LIKE predicate

The LIKE predicate performs pattern-matching (wildcard) queries. Its syntax is

<Field Name> *<NOT>* LIKE '*<String Pattern>*'

Follow these instructions to code the arguments in this predicate:

- **Field Name** specifies the name of the field to search. This field's data type must agree with the format of the string pattern you specify.

- **NOT** is an optional keyword that searches for catalog records that don't match the given pattern.

- **String Pattern** specifies a literal to use as a string-matching pattern. This literal can contain any combination of normal and wildcard characters. Table 11-3 lists the wildcard characters the LIKE predicate recognizes.

Table 11-3   Wildcard Characters

Name	Symbol	Description
Percent	%	Matches zero to many occurrences of the search pattern
Underscore	_	Matches any single character
Square brackets	[ ]	Matches any single character within a list or range specified within the square brackets
Caret	[^]	Matches any single character not within the specified range inside the square brackets

To use the percent (%), underscore (_), or left square bracket ([) as a literal (rather than as wildcard) character, surround it with square brackets. The right square bracket (]) matches itself unless preceded by a left square bracket.

The range character (-) matches itself unless it's inside square brackets and preceded and followed by a single character. The expression *[A-K]*, for example, matches any character in the range *A* through *K*.

Table 11-4 offers several examples that use wildcards as literals.

Table 11-4   Pattern Matching in the LIKE Clause

Pattern	Matches
LIKE 'd%'	The character *d* followed by any string of zero or more characters
LIKE 'd[%]'	The character *d* followed by the character %
LIKE '_n'	Any single character followed by the character *n*
LIKE '[_]n'	An underscore followed by the character *n*
LIKE '[a-cdf]'	The character *a*, *b*, *c*, *d*, or *f*
LIKE '[-acdf]'	The character -, *a*, *c*, *d*, or *f*
LIKE '[[]'	The character *[*
LIKE ']'	The character *]*
LIKE '[ab]cd]e'	The string *"acd]e"* or the string *"bcd]e"*

Code the MATCHES predicate

The MATCHES predicate searches for catalog fields that match a form of *regular expression*. Regular expressions invoke a powerful type of pattern matching first introduced years ago on UNIX. This makes the MATCHES predicate more powerful but also more complex than the LIKE predicate. The MATCHES predicate has the following syntax:

MATCHES (*<Field Name>*, '*<Grouped Search Pattern>*') > 0
MATCHES (*<Field Name>*, '*<Counted Search Pattern>*') > 0

Code the variable portions of this predicate as described below:

- **Field Name** specifies the name of the field to search. Its data type must be compatible with the format of the search pattern you specify.

- **Grouped Search Pattern** specifies a search for one or more distinct patterns.

- **Counted Search Pattern** specifies a search for repetitions of a single pattern. You can request exactly *m* matches, at least *m* matches, or between *m* and *n* occurrences of the search pattern

A grouped or counted search pattern is a string that contains ordinary characters and regular expressions (match symbols). Table 11-5 describes the regular expressions you can use with the MATCHES predicate.

Table 11-5   Match Symbols Used with the MATCHES Predicate

Name	Symbol	Description
Vertical bar			An escape character that invokes match processing for any of the remaining symbols in this table. Without the leading escape character, these symbols function as ordinary characters. Commas separating OR clauses in the matching terms must also be preceded by the escape character.
Asterisk	*	Matches zero or more occurrences of the search pattern.
Question mark	?	Matches zero or one occurrence of the preceding pattern.
Plus sign	+	Matches one or more occurrences of the preceding pattern.
Parentheses	( )	Used to delimit search patterns greater than one character.
Curly braces	{ }	Used to delimit a counted match.
Square Brackets	[ ]	Used to specify a range of characters in a pattern.

Indexing Service isn't case-sensitive to characters in a search pattern other than the match symbols.

The following example uses a grouped match. The pattern matches authors with the names *McAlister*, *McAllister*, *McAlllister*, and so on. Notice how vertical-bar escape characters precede the plus sign and the parentheses. Without the vertical bars, the predicate would search for the exact string *(MacAl+ister)*.

```
...WHERE MATCHES (DocAuthor, '|(MacAl|+ister|)' )> 0
```

The next example uses a counted match. The expression |{2|} evaluates to {2}, which specifies that exactly two instances of the pattern *Walla* must occur.

```
...WHERE MATCHES (DocText, '|(Walla|)|{2|}' ) > 0
```

To search for two or more occurrences of the word *Walla*, specify the counted match value as {2,}—that is, as |{2,|}. To specify two or three occurrences, code {2,3}—that is, as |{2,3|}.

Code the ARRAY predicate

The ARRAY (or VECTOR) predicate searches for an array of values. Its syntax is

> *<Field Name>*
>   *<Comparison Operator>*
>   *<ALL or SOME>* ARRAY [*<Array Elements>*]

Here are the requirements for coding each parameter in this predicate:

- **Field Name** specifies the name of the field you want to search. The data type of this field must agree with the format of the array elements you specify. A single field name can have multiple values, such as a vector property or a file attribute bitmask.

- **Comparison Operator** specifies how to compare the array elements. The acceptable values are those listed in Table 11-2.

- **ALL or SOME** specifies how to quantify the array elements.
    If you specify ALL, the test will succeed only if the condition is true between each element on the left side of the expression and each element on the right. The following test fails, for example, because the first element on the left isn't greater than the second element on the right side. For this test to succeed, all six comparisons would have to be *True*.

```
[1,2,3] > ALL ARRAY [1,2]
```

  If you specify SOME, the test will succeed if the condition is true between any element on the left and any element on the right. The following test succeeds because the second element on the left is greater than the second element on the right. For this test to fail, all six comparisons would have to be *False*.

```
[1,2,3] > SOME ARRAY [2,1]
```

  If you specify neither ALL nor SOME, the condition must be true between each element on the left and its ordinal counterpart on the right. If one side contains more values than the other, existent values are considered greater than nonexistent ones.

- **Array Elements** specify the elements in the array. You must include the square brackets when you specify the array elements. To specify an empty array, code *[]*.

Code the NULL predicate

The NULL predicate determines whether a given catalog field contains a defined value. Its syntax is

<Field Name> IS *<NOT>* NULL

Field Name specifies the name of a field in the catalog. *NOT*, if present, negates the expression.

The example below retrieves the *FileName* and *VPath* fields for all files within the Web location /webdbdev where the field *DocAuthor* is defined.

```
SELECT FileName, VPath
  FROM SCOPE('"/webdbdev"')
 WHERE DocAuthor IS NOT NULL
```

Coding the ORDER BY Clause

The ORDER BY clause sorts the result set on specified fields. To code this clause, follow this syntax:

ORDER BY *<Sort Field 1>* <ASC or DESC>, ..., *<Sort Field n>* <ASC or DESC>

Follow these instructions for coding the arguments:

- **Sort Field** specifies the name of the field to be sorted (or its ordinal position following the SELECT verb).

- **ASC or DESC** specifies the sorting order: ascending (ASC) or descending (DESC). If you don't specify a sort order, the default is ascending order. However, once you explicitly specify a sort order for a field, all subsequent fields will default to that order until you explicitly specify the sort order for another field.

Locating Additional Documentation

You can get additional information about the Windows 2000 Indexing Service at *http://windows.microsoft.com/windows2000/en/server/help*. To locate the Indexing Service topic, first open the Files and Printers topic as shown in Figure 11-2.

To find out more about the ADO access to the Indexing Service catalog, browse the MSDN Library at *http://msdn.microsoft.com/library*. Expand the following topics in the order listed:

Platform SDK
   Data Access Services
      Microsoft Data Access Components (MDAC) SDK
        Microsoft ActiveX Data Objects (ADO)
          Microsoft ADO Programmer's Reference
           Using Providers with ADO
             Microsoft OLE DB Provider for Microsoft Indexing Service.

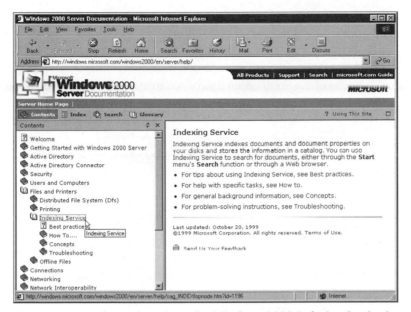

Figure 11-2 *Information about the Windows 2000 Indexing Service is available from Microsoft's Web site.*

Figure 11-3 illustrates this path.

If your server runs Windows NT 4.0 with the Windows NT Server Option Pack, you can find documentation under the heading Microsoft Index Server at the path */iishelp/iis/misc/default.asp*. To learn more about accessing Index Server

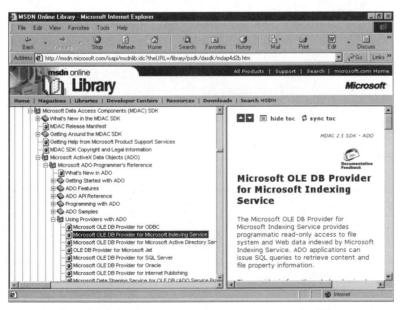

Figure 11-3 *Documentation on using ADO to search Indexing Service catalogs is available from this location.*

catalogs through ADO, open the Microsoft Index Server entry and then choose the topic, "SQL Access to Index Server Data." Figure 11-4 illustrates this location.

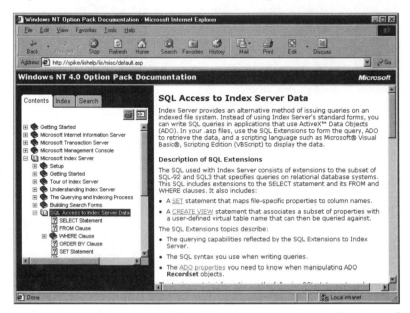

Figure 11-4   *The topic highlighted in this screen shot provides more information about accessing Index Server catalogs through ADO.*

Searching a Web Site

For a working example of all this technology, take a look at Figure 11-5. The Web page pictured accepts two fields from the Web visitor (search text and scope). If the scope is empty, the ASP code substitutes */webdbdev*. If the search text is empty, the code displays an error message. If search text is present, the code builds and runs a SQL statement containing the submitted values. If the search discovers no matching records, the code again quits with an error message. If the search does find matching records, the code runs a typical *Do While Not EOF* loop to display each record. In short, this page is quite typical of pages you've seen in the last few chapters, except that it accesses an Indexing Service catalog rather than an Access database.

The steps to create this page are relatively simple, given your knowledge of the previous chapters:

1. Create a new Web page with the usual structural elements and include statements. In the <body> section, create an HTML form with a text box named *qText*, a text box named *qScope*, and a Submit button named anything you want.

2. Insert the following statements in the <head> section of the Web page. These statements copy the submitted search text to a variable named *qText* and the submitted scope to a variable named *qScope*. If *qScope* is empty, the code supplies a default value of */webdbdev*.

```
<%
qText = Request("qText")
qScope = Request("qScope")
If qScope = "" Then
  qScope = "/webdbdev"
End If
%>
```

3. In the <body> section, after the HTML form code, insert the following code to exit with an error if the Web visitor submitted no search text:

```
<%
If qText = "" Then
  Response.Write "<p class=err>Enter text to search.</p>"
  Response.Write vbCrLf
Else
'  Code to run and display query will go here.
End If
%>
```

4. Open and close a connection to the Indexing Service data provider by replacing the comment in step 3 with these statements:

```
cnStIx = "provider=msidxs;data source=Interlacken"
Set cnIx = Server.CreateObject("ADODB.Connection")
cnIx.Open cnStIx, "", ""
'   Code to open and display recordset will go here.
cnIx.Close
```

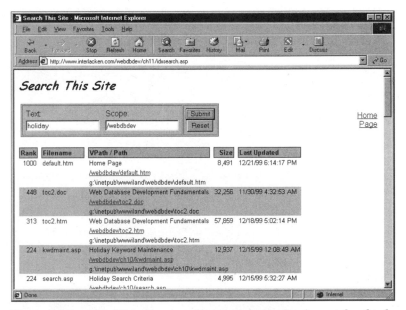

Figure 11-5 *This Web page searches an Indexing Service catalog for documents that contain given text and reside within a given scope.*

The *provider* value will always be *msidxs*, for Microsoft Indexing Service. The *data source* value is the name of the Indexing Service catalog you want to query. Contact your Web administrator for the name of your Web server's catalog.

5. Open and close a recordset containing any catalog records that match the Web visitor's criteria. This requires replacing the comment in step 4 with these statements:

```
Set rsIx = Server.CreateObject("ADODB.Recordset")
sql = "SELECT Rank, Filename, DocTitle, Path, VPath, Size, Write " & _
        "FROM SCOPE('" & Chr(34) & qScope & Chr(34) & "') " & _
        "WHERE (CONTAINS(Contents, '" & _
                    Chr(34) & qText & Chr(34) & _
                    "') > 0) " & _
            "AND (VPath NOT LIKE '%[_]vti[_]%') " & _
        "ORDER BY Rank DESC"
rsIx.Open sql, cnIx, adOpenForwardOnly
'   Code to display contents of recordset will go here.
rsIx.Close
```

Lines two through six of this code construct a SQL statement that looks like this:

```
SELECT Rank, Filename, DocTitle, Path, VPath, Size, Write
    FROM SCOPE('"/webdbdev"')
    WHERE (CONTAINS(Contents, '"holiday"') > 0)
        AND (VPath NOT LIKE '%[_]vti[_]%')
ORDER BY Rank DESC
```

The clause *SCOPE('"/webdbdev"')* restricts the search to files with URLs in the */webdbdev* folder tree. The WHERE clause searches for files containing the word *holiday* and not having the string *_vti_* in their virtual path (that is, in their URL).

As coded, the Search This Site page always searches for complete phrases. If you specify multiple words, Indexing Service will search for them as a single string. While the string *holiday photo* has matches, for example, *photo holiday* doesn't. If you want to provide more flexible options for your visitors, you'll need to write code that prompts for these criteria and constructs the necessary predicates.

6. To display any matching records, replace the comment in step 5 with the following code:

```
If rsIx.EOF Then
  Response.Write "<p class=err>No matching documents found. & _
    </p>" & vbCrLf
Else
  hits = 0
  Do While Not rsIx.EOF
    hits = hits + 1
    If hits Mod 2 = 0 Then
      bgcolor = "background-color: #cccccc"
```

```
          Else
            bgcolor = ""
          End If
          link = "<a href=" & _
                  Chr(34) & rsIx("VPath") & Chr(34) & _
                  ">" & rsIx("VPath") & "</a>"
'         Code to display one result record will go here.
          rsIx.MoveNext
       Loop
    End If
```

If the *rsIx* recordset is already at *EOF*, there are no matching records and the code simply displays a message. Otherwise, it initializes a count named *hits* to zero and runs a *Do While Not EOF* loop to display each record. When the *hits* counter is even (that is, when division by two yields a zero remainder) the code sets the variable *bgcolor* to the CSS code for a gray background; otherwise, it stores an empty value. For readability, subsequent code will include the *bgcolor* value as an attribute within each <tr> tag.

The link variable contains the HTML code to display each *VPath* value as a hyperlink.

7. The following HTML code displays each record. Replace the comment in step 6 with these statements:

```
%>
  <tr style="<%=bgcolor%>">
    <td align="right"><%=rsIx("rank")%></td>
    <td></td>
    <td align="left"><%=rsIx("filename")%></td>
    <td></td>
    <td align="left"><%=rsIx("DocTitle") %></td>
    <td></td>
    <td align="right"><%=formatnumber(rsIx("size"),0,,true)%></td>
    <td></td>
    <td align="left"><%=rsIx("write")%></td>
  </tr>
  <tr style="<%=bgcolor%>">
    <td align="right" colspan="4"></td>
    <td align="left" colspan="5"><%=link%></td>
  </tr>
  <tr style="<%=bgcolor%>">
    <td align="right" colspan="4"></td>
    <td align="left" colspan="5"><%=rsIx("Path")%></td>
  </tr>
  <%
```

Because the *VPath* and *Path* values received from the catalog are long strings, they don't display well in a single HTML table row. The preceding code therefore creates a set of three HTML table rows for each matching catalog record, visually grouping those sets by alternately shading them.

To view the complete HTML and ASP code for this page, open the sample file \webdbdev\ch11\idxsearch.asp using your favorite HTML or text editor.

Chapter Summary

This chapter explained how to search a full-text document index by using methods you've already learned for querying ordinary databases. This technique works with Microsoft Indexing Service for Windows 2000 as well as with Microsoft Index Server for Windows NT Server 4.0.

Chapter 12, "Managing Sessions," will explain how to retain information on a visitor-by-visitor basis as Web visitors traverse multiple pages in the same site.

Managing Sessions

In this chapter, you'll learn how to

- Use the Session object for storing temporary data about your site's visitors.

- Build a visitor registration and login system that uses the Session object.

All the ASP pages you've seen so far have passed data from one Web page to the next by means of a query string in a URL or a form field in a POST request. These methods have the advantage of simplicity, but only when the amount of data is relatively small. Passing dozens or hundreds of field values this way would be cumbersome at best. Using query strings or form fields also suffers from a lack of *persistence*, which means that if the Web visitor strays from the expected series of Web pages in the slightest way, he or she will need to start over from the beginning.

The ASP Session object solves both of these problems. IIS automatically creates a Session object for each visitor to your application, and within these objects you can save whatever data you want on a visitor-by-visitor basis. Even if the visitor wanders off to another site and then—within a reasonable period of time—returns, the session information will still be there.

Understanding the Session Object

Chapter 5, "Customizing Web Content with Server-Side Scripting," introduced the Session object. However, just in case that material seems a bit fuzzy right now, here's a high-level summary:

- Whenever a Web visitor accesses an ASP page in a given executable directory tree (that is, within a given IIS application) for the first time, the ASP software creates a new Session object identified by a session ID. The value of this session ID is stored in the Session object's *SessionID* property.

- When the ASP software responds to the Web visitor, it transmits the session ID value as a cookie.

- The browser—assuming it supports cookies—sends the session ID back to the server whenever the browser requests a page within the same executable folder tree.

- If the ASP software can find that particular session ID, it will use the associated Session object.

- If a request specifies a session ID that no longer exists—or if it doesn't specify a session ID at all—the ASP software creates and attaches a new Session object.

Using the Session object is easier than explaining it. To save information in the Session object, simply assign a value, as shown here:

```
Session("firstname") = "Jim"
```

After you assign this value, any ASP page in the same executable folder tree can retrieve the value by using essentially the same syntax. For example, after executing the following statement, the variable *fName* will contain the value *Jim*:

```
fName = Session("firstname")
```

If several Web visitors use the same application at the same time, each has his or her own Session object. The value of *Session("fName")* could, at the same time on the same server, be *Ann*, *Bill*, *Cynthia*, *Duane*, or any other value, depending on who requested the current execution. The ASP software keeps track of which Web visitor is which and always supplies each with the correct Session object.

Figure 12-1 shows an extremely simple Web page that uses the Session object. To see the complete listing of this page, open the sample file \webdbdev\ch12\sesssave.asp in your favorite text or HTML editor.

Figure 12-1 *This Web page saves two text box values to the ASP Session object.*

The two text boxes in this page are named *fName* and *sName*, and the Save button is named btnSave. The following piece of code, located in the <head> section, runs every time the ASP page loads:

```
<%
If Request("btnSave") <> "" Then
  Session("fName") = Request("fName")
  Session("sName") = Request("sName")
End If
%>
```

The condition in the first line is *True* only when the ASP page is running because a Web visitor clicked the Save button. If so, the next two statements save the values entered in the *fName* and *sName* text boxes as session variables named *fName* and *sName*.

If the condition is *False*, the page is probably running because the Web visitor clicked a hyperlink on a menu page or typed its URL into the browser's Address line. In such cases, the *Request("fName")* and *Request("sName")* fields are meaningless and the code doesn't update the Session object.

The value attributes of the two text boxes are coded, respectively, as follows:

```
value="<%=Session("fName")%>"
value="<%=Session("sName")%>"
```

Thus, in all cases, these text boxes display the values currently stored in the Session object. For further confirmation of what the Session object contains, take a look at the sessshow.asp page in Figure 12-2.

Figure 12-2   *This Web page lists and displays each value currently stored in a Web visitor's Session object.*

The Contents
collection is the
Session object's
default collection.

This page runs the following loop to retrieve and display all variables currently stored in the Session object. The Session.Contents collection contains these variables.

```
<%
For Each vbl in Session.Contents
  Response.Write "<tr>" & vbCrlf
  Response.Write "  <td>" & vbl & "</td>" & vbCrLf
  Response.Write "  <td>" & Session(vbl) &"</td>" & vbCrLf
  Response.Write "</tr>" & vbCrLf
Next
%>
```

You can learn a lot about the behavior of the Session object by testing various scenarios involving these two pages, as described in the following bullets:

- If you run the sesssave.asp page, save some *fName* and *sName* values, and then run the sessshow.asp page, sessshow.asp will display the values you saved despite the lack of any visible data connection between these two pages.

- If other Web visitors perform the same exercise at about the same time, no conflicts will result—each visitor has a different Session object.

- If you wait more than twenty minutes and then run the sessshow.asp page again, the *fName* and *sName* values will be blank because the Session object has timed out and IIS has destroyed it. (The timeout value of twenty minutes is a default that might be configured differently on your server.)

- If you quit and restart the browser, the sessshow.asp page will be blank because you've started a new session.

Session variables are variant data types and can thus contain any variable, array, or object that a VBScript variable can contain. Be aware, however, of the following two precautions:

- If an object's threading model isn't marked as *both*, storing it in the Session object locks the session to a single thread and thus reduces performance. This is a somewhat advanced consideration, but it's worth investigating if you expect high volumes for either an application or the server it runs on.

- If you store an array in a Session object, don't try to modify its elements directly. The following statement, for example, doesn't work because the expression *(2)* indexes the third session variable, not the third array element. (Both the array and the Session.Contents collection are zero-based.)

```
Session("MyArray")(2) = "Who cares?"
```

The preferred approach is to copy the whole array to a local variable, update the local variable, and then replace the array in the Session object.

```
locArray = Session("MyArray")
locArray(2) = "Who cares?"
Session("MyArray") = locArray
```

The Session object is handy when you need to build up data from different Web pages (as when building a customer order) and then process all the data when it's complete (as when the visitor actually submits the order).

Using the Session Object

Although you can use the Session object to hold information applicable to a single Web page, it's more common to use it to accumulate data from several Web pages that you expect your visitors to traverse in order. Here's how this works:

- Each page contains an HTML form with a Submit button that runs the same page. For example, the Submit button on page1.asp runs page1.asp; the Submit button on page2.asp runs page2.asp, and so on.

- ASP code at the start of each page checks the submitted data for completeness and accuracy. If the data is acceptable, the code performs any required application processing (such as updating the Session object or the database) and then uses the *Response.Redirect* method to advance to the next page. If the data is incomplete or otherwise unacceptable, the page redisplays itself with an error message.

The section titled "Using the Response Object" in Chapter 5 explained the *Response.Redirect* method. To briefly review, recall that the following statement displays the Web page at *url*, rather than the current page, on the visitor's browser:

Response.Redirect *<url>*

The *Response.Redirect* method has two different ways of working, depending on the URL you specify:

- If you specify a URL that resides on the server that's executing the ASP page, the *Response.Redirect* method simply tells the server to deliver the specified page instead of the current one. If, however, the server has already begun to deliver the page that contains the *Response.Redirect* statement, there's no way to call the transmitted portion back. The *Response.Redirect* method fails.

- If you specify a URL that resides on a different server, the *Response.Redirect* method creates a special HTTP header that tells the Web visitor's browser to retrieve the specified page. If the server has already begun to deliver HTML tags for the current page, however, it's too late to send additional HTTP headers. The *Response.Redirect* method fails.

Note   The ASP code can redirect the Web visitor to different pages, depending on the data accumulated so far.

Either way, you must execute the *Response.Redirect* statement before the Web server encounters the first HTML tag. If this isn't possible, execute a *Response.Buffer=True* statement before the first HTML tag. This tells the server not to transmit any part of the Web page until all processing is complete.

Build a page that requires visitor registration

More and more Web sites require visitors to register and log in before using all or part of the site. The site can use this information to save the visitor's preferences and interests, to customize the site's content based on those factors, and to send occasional e-mail. To require visitor registration for your own site, you must develop two components:

- A component that determines whether a Web visitor is logged in and, if not, switches the visitor to a login page. This component must be present in each Web page requiring registration.

- A registration and login page where visitors can create new accounts for themselves or log in to existing accounts.

A complete code listing of the first component follows. This code appears in the sample files as \webdbdev\ch12\secure.inc.

```
<%
If Session("loginemail") = "" Then
  Session("goback") = Request.ServerVariables("URL")
  Response.Redirect "login.asp"
End If
%>
```

The first statement in this code determines whether a Session object variable named *loginemail* exists and contains a value. Assuming that only the login process updates this variable, the existence of a value indicates that the Web visitor has logged in and that the Web server can process the rest of the page normally.

If no *Session("loginemail")* value is present, the Web visitor hasn't logged in. The code therefore saves the current URL in the Session variable *goback* and then redirects the Web visitor to a page called login.asp. If and when the visitor successfully logs in, the login.asp page will store the visitor's identity in *Session("loginemail")* and then redirect the visitor back to the location in *Session("goback")*.

Because such code typically needs to appear in a number of pages, it makes sense to store the code in a separate file and add it to each applicable Web page using a server-side include (SSI). This requires that each applicable page have an .asp filename extension and contain the following statement before the first HTML tag. (Of course, the filename secure.inc and its relative location will vary depending on your environment.)

```
<!-- #include file="secure.inc" -->
```

The sample file \webdbdev\ch12\secure.asp displayed in Figure 12-3 contains such a statement. If you put the secure.asp, secure.inc, and login.asp pages in the same directory on your Web server, you should find that any attempt to load the secure.asp page immediately switches you to the login.asp page.

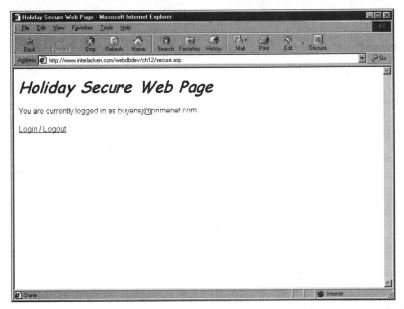

Figure 12-3 *This Web page automatically redirects Web visitors to a login page if they haven't logged in yet.*

Build a registration and login page

Figure 12-4 shows the login.asp page mentioned in the previous section. The message "You are currently not logged in" reports the current login status. To create a new login account, a Web visitor enters his or her e-mail address and a desired password, clicks the New Visitor: Yes option, and then clicks the Login button. If no such account yet exists, the page will do the following:

- Add the new account and password to a *visitors* table in the holiday.mdb database. This table has two fields, *email* and *paswd*, both of which are text. The *email* field is the table's primary key.

- Save the e-mail address in the Session object's *loginemail* variable.

- Redirect the visitor to whatever location it finds in the Session object's *goback* variable.

If a visitor tries to create a new account using the same e-mail address as an existing record in the *visitors* table, the page will return an error message.

If a visitor already has an account, he or she can log in by specifying the account's e-mail address and password, selecting New Visitor: No (the default), and then clicking the Login button. If the e-mail address and password match an existing record in the *visitors* table, the page will once again save the e-mail address in *Session("loginemail")* and redirect the visitor to the location in *Session("goback")*.

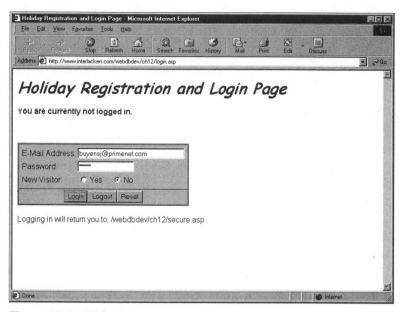

Figure 12-4   *Web visitors can use this Web page to register for access to a site and to recall that registration during future visits.*

Clicking the Logout button simply erases the current value of the Session object's *loginemail* variable.

The following procedure constructs this page.

1. Initialize a new Web page with the usual structural tags and an HTML form containing the following form elements:

- A text box with the name *email* and an initial value taken from the current *email* value in the Request object.

```
<input type="text" name="email" size="30"
       value="<%=Request("email")%>">
```

- A text box with the name *paswd* and an initial value taken from the current *paswd* value in the Request object.

```
<input type="password" name="paswd" size="15"
       value="<%=Request("paswd")%>">
```

- Two radio buttons, both named *newvisitor*. One should transmit a value of *y*; the other should transmit the value *n* and be checked when the page first displays.

```
<input type="radio" name="newvisitor" value="y">
<input type="radio" name="newvisitor" value="n" checked>
```

- Two pushbuttons: one titled Login and named *btnLogin*; the other titled Logout and named *btnLogout*.

```
<input type="submit" value="Login" name="btnLogin">
<input type="submit" value="Logout" name="btnLogout">
```

Arrange these elements in an HTML table and give them appropriate visual headings.

2. Insert the following statements before the first HTML tag in the Web page (that is, before the opening <html> tag):

```
<!-- #include file="../advbs.inc" -->
<%
fMsg = ""
iMsg = ""
loggedIn = False
' Code to process login will go here.
%>
```

The first statement includes the usual ADO named constants. Lines three and four initialize variables named *fMsg* and *iMsg* that will contain any fatal and informational messages, respectively. The fifth statement initializes a variable named *loggedIn* that indicates whether the Web visitor has completed a successful login during this execution of the Web page.

3. Replace the comment in step 2 with the following code to determine which button, if any, the Web visitor pressed:

```
If Request("btnLogin") <> "" Then
  ProcessLogin
Else
  If Request("btnLogout") <> "" Then
    Session("loginemail") = ""
  End If
End If
```

If the visitor clicked the Login button, this code runs a subroutine named *ProcessLogin*. The next few steps explain how to construct this subroutine. If the visitor clicked the Logout button, the code sets the Session object's *loginemail* value to a null string and then lets the rest of the Web page display normally. If the visitor clicked neither button, the script does nothing and the Web page again displays normally.

4. Begin creating the *ProcessLogin* subroutine by inserting the following statements immediately after the code you inserted in step 3:

```
Sub ProcessLogin()
' Code to process login will go here.
End Sub
```

5. The first step in processing a login is to verify that the visitor supplied both an e-mail address and a password. To do this, replace the comment in step 4 with the following code. If either or both fields are blank, the code stores an error message in the *fMsg* variable and exits the subroutine.

```
If Request("email") = "" Then
  If Request("paswd") = "" Then
```

(continued)

```
            fMsg = "Enter e-mail address and password."
            Exit Sub
        Else
            fMsg = "Enter e-Mail address."
            Exit Sub
        End If
    Else
        If Request("paswd") = "" Then
            fMsg = "Enter password."
            Exit Sub
        End If
    End If
End If
```

Note If you want to perform any additional processing on the e-mail or password fields, place the code here. For example, you might want to verify that each field has or exceeds a minimum length, or that the e-mail address contains an @ character. This is also a good spot to edit any additional fields you choose to collect from your visitors.

---

6. Create an ADO connection string for the holiday.mdb database, create a SQL statement that queries the *visitors* table for the given e-mail address, and then use these values to open and close an ADO recordset. This code belongs immediately after the code you entered in step 5.

```
cnStHol = "driver={Microsoft Access Driver (*.mdb)};" & _
          "dbq=" & Server.MapPath("../holiday/holiday.mdb")
sql = "SELECT * " & _
          "FROM visitors " & _
          "WHERE (email = '" & Request("email") & "') ; "
Set rsVis = Server.CreateObject("ADODB.Recordset")
rsVis.Open sql, cnStHol, adOpenDynamic, adLockOptimistic
' Code to add and/or log in Web visitor will go here.
rsVis.Close
```

At this point, you have two binary conditions to evaluate: whether the visitor is in the database and whether the visitor is requesting a new account. You can arrange these conditions and the responses in a typical truth table format as shown in Table 12-1.

Table 12-1   Conditions for Holiday Registration and Login Page

New Visitor	E-mail Address Not in Database	E-mail Address Exists in Database
Yes	Add visitor to database.	Reject request with the message "E-mail address already in use."
No	Reject request with the message "E-mail address not found."	If passwords match, log in visitor. If not, reject request with the message "Password not matched."

To create this table in code, enter the following statements in place of the comment in the code you entered previously in this step:

```
If rsVis.EOF Then
  If LCase(Request("newvisitor")) = "y" Then
'     Case 1: E-mail address not in database; new visitor.
  Else
'     Case 2: E-mail address not in database;
'             returning visitor.
  End If
Else
  If LCase(Request("newvisitor")) = "y" Then
'     Case 3: E-mail address in database; new visitor.
  Else
'     Case 4: E-mail address in database; returning visitor.
  End If
End If
```

7. In Case 1, the e-mail address is not in the database and the visitor requests a new account. Therefore, create a record for the new user and then set the *loggedIn* variable to *True*.

```
rsVis.Addnew
rsVis("email") = Request("email")
rsVis("paswd") = Request("paswd")
rsVis.Update
loggedIn = True
```

Note If you choose to collect any additional information from your visitors, be sure to save those fields between the *rsVis.Addnew* and *rsVis.Update* statements.

---

8. In Case 2, the e-mail address isn't in the database and the visitor isn't requesting a new account. Therefore, record a fatal error message.

```
fMsg = "E-Mail address not found."
```

9. In Case 3, the e-mail address is already in the database but the visitor is requesting a new account. Therefore, record a fatal error message.

```
fMsg = "E-Mail address already in use."
```

10. In Case 4, the e-mail address is in the database and the visitor isn't requesting a new account. If the visitor specified the password previously stored in the database, set the *loggedIn* variable to *True*. If the visitor didn't specify the correct password, record a fatal error message.

```
If Request("paswd") = rsVis("paswd") Then
  loggedIn = True
Else
  fMsg = "Password not matched."
End If
```

11. If any preceding step recorded a fatal error message, exit the subroutine with no further action. The following statement belongs after the *rsVis.Close* statement you added in step 6:

```
If fMsg <> "" Then
  Exit Sub
End If
```

12. If the subroutine completed a successful login (that is, if the *loggedIn* variable is *True*), save the e-mail address value in the visitor's Session object under the name *loginemail*. If the Session object doesn't specify a *goback* location, record an informational message. If, however, the page that sent the Web visitor to the login.asp page *did* specify a *goback* location, redirect the visitor to that location now.

```
If loggedIn Then
  Session("loginemail") = Request("email")
  If Session("goback") = "" Then
    iMsg = "Login successful"
  Else
    goback = Session("goback")
    Session("goback") = ""
    Response.Redirect goback
  End If
End If
```

13. To display the visitor's current login status, insert the following code anywhere within the body of the Web page:

```
<%
If Session("loginemail") = "" Then
  Response.Write "You are currently not logged in."
Else
  Response.Write "You are currently logged in as " _
    & Session("loginemail")
End If
%>
```

14. To display any fatal or informational messages that arise, insert the following code anywhere within the body of the Web page:

```
<p>
<span class="err"><%=fMsg%></span>
<span class="msg"><%=iMsg%></span> 
</p>
```

15. If you want to display the goback location, insert the following code wherever you want it to appear:

```
<p>Logging in will return you to: <%=Session("goback") %></p>
```

You've now coded the login.asp page. A complete listing of the ASP code from this example follows. For a complete listing, including the HTML, take a look at the file \webdbdev\ch12\login.asp on the CD.

```
<!-- #include file="../adovbs.inc" -->
<%
fMsg = ""
iMsg = ""
loggedIn = False
' Determine which button the Web visitor clicked and take
' appropriate action.
If Request("btnLogin") <> "" Then
  ProcessLogin
Else
  If Request("btnLogout") <> "" Then
    Session("loginemail") = ""
  End If
End If

Sub ProcessLogin ()
' Verify that the Web visitor submitted both an e-mail address
' and a password.
  If Request("email") = "" Then
    If Request("paswd") = "" Then
      fMsg = "Enter e-mail address and password."
      Exit Sub
    Else
      fMsg = "Enter e-Mail address."
      Exit Sub
    End If
  Else
    If Request("paswd") = "" Then
      fMsg = "Enter password."
      Exit Sub
    End If
  End If
' Build an ADO connection string.
  cnStHol = "driver={Microsoft Access Driver (*.mdb)};" & _
            "dbq=" & Server.MapPath("../holiday/holiday.mdb")
' Create and open an ADO Recordset object.
  sql = "SELECT * " & _
        "FROM visitors " & _
        "WHERE (email = '" & Request("email") & "') ; "
  Set rsVis = Server.CreateObject("ADODB.Recordset")
  rsVis.Open sql, cnStHol, adOpenDynamic, adLockOptimistic
' Add and/or log in Web visitor.
  If rsVis.EOF Then
    If LCase(Request("newvisitor")) = "y" Then
```

(continued)

```
'       E-mail address not in database; new visitor.
        rsVis.Addnew
        rsVis("email") = Request("email")
        rsVis("paswd") = Request("paswd")
        rsVis.Update
        loggedIn = True
      Else
'       E-mail address not in database; returning visitor.
        fMsg = "E-Mail address not found."
      End If
    Else
      If LCase(Request("newvisitor")) = "y" Then
'       E-mail address in database; new visitor.
        fMsg = "E-Mail address already in use."
      Else
'       E-mail address in database; returning visitor.
        If Request("paswd") = rsVis("paswd") Then
          loggedIn = True
        Else
          fMsg = "Password not matched."
        End If
      End If
    End If
    rsVis.Close
' Exit subroutine if a fatal error has occurred.
    If fMsg <> "" Then
      Exit Sub
    End If
' If a successful login has occurred and a goback location is
' specified, redirect to that location.
    If loggedIn Then
      Session("loginemail") = Request("email")
      If Session("goback") = "" Then
        iMsg = "Login successful"
      Else
        goback = Session("goback")
        Session("goback") = ""
        Response.Redirect goback
      End If
    End If
  End Sub
%>
```

As implemented, this example makes no provision for collecting additional data such as visitor name, demographics, mailing list enrollment, or security level. If your site has just a few such fields, you can handle them much as the example handled the password (except, of course, that the visitor won't need to reenter all these values correctly in order to log in again). If your site has many fields, you should probably separate your login and account maintenance functions into discrete Web pages.

Chapter Summary

This chapter explained how the Session object works and, as an example, showed you how to require and provide visitor registration for any or all Web pages in a site.

Part 4, "Advanced Topics," explained two advanced techniques that are useful whether or not your site is database oriented: the use of Microsoft Indexing Service for full text searching and the use of the Session object to store temporary data used by multiple Web pages.

Part 5, "Exchanging Data with XML," explains another technique so important that it deserves its own part of the book: eXtensible Markup Language (XML). XML promises to revolutionize data interchange in much the same way that HTML revolutionized document interchange. This makes XML highly relevant to the topic of Web database processing. Chapter 13, "Using XML at the Browser," explains the basics of XML and shows how to perform XML processing on your Web visitor's computer. Chapter 14, "Using XML at the Server," explains how XML can be used from ASP scripts, which allow the processing of XML data before presenting it to the client.

Part 5

Exchanging Data with XML

Using XML at the Browser

Estimated Time: 40 minutes

In this chapter, you'll learn

- The fundamental concepts of XML—eXtensible Markup Language.

- How to code several examples wherein the browser displays information that the Web server obtains from a database and delivers in XML format.

In recent years, XML has garnered tremendous praise, promise, and promotion. At the same time, simple explanations and practical examples of XML have remained rare to nonexistent. This chapter and the next (Chapter 14, "Using XML at the Server") try to resolve that discrepancy.

For both technological and aesthetic reasons, Web developers have up to now concentrated much more on data presentation than on data interchange. They think of Web pages as natural language documents marked up with simple formatting codes. This makes the information in those documents hard to update and hard to use for other purposes. If XML achieves its promise, however, that's all about to change.

Unlike HTML, which was designed to control the visual appearance of information, XML is totally and exclusively designed for transmitting structured data from one computer to another or from one application to another. XML provides no visual information at all. Visual presentation, if any, is totally at the control and discretion of the receiving program.

With XML, you code the data by attributes such as structure, information type, and storage format. Once you've coded your data into XML format, a formatting program translates it into a readable document. In short, a Web page becomes a structured data store with a presentation layer tacked on top of it.

If you're wondering why this material belongs in a book about Web database development, consider these facts:

- XML is for storing and transmitting structured data.

- Data stored in databases is, by definition, structured.

- The World Wide Web provides a fantastic way to store and transmit data.

The only missing element is the know-how to make all this work, and that's what this chapter and the next will provide.

Introducing XML

The next few topics will introduce the fundamental concepts of XML. Later topics in this chapter will explain how to construct useful examples that use XML on the browser, and the next chapter will explain how a Web server can use XML as well. The emphasis throughout will be on practical ways to get results.

Keep in mind, though, that this material is only an introduction. For more information about XML and its related technologies, browse Microsoft's Web site at *http://www.microsoft.com/xml*.

Keep in mind also that XML standards and XML software are still in the early stages of development. As a result, no one source of information can be correct for all environments. The XML environment described here is the one that comes with Microsoft Internet Explorer 5.0.

XML—eXtensible Markup Language

The first step in understanding XML is to brush aside a common preconceived notion: the belief that XML is some kind of super HTML with fantastic new presentation features that all browsers will support in a uniform way. In fact, XML's presentation capabilities are zero. XML only gets you the data; after that, you must use some other technology to sort, summarize, format, slice, dice, or make julienne fries of it.

The basic concept of XML is that to transmit, for example, the *catnr* field from a record in the holiday items database, you should surround it with tags like these:

```
<catnr>100</catnr>
```

Note   XML tag names must begin with a letter, an underscore (_), or a colon (:). Tag names beginning with the letters *xml*—in any combination of uppercase and lowercase—aren't allowed. The remaining characters can't be spaces, tabs, carriage returns, line feeds, colons, or angle brackets. Most other punctuation characters are allowed, but as a practical matter it's best to avoid them.

Both the start and end tags are mandatory, and their names are case-sensitive. Order multiple fields consecutively as shown here.

Note   If an XML tag contains no data, you can eliminate the end tag by placing a slash as the last character within the start tag. For example, the expressions <initial></initial> and <initial/> are equivalent.

The syntax of XML is much more demanding than that of HTML. In the case of HTML, it's the browser's job to make the best of whatever it receives. In the case of XML, it's the creating program's job to satisfy the required syntax.

```
<catnr>100</catnr>
<seqnr>100</seqnr>
<picname>scan395.jpg</picname>
<title>The Berjaya Eden Park Hotel</title>
<caption>This is where we stayed for four days in London.
That's Connie standing outside the front door.</caption>
<picdate>6/29/99</picdate>
```

To group these fields into a record, you surround them with another pair of tags named whatever you want: <itemrec> and </itemrec> tags, for example. To represent a table, surround one or more <itemrec>...</itemrec> groupings with another sensibly named pair of tags, such as <catalog> and </catalog>. Here's the result:

```
<catalog>
  <itemrec>
    <catnr>100</catnr>
    <seqnr>100</seqnr>
    <picname>scan395.jpg</picname>
    <title>The Berjaya Eden Park Hotel</title>
    <caption>This is where we stayed for four days in London.
    That's Connie standing outside the front door.</caption>
    <picdate>6/29/99</picdate>
  </itemrec>
  <itemrec>
    <catnr>100</catnr>
    <seqnr>200</seqnr>
    <picname>scan397.jpg</picname>
    <title>Inverness Terrace</title>
    <caption>These are the buildings across the street from
    our hotel. They're typical of the architecture in the
    district.</caption>
    <picdate>6/29/99</picdate>
  </itemrec>
</catalog>
```

Note   The XML standard requires that every XML document have a single *root element*, such as the catalog element in the example above. The root element contains all other elements, properly nested.

Notice how the well-named, well-structured field tags describe and organize the data. This, unlike the same data presented in an HTML table, is a format another program can deal with intelligently.

Of course, XML documents can accommodate much more complexity than the simple table, record, and field structure shown above. Many XML documents are more deeply nested than a database, table, record, and field metaphor can describe. XML documents can also contain natural language documents such as books, essays, poetry, plays, and brochures—texts normally not stored in a relational database. Therefore, XML developers often speak generically of *nodes* rather than specifically of database elements.

XML nodes can contain attributes as well as text. The following nodes, for example, contain an attribute named *currency*:

```
<price currency="USD">14.95</price>
<price currency="GBP">8.50</price>
```

This particular attribute informs whoever uses the XML document that the first price is given in U.S. dollars and the second in British pounds. An application could use this information to convert all prices to a Web visitor's local currency at current exchange rates. (Think of how convenient it would be if banks provided exchange-rate tables via the Web in XML format.)

Because XML consists entirely of plain text, computer programs can easily create XML documents. It's quite easy, for example, to imagine an ASP page that creates a database connection, runs a query, and formats the results as XML. Future database systems will no doubt have facilities to accept SQL statements and return XML result sets directly over the network.

Receiving and processing XML data takes a bit more work, because the receiving program must parse (pick apart) the XML code, create a matching structure in memory, load the data into that structure, and make the data available to the rest of the program. Any software that does this is called an *XML parser*.

Microsoft supplies a parser named msxml.dll with every copy of Internet Explorer 5.0 and later. This parser can load and process XML provided within a program, provided as a file on the local disk, or provided via HTTP from any computer on the network. As a bonus, you can load and run this parser not only within Internet Explorer 5.0, but also within any program that can load and run an ActiveX control. An ASP page, for example, can use msxml.dll to load one or more parsers, have each parser request data from a different source, and present consolidated data to the Web visitor.

DTD—The Document Type Definition

A *well-formed* XML document is one that conforms to all syntactical rules of XML. If you give the parser an ill-formed document, the parser will refuse to load it and will instead return an error code.

The parser can also check an XML document for *valid* content, but for this it needs a *document type definition* (DTD). A DTD tells the parser what tags are mandatory, what tags are optional, what values are allowable for any given tag, and so forth. If a document violates any of the rules in the DTD, the parser returns an error code and refuses to load the document. A document that passes muster against a DTD is both *well-formed* and *valid*.

DTDs have their own syntax, different from that of XML, HTML, CSS, or anything else. In localized applications where one person or team creates both the XML documents and all the programs that use them, creating DTDs frequently isn't worth the trouble. As the scope of an application grows, however, the value of using DTDs quickly becomes apparent.

Much to the chagrin of U.S. citizens, the Internal Revenue Service collects all federal taxes in the United States. Suppose this agency decided to accept electronic tax forms in XML format. As part of this endeavor, the IRS would probably create a DTD corresponding to each form a taxpayer could submit electronically. Developers of tax preparation software could use these DTDs to test their output for compliance with IRS standards, and the IRS could use the DTDs to test each electronic tax return for validity.

If banks decided to start providing exchange-rate data via XML, some central authority would probably construct a DTD for this purpose, and that DTD would become the standard for all currency exchange reporting by all banks. This would make it easy to use rates from any bank a developer or Web visitor wanted to patronize.

Further discussion of DTDs is beyond the scope of this book, but you can get more information from Microsoft's Web site or from any number of XML books.

XSL—Extensible Stylesheet Language

Because an XML document has no visual appearance, displaying XML data requires the use of some other technology. The most obvious approach is to write a script that loads an XML document into a parser, reads the data, and writes HTML. This is a common approach, and one that you can implement either on the browser or on the Web server.

Another approach involves loading an XML document into a parser on the browser and then, rather than creating a complete HTML stream, simply replacing portions of a Web page already on display. This is possible using the Dynamic HTML features found in Internet Explorer version 4.0 and later.

Note Both approaches described so far use the browser's Document Object Model, or DOM, to display XML data. If you hear XML developers speak of "using the DOM" to display data, this is what they mean.

A third approach involves loading an XML document into a so-called XML data source object (DSO) within the Web page. This approach has two primary advantages. First, script code can access the XML data using familiar ADO Recordset methods and properties. Second, you can *bind* HTML display elements to nodes within the XML DSO recordset. Each bound element then displays—automatically—the current value of the bound node. If a browser-side script invokes methods such as *moveFirst*, *moveNext*, *moveLast*, and *movePrevious*, the values of the bound display elements change correspondingly.

The fourth approach is the one actually proposed by the World Wide Web Consortium (W3C)—using Extensible Stylesheet Language. XSL encompasses two main components: a transformation language and a formatting language. The transformation language converts one XML document to another. Typical transformations include adding, recalculating, excluding, renaming, or reordering nodes. Many other kinds of transformation are, of course, possible.

The XSL formatting language is currently just a working draft. The working draft tries to accommodate formatting of the same XML data for a variety of different media, of which HTML is just one, and has aroused some controversy among the many concerned parties. As a result, there are currently no major implementations.

The Microsoft approach, at least for now, accomplishes formatting through transformation. The XSL capabilities in Internet Explorer perform XSL formatting by transforming one XML document into another that satisfies both HTML and XML syntax.

The XSL transformation language is organized around the concept of *templates*. An XSL template is basically a model collection of statements interspersed with XSL tags that repeat blocks of statements for each selected node in an XML document. Additional XSL tags substitute the values of specified nodes into the model statements.

An XSL style sheet is itself a valid XML document. To run the style sheet, you first load the data into one XML document object and the style sheet into another. Then you invoke the first object's *transformNode* method to create the text of a new XML document.

The section titled "Using XSL Stylesheets" later in this chapter provides a working example of how this technology works.

XML Namespaces

The capability to gather, consolidate, and process data from disparate sources is a key XML objective. This isn't possible, however, when different data providers use the same names to identify different kinds of data.

The most obvious solution is for each organization, developer, or application to prefix all names with a unique identifier. This eliminates any confusion between, say, a Part Number field defined by manufacturing company A and a Part Number field defined by casting director B. All element names defined within a given prefix are said to reside in that prefix's *namespace*.

The critical property of a namespace is obviously that it be unique; its specific content is irrelevant. Namespace identifiers could have been semi-random numbers generated by an algorithm or some code obtained from an issuing authority. The XML standard, however, is to use a Universal Resource Identifier (URI). In most cases, this is synonymous with using a Web site's URL.

Note   In theory, a URI identifies information in a way that's independent of its physical location. Web visitors who look up a URI could get the same information even if its physical location (its URL) changes. However, given the lack of a global URI directory system, URIs and URLs are currently the same.

To make a namespace available throughout a given XML document, include a tag such as the following prior to the first XML node element:

```
<?xml:namespace ns="http://www.interlacken.com/schema/ns" prefix="il" ?>
```

Then, for each node name that belongs in this namespace, precede its local name with the prefix *il* and a colon. Here's an example:

```
<il:catnr>100</il:catnr>
```

Note   Tag names not associated with any namespace are said to be *local*.

You can also define a namespace for use within a single node. The following code shows this technique in use.

```
<il:catnr xmlns:il="http://www.interlacken.com/schema/ns">100</il:catnr>
```

If you don't specify a prefix, the given namespace becomes the default; that is, it applies to all tag names that don't specify a prefix.

Because the examples within this book are self-contained, they don't use global namespaces. Doing so would simply make the examples more complex.

However, you should definitely assign namespaces—at least default ones—within any XML files you design for use beyond a single application.

Using the XML Document Object

Processing XML data requires first creating and then loading an XML Document Object. The Microsoft way of doing this involves an ActiveX control called Microsoft.XMLDOM. The following statements will create an instance of (that is, instantiate) this object in the environment indicated:

- Microsoft JScript

```
var mydoc = new ActiveXObject("Microsoft.XMLDOM");
```

- Microsoft VBScript

```
Dim xmldoc
Set xmldoc = CreateObject("Microsoft.XMLDOM")
```

- Microsoft Visual Basic

```
Dim xmldoc = new DOMDocument
```

Note   Microsoft calls the object that stores an XML document an *XMLDOMDocument* object. This object implements the XML parser and additional methods that support XML and XSL. Because its name is lengthy and hard to read, this book will simply call this object an XML DOM object.

Loading an XML Document Object

You can load data into an XML DOM object using either of two methods, both of which replace any data already in the object. The first method loads XML from a local file or from a Web location. The following example loads XML from a Web location; to load XML from a file, specify its location in the ordinary way (by explicit or implied drive letter, path, and filename).

XMLDoc.load("http://*<server>*/*<path>*/*<file>*.xml")

The second method loads XML from a string variable or literal. The following examples show this method in use.

```
strMbrXml = "<member>" & _
            "<fname>Steven</fname>" & _
            "<sname>Buchanan</sname>" & _
            "</member>")
XMLDoc.loadXML(strMbrXML)
```

The XML DOM object has four properties that control document parsing behavior. You can find these listed in Table 13-1.

For most tasks, only the *async* property merits attention, because the loading and parsing of an XML file occurs asynchronously by default. This means the XML DOM object can pass control to the next line of code before it finishes loading the XML document. To avoid this behavior (that is, to load the XML file synchronously) set the object's *async* property to *False*. To abort an asynchronous download, call the document object's *abort* method.

Table 13-1   XML DOM Properties that Affect Object Loading

Property	Value	Default	Description
async	True	●	The *load* method returns control to the caller almost immediately (before it finishes loading the document).
	False	○	The *load* method retains control until it completely loads the document or encounters an unrecoverable error.
validateOnParse	True	●	The parser should validate this document against any available DTDs.
	False	○	The parser tests only for well-formed XML even if an applicable DTD is present.
resolveExternals	True	●	The parser should resolve any external definitions (resolvable namespaces, DTD external subsets, and external entity references) independent of validation.
	False	○	The parser shouldn't resolve external definitions.
preserveWhiteSpace	False	○	The *xml* property will contain a single newline or space character wherever any white space occurred in the original document.
			The *text* property will contain no leading or trailing white space characters, and a single space character where any sequence of white space characters occurred in the original document.
			Any *xml:space* attributes within the XML document override these settings.
	True	●	All white space characters in the original document are preserved.

Obtaining Document Information

The following properties provide information about any document loaded into an XML DOM object:

- *doctype* contains the name of the DTD that validated the document. For XML documents without a DTD and for HTML documents, this property is *NULL*.

- *implementation* provides access to the *XMLDOMImplementation* object that handles this document. You can use this object to determine whether certain features are available for a given document.

- *parseError* provides access to an *XMLDOMParseError* object. This object provides information about the most recent parsing error. Table 13-2 lists the properties available.

- *readyState* indicates the current state of the XML document. Table 13-3 lists the possible values.

- *url* returns the URL from the last successful load. While a document is being loaded, this property is *NULL*. Saving a loaded document to a different location doesn't change this property.

Table 13-2   *XMLDOMParseError* Object Properties

Property	Description
errorCode	Contains the error code of the last parse error.
filepos	Contains the absolute file position where the error occurred.
line	Specifies the line number that contains the error.
linepos	Contains the character position within the line where the error occurred.
reason	Explains the reason for the error. (Warning: following certain kinds of errors, this object might not be available.)
srcText	Returns the full text of the line containing the error.
url	Contains the URL of the XML document containing the last error.

Table 13-3   Values of the *readyState* Property

Status	Value	Description
LOADING	1	The load is proceeding but hasn't started parsing data.
LOADED	2	The load is reading and parsing data, but the object model still isn't available.
INTERACTIVE	3	Some data has been read and parsed, and is now available in read-only mode.
COMPLETED	4	The load process is complete, successful or not.

Loading XML Documents Asynchronously

When you load an XML document and the XML DOM object's *async* property is *True* (the default), it's your responsibility not to use the XML DOM object until its *readyState* property equals 4. There are two ways to verify this:

- Write a subroutine or function that checks the *readyState* property. If it's not equal to 4, set a timer to run the routine again after some delay.

If *readyState* equals 4, check the value of the *parseError* property. If it's zero, no errors occurred and you can use the XML DOM object. If it's nonzero, you should report the error and terminate processing.

* Provide an *onreadystatechange* event handler. This is a subroutine or function the XML DOM object will call every time it changes the value of its *readyState* property. When *readyState* is 4, proceed as described in the previous bullet. Table 13-4 lists three ways to invoke an *onreadystatechange* event handler.

Table 13-4   Invoking an *onreadystatechange* Event Handler

Method	Sample Code	Environment
Inline HTML	`<ELEMENT onreadystatechange = "<handler>" ... >`	All platforms
Event property	`<object>.onreadystatechange = <handler>`	JScript only
Named script	`<SCRIPT FOR = <object> EVENT = onreadystatechange>`	Internet Explorer only

Asynchronous parsing lets your Web page continue with other processing while an XML DOM object receives and parses an XML file. If, however, the time to load the object is short (or if—without the XML data—the Web page is blank or useless anyway), asynchronous parsing probably isn't worth the extra coding effort. The following statements turn off asynchronous parsing. You must set these values after creating the XML DOM object and before loading it:

* Jscript

```
<object>.async = "false"
```

* VBScript

```
<object>.async = False
```

Getting Data from an XML Document

Once you've loaded an XML DOM object with data, the following expression points to the document's *root node*—that is, to the node that the outermost pair of XML tags define.

<tag id>.documentElement

If you loaded an XML DOM object named *xmlDoc* with the following XML document, *xmlDoc.documentElement* would point to the *items* node.

```
<items>
<itemrec>
  <catnr>100</catnr>
  <seqnr>100</seqnr>
  <picname>scan395.jpg</picname>
  <title>The Berjaya Eden Park Hotel</title>
```

```
  <caption>This is where we stayed for four days in London. That's Connie
standing outside the front door.</caption>
  <picdate>6/29/99</picdate>
</itemrec>
</items>
```

The root node (and every other node, for that matter) contains a *childNodes* object that maintains a list of all subordinate nodes. Given a zero-based index (that is, a subscript), the *item* method of a *childNodes* object returns a pointer to any desired node. The expression that accesses the first *itemrec* node within the *items* node is therefore as follows:

```
xmlDoc.documentElement.childNodes.item(0)
```

The expression to access the second *itemrec* node, if there were one, would be:

```
xmlDoc.documentElement.childNodes.item(1)
```

The expression *xmlDoc.documentElement.childNodes.length* returns the number of available child nodes. Thus, iterating through all children of the *items* node involves nothing more than iterating the *item* index from zero to *xmlDoc.documentElement.childNodes.length* minus one.

Shortcutting Long Object Expressions

Because expressions such as the following are tedious to work with, most developers save pointers to intermediate objects and then use them as shortcuts.

```
xmlDoc.documentElement.childNodes.item(1).childNodes.item(3)
```

For example, instead of coding this:

```
dpname = xmlDoc.documentElement.childNodes.item(1).childNodes.item(3)
```

they might code this:

```
rootnode = xmlDoc.documentElement
dtitle = rootnode.childNodes.item(1).childNodes.item(3)
```

or this:

```
currec = xmlDoc.documentElement.rootnode.childNodes.item(1)
dtitle = currec.childNodes.item(3)
```

This code works because Jscript and VBScript object variables contain pointers to objects, and not the objects themselves. Thus, after executing a statement like this:

```
rootnode = xmlDoc.documentElement
```

the *rootnode* variable points to the same object as *xmlDoc.documentElement*. The *rootnode* variable doesn't contain a completely new copy of that object.

Of course, each of these subnodes (that is, each of these *itemrec* nodes) contains its own *childNodes* object, with pointers to the *catnr*, *seqnr*, *picname*, *title*, *caption*, and *picdate* nodes. The expression to access the first *catnr* node is therefore as follows:

```
xmlDoc.documentElement.childNodes.item(0).childNodes.item(0)
```

The expression to access the *title* node of the second *itemrec* node (if there were one) would be

```
xmlDoc.documentElement.childNodes.item(1).childNodes.item(3)
```

If such an expression seems difficult to work with, take heart in the fact that most developers feel the same way. The sidebar "Shortcutting Long Object Expressions" describes a way to avoid this nuisance.

Build a simple page that displays XML data

At this point you should be ready to code a simple Web page that displays data provided in XML format. Such a page appears in Figure 13-1.

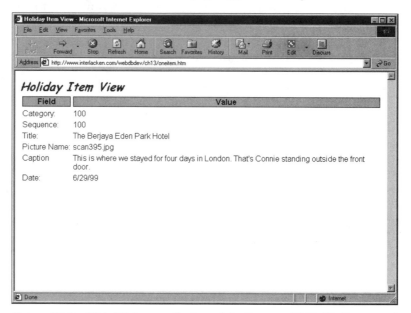

Figure 13-1 *This Web page displays data from an XML file it accessed over the network.*

The completed source code for this exercise appears within the sample files as \webdbdev\ch13\oneitem.htm. The XML file that contains the data is named \webdbdev\ch13\holicat.xml. This file contains several records similar to the one listed here.

```
<items>
<itemrec>
  <catnr>100</catnr>
  <seqnr>100</seqnr>
```

```
<picname>scan395.jpg</picname>
<title>The Berjaya Eden Park Hotel</title>
<caption>This is where we stayed for four days in London. That's Connie
standing outside the front door.</caption>
<picdate>6/29/99</picdate>
</itemrec>
</items>
```

Follow these steps to build this page:

1. Initialize a new, empty Web page with the usual structural elements, plus any style embellishments you want to use.

```
<html>
<head>
<link rel="stylesheet" type="text/css"
      href="../holiday/holiform.css">
<title>Holiday Item View</title>
</head>
<body>
<h2>Holiday Item View</h2>
<!-- Code to load and display XML data will go here. -->
</body>
</html>
```

2. Replace the comment in step 1 with a script block and declare any variables you plan to use. Here are the required statements:

```
<script language="JavaScript">
var dcatnr, dseqnr, dpname, dtitle, dcaptn, dpdate
var rootElem;
// Code to load XML DOM object and retrieve data will go here.
</script>
```

3. Create an XML DOM object, set its *async* property to *false*, and load the XML file holicat.xml. These statements must replace the comment in step 2.

```
var xmlDoc = new ActiveXObject("Microsoft.XMLDOM");
xmlDoc.async = "false";
xmlDoc.load("holicat.xml");
```

Setting the *async* property to *false* ensures that any statements following the *xmlDoc.load* statement won't execute until the *load* method finishes its work.

4. Test the success of the *xmlDoc.load* operation by testing the value of the *xmlDoc.parseErrror* property. If this property is zero, the load worked. If not, display the error message contained in the *xmlDoc.parseError.reason* property. This code should immediately follow that from step 3.

```
if (xmlDoc.parseError == 0) {
// Code to retrieve field values will go here.
```

(continued)

```
    }else{
      alert(xmlDoc.parseError.reason);
    }
```

5. If the load worked, store a pointer to the XML document's root element and then retrieve fields one through six of the root element's first child node. Save each value in a Jscript variable. This code should replace the comment in step 4.

```
    rootElem = xmlDoc.documentElement;
    dcatnr=rootElem.childNodes.item(0).childNodes.item(0).text;
    dseqnr=rootElem.childNodes.item(0).childNodes.item(1).text;
    dpname=rootElem.childNodes.item(0).childNodes.item(2).text;
    dtitle=rootElem.childNodes.item(0).childNodes.item(3).text;
    dcaptn=rootElem.childNodes.item(0).childNodes.item(4).text;
    dpdate=rootElem.childNodes.item(0).childNodes.item(5).text;
```

6. Follow the </script> tag you created in step 2 with the HTML code to display whatever structural elements and titles you want to use for presenting the data. Then insert a one-line script such as the following wherever you want a data value to appear.

```
    <script>document.write(dcatnr)</script>
```

To complete step 6, the sample file for this exercise uses an HTML table. You can see how this works in the complete HTML listing that follows.

```
<html>
<head>
<link rel="stylesheet" type="text/css"
      href="../holiday/holiform.css">
<title>Holiday Item View</title>
</head>
<body>
<h2>Holiday Item View</h2>
<script language="JavaScript">
var dcatnr, dseqnr, dpname, dtitle, dcaptn, dpdate
var rootElem;
// Create and load an XML DOM object.
var xmlDoc = new ActiveXObject("Microsoft.XMLDOM");
xmlDoc.async = false;
xmlDoc.load("holicat.xml");
// If successful, retrieve data values from the first record;
// otherwise, display the error message from the parser.
if (xmlDoc.parseError == 0) {
  rootElem = xmlDoc.documentElement;
  dcatnr=rootElem.childNodes.item(0).childNodes.item(0).text;
```

```
    dseqnr=rootElem.childNodes.item(0).childNodes.item(1).text;
    dpname=rootElem.childNodes.item(0).childNodes.item(2).text;
    dtitle=rootElem.childNodes.item(0).childNodes.item(3).text;
    dcaptn=rootElem.childNodes.item(0).childNodes.item(4).text;
    dpdate=rootElem.childNodes.item(0).childNodes.item(5).text;
}else{
  alert(xmlDoc.parseError.reason);
}
</script>
<table border="0" cellpadding cellspacing="5">
  <tr>
    <th>Field</th>
    <th>Value</th>
  </tr><tr>
    <td>Category:</td>
    <td><script>document.write(dcatnr)</script></td>
  </tr><tr>
    <td>Sequence:</td>
    <td><script>document.write(dseqnr)</script></td>
  </tr><tr>
    <td valign=="top">Title:</td>
    <td><script>document.write(dtitle)</script></td>
  </tr><tr>
    <td>Picture Name:</td>
    <td><script>document.write(dpname)</script></td>
  </tr><tr>
    <td valign=="top">Caption</td>
    <td><script>document.write(dcaptn)</script></td>
  </tr><tr>
    <td>Date:</td>
    <td><script>document.write(dpdate)</script></td>
  </tr>
</table>
</body>
</html>
```

Build a page that displays XML data asynchronously

In the example just shown, setting the XML DOM object's *async* property to *false* forced script execution to halt while the XML DOM object loaded the specified XML file. This has the effect of delaying whatever the remaining code was supposed to do.

If this delay isn't acceptable, you can let the *async* property remain *True* (the default). This lets the rest of your script continue executing while the XML DOM object loads the specified XML document. However, it also demands that you deal with two other problems, as described on the next page.

- Before your script can reliably access the loaded XML document, it must verify that the load operation is complete. In general, there are two ways to do this:

  - The script runs a function that checks the XML DOM object's *ready-State* property. If this property is 4 (meaning *completed*), the script processes the XML document. If it isn't, the script sets a timer to run the check function again after some time interval. The sample Web page oneitema.htm, contained in the sample files, will illustrate this method.

  - The script can tell the XML DOM object to call a certain function whenever the value of its *readyState* property changes. When this function determines that the *readyState* property is 4, it processes the completed XML document. The sample Web page oneitemb.htm will illustrate this.

- Once the XML DOM object is loaded, the browser will most likely have finished displaying the Web page (except, of course, for any XML data you want to display). To display values from the XML document, you must therefore use the Dynamic HTML features introduced in Internet Explorer 4.0.

The following are the most common Dynamic HTML properties used when displaying XML data:

- *innerText* includes all text between an opening and closing pair of HTML tags. Take a look at the following example:

  ```
  <span id=product>Jelly<br>Beans</span>
  ```

  The value of *product.innerText* would initially be *Jelly* and *Beans* on separate lines. If you replaced *product.innerText* with the string *Bonbons*, the Web visitor would see the word *Bonbons*. If you replaced *product.innerText* with *Gum
Drops*, the Web visitor would see *Gum
Drops* (including the angle brackets).

- *innerHTML* includes all text and HTML tags between an opening and closing pair of HTML tags.

  Given the example above, the value of *product.innerHTML* would initially be *Jelly
Beans*). If you replaced *product.innerHTML* with the string *Bonbons*, the Web visitor would see the word *Bonbons*. If you replaced *product.innerHTML* with *Gum
Drops*, the Web visitor would see the words *Gum* and *Drops* on separate lines.

A *span,* by the way, is simply a named block of Web page content. It introduces no formatting of its own (although you can, of course, assign formatting through the *style=* or *class=* attributes). A span begins where you put a <span> tag and ends where you put a </span> tag.

Given the preceding information, here's the procedure to create an asynchronous version of the previous example. You can find the completed code among the sample files as ch13\oneitema.htm.

1. Initialize a new, empty Web page with the usual structural elements, plus any style embellishments you want to use.

```
<html>
<head>
<link rel="stylesheet" type="text/css"
      href="../holiday/holiform.css">
<title>Holiday Item View</title>
<!-- Code to load and display XML data will go here. -->
</head>
<body>
<h2>Holiday Item View</h2>
</body>
</html>
```

2. Replace the comment in step 1 with a <script> block, create an XML DOM object named *xmlDoc*, and tell it to start loading the file holicat.xml. Initialize a counter called *xmlwait* to zero.

```
<script language="JavaScript">
var xmlDoc = new ActiveXObject("Microsoft.XMLDOM");
xmlDoc.load("holicat.xml");
xmlwait = 0
// Functions to check load completion will go here.
</script>
```

3. Lay out the body of the Web page as you want it to appear. Insert the following tags wherever you want the *catnr*, *seqnr*, *title*, *picname*, *caption*, and *picdate* values to appear.

```
<span id="dcatnr"></span>
<span id="dseqnr"></span>
<span id="dtitle"></span>
<span id="dpname"></span>
<span id="dcaptn"></span>
<span id="dpdate"></span>
```

4. Insert the following code somewhere near the bottom of the <body> section. This will display the amount of time the XML document took to load.

```
<p>XML Response time: <span id="waitsec">0</span> second(s).</p>
```

5. Add an *onload* attribute to the <body> tag as shown here. This tells the browser to run the script function *CheckState()* whenever it finishes loading the <body> section.

```
<body onload="CheckState();">
```

For an explanation of why this technique is necessary, refer to the sidebar titled, "Asynchronous Timing Factors."

Asynchronous Timing Factors

When you load an XML document synchronously and display its contents via Dynamic HTML, you must ensure that the entire body section is loaded before you insert any XML values. Otherwise, if the XML document happens to load faster than the rest of the Web page, you might try to store an XML value in a span that didn't exist yet.

One way to achieve this is by loading the XML document in a function invoked by the <body> tag's *onload=* attribute. A function invoked this way runs only after the entire Web page is loaded.

6. Add the following function to the <script> block already in the <head> section. This code will replace the comment in step 2.

```
function CheckState() {
  if (xmlDoc.readyState == "4")
    GetData();
  else
    xmlwait = xmlwait + 1;
    waitsec.innerText = xmlwait;
    window.setTimeout("CheckState()", 1000);
}
```

If this function finds that the *xmlDoc* object's *readyState* property is 4—meaning *complete*—it executes the *GetData()* function. Otherwise, it increments the response time counter *xmlwait* by 1, displays that value within the message created in step 4, and then sets a timer to run the *CheckState()* function again after 1000 milliseconds.

7. Add the following function immediately after the code you added in step 6. As in the previous example, this code retrieves data values from the first record in the XML document. In this case, however, the code copies those values into the *innerText* properties of the <span> elements you created in step 3, thus displaying them to the Web visitor.

```
function GetData() {
  curRec = xmlDoc.documentElement.childNodes.item(0);
  dcatnr.innerText = curRec.childNodes.item(0).text;
  dseqnr.innerText = curRec.childNodes.item(1).text;
  dpname.innerText = curRec.childNodes.item(2).text;
  dtitle.innerText = curRec.childNodes.item(3).text;
  dcaptn.innerText = curRec.childNodes.item(4).text;
  dpdate.innerText = curRec.childNodes.item(5).text;
}
```

As shown in Figure 13-2, this Web page produces essentially the same results as the previous one. The only difference is the response time message at the bottom of the display.

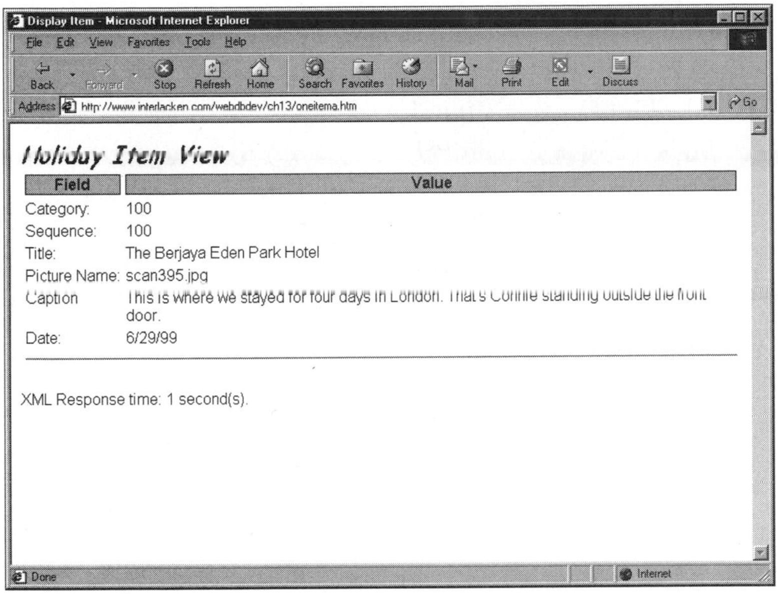

Figure 13-2 *The XML document displayed in this Web page loaded asynchronously—that is, while the browser continued to work on other parts of the Web page.*

The complete HTML listing for this page appears here:

```
<html>
<head>
<link rel="stylesheet" type="text/css"
     href="../holiday/holiform.css">
<title>Display Item</title>
<script language="JavaScript">
// Create XML DOM object, and load the .xml document.
var xmlDoc = new ActiveXObject("Microsoft.XMLDOM");
xmlDoc.load("holicat.xml");
xmlwait = 0
// Check if XML DOM object is completely loaded.
// If so, run GetData() function.
// If not, wait 1 second and then try again.
function CheckState() {
  if (xmlDoc.readyState == "4")
    GetData();
  else
    xmlwait = xmlwait + 1
    waitsec.innerText = xmlwait
    window.setTimeout("CheckState()", 1000)
}
// Copy values from first XML record to spans in Web page.
function GetData() {
  curRec = xmlDoc.documentElement.childNodes.item(0);
```

(continued)

```
        dcatnr.innerText = curRec.childNodes.item(0).text;
        dseqnr.innerText = curRec.childNodes.item(1).text;
        dpname.innerText = curRec.childNodes.item(2).text;
        dtitle.innerText = curRec.childNodes.item(3).text;
        dcaptn.innerText = curRec.childNodes.item(4).text;
        dpdate.innerText = curRec.childNodes.item(5).text;
    }
</script>
</head>
<body onload="CheckState();">
<h2>Holiday Item View</h2>
<table border="0" cellpadding cellspacing="5">
    <tr>
        <th>Field</th>
        <th>Value</th>
    </tr><tr>
        <td>Category:</td>
        <td><span id="dcatnr"></span></td>
    </tr><tr>
        <td>Sequence:</td>
        <td><span id="dseqnr"></span></td>
    </tr><tr>
        <td valign="top">Title:</td>
        <td><span id="dtitle"></span></td>
    </tr><tr>
        <td>Picture Name:</td>
        <td><span id="dpname"></span></td>
    </tr><tr>
        <td valign="top">Caption</td>
        <td><span id="dcaptn"></span></td>
    </tr><tr>
        <td>Date:</td>
        <td><span id="dpdate"></span></td>
    <tr>
        <td colspan="2">
          <hr>
        </td>
</table>
<p>XML Response time: <span id="waitsec">0</span> second(s).</p>
</body>
</html>
```

Build an asynchronous page that doesn't use timers

Using a timer to poll the *readyState* property might occasionally seem slow or awkward. If the XML document in the previous example takes 1.1 seconds to load, for example, the Web visitor will still have to wait 2 seconds. This wait could be reduced if the XML DOM object could just wake up a piece of code whenever loading is complete. Replacing the <body> tag and the <script> block in the head section with the following code does just that.

```
<script language="JavaScript">
var xmlDoc;
xmlDoc = new ActiveXObject("Microsoft.XMLDOM");
xmlDoc.onreadystatechange = ChkStateChange;

function StartLoad() {
  xmlDoc.load("holicat.xml");
}
function ChkStateChange(){
  var state = xmlDoc.readyState;
  loadstat.innerText = state;
  if (state == 4) {
    if (xmlDoc.parseError == 0) {
      GetData();
    }else{
      alert(xmlDoc.parseError.reason);
    }
  }
}

function GetData() {
  curRec = xmlDoc.documentElement.childNodes.item(0);
  dcatnr.innerText = curRec.childNodes.item(0).text;
  dseqnr.innerText = curRec.childNodes.item(1).text;
  dpname.innerText = curRec.childNodes.item(2).text;
  dtitle.innerText = curRec.childNodes.item(3).text;
  dcaptn.innerText = curRec.childNodes.item(4).text;
  dpdate.innerText = curRec.childNodes.item(5).text;
}
</script>
</head>
<body onload="StartLoad();">
```

The first three lines in the <script> block create an XML DOM object named *xmlDoc* in the usual way. The following statement then tells the *xmlDoc* object that whenever it changes the value of its *readyState* property, it should call a function named *ChkStateChange*:

```
xmlDoc.onreadystatechange = ChkStateChange
```

The <body> tag specifies that upon loading, the Web page should run a function called *StartLoad*. This is the first function defined within the script block above, and it simply invokes the *xmlDoc* object's load method.

As loading proceeds, the *xmlDoc* object keeps the *readyState* property updated. Whenever it changes this property, the *xmlDoc* object calls the *ChkStateChange* function. When *ChkStateChange* notices that *readyState* is 4, it calls the *GetData* function to update the Web page with the desired data.

Notice that once the command to load *xmlDoc* is given, this code has no mechanism to prevent updating a part of the Web page that hasn't loaded yet.

The only recourse is to defer loading the *xmlDoc* object until after the Web page is loaded. For a further discussion of this issue, refer to the sidebar, "Asynchronous Timing Factors," earlier in this chapter.

To view a complete Web page that uses this technique, look at the sample file \webdbdev\ch13\oneitemb.htm. This page produces essentially the same results as the previous two examples.

Saving an XML Document

The *save* method writes an XML DOM object's current document to a file or to another object. The save location can be a filename specified as a string, an Active Server Pages *Response* object, another XML DOM object, or any custom object that supports persistence. The following ASP code saves the XML document to a file named sample.xml:

```
<%
Dim xmldoc
Set xmldoc = Server.CreateObject("Microsoft.XMLDOM")
xmldoc.async = false
xmldoc.load(Request)
xmldoc.save(Server.MapPath("sample.xml"))
%>
```

The following statement treats the body of an HTTP request as XML data and loads it into the *xmldoc* object:

```
xmldoc.load(Request)
```

The following statement would send the XML document contained in the *xmldoc* object back to a Web visitor as XML text:

```
xmldoc.save(Response)
```

Using the XML Data Source Object

If accessing data in an XML DOM object seems difficult and awkward compared to accessing data in an ADO recordset, you're in luck. The XML data source object loads an XML document into a subordinate XML DOM object and then provides access using familiar ADO methods and properties.

There are two ways to create an XML DSO:

- You can use the OBJECT element to directly load an instance of the XML DSO. For example, the following code, located anywhere in a Web page's <body> section, directly loads an instance of the XML DSO:

```
<OBJECT width=0 height=0
    classid="clsid:550dda30-0541-11d2-9ca9-0060b0ec3d39"
    id="ex1dso">
</OBJECT>
```

- You can use an XML data island. The section "Using XML Data Islands" will describe this topic specifically.

To access XML data via the DSO, first use the DSO's *XMLDocument* property to find its XML DOM object, and then load the XML DOM object in the usual way. The following code loads the XML DOM object contained within the XML DSO created just above. It runs after the rest of the Web page is loaded.

```
<SCRIPT for=window event=onload>
    var doc = ex1dso.XMLDocument;
    doc.load("yourdata.xml");
    if (doc.documentNode == null)
    {
        YourErrorHandler(doc);
    }
</SCRIPT>
```

If you'd rather not load the XML data from another file, you can code it within the OBJECT element. The following example shows how to do this.

```
<OBJECT width=0 height=0
    classid="clsid:550dda30-0541-11d2-9ca9-0060b0ec3d39"
    id="ex2dso">
<members>
  <member>
    <fname>Steven</fname>
    <sname>Buchanan</sname>
  </member>
</members>
</OBJECT>
```

The following script code loads this XML into this DSO:

```
<SCRIPT for=window event=onload>
    var doc = ex2dso.XMLDocument;
    doc.loadXML(ex2dso.altHtml);
    if (doc.documentNode == null)
    {
        HandleError(doc);
    }
</SCRIPT>
```

Navigate an XML document by using DSO

The Web page in Figure 13-3, catbrowse.htm, loads an XML file into an XML DSO and displays one record at a time. However, unlike the previous examples, this page provides a way for Web visitors to move forward and backward through the XML document. It also illustrates the use of bound data elements that—compared to other methods—saves some code.

The XML data in this example comes from an ASP page named holicat.asp. The next chapter will explain in detail how this page works. For now, it's enough to know that requesting *holicat.asp?qcatnr=200* from the Web server returns all *item* records in the holiday.mdb database that are coded with category number 200.

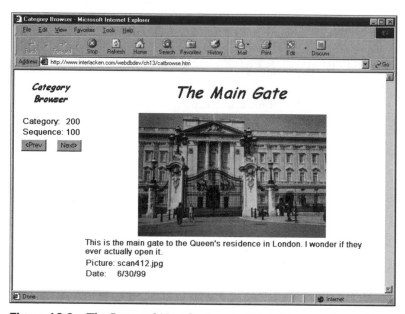

Figure 13-3   *The Prev and Next buttons in this Web page change the current record pointer in an XML DSO recordset. Page elements bound to that recordset will then display new values automatically.*

Because holicat.asp is an ASP file, it contains program code rather than XML code. Running the program code produces the XML shown in Figure 13-4. You might want to test this page directly, as shown in the figure, before using it in the remaining examples.

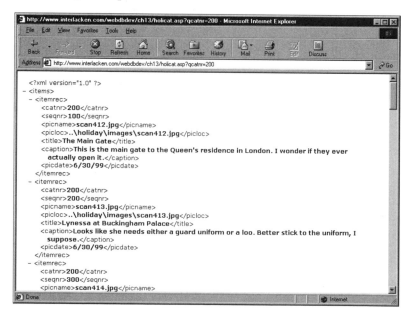

Figure 13-4   *Requesting the holicat.asp page from a properly configured Web server returns this XML stream.*

Here are the steps required to create catbrowse.htm:

1. Initialize a new, empty Web page with the usual structural elements. Add any style embellishments you want to use.

```
<html>
<head>
<link rel="stylesheet" type="text/css"
        href="../holiday/holiform.css">
<title>Holiday Category Browser</title>
<!-- Code to load and display XML data will go here. -->
</head>
<body>
</body>
</html>
```

2. Add an XML DSO named *xmldso* immediately after the <body> tag. This requires the following code:

```
<object width="0" height="0" id="xmldso"
  classid="clsid:550dda30-0541-11d2-9ca9-0060b0ec3d39">
</object>
```

3. Add a pair of <script> and </script> tags immediately after the code you added in step 2. Between these tags, create a function that loads the XML DSO you created in step 2 with the XML returned by the URL *holicat.asp?qcatnr=200*.

```
<script language="JavaScript">
function OpenDSO() {
  xmldso.XMLDocument.load("holicat.asp?qcatnr=200");
  if (xmldso.XMLDocument.parseError != 0) {
    alert("XML load failed.");
  }
}
</script>
```

Because holicat.asp is an ASP page, you must load this file from a properly configured Web server and not from a location on your disk.

4. To run the *OpenDSO* function from step 3 whenever the Web page opens, add an *onload* attribute to the <body> tag, as shown here.

```
<body onload="OpenDSO();">
```

5. Lay out the rest of the Web page however you want. Then insert the following expressions after the script block added in step 3 and wherever you want the *catnr*, *seqnr*, *title*, *caption*, *picname*, and *picdate* fields to appear.

```
<span datasrc="#xmldso" datafld="catnr"></span>
<span datasrc="#xmldso" datafld="seqnr"></span>
<span datasrc="#xmldso" datafld="title"></span>
<span datasrc="#xmldso" datafld="caption"></span>
```

(continued)

```
<span datasrc="#xmldso" datafld="picname"></span>
<span datasrc="#xmldso" datafld="picdate"></span>
```

The *datasrc* attributes in these expressions point to the data source that contains the data to display, namely the *xmldso* object created in step 2 and loaded in step 3. The *datafld* attributes specify the name of the field (from that data source) to display.

Specifying *datasrc* and *datafld* attributes for an HTML element *binds* that element to the corresponding data source. Whatever value the current record in that data source contains, the bound element will dynamically display it.

6. Insert the following expression wherever you want the full-size picture to appear. The holicat.asp page constructs the *picloc* field by prefixing the contents of the *picname* field with *../holiday/images/*.

```
<img datasrc="#xmldso" datafld="picloc">
```

7. To support forward and backward movement through the XML document, create two buttons by adding the following statements to your page layout. They needn't reside within an HTML form.

```
<input type="button" value="&lt;Prev" onclick="mvprev()">
<input type="button" value="Next&gt;" onclick="mvnext()">
```

8. To make the Prev button work, insert the following function after the *OpenDSO* function you created in step 3. Notice that the name of the function, *mvprev*, was specified as an *onclick* event in step 7.

```
function mvprev() {
  if (xmldso.recordset.bof){
    alert("Already at bof")
  }else{
    xmldso.recordset.movePrevious()
    if (xmldso.recordset.bof){
      xmldso.recordset.moveFirst();
      alert("This is the first record.");
    }
  }
}
```

Because this function moves backward through the XML DSO recordset, the first order of business is to verify that the recordset isn't at *bof* (beginning of file). If it is at *bof*, trying to move backward will produce an error, so instead the script simply exits with a message.

If the recordset isn't at *bof*, the script uses the recordset's *movePrevious* method to move one record closer to the beginning. If this results in a *bof* condition, the script positions to the beginning of the recordset by using its *moveFirst* method and so informs the Web visitor.

Changing the current record position in the *xmldso* recordset automatically updates any bound elements that reference *#xmldso* in a *datasrc* attribute.

9. Immediately after the *mvprev* function you created in step 8, create a *mvnext* function that responds to the Next button. The *mvnext* function is almost a mirror image of the *mvprev* function, changing *bof* to *eof*, *movePrevious* to *moveNext*, and *moveFirst* to *moveLast*.

```
function mvnext() {
  if (xmldso.recordset.eof){
    alert("Already at eof")
  }else{
    xmldso.recordset.moveNext()
    if (xmldso.recordset.eof){
      xmldso.recordset.moveLast();
      alert("This is the last record.");
    }
  }
}
```

To view a completed version of this Web page, open the sample file \webdbdev\ch13\catbrowse.htm. To see the page in action, use Internet Explorer 5.0 or above to open /webdbdev/ch13/catbrowse.htm from your ASP-enabled Web server.

Using XML Data Islands

Directly creating XML DOM and XML DSO objects can at times be tedious and complex. XML data islands provide a more direct way of doing the same job.

An XML data island is basically an "island" of data that resides inside a Web page. Such islands provide all the capabilities of XML DOM and XML DSO, but you create them with a single HTML tag. Here's an example:

```
<XML id="xmlmems" src="members.xml"></XML>
```

This statement creates an XML DSO (including an accompanying XML DOM object) and then loads the XML DOM object from members.xml. If you prefer to store the XML data inside the Web page, you can omit the *src* attribute and put the XML code between the <XML> and </XML> tags, as shown here:

```
<XML ID="xmlmems">
<members>
  <member>
    <fname>Steven</fname>
    <sname>Buchanan</sname>
  </member>
</members>
</XML>
```

You can access the data in an XML data island in at least three ways:

- You can use the island as a data source and bind HTML elements to it.

- You can access fields within the island's recordset object: for example, *xmlmems.recordset("fname")*.

- You can access the island's built-in XML DOM object.

Relating XML Data Islands and XML DOM Objects

Like all other XML DOM objects, the XML DOM object inside an XML data island opens asynchronously by default. This creates no issues when you access data through data binding or through the recordset object: the built-in Microsoft code seems to wait properly for the data to arrive.

When accessing an XML data island's XML DOM object directly, however, you might be better off avoiding asynchronous loading. The following code accomplishes this by setting the *async* property and opening the XML DOM object explicitly. Note the absence of a *src* attribute in the <XML> tag itself.

```
<XML id="xmldso"></XML>
<script>
xmldso.XMLDocument.async = "false"
xmldso.XMLDocument.load("holicat.asp?qcatnr=200&thumb=y")
</script>
```

To access an XML data island's XML DOM object, use the expression *<id>.XMLDocument*, where *<id>* is the *id=* attribute coded in the <XML> tag.

To access the first record within an XML data island's XML DOM object, use either of the following expressions:

```
curRec = xmldso.XMLDocument.documentElement.childNodes.item(0)
curRec = xmldso.documentElement.childNodes.item(0)
```

Because the *XMLDocument* property doesn't appear in the second expression, the *documentElement* property retrieves the XML root element. After executing either of these statements, you could access the first field in the first record by using this expression:

```
curRec.childNodes.item(0).text
```

Use data binding to display an entire XML data island

The Web page shown in Figure 13-5 displays all the records in a single XML document loaded into an XML data island. Furthermore, the Web page does this using no script code whatsoever.

The <body> section of this Web page appears in the following code, with portions relevant to the XML data island appearing in blue. The second line defines the XML data island. The *id* attribute gives the island a name and the *src* attribute gives it the name of an XML file to load. Once again, this file comes from the holicat.asp example discussed in the next chapter. The query string variable *thumb=y* tells the holicat.asp file to create the *picloc* field by prefixing the *picname* field with *../holiday/images/thumb/* rather than *../holiday/images/*.

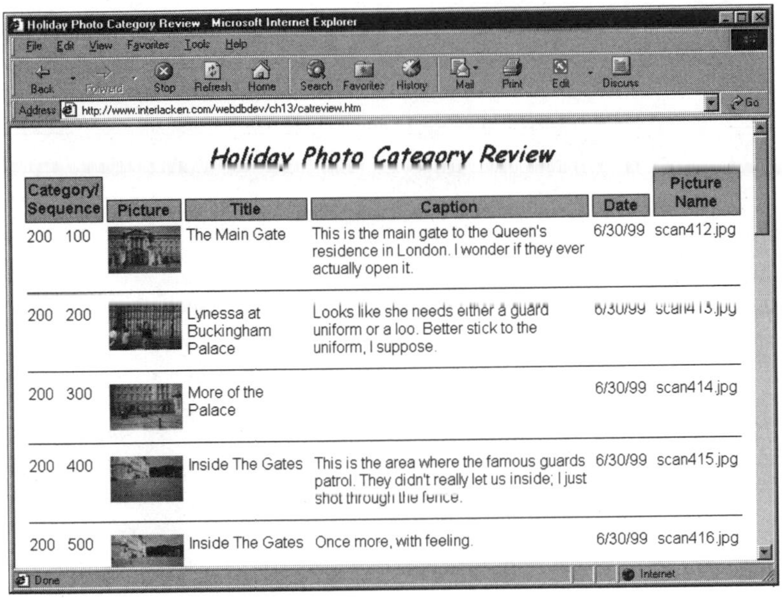

Figure 13-5 *This page works entirely by means of an XML data island and data binding. There's no underlying script code at all.*

```
<body>
<XML id="xmldso" src="holicat.asp?qcatnr=200&thumb=y"></XML>
<h2 align="center">Holiday Photo Category Review</h2>
<table datasrc="#xmldso" cellspacing="4">
  <thead>
    <tr>
      <th rowspan="2" colspan="2">Category/<br>
        Sequence</th>
      <td colspan="4"> </td>
      <th rowspan="2">Picture<br>
        Name</th>
    <tr>
      <th>Picture</th>
      <th>Title</th>
      <th>Caption</th>
      <th>Date</th>
  </thead>
  <tr>
    <td valign="top"><span datafld="catnr"></span></td>
    <td valign="top"><span datafld="seqnr"></span></td>
    <td valign="top" align="center"><img datafld="picloc"></td>
    <td valign="top"><span datafld="title"></span></td>
    <td valign="top"><span datafld="caption"></span></td>
```

(continued)

```
    <td valign="top"><span datafld="picdate"></span></td>
    <td valign="top"><span datafld="picname"></span></td>
  </tr>
  <tr>
    <td colspan="7">
      <hr size="1" color="#000000">
    </td>
  </tr>
</table>
</body>
```

Notice that the <table> tag in line four contains a *datasrc* attribute. This invokes a special process whereby all normal rows coded between the <table> and </table> tags get repeated once for each record in the given data source. The only exceptions are rows coded between <thead> and </thead> tags, or between <tfoot> and </tfoot> tags. Although seldom used, these official HTML tags respectively mark a table's heading and footing. Enclosing the first two rows of the table between <thead> and </thead> tags keeps the data binding process from repeating them for each record.

The table cells in the third HTML table row each contain a <span> or an <img> tag with a *datafld* attribute. This controls which fields appear in which cells. These tags contain no *datasrc* tags because the <table> tag has already specified the data source.

More Ways to Traverse XML Documents

The preceding sections have described two primary ways to access data loaded into an XML DOM object. The first of these involves indexing numerically into the DOM, and the second involves binding HTML elements to XML DSOs. This section demonstrates three more ways to do the same thing:

- Indexing numerically through all children of a node and watching for desired names

- Using a built-in method that searches all of a given node's children for a given name

- Accessing the field objects in an XML DSO recordset

Why so many ways of doing the same thing? A desire to provide flexibility might have something to do with it; so might the fact that XML is a new technology searching for acceptance. Regardless, you might as well have a full assortment of tools at your disposal and be capable of interpreting any code you acquire from others.

The Web page that demonstrates all these techniques appears in Figure 13-6. Displaying the same results three times might seem a bit unusual, but it efficiently illustrates all three techniques.

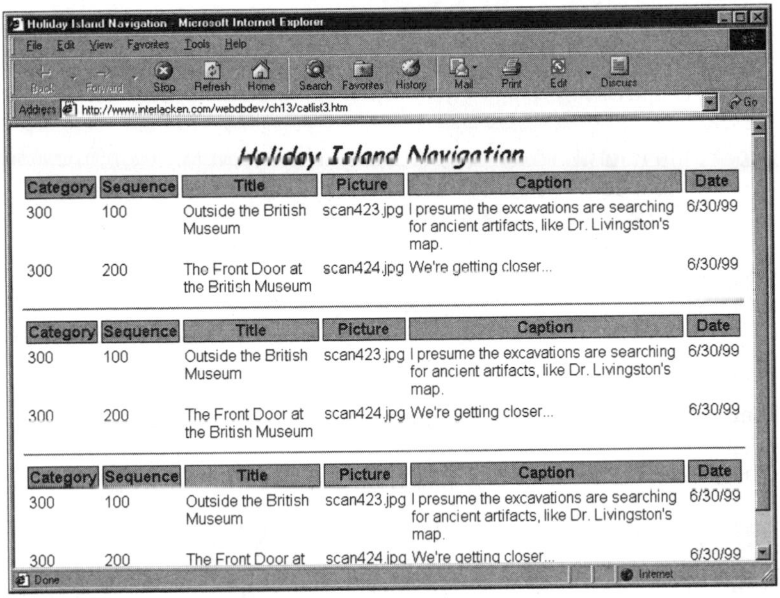

Figure 13-6 *This Web page shows how to achieve the same results three different ways.*

The data in all three cases comes from an XML data island created by the following code. To keep the example simple, the XML data is coded inline and contains only two records.

```
<xml id=catalog>
  <items>
    <itemrec>
      <catnr>300</catnr>
      <seqnr>100</seqnr>
      <title>Outside the British Museum</title>
      <picname>scan423.jpg</picname>
     <caption>I presume the excavations are searching for ancient artifacts,
     like Dr. Livingston's map.</caption>
      <picdate>6/30/99</picdate>
    </itemrec>
    <itemrec>
      <catnr>300</catnr>
      <seqnr>200</seqnr>
      <title>The Front Door at the British Museum</title>
      <picname>scan424.jpg</picname>
      <caption>We're getting closer...</caption>
      <picdate>6/30/99</picdate>
    </itemrec>
  </items>
</xml>
```

The HTML table structure and heading rows are duplicated exactly for all three cases.

```
<table cellspacing="4">
  <tr>
    <th>Category</th>
    <th>Sequence</th>
    <th>Title</th>
    <th>Picture</th>
    <th>Caption</th>
    <th>Date</th>
  </tr>
<script>
// Code to display XML data goes here.
</script>
</table>
```

Index through fields and watch for names

Referring to the inline XML listed in the preceding section, you should be able to verify the following:

- *catalog* is the name of the XML document.

- *catalog.documentElement* refers to the root node within the document: the *items* node.

- *catalog.documentElement.childNodes.length* returns the number of child nodes subordinate to the *items* node—that is, the number of *itemrec* nodes.

- *catalog.documentElement.childNodes.item(0)* refers to the first child node subordinate to the *items* node—that is, to the first *itemrec* node.

- *catalog.documentElement.childNodes.item(0).childNodes.length* returns the number of child nodes subordinate to the first *itemrec* node—that is, the number of fields in a given *itemrec* node.

- *catalog.documentElement.childNodes.item(0).childNodes.item(0)* refers to the first child node subordinate to the first *itemrec* node—that is, to the first *catnr* node.

Given these observations and the freedom to create some intermediate object variables, it isn't terribly difficult to construct a loop that examines all fields in all records. Here's the procedure:

1. Establish a variable named *rset* as an alias for *catalog.documentElement.childNodes*—that is, for the object that contains all children of the *items* node.

```
rset = catalog.documentElement.childNodes
```

2. Write a loop that iterates through each child of the *rset* object (through each *itemrec* node).

```
for (rnum = 0; rnum < rset.length ; rnum++){
// Code to process each record goes here.
}
```

Recall that any array of XML nodes is zero-based. The loop therefore initializes *rnum* (record number) to zero, increments it by one after each iteration, and continues while *rnum* is less than the number of *itemrec* nodes. If there are two records, the loop increments *rnum* from zero to one.

3. Replace the comment in step 2 with a statement that establishes *crec* as an alias for *rset.item(rnum).childNodes*—that is, for the object that contains all children of the current *itemrec* node.

```
crec = rset.item(rnum).childNodes
```

4. Write a loop that iterates through each child of the *crec* object (through each field in the current *itemrec* node).

```
for (fnum = 0 ; fnum < crec.length ; fnum++) {
// Code to process each field goes here.
}
```

5. Within the loop you wrote in step 4, the expression *crec.item(fnum).tagName* returns the name of the current field, and the expression *crec.item(fnum).text* returns its value. The following code tests for each desired value of *crec.item(fnum).tagName* and, if one is found, saves the corresponding value in an appropriate temporary variable. Replace the comment in step 4 with this code:

```
switch (crec.item(fnum).tagName) {
  case "catnr":
    dcatnr = crec.item(fnum).text;
    break;
  case "seqnr":
    dseqnr = crec.item(fnum).text;
    break;
  case "title":
    dtitle = crec.item(fnum).text;
    break;
  case "picname":
    dpname = crec.item(fnum).text;
    break;
  case "caption":
    dcaptn = crec.item(fnum).text;
    break;
  case "picdate":
    dpdate = crec.item(fnum).text;
    break;
}
```

6. When all fields for the current record have been examined (when the inner loop ends), write out one row of the HTML table using the following code:

```
document.writeln("<tr>")
document.writeln("<td valign=top>" + dcatnr + "</td>");
document.writeln("<td valign=top>" + dseqnr + "</td>");
document.writeln("<td valign=top>" + dtitle + "</td>");
document.writeln("<td valign=top>" + dpname + "</td>");
document.writeln("<td valign=top>" + dcaptn + "</td>");
document.writeln("<td valign=top>" + dpdate + "</td>");
document.writeln("</tr>")
```

7. There's no guarantee that every *itemrec* node will contain all six child nodes processed in step 5. If any child node were missing, the code in step 5 would never replace the corresponding temporary variable and values from one node would be carried over to another. To guard against this possibility, insert the following code to erase each temporary variable:

```
dcatnr = ""
dseqnr = ""
dtitle = ""
dpname = ""
dcaptn = ""
dpdate = ""
```

This code belongs immediately before the loop coded in step 4.

The complete script code for this method of accessing XML data appears here:

```
rset = catalog.documentElement.childNodes
for (rnum = 0; rnum < rset.length ; rnum++){
  crec = rset.item(rnum).childNodes
  dcatnr = ""
  dseqnr = ""
  dtitle = ""
  dpname = ""
  dcaptn = ""
  dpdate = ""
  for (fnum = 0 ; fnum < crec.length ; fnum++) {
    switch (crec.item(fnum).tagName) {
      case "catnr":
        dcatnr = crec.item(fnum).text;
        break;
      case "seqnr":
        dseqnr = crec.item(fnum).text;
        break;
      case "title":
        dtitle = crec.item(fnum).text;
        break;
```

```
        case "picname":
          dpname = crec.item(fnum).text;
          break;
        case "caption":
          dcaptn = crec.item(fnum).text;
          break,
        case "picdate":
          dpdate = crec.item(fnum).text;
          break;
    }
  }
  document.writeln("<tr>")
  document.writeln("<td valign=top>" + dcatnr + "</td>");
  document.writeln("<td valign=top>" + dseqnr + "</td>");
  document.writeln("<td valign=top>" + dtitle + "</td>");
  document.writeln("<td valign=top>" + dpname + "</td>");
  document.writeln("<td valign=top>" + dcaptn + "</td>");
  document.writeln("<td valign=top>" + dpdate + "</td>");
  document.writeln("</tr>")
}
```

Search child nodes for a given name

The XML DOM object has a method called *getElementsByTagName* that locates children by name. This eliminates the need to numerically index through a record's fields in search of the field names you want. As you'll see in this section, this can simplify your code if you know ahead of time what names exist within the data. This code is simpler than in the last example because it doesn't need a nested loop to iterate through the fields and because it doesn't need a case structure to test all the field names.

```
rset = catalog.documentElement.childNodes
for (rnum = 0 ; rnum < rset.length ; rnum++) {
  cnode = rset.item(rnum);
  dcatnr = cnode.getElementsByTagName('catnr').item(0).text
  dseqnr = cnode.getElementsByTagName('seqnr').item(0).text
  dtitle = cnode.getElementsByTagName('title').item(0).text
  dpname = cnode.getElementsByTagName('picname').item(0).text
  dcaptn = cnode.getElementsByTagName('caption').item(0).text
  dpdate = cnode.getElementsByTagName('picdate').item(0).text
  document.writeln("<tr>")
  document.writeln("<td valign=top>" + dcatnr + "</td>");
  document.writeln("<td valign=top>" + dseqnr + "</td>");
  document.writeln("<td valign=top>" + dtitle + "</td>");
  document.writeln("<td valign=top>" + dpname + "</td>");
  document.writeln("<td valign=top>" + dcaptn + "</td>");
  document.writeln("<td valign=top>" + dpdate + "</td>");
  document.writeln("</tr>")
}
```

When using the *getElementsByTagName* method, keep in mind that it only returns the first matching node. This can produce unexpected results if you search a multilevel node that contains more than one instance of the same tag name.

Access XML DSO recordset fields

The simplest way to extract information from an XML document—especially if you're conversant with ADO conventions—is to use the XML DSO's recordset object. The familiar *moveFirst*, *movePrevious*, *moveNext*, and *moveLast* methods modify the current record position, and you can access field values using familiar ADO properties. The following code produces the same results as the previous two examples:

```
while (catalog.recordset.eof == 0) {
  document.writeln("<tr>");
  document.writeln("<td valign=top>" + catalog.recordset("catnr")
                 + "</td>");
  document.writeln("<td valign=top>" + catalog.recordset("seqnr")
                 + "</td>");
  document.writeln("<td valign=top>" + catalog.recordset("title")
                 + "</td>");
  document.writeln("<td valign=top>" + catalog.recordset("picname")
                 + "</td>");
  document.writeln("<td valign=top>" + catalog.recordset("caption")
                 + "</td>");
  document.writeln("<td valign=top>" + catalog.recordset("picdate")
                 + "</td>");
  document.writeln("</tr>");
  catalog.recordset.moveNext();
}
```

This method has two primary disadvantages. First, it's only suited to XML documents structured as tables containing records and fields. Using this method to access a theatrical script or a technical document coded in XML, for example, would be difficult at best. Second, the recordset methods and properties are proprietary to Microsoft. This makes your code less portable to other parsers.

Using XSL Stylesheets

This final example demonstrates the use of XSL to create an HTML document that displays the data in an XML document.

Display XML data with an XSL stylesheet

As you might recall, Microsoft has implemented only the transformation portion of XSL, and transformation involves reading through an XML document and substituting values into templates. A Web page that orchestrates this process appears here.

```
<html>
<head>
<link rel="stylesheet" type="text/css"
      href-"../holiday/holiform.css">
<SCRIPT LANGUAGE="JavaScript" FOR="window" EVENT="onload">
var source = new ActiveXObject("Microsoft.XMLDOM");
source.async = "false";
source.load("holicat.asp?qcatnr=200");
var style = new ActiveXObject("Microsoft.XMLDOM");
style.async = "false";
style.load("catrevxsl.xsl");
document.all.item("xslContainer").innerHTML =
  source.transformNode(style.documentElement);
</SCRIPT>
<title>Holiday Photo Category Review</title>
</head>
<body>
<h2 align="center">Holiday Photo Category Review</h2>
<div id="xslContainer"></div>
</body>
</html>
```

The script highlighted in blue runs immediately after the current window has loaded. Including the same code in a function and calling that function from the <body> tag's *onload* attribute would have accomplished the same result.

The first three lines in the script should be familiar: they create an XML DOM object and load it with all the items records in the Holiday database that have a category code of 200. This data comes from the same ASP page that the previous few examples used.

The next three lines load an XSL style sheet in exactly the same way. This is possible because an XSL style sheet is itself an XML document.

The last statement in the script sets the *innerHTML* property of an object named *xslContainer* to the output of a *transformNode* method. Take a look at the following expression:

```
source.transformNode(style.documentElement);
```

- *source* is the name of the XML DOM object that contains the data to be formatted.

- *transformNode* is the method that performs the transformation.

- *style* is the name of the XML DOM object that contains the template.

- *documentElement* points to the beginning of the style sheet.

The code *<div id="xslContainer"> </div>* later in the Web page defines an empty division named *xslContainer*. This division's *innerHTML* property receives and displays the output of the transformation.

Note   The primary difference between a <div> and a <span> is that a <div> causes
line breaks before and after itself.

The template file itself, catrevxsl.xsl, appears here.

```xml
<?xml version="1.0"?>
<xsl:stylesheet xmlns:xsl="url:xsl">
  <xsl:template match="/">
    <table  cellspacing="4">
      <tr>
        <th rowspan="2" colspan="2">Category/<br/>Sequence</th>
        <td colspan="4" style="color:white">X</td>
        <th rowspan="2">Picture<br/>Name</th>
      </tr>
      <tr>
        <th>Picture</th>
        <th>Title</th>
        <th>Caption</th>
        <th>Date</th>
      </tr>
      <xsl:for-each select="items/itemrec">
      <tr>
        <td valign="top"><xsl:value-of select="catnr"/></td>
        <td valign="top"><xsl:value-of select="seqnr"/></td>
        <td valign="top" align="center"><img>
          <xsl:attribute name="src">
          ../holiday/images/thumb/<xsl:value-of select="picname"/>
          </xsl:attribute>
        </img></td>
        <td valign="top"><xsl:value-of select="title"/></td>
        <td valign="top"><xsl:value-of select="caption"/></td>
        <td valign="top"><xsl:value-of select="picdate"/></td>
        <td valign="top"><xsl:value-of select="picname"/></td>
      </tr>
      </xsl:for-each>
    </table>
  </xsl:template>
</xsl:stylesheet>
```

This listing contains the following significant features, some of which are
highlighted in blue:

- The opening <xsl:stylesheet> tag (and its closing </xsl:stylesheet> counterpart) identify this document as an XSL style sheet.

- The <xsl:template> tag and its </xsl:template> counterpart mark the beginning and end of a template. The attribute match="/" includes
  (matches) all records in the XML document.

- The next 12 lines, shown in black type, will appear in the output "as is." This is XML code, however, and must satisfy the XML parser. Note the <br/> tag in the third of these lines. For example, the slash before the closing ">" character satisfies the XML requirement that all tags be closed. The fourth line preserves line height by displaying a white X rather than a nonbreaking space because the string   violates XML syntax.

- The <xsl:for-each select="items/itemrec"> tag repeats everything between itself and its closing </xsl:for-each> tag, once for each *itemrec* node within an *items* node.

- Within this loop, tags like <xsl:value-of select="catnr"/> select and substitute field values. Note once again the slash preceding the closing > character, which eliminates the need for a closing tag.

- Creating an output <img> tag requires special precautions. For one thing, this is XML, which requires a closing </img> tag. For another, you can't have one XML tag inside another; the following expression is therefore invalid:

```
<img src='<xsl:value-of select="picname">'>
```

   Instead, the required approach is to first define the <img> and </img> tags, and then place an <xsl:attribute> tag (and its closing counterpart) between them. Finally, place the desired attribute value between the <xsl:attribute> and </xsl:attribute> tags. The code that does this appears here:

```
<img>
  <xsl:attribute name="src">
  ../holiday/images/thumb/<xsl:value-of select="picname"/>
  </xsl:attribute>
</img>
```

The result of these machinations, as seen in Figure 13-7, matches those from the example in Figure 13-5.

To view the Web page for this example, open the sample file \webdbdev\ch13\catrevxsl.htm. To view the template, open \webdbdev\ch13\catrevxsl.xsl. Creating the display seen in Figure 13-7 requires use of the holicat.asp page described in the next chapter. Using an ASP page, of course, requires loading it from a fully configured Web server.

At this point, it's no doubt obvious that coding data in XML format and then writing code that transforms it into HTML creates more work and less compatibility than simply coding the Web page from scratch. However, this observation holds true only for single Web pages. The power of XML quickly becomes apparent if you have thousands of documents that you need to present in multiple formats (for example, to suit the needs of various browsers). XML lets you code the data only once, no matter how many presentation formats you need, and it requires coding the transformations only once, no matter how many documents they process.

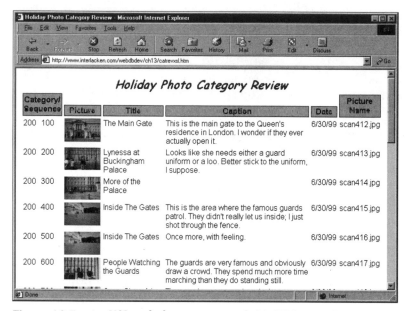

Figure 13-7 *An XSL stylesheet constructed this Web page from a template.*

This chapter explained the fundamentals of XML—eXtensible Markup Language—and provided several examples of how to use XML-coded database information at the Web visitor's browser.

Chapter 14, "Using XML at the Server," will illustrate some ways to support and use XML on a Web server.

Using XML at the Server

In this chapter, you'll learn how to

- Create XML text from conventional database queries.
- Use Microsoft XML objects in ASP pages.

XML deals with the storage, description, and interchange of data—not with its visual presentation. That's why the examples in the previous chapter used HTML to display the data, even though they received it as XML.

Because the various XML programming objects make no use of the computer's display system, you can run them on a server (a Web server, for example) as easily as on a client (a Web browser). An ASP page can create, load, transmit, and receive XML data—plus access conventional databases—in any combination. This gives you tremendous flexibility in developing applications that best meet your Web visitors' needs.

Why process XML data on the server? For many reasons, but these three are perhaps the most important:

- Some or all of your visitors use browsers that lack XML support.
- The amount of XML data is too large for transmission to the client in a reasonable amount of time.
- Once you make XML data available to your own Web pages, it's available to pages from other sites as well. These other sites might use the data in ways you neither intend nor approve.

Of course, there are also drawbacks:

- Creating, loading, parsing, and traversing XML documents on a server consumes more resources than delivering ordinary Web pages.
- Clients that—with an XML document loaded on the browser—could navigate, filter, sort, or otherwise requery a small recordset locally might instead need to submit additional, resource-consuming server transactions.
- Microsoft doesn't support the use of XML objects to access network resources when the XML object runs within an ASP page. An ASP page should only access XML resources located in the Web server's file system or within

the script itself. Retrieving XML data (or, for that matter, any sort of data) from another server consumes resources for much longer periods of time than retrieving data locally.

The net result is that neither client-based nor server-based XML processing is preferable in all cases. Only by knowing and understanding both approaches can you choose the right technique at the right time.

Generating XML for Clients

The first and perhaps most common use of XML on Web servers is providing XML data for clients to use. This section will describe two ways of doing just that.

Create XML code explicitly

The first and simplest order of business is to explain, as promised, the holicat.asp page used by several examples in the previous chapter. The complete code listing for this page appears here.

```
<% Response.ContentType = "text/xml" %>
<!-- #include file="../adovbs.inc" -->
<%
' Write XML version header.
Response.Write "<?xml version=" & _
  Chr(34) & "1.0" & Chr(34) & "?>" & vbCrLf
catnr = Request("qcatnr")
If catnr = "" Then
  catnr = 100
End If
If Request("thumb") = "" Then
  picPath = "..\holiday\images\"
Else
  picPath = "..\holiday\images\thumb\"
End If
' Create and open ADO Connection object.
Set cnHol = Server.CreateObject("ADODB.Connection")
cnStHol = "driver={Microsoft Access Driver (*.mdb)};" & _
          "dbq=" & Server.MapPath("../holiday/holiday.mdb")
cnHol.Open cnStHol,"",""
' Create and open ADO Recordset object.
Set rsItm = Server.CreateObject("ADODB.Recordset")
sql = "SELECT * " & _
      "FROM items " & _
      "WHERE (catnr=" & catnr & ") " & _
    "ORDER BY seqnr "
' Write XML tag for root element.
Response.Write "<items>" & vbCrLf
rsItm.Open sql, cnHol, adOpenStatic, adLockReadOnly
```

```
' Write an XML node for each record and
' child nodes for each field.
Do While Not rsItm.EOF
  Response.Write _
    "<itemrec>"   & vbCrLf & _
    "  <catnr>"   & rsItm("catnr")   & "</catnr>" & vbCrLf & _
    "  <seqnr>"   & rsItm("seqnr")   & "</seqnr>" & vbCrLf & _
    "  <picname>" & rsItm("picname") & "</picname>" & vbCrLf & _
    "  <picloc>"  & picPath & rsItm("picname") & _
                    "</picloc>" & vbCrLf & _
    "  <title>"   & rsItm("title")   & "</title>" & vbCrLf & _
    "  <caption>" & rsItm("caption") & "</caption>" & vbCrLf & _
    "  <picdate>" & rsItm("picdate") & "</picdate>" & vbCrLf & _
    "</itemrec>"  & vbCrLf
  rsItm.MoveNext
Loop
' Write XML tag to close root element.
Response.Write "</items>" & vbCrLf
rsItm.Close
cnHol.Close
%>
```

Most of this code should be familiar by now, but note these important details:

- This ASP page creates no HTML statements at all—not even the usual structural tags <html>, <head>, and <body>.

Note Some HTML editors automatically supply and later save required HTML tags such as <html> and <head> if not found in an input file. These tags will cause parse errors when you later run the page and try to load the output as XML. To avoid this problem, you might have to use another editor for ASP files that produce XML. Microsoft FrontPage 2000 suffers from this problem; Microsoft Visual InterDev doesn't.

- The very first line sets the response content type to *text/xml*. This tells the browser that the incoming data consists of XML.

- The first executable line (the fifth line in the listing) writes the XML identification string *<?xml version="1.0" ?>*. This further identifies the response as XML.

- The code opens an ordinary ADO recordset using the same methods and arguments as pages in earlier chapters.

- The code always writes opening and closing XML tags for a root element named *items*.

- The code writes out opening and closing <itemrec> tags for each member of the result set. Within those tags, the code writes opening and closing tags surrounding each field value. Here's sample output from one result set record: The variable portions appear in blue.

```
<itemrec>
  <catnr>100</catnr>
  <seqnr>100</seqnr>
  <picname>scan395.jpg</picname>
  <picloc>..\holiday\images\scan395.jpg</picloc>
  <title>The Berjaya Eden Park Hotel</title>
  <caption>This is where we stayed for four days in London.
  That's Connie standing outside the front door.</caption>
  <picdate>6/29/99</picdate>
</itemrec>
```

Coding an XML-producing ASP page and then coding an XML-enabled Web page to read and format the data is arguably more difficult and time-consuming than creating a non-XML ASP page that produces the same visual result. For one thing, the XML approach requires that you create two Web pages instead of one. For another, it requires dealing with the new and often confusing technology of XML.

The payoff comes when one XML-producing ASP page drives several XML-displaying HTML pages. This leverages the time you spend writing the database code over several Web pages. It also divides work between a database specialist who writes and maintains the database code, and a Web page designer who devises and maintains the best presentation. And of course, the wider the applicability and distribution of the XML data, the greater the benefits of writing an ASP page that creates it.

Save a recordset as XML

Although the example in the previous section isn't terribly complex, it raises the question of whether ADO itself might have some facility for delivering a given query or recordset as XML. ADO knows all the records and field names, so why can't it write them out in XML format?

These kinds of facilities are just beginning to appear in database systems. In the case of ADO, built-in XML features are included with Microsoft Data Access Components (MDAC) 2.5 and later. MDAC 2.5 is the version that ships with Microsoft Windows 2000. You can also find a copy on the companion CD in the folder \software\mdac\. The latest version will always be available from *http://www.microsoft.com/data*.

A Stream object behaves much like a disk file, except that it only exists temporarily in memory.

Here are the steps required to convert an ADO recordset to XML text using MDAC 2.5:

1. Create and open an ADO recordset in the usual way.

2. Create an ADO Stream object. This is a new type of object that accepts and later supplies binary or text data. The following ASP statement creates a Stream object named *stm*:

```
Set stm = CreateObject("ADODB.Stream")
```

3. Use the recordset's *Save* method to dump the recordset's schema and data—formatted as XML—to the Stream object. The following statement saves the recordset *rsItm* to the stream *stm* as XML. The parameter *adPersistXML* is a constant in the adovbs.inc file; its value is 1.

```
rsItm.Save stm, adPersistXML
```

4. Use the Stream object's *ReadText* method to copy the stream's contents into a text variable.

```
XMLtext = stm.ReadText
```

5. Send the contents of the text variable to the Web visitor by writing it into the Response object.

```
Response.Write XMLtext
```

The following listing shows an ASP page that performs these steps. Otherwise, this page is the same as the one in the previous section. The modified statements appear in blue type.

```
<% Response.ContentType = "text/xml" %>
<!-- #include file="../adovbs.inc" -->
<%
Dim stm
Response.Write "<?xml version=" & _
  chr(34) & "1.0" & chr(34) & "?>" & vbCrLf
catnr = Request("qcatnr")
If catnr = "" Then
  catnr = 100
End If
If Request("thumb") = "" Then
  picPath = "..\holiday\images\"
Else
  picPath = "..\holiday\images\thumb\"
End If
' Create and open ADO Connection object.
Set cnHol = Server.CreateObject("ADODB.Connection")
cnStHol = "driver={Microsoft Access Driver (*.mdb)};" & _
          "dbq=" & Server.MapPath("../holiday/holiday.mdb")
cnHol.Open cnStHol,"",""
' Create and open ADO Recordset object.
Set rsItm = Server.CreateObject("ADODB.Recordset")
sql = "SELECT * " & _
        "FROM items " & _
        "WHERE (catnr=" & catnr & ") " & _
    "ORDER BY seqnr "
rsItm.Open sql, cnHol, adOpenStatic, adLockReadOnly
' Create Stream object,
' dump recordset to Stream object as XML,
```

(continued)

```
' copy Stream object to text variable, and
' write text variable to Response object.
Set stm = CreateObject("ADODB.Stream")
rsItm.Save stm, adPersistXML
XMLtext = stm.ReadText
Response.Write XMLtext
rsItm.Close
cnHol.Close
```

This approach has two drawbacks. First, it requires MDAC 2.5, which might not be installed or available on your server. Second, there are no options to control the structure of the resulting XML. Whatever the recordset's *Save* method decides you need, that's what you get.

Figure 14-1 and Figure 14-2 illustrate the results of running the ASP page listed above. At the first level are two nodes named *s:Schema* and *rs:data*. The *s:Schema* node describes the fields in the recordset in a way that ADO's *Recordset.Open* method can understand. (This is useful if you ever want to load the saved data as an ADO recordset rather than an XML DOM object.) The *rs:data* node contains a *z:row* node for each record that was present when the recordset's *Save* method ran. The fields within each row appear as XML attributes (for example, *catnr="100"*).

The JavaScript code that makes the browser run this ASP page and load the output into an XML DOM object should be familiar from the previous chapter:

```
var xmlDoc = new ActiveXObject("Microsoft.XMLDOM");
xmlDoc.async = false;
xmlDoc.load("savasxml.asp");
```

The following statement sets up an alias to the *rs:data* node. Recall that this is the second node under the document root (which is always at <id>.documentElement), and that the index is zero-based.

```
xmlRsData = xmlDoc.documentElement.childNodes.item(1);
```

Given this alias, the number of *z:row* nodes is *xmlRsData.childNodes.length* and the first one is at *xmlRsData.childNodes.item(0)*. Because the field values within each row are attributes rather than nodes in their own right, you must use the *getAttribute* method to retrieve each value. Here are the statements required to copy each data value from the first row into some ordinary script variables:

```
dcatnr = xmlRsData.childNodes.item(0).getAttribute("catnr");
dseqnr = xmlRsData.childNodes.item(0).getAttribute("seqnr");
dpname = xmlRsData.childNodes.item(0).getAttribute("picname");
dtitle = xmlRsData.childNodes.item(0).getAttribute("title");
dcaptn = xmlRsData.childNodes.item(0).getAttribute("caption");
dpdate = xmlRsData.childNodes.item(0).getAttribute("picdate");
```

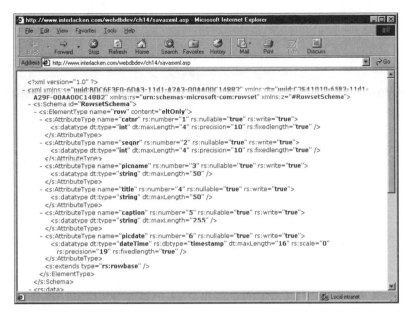

Figure 14-1   *An ADO recordset's* Save *method begins by saving a description of the recordset within a node called* <s:schema>.

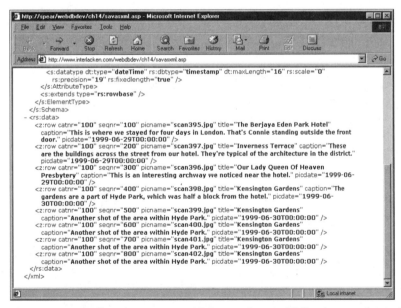

Figure 14-2   *When you save an ADO recordset as XML, the recordset's data appears within a node called* <rs:data>. *Column values appear as XML attributes of child nodes called* <z:row>.

Figure 14-3 shows a Web page that runs the saveasxml.asp page and displays the first record of the results. These results are remarkably similar to those shown in Figure 13-2 in the previous chapter (on page 373); only the source ASP page and the method of accessing field data changed. You can find this file among the sample files at \webdbdev\ch14\saveasxml.htm.

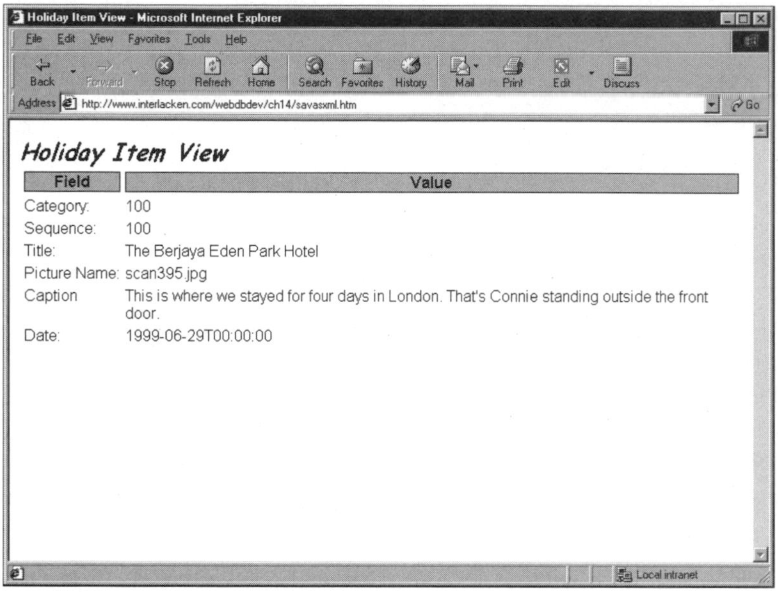

Figure 14-3   *This Web page displays XML data obtained by saving an ADO recordset as XML.*

Loading XML on the Server

Although Microsoft designed the *Microsoft.XMLDOM* object to run within a Web browser, nothing prevents it from running on a server. In fact, Figure 14-4 shows a Web page that does just that. Notice that the browser in that figure is Netscape Navigator 4.03, a browser that can't load *Microsoft.XMLDOM* (or, for that matter, any other ActiveX object).

The ASP script code that creates these results follows. The first line of code creates an XML DOM object. The second line specifies asynchronous loading, and the third line loads the XML file whose disk location corresponds to the URL *../ch14/holicat.xml*. The remainder of the code checks for parse errors and either writes an error message to the response string or saves each field value from the first record to variables named *dcatnr*, *dseqnr*, and so forth. Tags such as <%=dcatnr%> and <%=dseqnr%> will display the saved field values in an HTML table.

```
<%
Set xmlDoc = Server.CreateObject("Microsoft.XMLDOM")
xmlDoc.async = False
xmlDoc.load(Server.MapPath("../ch14/holicat.xml"))
If xmlDoc.parseError Then
  Response.Write "<p class=err>" & xmlDoc.parseError.reason & _
    "</p>" & vbCrLf
```

```
Else
  Set rootElem = xmlDoc.documentElement
  dcatnr=rootElem.childNodes.item(0).childNodes.item(0).text
  dseqnr=rootElem.childNodes.item(0).childNodes.item(1).text
  dpname=rootElem.childNodes.item(0).childNodes.item(2).text
  dtitle=rootElem.childNodes.item(0).childNodes.item(3).text
  dcaptn=rootElem.childNodes.item(0).childNodes.item(4).text
  dpdate=rootElem.childNodes.item(0).childNodes.item(5).text
%>
<!-- HTML table that displays results will appear here. -->
<%
End If
%>
```

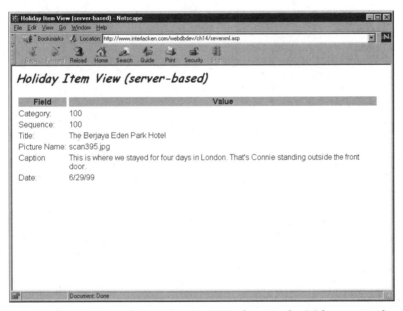

Figure 14-4 *This Web page queries XML data on the Web server and transmits ordinary HTML to the browser. The browser in this screen shot is Netscape Navigator 4.03, which provides no XML support.*

Using an ASP Page as an XML Gateway (Not)

If you were in a devious (or at least experimental) frame of mind, you might wonder if the *xmlDoc.load* method, running within an ASP page, would accept a network location such as *http://www.interlacken.com/webdbdev/ch14/holicat.asp*. (This URL delivers an XML document.) After all, the *xmlDoc.load* method works fine with the same ActiveX control running in a browser. If you try it with asynchronous loading turned off, you'll probably find that it works within an ASP page as well. Nevertheless, Microsoft neither recommends nor supports this approach, for the reasons described on the next page.

(continued)

Using an ASP Page as an XML Gateway (Not) *(continued)*

- All Microsoft XML objects, including the *Microsoft.XMLDOM* object, use network calls designed for client machines and not for servers. These calls provide enhanced performance on lightly loaded systems—but degraded performance on heavily loaded systems. Because servers are usually heavily loaded, you should avoid using any software that makes client-style networking calls.

- ASP pages that wait for a response from another system might remain in memory an unusually long time. If this happens frequently, it can consume unusual amounts of server resources.

- ASP pages have no built-in timer objects. This makes it difficult or impossible to retrieve XML objects from several remote sites at once or, for that matter, to use asynchronous retrieval for any other purpose. As to why Microsoft provides no timers for ASP pages, review the previous bullet.

For more information about these limitations, search Microsoft's Web site for article Q237906: PRB: Loading Remote XML or Sending XML HTTP Requests from Server Is Not Supported.

Transmitting XML Objects

Several earlier examples used the holicat.asp page to obtain customized XML data from a network location. These examples first created an XML DOM object, and then used it to load an XML document from a network location such as *holicat.asp?qcatnr=200*. This is nothing more than a relative URL with a query string. The same code would work perfectly well with a fully qualified URL such as *http://www.interlacken.com/webdbdev/ch13/holicat.asp?qcatnr=200*.

This technique certainly works, but query strings can contain only a limited amount of information. Query strings can't transmit larger, more variable, more complex kinds of data, such as an entire customer order. For such applications, it makes more sense for both the request and the response to be XML documents. The XMLHttpRequest object (*Microsoft.XMLHTTP*) supports this kind of operation.

Controlled by a script, the XMLHttpRequest object does the following:

Using the XMLHttpRequest object is a background process that doesn't reload the current Web page.

- Requests a document from a local or remote Web server, just as a browser would

- Transmits an XML document as the body of that request

- Interprets the body of the Web server's response as an XML document

The target location must be an ASP page or another server-side process that

- Loads the XML document submitted with the request

- Reacts to the XML document's content

- Supplies an XML document with its response

Table 14-1 lists the XMLHttpRequest object methods. Table 14-2 lists the XMLHttpRequest object properties.

Table 14-1   XMLHttpRequest Object (*Microsoft.XMLHTTP*) Methods

Name	Description
abort	Stops waiting for an HTTP response
getAllResponseHeaders	Returns all the HTTP headers received with a response
getResponseHeader	Returns a specific HTTP header received with a response
open	Initializes a request and specifies its method (*GET* or *POST*), URL, and authentication information
send	Sends an HTTP request to the server and receives a response
setRequestHeader	Specifies the name and value of an HTTP header

Table 14-2   XMLHttpRequest Object (Microsoft.XMLHTTP) Properties

Name	Access	Description
onreadystatechange	Read/write	Specifies an event handler to call when the *readystate* property changes
readyState	Read-only	Reports the current state of a request
responseBody	Read-only	Returns the body of a response as an array of unsigned bytes
responseStream	Read-only	Returns the body of a response as an *Istream*
responseText	Read-only	Returns the body of a response as a string
responseXML	Read-only	Returns the body of a response as an XML DOM object
status	Read-only	Returns the HTTP status code the Web server returned with its response (200 or 404, for example)
statusText	Read-only	Returns the HTTP response line the Web server returned with its response (*OK* or *File not found*, for example)

The following is typical client code that uses a *Microsoft.XMLHTTP* object. The first line creates an ordinary XML DOM object and the second is a placeholder for whatever code loads the new *xmlDoc* object with application data.

```
var xmlDoc = new ActiveXObject ("Microsoft.XMLDOM");
// Code to load xmlDoc with data goes here.
var xmlhttp = new ActiveXObject ("Microsoft.XMLHTTP");
xmlhttp.open("POST", "http://<server>/<path>/<page>.asp", false);
xmlhttp.send(xmlDoc);
```

The third statement creates the *Microsoft.XMLHTTP* object. The fourth statement uses the *open* method to initialize the request (that is, to specify information used later for connecting to a Web server). The *Send* method used in the last line specifies the XML document that forms the body of the request and transmits the entire request to the given URL, thereby initiating the actual connection. This XML document can be a string variable, a literal, or a stream object containing XML code, it can also be an XML DOM object.

Table 14-3 lists the arguments the *open* method can take.

Table 14-3   Parameters for the XMLHttpRequest Obect's *open* Method

Parameter	Type	Description
Method	String	HTTP method used to open the connection, such as GET, POST, PUT, or PROPFIND.
Url	String	Requested URL. This can be an absolute URL such as *http://Myserver/Mypath/* or a relative one such as */Mypath/xml/.*
Async	Boolean	Indicator of whether the call is asynchronous. The default is *true* (the call returns immediately).
User	String	Name of the user for authentication. If this parameter is NULL ("") or missing and the site requires authentication, the component displays a logon window.
Password	String	Password for authentication. This parameter is ignored if the user parameter is NULL ("") or missing.

If you specified *False* as the third parameter of the *open* method (that is, as the *async* parameter) the script will pause while the *Microsoft.XMLHTTP* object submits the Web request and waits for a response. If you specified *true*, the script will continue executing; you'll need to specify an *onreadystatechange* routine that watches for the response to be complete and takes appropriate action.

Note   If you use the same *Microsoft.XMLHTTP* object more than once, you should clear the request headers and the response body between each use.

When the request does complete, the *responseBody, responseStream, responseText*, and *responseXML* properties provide access to the results. Table 14-1 has already described these properties.

Figure 14-5 illustrates a simple Web page that uses a *Microsoft.XMLHTTP* object. The name of this page is getcats.htm. Here's how it works:

- By repeatedly entering category numbers and clicking the Add button, the Web visitor builds a list of Holiday Photo categories to query. This is a local operation requiring no interaction with the Web server.

- When the Web visitor clicks the Run Query button, the Web page builds an XML document that contains a *catrec* node and a *catnr* child node for each value listed in the Categories Specified list box.

- A *Microsoft.XMLHTTP* object submits this XML document to the relative URL *getcats.asp*.

- On startup, the getcats.asp page opens the incoming XML document, opens the *category* table of the *Holiday* database, and creates a new, empty XML DOM object.

- The getcats.asp page then scans the submitted XML document for nodes named *catnr*.

- For each *catnr* node it finds, the getcats.asp page searches the *categories* table for the corresponding category number and adds three nodes to the new XML DOM object it created: one *catrec* node and two child nodes. The child nodes are named *catnr* and *desc*. Each *catnr* node contains a value submitted by the Web visitor, and the corresponding *desc* node contains the matching *catdesc* value from the *categories* table.

- The getcats.asp page saves the new XML document to the Response object and then exits.

- Script execution in the getcats.htm page resumes when the *Microsoft .XMLHTTP* object receives a response from the getcats.asp page.

- The *Microsoft.XMLHTTP* object's *responseXML* property will contain a copy of the XML document that getcats.asp saved to the Response object. The script displays this document by creating an HTML table row for each second-level node and an HTML table cell for each third-level node in that XML document. (Of course, there's only one first-level node: the root node).

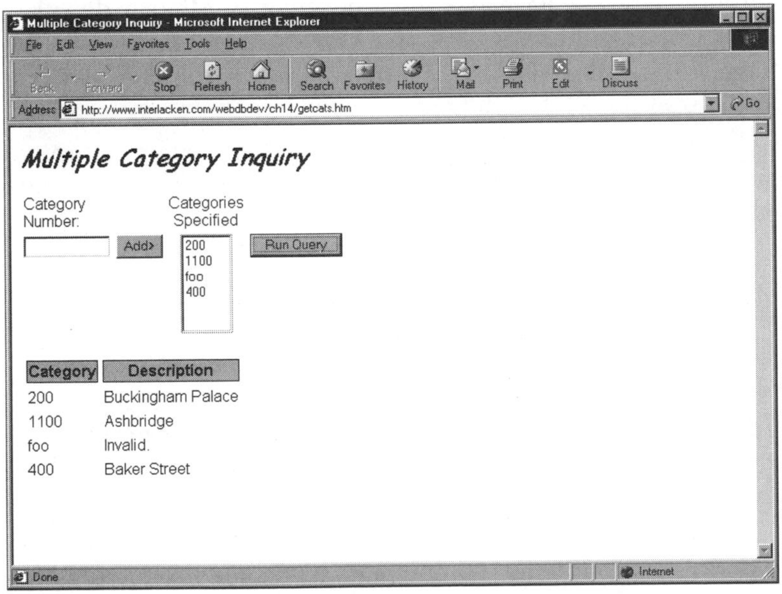

Figure 14-5   *This Web page collects several category numbers and sends them to a Web server as an XML document. The Web server responds with another XML document that this Web page then displays.*

The following sections describe the procedures to construct these Web pages.

Build the getcats.asp page

The getcats.asp page loads an XML document from the IIS *request* object, searches the document for nodes named *catnr*, and looks up the value of each. Its response is another XML document having the following structure. There will be one *<catrec>* structure for each *catnr* node found in the submitted XML document. Variable portions appear in blue.

```
<categories>
  <catrec>
    <catnr>100</catnr>
    <desc>Berjaya Eden Park Hotel</desc>
  </catrec>
</categories>
```

1. Initialize a new Web page with the following statements. Don't include any of the usual <html>, <head>, or <body> tags.

```
<% Response.ContentType = "text/xml" %>
<!-- #include file="../adovbs.inc" -->
<%
Response.Write "<?xml version=" & _
  Chr(34) & "1.0" & Chr(34) & "?>" & vbCrLf
' Main processing code will go here.
%>
```

   The first line modifies the HTTP *ContentType* header to identify the output of this ASP page as XML rather than HTML (the default). The second line includes the usual ADO database constants. The fourth line also identifies the output of this page as XML, this time by inserting an XML tag at the start of the response body.

2. Open and close an ADO Recordset object that contains all the records in the *categories* table of the holiday.mdb database. These statements should hold no surprises; insert them in place of the comment in step 1.

```
sql = "SELECT * FROM categories ORDER BY catnr ; "
cnStHol = "driver={Microsoft Access Driver (*.mdb)};" & _
          "dbq=" & Server.MapPath("../holiday/holiday.mdb")
Set rsCat = Server.CreateObject("ADODB.Recordset")
rsCat.Open sql, cnStHol,adOpenStatic, adLockReadOnly
' Code to open and process incoming XML document will go here.
rsCat.Close
```

3. Create an XML DOM object and, within it, create a node named *categories*. Also code the statement that will send this document back to the requesting Web visitor. These statements should replace the comment in step 2.

```
Set xmlRsp = Server.CreateObject("Microsoft.XMLDOM")
Set newNode = xmlRsp.createElement("categories")
xmlRsp.appendChild(newNode)
' Code to load XML document xmlRsp with data will go here.
xmlRsp.save(response)
```

To learn how the second and third statements work, refer to the sidebar "Creating New XML Document Nodes with Code" on page 411.

An XML DOM object's *save* method can copy it to other objects of various kinds. One of these is the ASP page's Response object. Saving an XML DOM object to the response object sends a copy of the XML DOM object to the requesting Web visitor.

4. Create an XML DOM object named *xmlReq* and load it from the ASP page's *request* object. This loads a copy of the XML document the Web visitor's browser script specified when it invoked the *Microsoft.XMLHTTP* object's *send* method. These statements should replace the comment you added in step 3.

```
Set xmlReq = Server.CreateObject("Microsoft.XMLDOM")
xmlReq.load(request)
```

5. If attempting to load the ASP *request* object as an XML document created a parse error, add the error message to the *xmlRsp* document as if it were a node. The invoking Web page will display a copy of the *xmlRsp* object, which ensures that the visitor will see the message. Otherwise, scan the well-formed XML document for categories to look up.

```
If xmlReq.parseError Then
  AddCatnrNode "", xmlReq.parseError.reason
Else
' Code to scan for category requests will go here.
End If
```

Step 8 will explain how the *AddCatnrNode* subroutine adds a node to the *xmlRsp* document.

6. Replace the comment in step 5 with the following statements, which step through the entire *reqRst* document looking for nodes named *catnr*. Upon finding such a node, call a subroutine named *FindCatnr* and pass it the node's text value (that is, its category number) as an argument.

```
Set reqRst = xmlReq.documentElement.childNodes
For rnum = 0 to reqRst.length - 1
  Set reqRcd = reqRst.item(rnum).childNodes
  For fnum = 0 to reqRcd.length - 1
    If (reqRcd.item(fnum).tagName = "catnr") Then
      FindCatnr(reqRcd.item(fnum).text)
    End If
  Next
Next
```

If this code doesn't seem familiar, review "Indexing Through Fields and Watching For Names" in the previous chapter.

7. Add the code for the *FindCatnr* subroutine immediately after the code you added in step 2. This routine accepts one argument: a category number.

- If the argument isn't numeric, the routine passes the given category number and the message "Invalid" to the *AddCatnrNode* subroutine described in step 8.

- If the argument is numeric, the routine tries to find a matching record in the *rsCat* recordset opened in step 2. If it finds a match, it calls *AddCatnrNode* with the given category number and the *catdesc* field from the *rsCat* recordset as arguments.

- If the argument is numeric but the routine can't find a matching record, it calls *AddCatnrNode* with the given category number and the message "Not found" as arguments.

```
Sub FindCatnr (acatnr)
  If IsNumeric(acatnr) Then
    rsCat.MoveFirst
    rsCat.find "catnr = " & acatnr
    If rsCat.EOF Then
      AddCatnrNode acatnr, "Not found."
    Else
      AddCatnrNode acatnr, rsCat("catdesc")
    End If
  Else
      AddCatnrNode acatnr, "Invalid."
  End If
End Sub
```

8. Add the code for the *AddCatnrNode* subroutine immediately after the code you added in step 7. This routine accepts two arguments—a category number and a description or message—and adds them to the document that the ASP page will return to the Web visitor's script. Here's how this happens:

- First the subroutine creates a node named *catrec* and appends it to the last child of the *xmlRsp* document's root (that is, to the node named *categories* that you created in step 3.)

- Next it creates a node named *catnr*, appends it to the *catrec* node created in the previous bullet, and assigns it the value provided in the first argument.

- Finally it creates a node named *desc*, appends it to the *catrec* node created in the first bullet, and assigns it the value provided in the second argument.

```
Sub AddCatnrNode (acatnr, adesc)
  Set newNode = xmlRsp.createElement("catrec")
  xmlRsp.lastChild.appendChild(newNode)

  Set newNode = xmlRsp.createElement("catnr")
  xmlRsp.lastChild.lastChild.appendChild(newNode)
  xmlRsp.lastChild.lastChild.lastChild.text = acatnr

  Set newNode = xmlRsp.createElement("desc")
  xmlRsp.lastChild.lastChild.appendChild(newNode)
  xmlRsp.lastChild.lastChild.lastChild.text = adesc
End Sub
```

This completes the code for the getcats.asp page.

Creating New XML Document Nodes with Code

Adding a node to a parsed XML DOM document is a two-step process. First you must create the node using one of the methods listed in Table 14-4. The following code creates a node element named *something*:

```
Set newNode = xmlRsp.createElement("something")
```

This creates an independent node; that is, a node with no parent. To give the node a parent, use the *appendChild* method as shown here:

```
xmlDoc.appendchild(newNode)
```

This statement appends a node to the root of an XML document named *xmlDoc*. To append a new node to some other existing element, use the *appendChild* method with that element. The following statement appends the *newNode* node to the second node located within the document root.

```
xmlDoc.documentElement.childNodes.item(1).appendchild(newNode)
```

Any node you insert will automatically become the last child under its parent. Thus, if you're inserting several nodes consecutively, it might be convenient to address them using the *lastChild* property. Suppose, for example, you inserted a *"record"* node by using the following statements.

```
Set newNode = xmlRsp.createElement("record")
xmlDoc.lastChild.appendchild(newNode)
```

This node would become the last child of the root element's last child. The following statement would append a node named *"field1"* to that node:

```
Set newNode = xmlRsp.createElement("field1")
xmlDoc.lastChild.lastChild.appendchild(newNode)
```

To assign a value to a newly created node, modify its text property:

```
xmlRsp.lastChild.lastChild.lastChild.text = acatnr
```

Table 14-4   XML DOM Methods That Create, Remove, and Replace Nodes

Method Name	Description
cloneNode	Creates a new node that's an exact clone of the node invoking the method
createAttribute	Creates a new attribute with a specified name
createCDATASection	Creates a CDATA section node that contains supplied data
createComment	Creates a comment node that contains the supplied data
createDocumentFragment	Creates an empty document fragment object
createElement	Creates an element node having a specified name
createEntityReference	Creates a new entity reference object
createNode	Creates a node using a supplied type, name, and namespace
createProcessingInstruction	Creates a processing instruction node that contains a supplied target and data
createTextNode	Creates a text node that contains supplied data
insertBefore	Inserts a child node to the left of the specified node or at the end of the list
removeChild	Removes the specified child node from the list of children and returns it
replaceChild	Replaces the specified old child node with the supplied new child node in the set of children of this node, and then returns the old child node

The complete source listing follows. Remember, it contains no HTML elements at all—just script code.

```
<% Response.ContentType = "text/xml" %>
<!-- #include file="../adovbs.inc" -->
<%
Response.Write "<?xml version=" & _
  chr(34) & "1.0" & chr(34) & "?>" & vbCrLf
' Create and open ADO Recordset object.
sql = "SELECT * FROM categories ORDER BY catnr ; "
cnStHol = "driver={Microsoft Access Driver (*.mdb)};" & _
        "dbq=" & Server.MapPath("../holiday/holiday.mdb")
Set rsCat = Server.CreateObject("ADODB.Recordset")
rsCat.Open sql, cnStHol,adOpenStatic, adLockReadOnly
' Create and initialize XML document for response.
Set xmlRsp = Server.CreateObject("Microsoft.XMLDOM")
Set newNode = xmlRsp.createElement("categories")
xmlRsp.appendChild(newNode)
```

```
' Create and load XML document from request.
Set xmlReq = server.createobject("Microsoft.XMLDOM")
xmlReq.load(Request)
' If the submitted document failed to parse, report the
' condition. Otherwise, step through the document and
' perform a lookup on the value of each catnr node.
If xmlReq.parseError Then
  AddCatnrNode "", xmlReq.parseError.reason
Else
  Set reqRst = xmlReq.documentElement.childNodes
  For rnum = 0 to reqRst.length - 1
    Set reqRcd = reqRst.item(rnum).childNodes
    For fnum = 0 to reqRcd.length - 1
      If (reqRcd.item(fnum).tagName = "catnr") Then
        FindCatnr(reqRcd.item(fnum).text)
      End If
    Next
  Next
End If
' Copy the response XML document to the Response object.
xmlRsp.save(response)
' Close the ADO recordset.
rsCat.Close
' If the category number supplied as an argument is numeric
' and found in the categories table, add it and its description
' to the response XML object. Otherwise, add it and an error to
' that document.
Sub FindCatnr (acatnr)
  If IsNumeric(acatnr) Then
    rsCat.MoveFirst
    rsCat.Find "catnr = " & acatnr
    If rsCat.EOF Then
      AddCatnrNode acatnr, "Not found."
    Else
      AddCatnrNode acatnr, rsCat("catdesc")
    End If
  Else
      AddCatnrNode acatnr, "Invalid."
  End If
End Sub
' Create a new catrec node and two child nodes (for catnr and
' desc) to the response XML object.
Sub AddCatnrNode (acatnr, adesc)
  Set newNode = xmlRsp.createElement("catrec")
  xmlRsp.lastChild.appendChild(newNode)
  Set newNode = xmlRsp.createElement("catnr")
  xmlRsp.lastChild.lastChild.appendChild(newNode)
```

(continued)

```
    xmlRsp.lastChild.lastChild.lastChild.text = acatnr
    Set newNode = xmlRsp.createElement("desc")
    xmlRsp.lastChild.lastChild.appendChild(newNode)
    xmlRsp.lastChild.lastChild.lastChild.text = adesc
End Sub
%>
```

Build the getcats.htm page

The getcats.htm page collects a list of category numbers from the Web visitor and submits them to the getcats.asp page as a single XML document. Because the script involved in running this page is run on the client, the language used is JavaScript. When the getcats.asp page responds with an XML document containing those category numbers plus descriptions, the getcats.htm page displays the document using an HTML table.

Here's the procedure to create this Web page:

1. Initialize a new Web page with all the normal HTML tags (<html>, <head>, <body>, and so on).

2. Create an HTML form named *frmReq*. Within it, create the following form elements, arranged as you wish:

   • A text box named *txtCatnr*:

     ```
     <input type="text" name="txtCatnr" size="11">
     ```

   • A button named btnAdd. This button's *onclick* method must run a function called *AddCat*.

     ```
     <input type="button" value="Add&gt;" name="btnAdd"
     onclick="AddCat()">
     ```

   • A selection list named *lstCatnr*:

     ```
     <select size="6" name="lstCatnr"></select>
     ```

   • A button named btnQuery. This button's *onclick* method must run a function called *GetCatInfo*.

     ```
     <input type="button" value="Run Query" name="btnQuery" _
     onclick="GetCatInfo()">
     ```

3. Beneath the HTML form, create a division named *catinfo*:

   ```
   <div id=catinfo></div>
   ```

4. Add a pair of <script> and </script> tags between the Web page's <head> and </head> tags.

5. Enter the code for the *AddCat* function between the <script> and </script> tags you added in step 4.

   This function runs whenever the Web visitor clicks the btnAdd button. Its first statement copies the current value from the *txtCatnr* text box into a variable named *txt*. If this value isn't empty, the function proceeds as follows:

- It copies the number of items in the *lstCatnr* list into a variable named *pos*.

- It creates a new Option object with the name *opt*. Its option text and value are both equal to the value saved in *txt*.

- It attaches this object to the *lstCatnr* list box at position *pos*. (If the list box already contains 3 items, they'll be numbered 0, 1, and 2. The proper index for a new option is therefore 3.)

- It erases the value in the *txtCatnr* text box. This makes it easier for the Web visitor to enter the next category code.

```
function AddCat(){
   txt = document.frmReq.txtCatnr.value;
   if (txt != "") {
     pos = document.frmReq.lstCatnr.options.length;
     var opt = new Option (txt, txt);
     document.frmReq.lstCatnr.options[pos] = opt;
     document.frmReq.txtCatnr.value = "";
   }
}
```

By repeatedly entering values in the *txtCatnr* text box and clicking the btnAdd button, the Web visitor can add as many category codes to the *lstCatnr* list box as he or she likes.

6. To define the *GetCatInfo* function, enter the following code immediately after the code you added for the *AddCat* function:

```
function GetCatInfo() {
// Procedural statements will go here.
}
```

7. As its first task, *GetCatInfo* needs to create an XML document that contains a *catnr* tag for each category number the Web visitor added to the *listCatnr* list box. To start this process, replace the comment in step 6 with these statements to create a root node:

```
   xml = "<categories>";
// Code to create <catnr> nodes will go here.
   xml = xml + "</categories>";
```

8. Insert the following code to loop through each entry in the *lstCatnr* list box. This code should replace the comment in step 7.

```
   for (itm=0;
        itm < document.frmReq.lstCatnr.options.length;
        itm++) {
// Code to create one catnr node will go here.
   }
```

The expression *document.frmReq.lstCatnr.options.length* returns the number of items in the *lstCatnr* list box.

9. To create the individual *catnr* nodes, replace the comment in step 8 with these statements:

```
xml = xml + "<catrec>";
xml = xml + "<catnr>"
           + document.frmReq.lstCatnr.options[itm].value
           + "</catnr>";
xml = xml + "</catrec>";
```

The expression *document.frmReq.lstCatnr.options[itm].value* returns the value of option number *itm* in the list box *lstCatnr*.

10. As its second major task, the *GetCatInfo* function needs to send the XML document built in steps 7 through 9 to the getcats.asp page. This requires the following statements, inserted after the last statement you added in step 7.

```
var xmlhttp = new ActiveXObject("Microsoft.XMLHTTP");
xmlhttp.open("POST", "getcats.asp", "false");
xmlhttp.send(xml);
```

As explained earlier in this chapter, the Microsoft.XMLHTTP object sends an XML document to another Web location and receives an XML document in return. In this case, it's sending the document contained in the string variable *xml* to the ASP page getcats.asp. The *false* parameter turns off asynchronous retrieval; that is, it makes the script pause until the operation completes successfully, times out, or otherwise fails.

11. The third major task *GetCatInfo* needs to accomplish is receiving and displaying the XML document that the getcats.asp page creates.

As with all HTTP requests, a status code of 200 means OK. Anything else indicates an error. Therefore, insert the following statement after the code you added in step 10:

```
if (xmlhttp.status == 200) {
// Code to process successful HTTP response goes here.
}else{
  rslt = "<p class=err>"
         + xmlhttp.status + " "
         + xmlhttp.statusText + "</p>";
}
```

The expression *xmlhttp.status* returns the status code from the last *send* operation that the xmlhttp object performed. The expression *xmlhttp.status-Text* returns the corresponding message.

12. If the xmlhttp object's *send* operation succeeded, start creating an HTML table to display the results. The following code should replace the comment in step 11:

```
rslt = "<table cellspacing=5>";
rslt = rslt + "<tr><th>Category</th>" +
                  "<th>Description</th></tr>";
// Code to create detail rows and columns will go here.
rslt = rslt + "</table>";
```

13. The XML document that the getcats.asp page sent will be in the xmlhttp object's responseXML child object. The following loop traverses this object, creating `<tr>` and `</tr>` tags for each child of the root element (that is, for each *catrec* node) and `<td>` and `</td>` tags surrounding each value found in a child of a *catrec* node. The following HTML is typical of this pattern: Variable portions appear in blue.

```
<tr>
  <td>100</td>
  <td>Berjaya Eden Park Hotel</td>
</tr>
```

Insert the following statements in place of the comment you entered in step 12:

```
rset = xmlhttp.responseXML.documentElement.childNodes;
for (rnum = 0; rnum < rset.length ; rnum++){
  crec = rset.item(rnum).childNodes;
  rslt = rslt + "<tr>";
  for (fnum = 0 ; fnum < crec.length ; fnum++) {
    rslt = rslt + "<td>" + crec.item(fnum).text + "</td>";
  }
  rslt = rslt + "</tr>";
}
```

14. The last step is to display the HTML now contained in the variable *rslt*. To do this, insert the following statement as the last in the *GetCatInfo* function:

```
catinfo.innerHTML = rslt;
```

This completes the essential parts of the getcats.htm Web page. A complete listing of the *AddCat* and *GetCatInfo* functions follows. To see these integrated with the HTML, open the sample file \webdbdev\ch14\getcats.htm with your favorite HTML or text editor.

```
function AddCat(){
// Get the current value of the txtCatnr text box and add it
// to the lstCatnr list box.
  txt = document.frmReq.txtCatnr.value;
  if (txt != "") {
    pos = document.frmReq.lstCatnr.options.length;
    var opt = new Option (txt, txt);
    document.frmReq.lstCatnr.options[pos] = opt;
    document.frmReq.txtCatnr.value = "";
  }
}
function GetCatInfo() {
// Create an XML document root.
  xml = "<categories>";
// Create a catrec node and a catnr child node for each value
// in the lstCatnr list box.
```

(continued)

```
    for (itm=0;
        itm < document.frmReq.lstCatnr.options.length;
        itm++) {
  xml = xml + "<catrec>";
  xml = xml + "<catnr>"
                + document.frmReq.lstCatnr.options[itm].value
                + "</catnr>";
  xml = xml + "</catrec>";
// Create a closing tag for the XML document root.
  xml = xml + "</categories>";
// Send the XML document to the getcats.asp page and wait
// for a response.
  var xmlhttp = new ActiveXObject("Microsoft.XMLHTTP");
  xmlhttp.open("POST", "getcats.asp", "false");
  xmlhttp.send(xml);
// If the ASP page responded OK (status 200), create an HTML table
// that contains a row for each level 2 node and a detail for each
// level 3 node (level 1 being the document root).
// Otherwise, display the bad status code and
// corresponding message.
  if (xmlhttp.status == 200) {
    rslt = "<table cellspacing=5>";
    rslt = rslt + "<tr><th>Category</th>" +
                        "<th>Description</th></tr>";
    rset = xmlhttp.responseXML.documentElement.childNodes;
    for (rnum = 0; rnum < rset.length ; rnum++){
      crec = rset.item(rnum).childNodes;
      rslt = rslt + "<tr>";
      for (fnum = 0 ; fnum < crec.length ; fnum++) {
        rslt = rslt + "<td>" + crec.item(fnum).text + "</td>";
      }
      rslt = rslt + "</tr>";
    }
    rslt = rslt + "</table>";
  }else{
    rslt = "<p class=err>"
            + xmlhttp.status + " "
            + xmlhttp.statusText + "</p>";
  }
  catinfo.innerHTML = rslt;
}
```

Using XSL on the Server

You can use the XML DOM object's *transformNode* method as easily on the server as you use it on the browser. Although doing so obviously consumes server resources, it requires no XSL support on the browser. Running XSL on the server might also be advantageous when there's too much data to send to the browser.

In the previous example, the getcats.asp page built an XML document from scratch and then wrote it into the *response* stream by using the document's *save* method. This works perfectly well, but suppose the categories in the *response* need to be sorted by category number. An XML DOM object has no built-in methods for sorting (or otherwise rearranging) its nodes, but XSL easily performs this kind of transformation. In essence, XSL can transform the unsorted XML document to a new, sorted XML document.

Build an XSL stylesheet that sorts an XML document

The following steps create an XSL stylesheet that transforms the *xmlRsp* document in the previous example into a new document sorted according to the contents of the *catnr* node:

1. Create a new, empty text file and add the XML header line:

   ```
   <?xml version="1.0"?>
   ```

2. Beneath the line created in step 1, add the tags that define the start and end of an XSL stylesheet:

   ```
   <xsl:stylesheet xmlns:xsl="uri:xsl">
   <!-- Code for XSL template will go here. -->
   </xsl:stylesheet>
   ```

3. Replace the comment in step 2 with the tags that define the start and end of an XSL template:

   ```
   <xsl:template match="/">
   <!-- Body of XSL template will go here. -->
   </xsl:template>
   ```

   The attribute *match="/"* applies this template to all nodes in the source XML document.

4. Replace the comment in step 3 with the desired root element tags. The template will write these tags only once.

   ```
   <categories>
   <!-- Code to create child nodes will go here. -->
   </categories>
   ```

5. Create a *for-each* loop that creates one set of output statements for each *catrec* node found in the input XML document. Do this by replacing the comment in step 4 with this code:

   ```
   <xsl:for-each select="categories/catrec" order-by="+ catnr">
   <!-- Code to create output catrec nodes will go here. -->
   </xsl:for-each>
   ```

   The *order-by* attribute specifies that the *for-each* loop should process *catrec* nodes in ascending order by *catnr* child node value. This is what produces the sorted output.

6. To create the text of each output *catrec* node, replace the comment in step 5 with the following code:

```
<catrec>
  <catnr><xsl:value-of select="catnr"/></catnr>
  <desc><xsl:value-of select="desc"/></desc>
</catrec>
```

The <xsl:value-of> tags replace themselves with the current *catnr* and *desc* node values from the input XML document.

The complete listing appears below. The XSL tags appear in blue. You can find this code in the sample file \webdbdev\ch14\getcats2.xsl.

```
<?xml version="1.0"?>
<xsl:stylesheet xmlns:xsl="uri:xsl">
<xsl:template match="/">
  <categories>
  <xsl:for-each select="categories/catrec" order-by="+ catnr">
    <catrec>
      <catnr><xsl:value-of select="catnr"/></catnr>
      <desc><xsl:value-of select="desc"/></desc>
    </catrec>
  </xsl:for-each>
  </categories>
</xsl:template>
</xsl:stylesheet>
```

Run an XSL stylesheet on a Web server

To modify the getcats.htm example so that it uses the stylesheet created in the previous section, follow these steps:

1. Copy the getcats.htm and getcats.asp pages from the previous example to two new files named getcats2.htm and getcats2.asp.

2. Open the getcats2.asp page, and find the following statement:

```
xmlRsp.save(response)
```

and replace it with this code:

```
Set xmlSty = Server.CreateObject("Microsoft.XMLDOM")
xmlSty.async = False
xmlSty.load(Server.MapPath("getcats2.xsl"))
If xmlSty.parseError Then
  AddCatnrNode "", xmlSty.parseError.reason
  xmlRsp.save(response)
Else
  Response.Write xmlRsp.transformNode(xmlSty.documentElement)
End If
```

The first three statements in this code create a new XML DOM object, set its asynchronous mode to *False*, and load the getcats2.xsl stylesheet file from the physical location that corresponds to the relative URL getcats2.xsl.

If loading the stylesheet results in a parse error, the code calls the *AddCatnrNode* routine to add a node containing the error message to the xmlRsp object, and then delivers that object to the xmlhttp object in the getcats2.htm page as before.

If loading the stylesheet succeeds, the xmlRsp object's *transformNode* method applies it. The code then writes the results (which consist of XML text) directly into the ASP Response object.

3. By default, all XML node values are strings. Sorting the *catnr* values 100, 500, and 1000 therefore produces the following results:

```
100
1000
500
```

To sort these values numerically requires coding the XML data type of each *catnr* code as *number*. To do this, locate the following line within the *AddCatnrNode* subroutine in the getcats2.asp page:

```
xmlRsp.lastChild.lastChild.lastChild.text = acatnr
```

Follow it with this code:

```
If IsNumeric(acatnr) Then
  xmlRsp.lastChild.lastChild.lastChild.dataType = "number"
End If
```

Notice that some *catnr* nodes might contain non-numeric values. This can occur because of bad input from the Web visitor or because the node actually contains an error message. Assigning a data type of *number* to a node containing non-numeric data results in an error.

Sorting a collection of *catnr* fields—some with an assigned data type of *number* and others with a default data type of *text*—doesn't create an error. XSL simply sorts the text values first and follows them with all the sorted numeric values.

For more information about XML data types, refer to the sidebar "XML Data Types."

4. Also in the getcats2.htm page, locate the following JavaScript statement:

```
xmlhttp.open("POST", "getcats.asp", false);
```

and change it to access the getcats2.asp page instead, as shown here:

```
xmlhttp.open("POST", "getcats2.asp", false);
```

5. Still working in the getcats2.htm page, locate the following loop:

```
for (fnum = 0 ; fnum < crec.length ; fnum++) {
  rslt = rslt + "<td>" + crec.item(fnum).text + "</td>";
}
```

Replace the middle statement as shown here. This has the effect of right-aligning the displayed, numerically sorted category numbers.

```
for (fnum = 0 ; fnum < crec.length ; fnum++) {
  if (fnum == 0) {
    rslt = rslt + "<td align=right>";
  }else{
    rslt = rslt + "<td>";
  }
  rslt = rslt + crec.item(fnum).text + "</td>";
}
```

Figure 14-6 shows the completed Web page in action. Note that the category numbers in the response are in sequence even though the Web visitor specified them randomly. The invalid category number *foo* sorts first because it isn't numeric.

XML Data Types

By default, all XML values are strings. To override this assignment in XML code, you must first define an abbreviation for the *datatypes* namespace. It will probably be most convenient to do this by adding the following line of code prior to the first node in an XML document.

```
<?xml:namespace ns="urn:schemas-microsoft-com:datatypes"
                prefix="dt" ?>
```

Having done this, you can specify a data type for any node by coding *dt:dt="<datatype>"* within its opening tag, where *<datatype>* is a value from Table 14-5 or Table 14-6. To assign a data type in script code, assign a value to the node's *dataType* property as shown here, where <node> is a standard node identifier and *<datatype>* is again a value from Table 14-5 or Table 14-6.

<node>.dataType = *"<datatype>"*

Although a script can change the data type of an existing node, keep in mind that not all conversions are possible and that some might produce unexpected results. For example, you can't convert the string *giraffe* to a number, and converting the string *-99* to a *ui1* produces the positive result *99*.

Data types are more commonly found in DTDs than in ordinary XML code. When coded within a DTD, data types tell the parser to reject any document having one or more fields whose values don't conform to the specified types.

Table 14-5 contains rich XML data types that are supported by the Microsoft processor. Table 14-6 contains the primitive XML data types listed in the World Wide Web Consortium (W3C) XML 1.0 recommendation.

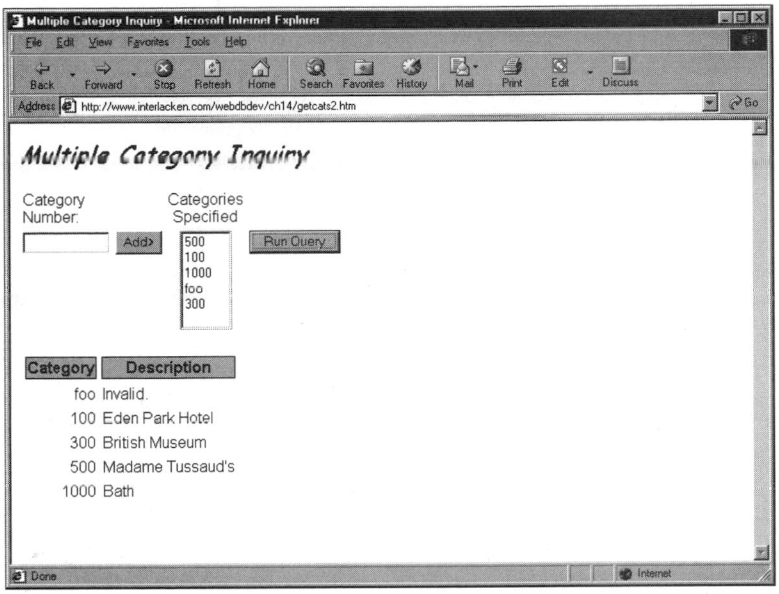

Figure 14-6 *An ASP page uses XSL on the Web server to sort the XML data displayed here.*

Table 14-5 Rich XML Data Types

Type	Description
bin.base64	A binary object encoded with MIME-style Base64.
bin.hex	Hexadecimal digits representing octets.
Boolean	0 or 1, where 0 means *false* and 1 means *true*.
char	A one-character string.
date	A date, but not a time, in a subset ISO 8601 format. Example: 1947-06-11.
dateTime	A date in a subset ISO 8601 format, with an optional time and no time zone. Fractional seconds can be precise up to nanoseconds. Example: 1947-06-11T18:39:09.
dateTime.tz	A date in a subset ISO 8601 format, with optional time and optional zone. Fractional seconds can be precise up to nanoseconds. Example: 1947-06-11T18:39:09-08:00.
fixed.14.4	The same as *number* but no more than 14 digits to the left of the decimal point and no more than 4 to the right.
float	A real number with no limit on digits. It can have a leading sign, fractional digits, and optionally an exponent. Punctuation can be present as in U.S. English. Values can range from 1.7976931348623157E+308 to 2.2250738585072014E-308.
int	A number with an optional sign, no fractions, and no exponent.
number	A number with no limit on digits. It can have a leading sign, fractional digits, and optionally an exponent. Punctuation can be present as in U.S. English. (Values have the same range as the largest significant number, R8: 1.7976931348623157E+308 to 2.2250738585072014E-308.)

(continued)

Table 14-5 *continued*

Type	Description
time	A time in a subset ISO 8601 format, with no date and no time zone. Example: 13:30:01.
time.tz	A time in a subset ISO 8601 format, with no date but an optional time zone. Example: 13:30:01-05:00.
i1	An integer represented in one byte. A number, with optional sign, no fractions, and no exponent. Examples: 1, 127, –128.
i2	An integer represented in two bytes. A number, with optional sign, no fractions, and no exponent. Examples: 1, 703, –32768.
i4	An integer represented in four bytes. A number, with optional sign, no fractions, and no exponent. Examples: 1, 703, –32768, 148343, –1000000000.
r4	A real number with seven-digit precision. It can have a leading sign, fractional digits, or an exponent. Punctuation can be present as in U.S. English. Values range from 3.40282347E+38F to 1.17549435E-38F.
r8	A real number with 15-digit precision, It can have a leading sign, fractional digits, or an exponent. Punctuation can be present as in U.S. English. Values range from 1.7976931348623157E+308 to 2.2250738585072014E-308.
ui1	An unsigned integer. The value must be an unsigned number with no fractions and no exponent. Examples: 1, 255.
ui2	An unsigned two-byte integer. The value must be an unsigned number with no fractions and no exponent. Examples 1, 255, 65535.
ui4	An unsigned four-byte integer. The value must be an unsigned number with no fractions and no exponent. Examples: 1, 703, 3000000000.
uri	A Universal Resource Identifier (URI). Example: *urn:schemas-microsoft-com:Office9*.
uuid	A series of hexadecimal digits representing octets. Embedded hyphens are optional and ignored. Example: 333C7BC4-460F-11D0-BC04-0080C7055A83.

Table 14-6   Primitive XML Data Types

Type	Description
entity	Represents the XML ENTITY type
entities	Represents the XML ENTITIES type.
enumeration	Represents an enumerated type (supported on attributes only)
id	Represents the XML ID type
idref	Represents the XML IDREF type
idrefs	Represents the XML IDREFS type
nmtoken	Represents the XML NMTOKEN type

Type	Description
nmtokens	Represents the XML NMTOKENS type
notation	Represents a NOTATION type
string	Represents a string type

Chapter Summary

This chapter illustrated how to create XML text from conventional database queries and how to use Microsoft XML objects in ASP pages. Server-based XML processing is useful not only for supporting client-based use of XML, but also in cases where browser compatibility or data transmissions times are an issue.

Part 5, "Exchanging Data with XML," provided a brief introduction to XML and the various Microsoft objects that process XML. Unlike most books, it did so in the context of practical examples. The complexity of working with XML will decrease as more data becomes available in XML format, as designers learn to use XML for mass-producing or mass-customizing Web pages, and, of course, as the technology matures.

Part 6, "Tuning and Debugging," will explain a series of techniques for getting your Web database pages to run quickly, reliably, and as designed.

Part 6

Tuning and Debugging

Chapter 15

Tuning Application Performance

Chapter Objectives   Estimated Time: 30 minutes

In this chapter, you'll learn

- How to reduce ASP resource utilization.

- How to reduce database resource utilization.

All the examples and text so far in this book have emphasized getting Web pages to work in the simplest, most obvious way possible. This has many advantages in terms of learning time, development time, and ongoing maintenance time. However, as so often happens, the most obvious approach isn't always the most efficient one. If everything goes right and your pages become a phenomenal success, you should expect to encounter a performance bottleneck or two.

ASP pages are, of course, subject to all the performance considerations applicable to ordinary HTML pages: avoid transmitting large amounts of text, avoid transmitting large images, and so on. Beyond that are two further areas to consider: the performance of your ASP code and the performance of your database system. This chapter offers specific recommendations to help improve your Web database performance.

Tuning ASP Pages

Designing databases and accessing them with ADO and ASP are significant challenges in and of themselves. Designing and tuning for best performance adds further constraints and complexity.

The best overall approach for tuning ASP performance is to

- Keep the ASP page from doing any work that isn't strictly necessary.

- Avoid practices that are especially resource-intensive.

- Keep ASP pages from doing exactly the same work over and over again.

Before diving headlong into tuning, however, make sure you're tuning the right component. Measure before attempting to correct. Concentrate on the slowest, most frequently used Web pages. Web server activity logs will be helpful in this regard. Don't try to solve database performance problems by optimizing ASP code, or vice versa.

Combine script blocks

Each transition between script code and HTML code creates work for the ASP processor. Therefore, it's better to have a few large blocks of script code rather than many small ones. It's also faster for one *Response.Write* statement to write a long string than for many such statements to write a series of short strings. Taken together, these two factors argue against heavy use of the <%=...%> syntax in frequently accessed ASP pages.

> **Note**   If a single ASP page uses two scripting languages, the server has to load two script interpreters. If it uses three scripting languages, it has to load three, and so on. Save your server—and your sanity—by coding everything in a single language.

Preload the Application object with useful data

If you have Web pages that run frequently and use resource-intensive methods to obtain relatively static data, you can probably improve performance by retrieving that data just once and storing it in the Application object.

To do this, place a file named global.asa in the root folder of your application (the folder that begins its executable folder tree), and within that file define a subroutine named *Application_OnStart*. Here's how this code should look:

```
<%
Sub Application_OnStart ()
' Place application startup code here.
End Sub
%>
```

The Web server will run this subroutine the first time any Web visitor requests any ASP page from your application (that is, from within your executable folder). For a simple example of how this works, think about the code that built connection strings for most of the examples in this book.

```
cnStHol = "driver={Microsoft Access Driver (*.mdb)};" & _
          "dbq=" & Server.MapPath("../holiday/holiday.mdb")
```

Every time a Web page containing this code runs, it asks the Web server to translate the relative URL *../holiday/holiday.mdb* to a physical file location. The server could easily end up performing this translation thousands of times an hour, always returning the same results. To avoid this duplicate work, you could place the following code in the global.asa file:

```
Application("HolidayDB") = _
    Server.MapPath("/webdbdev/holiday/holiday.mdb")
```

Then you could change the code that builds your connection strings to this:

```
cnStHol = "driver={Microsoft Access Driver (*.mdb)};" & _
          "dbq=" & Application("HolidayDB")
```

This way, the Web server needs to run the *Server.MapPath* method only once. There are, however, three caveats:

- When the global.asa file's *Application_OnStart* subroutine runs, the current URL will be that of the first ASP page a visitor requests after the Web server starts. In most cases, this means the current URL will be unpredictable. That's why the preceding example gives the *Server.MapPath* method the full URL */webdbdev/holiday/holiday.mdb* rather than a relative URL such as *../holiday/holiday.mdb*. Specifying locations relative to an unpredictable starting point is unlikely to produce the results you want.

- As with the Session object, you can't directly update an array contained in the Application object. The following expression updates the third variable in the Application object—not the third element in the array *MyArray*:

```
Application("MyArray")(2) = "six"
```

  To perform such an update, copy the entire array to a local variable, update the desired element locally, and then copy the entire array back to the Application object.

- Once the *Application_OnStart* subroutine has run, it won't run again until an administrator shuts down and restarts the Web server and a Web visitor requests an ASP page within your application's executable folder. If some other process makes a change that requires updating the Application object, that process should perform the update directly.

Suppose, for example, that a Web page displays a list of upcoming events stored in a database table named *events*. The Web page that displays this data might run thousands of time per day, but the list of events gets updated only once or twice a week. If this Web page's performance is a problem, it might be advantageous to store the *events* data as a string of HTML within the Application object rather than opening, querying, and closing the database for each request. In such a case, you would open the database and create the HTML in two locations:

- Within the global.asa file's *Application_OnStart* subroutine

- Within the Web page that updates the *events* table

You must call the *Application.Lock* method before updating the Application object anywhere outside the *Application_OnStart* subroutine. When the update is complete, call *Application.Unlock*.

Figure 15-1 shows a simple ASP page that displays the contents of the Application object. You can find this page among the sample files at \webdbdev\ ch15\showapp.asp.

You can store almost anything you like in the Application object: simple variables, application parameters, arrays, and objects—to name just a few. Remember, though, that everything in the Application object remains constantly in memory. Putting a few kilobytes of information into the Application object shouldn't present a problem, but storing information by the megabyte is a bad idea.

To save a text file in the Application object, first use the ASP FileSystem object to store each record into one element of an array, and then store the array in the Application object. Here's some code that does this:

```
Set fSys = Server.CreateObject("Scripting.FileSystemObject")
fNam = Server.MapPath("file2app.txt")
Set fObj = fSys.OpenTextFile(fNam)
fTbl = Split(Replace(fObj.ReadAll,Chr(10),""),Chr(13))
fObj.Close
Set fSys = Nothing
Application("fTbl") = fTbl
```

The first statement in this code creates a file system object. The second obtains the physical location of the text file file2app.txt, and the third opens it. The next statement uses the file object's *ReadAll* method to read the whole file into memory, the VBScript *Replace* function to remove all line feed characters, and the VBScript *Split* function to create an array of substrings delimited by carriage returns. The next two statements close the file and destroy the file system object. The last statement copies the table into the Application object.

There are several ways to save a recordset in the Application object:

- As an HTML string

- As a double-subscripted array (one subscript for record number and another for field number)

- As a single subscripted array containing one element per record (Each array element would contain field data in tab-separated format.)

- As an ADO Stream object (but only if your server runs ADO 2.5 or later)

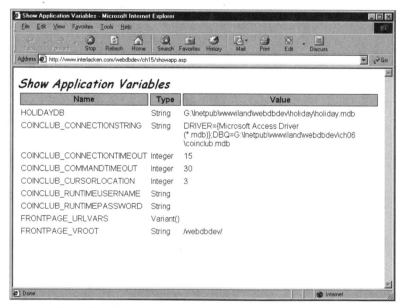

Figure 15-1 *This Web page displays the current contents of the Application object.*

Avoid retrieving the same data more than once

The preceding section explained how to avoid retrieving the same data in multiple Web pages. The same concepts apply to repeatedly obtaining the same data within a single Web page. Consider the following code, for example, which reads through a recordset. For each record, it searches the *desc* field to determine whether it contains a string named *qdesc* received from the Web visitor.

```
Do While Not rsItm.EOF
  If InStr(UCase(rsItm("desc")), UCase(Request("qdesc"))) Then
    Exit Do
  End If
  rsItm.MoveNext
Loop
```

If *rsItm.EOF* is *False* when the loop ends, the *Exit Do* statement must have executed and the record is positioned at the first matching record. If *rsItm.EOF* is *True*, there was no matching record.

More important, however, is that the loop evaluates the expression *UCase(Request("qdesc"))* once for each record in the recordset. If there are 50 records, that's 50 searches through as many as five collections in the Request object, plus 50 conversions to uppercase. The following code, which searches the Request object and converts the *qdesc* value to uppercase only once, is much more efficient:

```
sdesc = UCase(Request("qdesc"))
Do While Not rsItm.EOF
  If InStr(UCase(rsItm("desc")), sdesc) Then
    Exit Do
  End If
  rsItm.MoveNext
Loop
```

Retrieving values from collections of any type is relatively slow. If you need to access such a value more than once, store a copy in a local variable.

Use local variables rather than multiple object references

When Microsoft VBScript (or JavaScript) executes a statement like the following, it must search in order for the Catalog object, the DocumentElement object, the ChildNodes object, and the Item object (which turns out to be a method).

```
rset = Catalog.DocumentElement.ChildNodes.Item(0).Value
```

This is a lot of searching, and VBScript repeats it every time you access the same structure. The following code, for example, searches through these objects three times:

```
<td><%=Catalog.DocumentElement.ChildNodes.Item(0).Value %></td>
<td><%=Catalog.DocumentElement.ChildNodes.Item(1).Value %></td>
<td><%=Catalog.DocumentElement.ChildNodes.Item(2).Value %></td>
```

The following code would execute much faster because it only searches the object structure once:

```
<% Set curnode = Catalog.DocumentElement.ChildNodes %>
<td><%=curnode.Item(0).Value %></td>
<td><%=curnode.Item(1).Value %></td>
<td><%=curnode.Item(2).Value %></td>
```

The following code, of course, would be even better. For an explanation why, refer to the section "Combine script blocks" earlier in the chapter.

```
<%
Set curnode = Catalog.DocumentElement.ChildNodes
Response.Write _
   "<td>" & curnode.Item(0).Value & "</td>" & vbCrLf & _
   "<td>" & curnode.Item(1).Value & "</td>" & vbCrLf & _
   "<td>" & curnode.Item(2).Value & "</td>" & vbCrLf
%>
```

Avoid redimensioning arrays

VBScript has a *ReDim* statement that can change the size of an array. This command creates a new array of the requested size, optionally copies all the data from the old array, and then deletes the old array and replaces its address with that of the new one. This makes code such as the following time-consuming:

```
Dim CatArray()
Do While Not rsCat.EOF
   ReDim Preserve CatArray(UBound(CatArray) + 1))
   CatArray(UBound(CatArray)) = rsCat("catnr")
   rsCat.MoveNext
Loop
```

This loop reads all records in the rsCat recordset. For each record, it increases the size of the *CatArray* by one, and then stores the current category number in the last array element. (The *UBound* function returns the highest permissible subscript for an array.) This is quite processor-intensive.

The following loop does the same job much more efficiently because it redimensions the array only once:

```
Dim CatArray()
ReDim CatArray(rsCat.RecordCount - 1)
pos = 0
Do While Not rsCat.EOF
   CatArray(pos) = rsCat("catnr")
   pos = pos + 1
   rsCat.MoveNext
Loop
```

Code that originally dimensioned a large static array would run even faster. Rather than the statements shown above, code this:

```
Dim CatArray(100)
pos = 0
```

```
Do While Not rsCat.EOF
  If pos < UBound(CatArray) Then
    CatArray(pos) = rsCat("catnr")
    pos = pos + 1
  End If
Loop
```

This presumes, of course, that you're fairly certain there will never be more than 100 category codes. If this is a problem, dimension the array to 500 or 1000. If category codes are 32-bit integers, an array of 1000 will occupy only 4 kilobytes of memory. If *that's* a problem, it's time to upgrade your hardware.

Use the Dictionary object

VBScript's Dictionary object works like an array with alphanumeric subscripts. The section "Use the Dictionary object" in Chapter 5 ("Customizing Web Content with Server-Side Scripting") explained the details of using this object.

Indexing into a conventional array is much faster than indexing into a Dictionary object, but only if you already know the subscript. Consider, for example, the problem of searching a list. To use an array, you'd code this:

```
Dim animals(4)
animals(0) = "chicken"
animals(1) = "cow"
animals(2) = "goat"
animals(3) = "hog"
animals(4) = "sheep"
For pos = 0 to UBound(animals)
  If animals(pos) = Request("qanimal") Then
    Exit For
  End If
Next
If pos <= UBound(animals) Then
'  A match was found.
End If
```

This code requires resources for looping, calculating, indexing, and comparing five times. Contrast this with using the Dictionary object, which does the same job with no looping and no multiple comparisons:

```
Set animals = Server.CreateObject("Scripting.Dictionary")
animals("chicken") = "y"
animals("cow")     = "y"
animals("goat")    = "y"
animals("hog")     = "y"
animals("sheep")   = "y"
If animals(Request("qanimal")) = "y" Then
'  A match was found.
End If
```

Using the right tool for the job almost always produces the best results.

Use the <object> tag to create objects

There are two ways to create instances of ActiveX objects for use by an ASP page:

- Call the ASP Server object's *CreateObject* method. This is the method used throughout this book, and again here:

```
<%
Set cn = Server.CreateObject("ADODB.Connection")
%>
```

- Use the <object> tag as shown in the following code. This code is equivalent to that shown just above.

```
<object
runat="SERVER"
id="cn"
classid="Clsid:00000514-0000-0010-8000-00AA006D2EA4">
</object>
```

This code must appear outside of any <% and %> tags. The *runat="SERVER"* attribute makes it run immediately on the Web server rather than later on the browser.

Of these two approaches, the first is more readable but the second is faster. If you're having performance problems with a frequently used Web database page, creating its ADO and other ActiveX objects with <object> tags will provide some relief.

One way to find the class ID of an object is by looking in the HKEY_LOCAL_MACHINE\SOFTWARE\classes portion of the registry on the machine where the object is installed. Figure 15-2 shows the Microsoft Windows 2000 version of regedit.exe displaying this information.

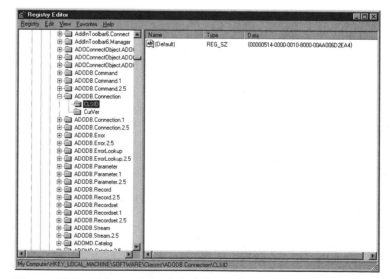

Figure 15-2   *This portion of the Microsoft Windows registry provides the class ID for each installed object.*

One disadvantage of using the <object> tag is that it *always* creates the object. When you use the *Server.CreateObject* method, you can decide during each page execution whether to create an object.

Avoid using the Request.ServerVariables collection

For performance reasons, the Web server doesn't construct the Request.Server-Variables collection unless an ASP page tries to access it. However, the first time you do access this collection, the server has to construct the entire collection. The server can't construct only the items you ask for. This can result in a noticeable performance hit.

If you're having performance problems with an ASP page that uses this collection, consider doing without it. Also, recall that the expression *Request("field1")* searches the following collections in this order: QueryString, Form, Cookies, ClientCertificate, and ServerVariables.

If you code *Request("field1")* and the field isn't present in the QueryString, Form, Cookies, or ClientCertificate collections, the ASP processor will create and search the ServerVariables collection. If you expect *field1* to be in the QueryString collection, code *Request.QueryString("field1")*. If you expect it to be in the Form collection, code *Request.Form("field1")*.

Be careful when using the Session object

Like anything else, creating and destroying Session objects requires its share of server resources. If an application or even an individual Web page doesn't use the Session object, you can save resources by not creating it.

To disable use of the Session object for a single Web page, code this before the first HTML or *Response.Write* statement:

```
<%@ EnableSessionState=False %>
```

To disable use of the Session object for an entire application, turn off the Enable Session State option shown in Figure 15-3. This is a Microsoft Internet Information Services (IIS) Web server setting that applies at the virtual directory level. To query or change this setting, open the Web server in Internet Services Manager, right-click the virtual directory, choose Properties, click the Configuration button in the resulting dialog box, and then select the App Options tab. This requires Administrator privileges.

Note that two Web pages using the same Session object can't execute at the same time. This normally isn't a problem because Web visitors submit only one request at a time—that is, they wait for a response before submitting another request. Nevertheless, disabling the Session object allows multiple ASP requests from the same visitor to execute at the same time.

Avoid using *Session_OnEnd* event procedures. These procedures reside within the global.asa file and execute whenever a session times out. Such routines consume resources long after the Web visitor is gone, they're difficult to debug, and if there's a system problem, they might never execute anyway. Whatever you need to accumulate and save, do it as the activity occurs.

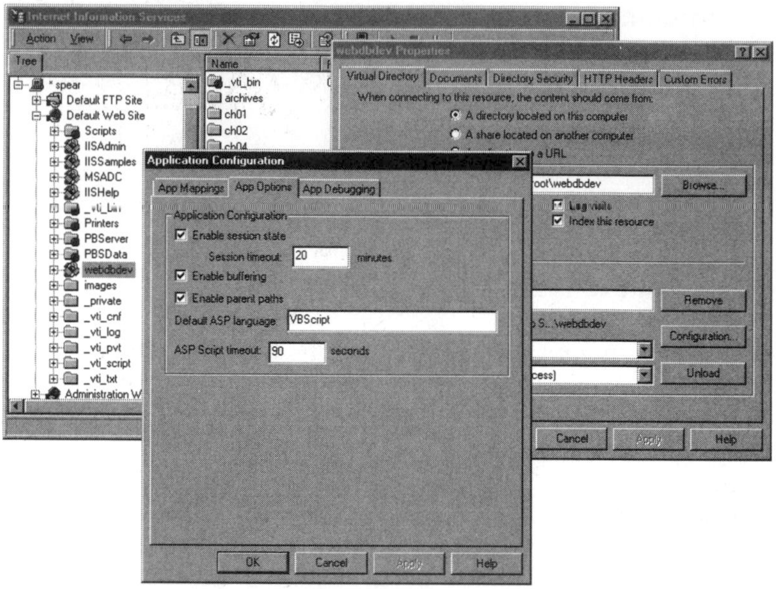

Figure 15-3   *Use Internet Services Manager to enable or disable use of the Session object for an executable folder.*

Buffer responses to the Web visitor

Buffering in this sense means holding ASP output in memory and sending it to the Web visitor only when complete. For some time, conventional wisdom held that this practice consumed more memory and CPU time than transmitting the response as the ASP page produced it. Current thinking, however, is the reverse: transmitting the response in many small packets consumes more resources than saving up the entire Web page and transmitting it in one burst.

The Enable Buffering option shown in Figure 15-3 configures buffering at the application level. In IIS 4.0, this value is unchecked by default. Reflecting the change in thinking, this value is checked by default in IIS 5.0 (which comes with Windows 2000). To override this setting for a particular Web page, code one of the following statements before the first HTML or *Response.Write* statement:

```
Response.Buffer=True
Response.Buffer=False
```

The Response.Flush *method immediately sends any buffered output to the Web visitor.*

Note that if the ASP page takes a noticeable amount of time to run, the Web visitor might perceive degradation with buffering turned on. This is because the visitor receives nothing until the entire ASP page finishes processing. With buffering turned off, the visitor might receive the page heading and titles before later parts of the Web page finish processing.

Check Response.IsClientConnected during lengthy processes

If, despite all efforts, your ASP page takes noticeable time to run, it's possible the Web visitor will tire of waiting and move on to another site. Once this happens, any further processing is a waste.

The *Response.IsClientConnected* property will be *False* if the Web visitor has disconnected from the server since the last *Response.Write*. If this is the case, you might as well terminate your script. Insert such checks throughout any long-running code.

Set realistic script timeouts

IIS will cancel any ASP page that runs beyond a configured number of seconds. The default is the ASP Script *Timeout* value that appears in Figure 15-3, which is usually 90 seconds. You can increase this for a specific page by inserting the following statement (where *<time>* is a number of seconds):

> Server.ScriptTimeout = *<time>*

Setting the timeout too short results in pages that consume resources and then fail before they complete normally. Setting the timeout too long can result in pages that consume resources either looping or waiting for something that will never happen.

Tip If an ASP page runs for 90 seconds on the Web server, the Web visitor will probably experience response times in the 100–120 seconds range. This is long enough that most Web visitors will tire of waiting and move on to another site. If you think your Web visitors will grow impatient after 30 seconds, you might as well set the *ScriptTimeout* value to 20 or 25 seconds.

Set efficient cache properties

If the information in an ASP page doesn't change often, consider setting the *Response.Expires* property to a fairly large value. Within the time limit you specify, the visitor's browser can cache and deliver copies of the page rather than requesting new copies from your Web server. To specify this property, code the following (where *<number>* is the number of minutes before the page expires):

> Response.Expires = *<number>*

Set this parameter to 0 to have the cached page expire immediately.

The *Response.CacheControl* property controls caching on proxy servers. Setting this property to *Public* specifies that proxy servers can cache the ASP output for later delivery to Web visitors. Every page thus cached represents a saving to your Web server, provided it's acceptable for the proxy server to deliver pages created in the past.

```
Response.CacheControl = "Public"
```

Unless you turn on buffering, you must set both the *Response.Expires* and *Response.CacheControl* properties prior to the first HTML or *Response.Write* statement.

Move processing to the browser

Moving code to the browser reduces Web server load in two ways. First, by moving work onto the Web visitor's computer, it reduces the amount of work per request the Web server needs to do. Second, by interacting directly with the Web visitor, browser-side scripts reduce the number of requests a Web visitor needs to make.

Input validation is an excellent function to run on the browser. The Web visitor gets faster response and the Web server gets fewer hits. Keep in mind, however, that some very old browsers don't support browser-side scripting, and some current browsers let Web visitors turn it off. Don't reduce server-side validation so much that outdated or mischievous visitors can compromise your system.

On output, consider transmitting small quantities of data to the browser and letting the Web visitor browse it using Dynamic HTML. For example, you could format a small item database into a JavaScript array or XML document and send it to the Web visitor for perusal. Doing this could eliminate several round trips to the server.

Tuning Database Usage

Database design and usage are generally greater performance factors than application design and coding. In practical terms, this means that tuning database usage generally provides greater payback than optimizing your application code. The best approach varies depending on the situation, but if other ASP pages on your server run fine and only the database pages are slow, it's definitely time to do some database tuning.

Design your database for efficiency

If you followed the recommendations from "Designing a Database" in Chapter 2 ("Understanding Database Concepts and Terms"), your database should have a sound fundamental design. If you didn't and now you have a mess, consider redesigning the database with all new table names and then creating stored queries that mimic the tables in the original database. This will keep your existing Web page running while you revise the high-hitting, long-running Web pages to use the new structure. Here are some additional tips to keep in mind:

- **Eliminate redundant data**   If you find yourself writing loops to update the same data in multiple records, it's definitely time to review your database design.

- **Don't make fields longer than necessary**   This wastes space and increases physical disk activity.

- **Use the proper data type for each field**   If the data consists of dates or times, use the Date/Time field format. If the field consists of integer values, don't store them as floating-point or currency. Using the proper data types makes life easier for both you and the database system.

- **Anticipate and support common access paths**   Real-world databases aren't designed in ivory towers. Be prepared to sacrifice a bit of theoretical purity for real-world performance.

Optimize your queries

Poorly constructed queries are among the most common causes of poor database performance. Here are some tips for getting the same results in significantly less time:

- Request no more data than necessary. If you don't need a field, don't specify it in a SELECT statement. If you only need the first record, set the recordset's *MaxRecords* property to 1. If you don't need data from a joined table, delete the JOIN statement.

- Given a choice between using WHERE and using HAVING, choose WHERE. Record selection specified on the WHERE clause occurs earlier in the retrieval process and speeds up overall database response.

- Make the database system do as much of the work as possible. In general, you're much better off telling the database system what you want than getting more data than you need and filtering or summarizing it yourself.

- Avoid large result sets.

- Avoid using criteria that require the database system to scan large numbers of records sequentially. Criteria involving IN, NOT IN, OR, and != (not equal) are examples of these.

- Column functions such as SUM are also resource-intensive, though generally less so than retrieving a large result set and performing the summation yourself. Use WHERE criteria to minimize the data processed by SUM or GROUP BY clauses.

Use stored procedures and stored queries

Stored procedures are blocks of script code that reside on the database server. Microsoft SQL Server, for example, supports stored procedures written in a language called Transact-SQL. Because stored procedures run in an environment closely bound to the database server, they're frequently the most efficient way to complete a series of database operations that depend on each other.

A stored query is a SQL statement stored within the database system. When you want to execute a stored query, you just send the database system its name and any replaceable parameters. "Using ADO Parameters" in Chapter 4 ("Accessing Tables and Records with ADO") explained how to run a stored query.

Query optimization is one of the first steps required to process any SQL statement. During this step, the database system analyzes the submitted SQL, analyzes the structure of the database, and develops (with any luck) an optimal strategy for efficiently retrieving the requested data. Most databases perform this step when you save a stored query, and not when an application runs it. With a conventional query, of course, the database system must optimize the query at run time. For this reason, running a stored query is often faster than running the same query supplied as text.

Avoid storing binary data in the database

Although Microsoft Access, SQL Server, and most other databases can store binary objects such as pictures and sounds, it's best to avoid this practice for Web database pages. For one thing, these objects make the database physically larger and thus increase search times. More importantly, though, retrieving data stored this way requires querying the database an additional time for each object you use on the same Web page.

To understand this problem, consider that an ASP page can't send the browser an image or a sound file along with the HTML. It can only send an <img> tag that gives that file's location. Thus, here's how displaying a picture stored in a database has to work:

1. The requested ASP page sends the browser an <img> tag that gives the *src=* attribute as another ASP page and that supplies the current record key as a query string.

2. When the browser receives this <img> tag, it dutifully requests that ASP page.

3. The second ASP page looks up the record specified in the query string, gets the picture data, and writes it into the Response object. This page will also override the *Response.ContentType* property to audio/wav, image/gif, image/jpeg, or whatever is appropriate.

It should be obvious at this point that running another ASP page, executing another query, and copying the data out of the database and into the Response object requires much more processing than delivering a simple .wav, .gif, or .jpg file. The best approach, therefore, is to store the picture, sound, or other binary file as a normal file on the Web server and record only its name in the database.

Pick the right cursor for the job

As described in "Open an ADO Recordset object" in Chapter 4, ADO provides four cursor options: forward-only, static, keyset, and dynamic. Each of these options provides different capabilities and different performance: forward-only is the least capable and fastest; dynamic is the most capable and slowest. Table 4-3 explained the capabilities of each cursor type.

If you're confused as to which cursor type to use, try them all! Testing all four possibilities won't take very long. If the Web page runs well with a forward-only cursor, leave it that way. Otherwise, try the static, keyset, and dynamic cursors in that order until the page starts working again. Alternatively, first get the page working with a dynamic cursor, and then try using the keyset, static, and forward-only cursors until something fails.

The *LockType* property also has an effect on performance. If your Web page doesn't update a recordset, open it with a read-only lock. Otherwise, try optimistic locking. If that seems to produce too many "Record in use" failures when you issue the *Update* method, try pessimistic locking.

Use connection pooling

Opening a connection is a relatively time-consuming process. IIS therefore supports a feature called *connection pooling* that retains Connection objects for some period of time after an ASP page releases them. If another page requests a similar connection (that is, one for the same driver, database, username, and password), IIS can reuse the discarded object rather than create a new one.

The Web server's administrator can enable or disable connection pooling on a driver-by-driver basis. This involves the Set Connection Pooling Attributes dialog box shown in Figure 15-4. An administrator can display this dialog box in Windows 2000 by choosing Data Sources (ODBC) from the Start program's Administrative Tools menu, or on Microsoft Windows NT 4.0 by opening the ODBC Control Panel Applet. In either case, the administrator should select the Connection Pooling tab.

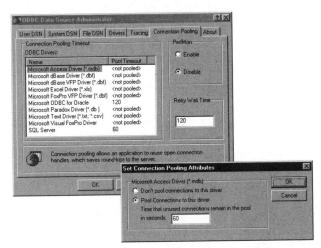
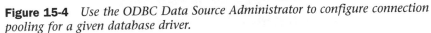

Figure 15-4 *Use the ODBC Data Source Administrator to configure connection pooling for a given database driver.*

To activate connection pooling for a particular driver, double-click the driver name and specify Pool Connections To This Driver in the resulting dialog box. The timeout value will default to 60 seconds, but you can override this. Click OK when your entries are correct.

The PerfMon Enable and Disable choices control whether ODBC Connection Pooling counters will be visible in the Windows 2000 Performance application or the Windows NT Performance Monitor. These counters provide feedback on the effectiveness of your current connection-pooling settings.

The Retry Wait Time setting specifies the amount of time ODBC will wait before making a second (or subsequent) connection attempt to the same database server.

Don't store ADO objects in the Session object

Before the availability and widespread use of connection pooling, developers often stored Connection and even Recordset objects within the Session object.

The idea was that opening one Connection object per session was better than opening one Connection object per Web page. It turns out that these connections remained open not for the brief instant that an ASP page ran, but for the duration of the session (which was the time the visitor spent browsing the site plus 20 minutes). This meant that the server reached capacity sooner with Connection objects persistently stored in the Session object than it would have with Connection objects created and released on a page by page basis. In short, use connection pooling rather than the Session object to reduce connection times.

Storing Recordset objects in the Session object might seem attractive because you can retain position and locking states in the database as the Web visitor traverses the site. If you have many Web visitors, however, this can once again result in many recordsets being open at the same time and a net decrease in server capacity. If the visitor wanders off without executing some kind of log-off page, the recordset remains open for 20 minutes after he or she leaves. Any pessimistically locked records will remain unavailable to other Web visitors for the same period of time. And finally, you can't store a Recordset object in the Session object without also storing its Connection object, which leads to all the problems described in the previous paragraph. In summary, don't store ADO objects in the Session object.

Create useful indexes

In the context of databases, an index is a table of values that exist within another table. However, the sequence of records in an index is different than the sequence of records in the original table. Here's how this works:

Suppose that your database has an employee table with employee number as its primary key.

Most database systems can support multiple indexes per table.

- The database system would automatically create a primary key index that contained the employee number and physical location of each record in the employee table.

- Pointers within the primary key index would significantly speed up reading or searching the index in employee number order, making it much faster than sorting or searching the employee table directly.

- Whenever an application added, changed, or deleted a record in the employee table, the database system would automatically update the primary key index accordingly.

When you ask the database system to process a SQL statement, the query optimizer takes note of any applicable indexes and uses them to speed up processing. If the query asks for a specific primary key, for example, the optimizer will no doubt decide to search for it using the primary key index.

If you queried the same table for all employee surnames beginning with the letter B, the database system would have to read through every record in the employee table looking for surnames that begin with that letter. If you asked for these records in surname sequence, the database system would construct a temporary index of the found records and use it to retrieve the matching records in the requested order. Creating a temporary index involves much more work than using an existing index to do the same thing.

Although indexes speed lookup and often eliminate the need for sorting, they aren't free. For one thing, indexes consume additional disk space. For another, whenever an application adds, modifies, or deletes a record in an indexed table, the database system also needs to update all the indexes. This can be a significant performance hit.

In general, indexing a given field will be more attractive to the extent that the following conditions are true:

Finding a key in an index is faster than finding it in the database itself because the index is smaller, and because the index is organized in the proper sequence.

- The table that contains the field is large.

- The field is frequently used for selecting, joining, and sorting.

- Record creations, record deletions, and updates to the specific field are infrequent.

However, there's no hard-and-fast rule: you should be willing to create or delete indexes and then monitor the resulting performance.

Figure 15-5 shows how to index a field in Access. Open the table in design mode, select the field you want to index, and set the Indexed property to Yes (Duplicates OK) or Yes (No Duplicates). If you select the Yes (No Duplicates) option, Access will reject any attempt to add a second record that has the same value as an existing one.

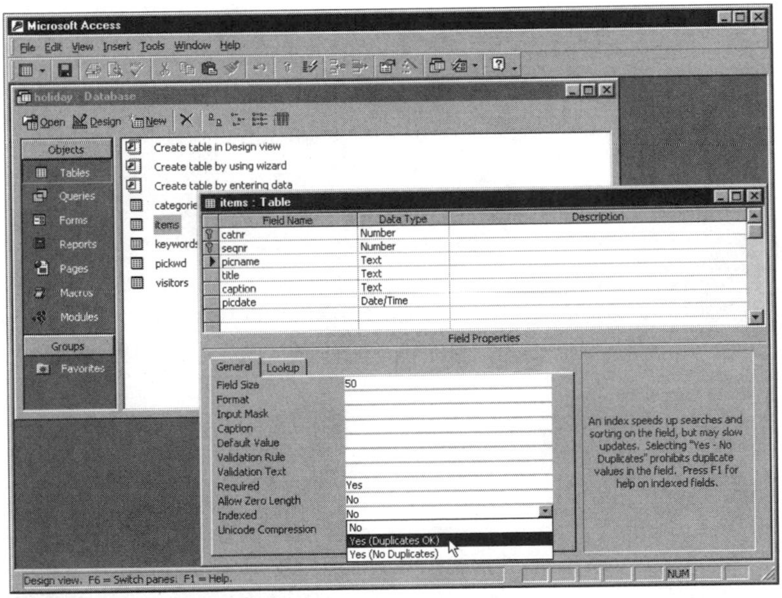

Figure 15-5   *To create or delete indexes for fields in an Access table, modify the field's Indexed property.*

Consider migrating to SQL Server

All the examples in this book use Access databases for three reasons: Access is widely available, easy to use and administer, and cheap to license. Nevertheless,

Access lacks the performance and stability of a well-configured SQL Server installation. If use of your application starts to exceed several hits a minute, or if your database grows larger than 10 or 20 megabytes, you should probably consider upgrading to SQL Server.

Access 2000 includes an Upsizing Wizard that automates the process of converting an Access database to SQL Server. Figure 15-6 shows the command necessary to start this wizard. Because the wizard will ask you for logon credentials and SQL Server configuration settings, it's probably best to have your SQL Server Administrator run this wizard for you or with you.

The wizard will create a SQL Server database equal in structure to your existing Access database, and will optionally duplicate your existing data as well. If you've used an ODBC system data source name (DSN) in all your connection strings, you can just redefine that system DSN so it points to the SQL Server database. Otherwise, you'll need to change all your connection strings. This might be a good time to start using system DSNs, or at least storing the connection string in the Application object.

Don't be surprised if some of your Web pages stop working after you convert a database to SQL Server. SQL Server and Access are two different database systems and it's normal for them to handle certain details differently. Consider testing mandatory prior to finalizing your conversion.

Administering SQL Server is normally the work of professionals and is clearly beyond the scope of this book. If you need to become a SQL Server administrator, you should seek out the proper training and reference materials. Otherwise, be sure to establish a good working relationship with the administrator you'll be working with.

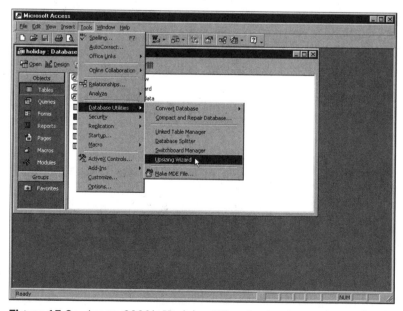

Figure 15-6 *Access 2000's Upsizing Wizard migrates an Access database to SQL Server.*

Testing Performance Regularly

Performance is the opposite of entropy—it decreases all the time. Review performance regularly, at least by running your own Web pages and seeing if they appear sluggish compared to a week or a month ago.

The Performance snap-in that comes with Windows 2000, the Network Monitor that comes with System Management Server (SMS), and even the Task Manager are valuable tools for measuring overall system performance. The IIS Resource Kit contains even more tools.

Chapter Summary

This chapter provided a series of tips for improving the performance of Web database pages. It centered primarily on two areas: ASP performance and database performance.

Chapter 16, "Debugging," offers some tips for debugging Web databases that don't provide expected results or that fail completely.

Debugging

Chapter Objectives   Estimated Time: 30 minutes

This chapter will

- Present some useful hints and techniques for testing, diagnosing, and correcting Web databases pages.

- Briefly introduce Microsoft Script Debugger.

At least a thousand and one things can go wrong with a given Web database page, and sooner or later you're bound to experience every one of them. There's a lot of software involved in processing a Web database page, and each component has its own requirements and eccentricities.

Neither this chapter nor any other can present a detailed procedure for debugging any single Web database problem. At some point, you must understand how the software works, what your page is supposed to be doing, and how to make at least a shrewd guess at what an error message means. This chapter will, however, present a general approach for debugging as well as solutions to common pitfalls. It concludes with a brief description of Microsoft Script Debugger, which provides source-level interactive debugging of ASP pages.

General Debugging Tips

This section presents a number of tips and suggestions for getting Web database pages to work. To learn the cause of specific errors, type the error number or message into the Web page at *http://www.microsoft.com/search* and look for a match. You'll often find good information from MSDN, the Microsoft Internet Information Services (IIS) Web site, or in the Microsoft Knowledge Base.

Verify the ASP environment

If running a simple ASP page such as the following doesn't display the expected message ("It worked."), your Web server isn't configured to run ASP pages. (You can find this file within the sample pages at \webdbdev\ch16\itworked.asp.)

```
<html>
<head>
<title>It worked.</title>
</head>
```

(continued)

```
<body>
<%="<H1>It worked.</H1>"%>
</body>
</html>
```

ASP pages can run only on a Web server running Microsoft Internet Information Services or Microsoft Personal Web Server and only if they reside in a folder tree that has Script Execute permissions. You can't, for example, load an ASP page directly from your hard disk into your browser, as you might when previewing an ordinary Web page. Similarly, you can't run ASP pages by switching to Preview mode in Microsoft FrontPage or Quick View mode in Microsoft Visual InterDev. These modes work by storing and displaying the Web page temporarily on disk and not by processing the page on a Web server.

Set Execute Permissions from Internet Services Manager

If your Web server is IIS for Microsoft Windows 2000 or Microsoft Windows NT 4, you can configure execute folders using the Internet Services Manager snap-in for MMC. Figure 16-1 shows how to do this. The setting Execute Permissions: Scripts Only specifies that ASP pages within the given folder can execute, but compiled programs having .exe or .dll filename extensions cannot. For compiled programs to execute, you must set Execute Permissions to Scripts and Executables.

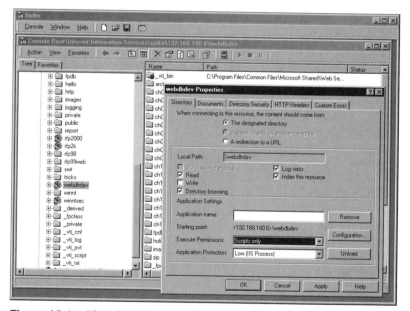

Figure 16-1   *This dialog box configures a Web server to execute scripts in a given folder tree.*

Set Execute Permissions from Within FrontPage

If you're the administrator of a server-based FrontPage Web, you can grant or revoke script execute permissions from within FrontPage. Simply right-click the folder you want to configure, choose Properties from the pop-up menu, and then configure the check box titled Allow Scripts To Be Run. Figure 16-2 shows this dialog box.

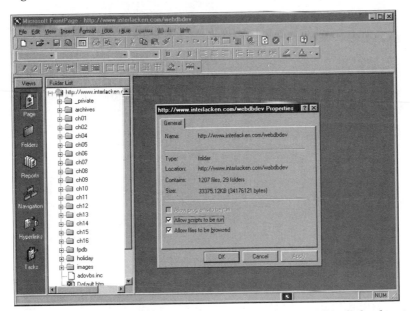

Figure 16-2 *Administrators of FrontPage Webs can use this dialog box to mark folders within their Webs as executable.*

Set Execute Permissions by Using Personal Web Manager

If you're using PWS for Windows 95 or Windows 98, use the Personal Web Manager application to configure executable directories. After starting Personal Web Manager, click the Advanced icon. If the folder you want to configure appears in the Virtual Directories box, select it and then click the Edit Properties button shown in Figure 16-3. Check the Access box titled Scripts, and then click OK.

If the folder you want to configure doesn't appear, click the Add button. An Add Directory dialog box similar to the Edit Directory box shown in Figure 16-3 will appear. In the Directory box, enter the folder's physical drive letter and path. In the Alias box, enter the URL path you want the folder to have. Finally, configure Access permissions as before.

The Personal Web Manager tool is also available for managing Internet Information Services in Windows 2000 Professional.

Note For an extra measure of security, many Web administrators turn off Read access to executable directories. This provides an additional level of assurance that Web visitors can't download and inspect your ASP code or other files residing in the same directory.

Don't forget to give your ASP file a .asp filename extension.

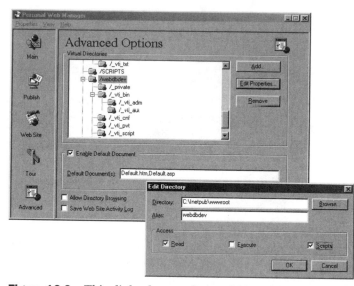

Figure 16-3 *This dialog box configures folder trees as executable in PWS for Windows 95 and Windows 98.*

Test early and test often

Saving and running an ASP page is such a rapid operation that you might as well test each part of your code as soon as you write it. If you test successfully, code another small function, and then test again, there's little doubt where any problems lie.

Conversely, if you're debugging some code that's already grown large, try commenting out the code one logical function at a time (beginning, of course, from the page's innermost workings). When the problem goes away, the last thing you commented out is probably its source.

Find the error message

Microsoft VBScript, IIS, and ADO error messages can appear on server-generated error pages or inline with the response HTML. (The exact location depends largely on the location of the malfunctioning code.) Sometimes, however, an inline error message will appear in a spot the browser won't display: for example, within a <select> </select> drop-down list but not between <option> and </option> tags. As shown in Figure 16-4, such a message will be visible only after you use your browser's View Source command. (IIS 5.0, which comes with Windows 2000, is better than prior versions at not hiding messages this way. This particular error, for example, produces a clearly visible error page.)

If your page isn't working and there's no obvious error message, try using the browser's View Source command and looking through the raw HTML. Using the View Source command is also a good way to check your ASP page's HTML for validity.

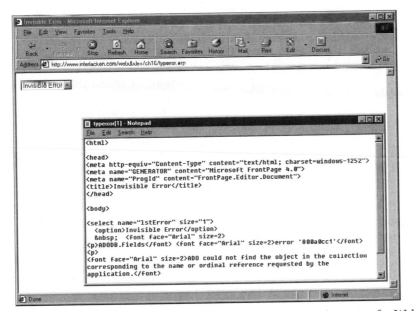

Figure 16-4 *ASP and ADO error messages might appear in parts of a Web page that the browser doesn't display. In such cases, use the browser's View Source command.*

Don't use On Error Resume Next *while testing*

Another reason that you might not get useful error messages is that you've turned them off! Once you've executed an *On Error Resume Next* statement, your script will keep running despite all errors and without displaying error messages until one of the following occurs:

- You execute an *On Error GoTo 0* statement.

- You leave the subroutine or function that executed the *On Error Resume Next* statement.

- The script ends.

In any case, the *On Error Resume Next* statement is no substitute for good coding. You should strive to produce code that never creates run-time errors except in certain conditions where the Web visitor submits invalid requests. (For example, if the Web visitor tries to add a record that already exists or supplies data that's the wrong format for a field, you might prefer writing code that traps and handles a database error over writing your own validation code.)

Note There are two viewpoints regarding validation of database activity. One viewpoint holds that to minimize load on the database system, the code in the application program should perform as much validation as possible. The other view contends that validation should occur at the database level so that it's consistent across all applications. Of course, neither view is completely right or wrong; you, as a developer, must strike an appropriate balance based on your particular needs.

Write messages to yourself

If you need to know the value of a certain variable or property, it's often help-ful to display it in a message written to the Response object. The first statement in the following code will print the number of items found in a particular recordset. Comparing this information with the results of the subsequent loop might be useful in determining what's wrong with the code.

```
Response.Write "<p>Items found: " & rsItm.RecordCount & "</p>"
Do While Not rsItm.EOF
'   Code that doesn't seem to be executing appears here.
   rsItm.MoveNext
Loop
```

Use the Option Explicit *statement*

VBScript can check for the existence and correct spelling of all the variables and constants in your program. To activate this feature, add the following statement before any other ASP or HTML code in your Web page:

```
<% Option Explicit %>
```

With this statement in effect, VBScript will no longer create variables on the fly, as you use them. Instead, you must declare variables using *Dim* statements such as the following:

```
Dim pos, cnt
Dim rsItm
```

If you forget to declare a variable, VBScript will produce a message like this:

```
Microsoft VBScript runtime error '800a01f4'
Variable is undefined: 'cursVal'
/webdbdev/ch16/supports.asp, line 25
```

If the offending variable is valid but isn't local to a subroutine or a function, declare it with a *Dim* statement placed after the first <% tag in the Web page. If it's local to a subroutine or function, place it after the *Sub* or *Function* declaration.

If the offending variable isn't valid, correct its spelling.

Don't forget the adovbs.inc file

If at all possible, use the version of adovbs.inc that came with the version of MDAC installed on your Web server.

If you don't use *Option Explicit*, forgetting an include file can cause a number of problems. For example, if you use any ADO named constants, and you for-get to include the adovbs.inc file, VBScript will create variables with the same names as those ADO constants. If used as strings, these variables will be empty; if used numerically, they will contain zero. Either way, this usually results in an error message such as this:

```
ADODB.Recordset error '800a0bb9'
The application is using arguments that are of the wrong type,
are out of acceptable range, or are in conflict with one another.
```

The invalid arguments, of course, are those variables with empty or zero values. The solution is to include the adovbs.inc file as explained in "Using ADO Named Constants" in Chapter 3, "Accessing Databases with ADO and ODBC."

If you always begin your VBScript code with an Option Explicit statement, you can avoid this type of problem.

Debug SQL statements in Microsoft Access

The section titled, "Let Access create your SQL statements," in Chapter 2 ("Understanding Database Concepts and Terms") described how to develop a query in Microsoft Access, display the corresponding SQL statement, and then cut and paste it into your Web page. Don't overlook the reverse process for debugging SQL statements that Web pages construct.

If you have a SQL statement that either fails completely or doesn't produce the result you want, follow these steps:

1. Display the SQL statement on the Web page by adding a statement such as the following to your ASP code:

```
Response.Write "<p>" & strSQL & "<p>" & vbCrLf
```

2. Run the ASP page, and make sure the SQL statement appears in the browser window.

3. Start Access, and open the database the ASP page is trying to access.

4. Create a new query, and switch from Design View to SQL View.

5. Copy the SQL statement displayed in step 2 to the clipboard.

6. Paste the clipboard contents into the SQL View window you opened in step 4.

7. Run the SQL statement by switching Access to Datasheet View.

The chances are good that Access will provide a more informative message than ADO. In addition, you can probably correct the query in Design View and test it in Datasheet View. Once the query works, you can either paste it back into the Web page—as described in Chapter 2—or display the corrected query in SQL View, note the changes, and incorporate them into your code.

Before executing a query pasted into Access, you must change any single quotes surrounding text literals back to double quotes.

Choose the correct cursor and locking

If ADO methods and properties don't seem to be performing as documented, you might be using the wrong type of cursor or locking. For more details on choosing these options, consult "Open an ADO Recordset object" in Chapter 4, "Accessing Tables and Records with ADO."

You can use the *Recordset.Supports* method to determine the capabilities of an open recordset. Figure 16-5 illustrates a Web page that does this for the *items* table of the holiday.mdb database. To test the capabilities of a recordset that opens this table, choose a cursor type, choose a lock type, and click Open. The HTML table that occupies most of the page will display the resulting recordset's capabilities. You can find this page among the sample files at \webdbdev\ch16\supports.asp.

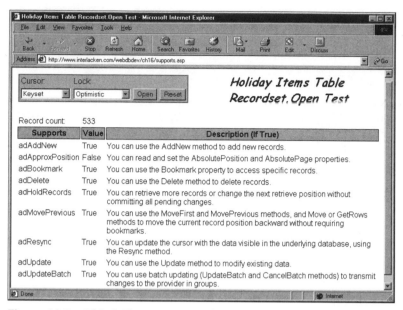

Figure 16-5 *This Web page reports the capabilities of a recordset opened with specified options.*

This page works by opening the recordset in the usual way, and then querying the *Recordset.Supports* method for each named constant listed in the Supports column. For example, the first cell under the Value heading displays the value of the expression *RsItm.Supports(adAddNew)*. By modifying the connection string and table name in this Web page, you can experiment with the capabilities of any database you like.

If you run this Web page, you might notice that whenever you try to open the recordset with a dynamic cursor, you actually get a keyset cursor. This is a limitation of Microsoft Access. You might also notice that whenever you open the recordset as forward-only, the record count is –1. A forward-only cursor asks the database system for only a few records at a time and has no way of determining how many records follow those received. Thus, it can't supply a record count.

Configure application settings for testing

Configuring your Web application for testing will make finding bugs a lot easier. Figures 16-6 and 16-7 show the four tabs of the Application Configuration dialog box for Windows 2000 Web servers. The corresponding dialog box for Windows NT 4.0 is quite similar.

To display these boxes, follow these steps:

1. Start Internet Services Manager.

2. Open Internet Information Services on Windows 2000 or Internet Information Server on Windows NT 4.0.

3. Right-click the IIS entry for a computer, a virtual Web server, or a virtual directory, and then choose Properties.

4. If in step 3 you selected a computer, select the IIS tab, set Master Properties to WWW Service, and click the Edit button.

5. If in step 3 you selected a virtual directory, select the Directory tab. Otherwise, select the Home Directory tab.

6. Click the Configuration button.

Note If the Configuration button is dimmed, the current folder isn't the root of an IIS application. If the application root resides elsewhere, close the dialog box, reposition to the application root, and then go back to step 3. If the current folder should become the root of a new application, click the Create button in the Application Settings box.

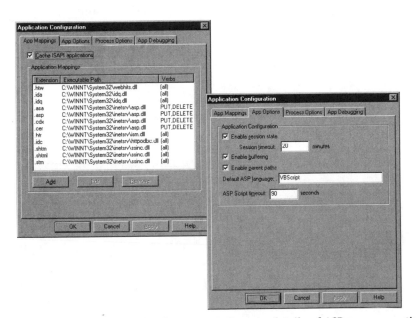

Figure 16-6 *These dialog boxes control many details of ASP page execution.*

The following sections list some dos and don'ts regarding this group of settings as related to testing. For further details on any specified field, click the Help button at the bottom of the dialog box. None of these options is configurable on PWS for Windows 95 and Windows 98.

App Mappings

These settings are available at all three configuration levels on both Windows 2000 and Windows NT 4.0.

- **Do** check the Cache ISAPI Applications box. If this box is unchecked, every time a visitor requests a Web page IIS will initialize the ASP environment, create Application and Session objects, run the global.asa file, process and deliver the requested ASP file, delete the Session and Application objects, and then shut down the ASP environment.

This means the Session object won't work for passing information from one page to another. In addition, if you request an ASP page while a previous session is still in progress, the second request will fail.

App Options

These settings are available at all three configuration levels on both Windows 2000 and Windows NT 4.0:

- **Do** check the Enable Session State box if any pages in your application use the *Session* object. This is the default.

- **Do** check the Enable Buffering box to improve performance and ease requirements that all modifications to HTTP header information precede output of the first HTML statement. This is the default on Windows 2000 but not on Windows NT 4.0.

- **Do** review the ASP Script Timeout value. This is the amount of time an ASP page will run if your page goes into a loop.

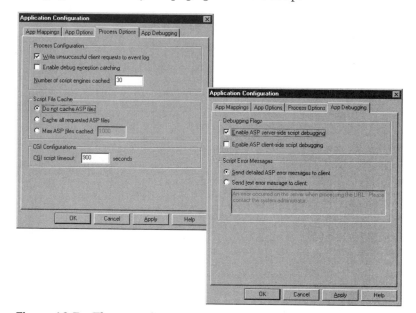

Figure 16-7 *These are the remaining tabs in the dialog box shown in Figure 16-6. The Process Options tab will not appear in some circumstances.*

Process Options

On Windows NT 4.0, this tab will only appear on the master properties for the entire computer. On Windows 2000, it also appears on the tab that configures a virtual server. The Process Options tab isn't available for a particular virtual directory.

- **Do** check the box titled Write Unsuccessful Client Requests To Event Log. When Web pages fail, this option will cause IIS to log error messages in the Windows Event Log. Some of these messages appear nowhere else. For performance reasons, you might want to turn this box off in a production environment.

- **Don't** check the box titled Enable Debug Exception Catching. When this box is checked, Active Server Pages sends a general error message when *Server.CreateObject* fails. When the box is unchecked, ASP sends a specific error message from the component. Production Web servers will usually have this box checked.

- **Do** check Do Not Cache ASP Files if you update ASP files by saving them directly into the Web server's file system. Otherwise, you might find a file in use when you try to save it. In this case, testing that file might actually test an older copy still held in memory.

    When the FrontPage Server Extensions update an ASP page, they tell the Web server to discard any cached copies of those Web pages. Therefore, you don't need to turn off ASP file caching if you use FrontPage, Visual InterDev, or the Microsoft Office 2000 Web Folders feature to save ASP files into a server-based FrontPage Web.

    Production Web servers should use one of the options that allow caching.

App Debugging

These settings are available at all three configuration levels on both Windows 2000 and Windows NT 4.0:

- **Do** check Enable ASP Server-Side Script Debugging if you plan to debug using the Microsoft Script Debugger described later in this chapter. Never check this box on a production server. If you do, failed ASP pages will stall the Web visitor and initiate debugging sessions.

- **Do** ignore the option Enable ASP Client-Side Script Debugging. It isn't implemented in any Microsoft Web server up to and including IIS 5.0. Later versions might include this feature. For now, checking this option will have no effect.

- **Do** check Send Detailed ASP Error Messages To Client. When debugging, you want all the information you can get. In production, a kinder, gentler message might be preferable.

Configure Windows permissions

In Chapter 6 ("Organizing Your Web Environment"), the section "Managing Windows 2000 and Windows NT Security for Web Pages" explained how Microsoft Web servers for Windows 2000 and Windows NT 4.0 first try to access Web resources using a so-called "Anonymous" user account and how, if that access fails, such Web servers prompt the Web visitor for a more capable Windows username and password.

To avoid granting security in several locations for each new Web user, grant permissions once to a group and then add all Web users to that group.

The same section also explained that whatever account succeeds in accessing the Web page is also the account used for accessing the ASP script interpreter, the database software, the database itself, and any other ActiveX controls or system services the Web page uses. Each account must also have the Log On Locally user right. If access to any of these resources fails, processing the ASP page will fail.

To determine whether your ASP pages aren't working because of NTFS security, temporarily add the Anonymous user account to the local system's Administrators group, then stop and restart the Web server. If your ASP pages start working, your prior problems are security-related. To remedy the situation, take the Anonymous user account out of the Administrators group and then search for the resource it can't access.

Warning   Never use an Administrator account for anonymous Web access. Doing so creates a major security breach.

Granting the Log On Locally User Right to a User or a Group

To grant a user or a group the Log On Locally right in Windows 2000, open the Group Policy MMC Snap-In, navigate to User Rights Assignment, open the Log On Locally policy, and click the Add button. Figure 16-8 shows this operation in progress.

To grant this right in Windows NT 4.0, start User Manager, select User Rights from the Policies menu, select the Log On Locally right, and then click the Add button.

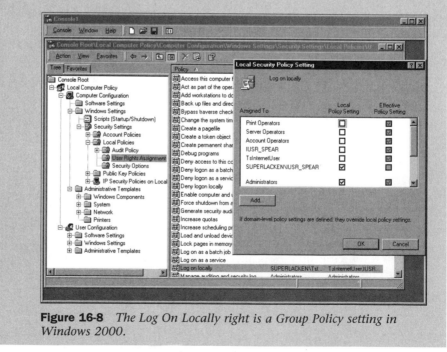

Figure 16-8   *The Log On Locally right is a Group Policy setting in Windows 2000.*

An additional issue arises when accessing resources (such as Access or SQL Server databases) located on other computers. Specifically, the default Anonymous account (created during IIS setup) is a local account having no security privileges on any other machine. The recommended solution is to create a Domain account usable on both systems, configure this account with all required permissions and user rights, and then make it the Anonymous Web server account for at least the virtual directory that accesses the remote resource. If this advice doesn't make sense, consult your security administrator, your Web server Administrator, or a book that explains Windows account administration.

Debugging with Microsoft Script Debugger

Microsoft provides an application called Script Debugger that provides source-level, interactive debugging of both server-side scripts (such as VBScript code in ASP pages) and browser-side scripts (such as JavaScript code that runs on the browser). Using Script Debugger, you can view your script as it runs, halt it for inspection, execute a line at a time, set breakpoints, inspect and modify variables, inspect and modify object-properties, and so on, all through an integrated graphical user interface.

Script Debugger has no remote debugging capability. To interactively debug a browser-side script, you must run Microsoft Internet Explorer and Script Debugger on the same computer. To interactively debug an ASP page, you must run Internet Explorer, Script Debugger, and the Web server all on the same computer. Furthermore, the Web server must be one of the following:

- Internet Information Services for Windows 2000

- Internet Information Server 4.0 for Windows NT Server 4.0

- Personal Web Server 4.0 for Windows NT Workstation 4.0

Microsoft Personal Web Server for Windows 95 and Windows 98 is a notable omission from this list. Interactive debugging doesn't work in these versions of Windows. If you currently test Web pages on a Windows 95 or Windows 98 computer and want to interactively debug ASP pages, consider upgrading to Windows 2000.

In practical terms, the best platforms for debugging ASP scripts interactively are likely to be Windows 2000 Professional or Windows NT Workstation 4.0. Debugging on a production server can degrade service to Web visitors.

Install and enable Script Debugger

To debug server-side scripts on a Windows NT 4.0 computer, you must install the version of Script Debugger that comes with the Windows NT 4.0 Option Pack. The version of Script Debugger that comes with Internet Explorer 4.0 and later versions provides only browser-side debugging.

Note Visual InterDev includes script debugging as a built-in feature. Therefore, you shouldn't install freestanding versions of Script Debugger on any computer that contains Visual InterDev. For more information on this topic, refer to the Visual InterDev documentation.

To install Script Debugger on Windows 2000, open the Add/Remove Programs applet in Control Panel and then click the Add/Remove Windows Components icon. Figure 16-9 shows this operation in progress.

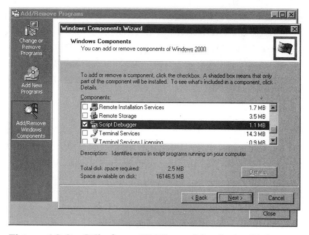

Figure 16-9 *Windows 2000 provides Script Debugger as an installation option.*

To enable browser-side script debugging, follow these steps:

1. Start Internet Explorer.

2. Choose Internet Options from the Tools menu.

3. Click the Advanced tab.

4. Locate the option Disable Script Debugging, and make sure it isn't checked. Figure 16-10 shows the correct setting.

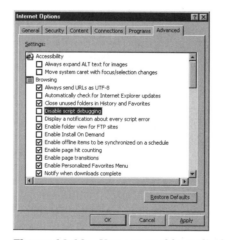

Figure 16-10 *You can enable or disable browser-side scripting by configuring this dialog box in Internet Explorer.*

To enable server-side debugging, the option Enable ASP Server-Side Script Debugging shown in Figure 16-7 must be checked for the executable folder tree that contains the script you want to debug. This is a setting the Web server's administrator configures using Internet Services Manager.

Invoke Script Debugger

You can invoke the Script Debugger in four ways:

- **From the Start menu**   You can start Script Debugger manually by following the appropriate path:

  - **Windows 2000**   Click Start, Programs, Accessories, Microsoft Script Debugger, and finally Microsoft Script Debugger.

  - **Windows NT 4.0**   Click Start, Programs, Windows NT 4.0 Option Pack, Microsoft Script Debugger, and then Microsoft Script Debugger.

  When opened in this way, Script Debugger can open, edit, and save Web files with about the same functionality as Notepad; color-coding is the only enhancement. However, you can't initiate debugging of any pages you open.

- **From Internet Explorer**   Choose Script Debugger from the View menu, and then choose Open. This option will be absent if, in the dialog box of Figure 16-10, you chose to disable script debugging. You can initiate browser-side debugging from Internet Explorer, but not server-side debugging.

- **From your script**   In VBScript, the *Stop* command will open the debugger, tell it to open the current page, and position it to the current statement. In Jscript, the equivalent command is *debugger*.

- **Automatically**   If the browser detects a browser-side scripting error and debugging is enabled, the browser will display a prompt asking if you want to debug the error. If the ASP processor detects a server-side scripting error and debugging is enabled, it starts Script Debugger immediately. In either case, Script Debugger will automatically display on the Web server's console the page and statement that contains the error.

All four of these methods load Script Debugger, but only the last two methods can initiate an ASP debugging session.

In addition to any open document windows, Script Debugger displays up to three windows of its own. You can hide or display these windows by choosing options on the View menu or by clicking toolbar buttons. Figure 16-11 shows how to locate these options.

The three windows provide the functions listed below:

- **Running Documents**   Lists two groups of Web pages, one for Microsoft Active Server Pages and one for pages running in Microsoft Internet Explorer. To debug any listed document, double-click its entry. The characteristics of these groups are listed here:

  - **Microsoft Active Server Pages**   Lists any ASP pages the server is currently executing. Note that an ASP page will appear under this entry only if the Web server temporarily suspends execution of that page. The Web server does this only if debugging is in effect for the given executable folder and the Web page either fails or executes a *Stop* or *debugger* statement (in VBScript and JScript, respectively).

- **Microsoft Internet Explorer**   Lists any Web pages currently displayed in your browser. Note, however, that double-clicking an ASP page under this entry loads only the code that Internet Explorer receives: that is, the response HTML and any browser-side scripts it contains.

- **Call Stack**   Lists any subroutines or functions currently running.

- **Command Window**   Accepts typed commands and displays the results. You can use this window to query or modify variables and properties in your script or to run any script statement directly.

    The command window always uses the language of the currently executing statement. If you're running a block of VBScript code, the command window expects VBScript statements. If you're running a block of JScript code, it expects JScript statements.

    To display a variable or a property in VBScript, enter a question mark, a space, and the name of the variable or property. To display a variable or a property in JScript, simply enter its name.

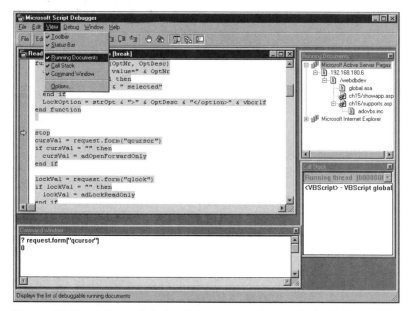

Figure 16-11 *Microsoft Script Debugger can interactively display values, modify values, and trace the flow of execution in an ASP page.*

Starting an ASP debugging session is a somewhat indirect process, and it might cause the browser to time out. To understand why this is so, consider the flow of control:

1. The browser requests the page.

2. The Web server detects a serious error or a *Stop* statement and finds that server-side debugging is in effect.

3. The Web server halts the script.

4. The Web server looks for a running copy of Script Debugger. If it finds one, it tells Script Debugger to start a debugging session. If it can't find a running copy of Script Debugger, it starts one and proceeds as before.

5. The developer debugs the Web page.

6. The browser either times out or displays the resulting Web page, depending on how long the developer spends debugging.

The Command Window in Figure 16-11 shows how to query a property in VBScript; simply enter a question mark, a space, and the name of the property. In the figure, *request.form("qcursor")* contains the value 0. You can query ordinary variables, arrays, and other expressions the same way. To change the value of a variable or a property—or to invoke a method—simply type the necessary line of code into the Command Window. For example, to change the value of the variable *cursVal* to *3*, type the following statement and then press Enter.

```
cursVal = 3
```

Table 16-1 summarizes the commands to execute one statement at a time, to execute one procedure at a time, or to run all code up to a certain statement. You can issue these commands from the Debug menu, by function key, or from the toolbar.

Table 16-1   Microsoft Script Debugger Commands

Menu Command	Function Key	Icon	Description
Run	F5		Initiates or resumes execution of the selected document.
Break at Next Statement			Initiates debugging at the first statement in the currently selected document. If you select a document in the Running Documents window and then choose this command, the next execution of that document will start a debugging session.
Stop Debugging	Shift+F5		Closes the debugging session on the currently selected document.
Step Into	F8		Executes the current script statement and then halts. If the current statement calls another procedure, the debugger will enter that procedure and pause at the first statement.
Step Over	Shift+F8		Executes the current script statement and then halts. If the current statement calls another procedure, the debugger runs the entire procedure and pauses at the first statement after the current statement.

(continued)

Table 16-1 *continued*

Menu Command	Function Key	Icon	Description
Step Out	Ctrl+ Shift+F8		Executes all remaining statements in the current procedure and pauses just after the statement that called it.
Toggle Breakpoint	F9		Sets or clears a breakpoint at the currently selected statement. The script will halt whenever it reaches a statement flagged as a breakpoint. Breakpoints exist only for the duration of the current debugging session.
Clear All	Ctrl+ Shift+F9		Clears all breakpoints in the current script.

To interactively debug procedures in the global.asa file you must place *Stop* or *debugger* statements in those procedures. To activate the *Session_OnStart* and *Session_OnEnd* procedures, quit and restart your browser—this opens a new session. To activate the *Application_OnStart* and *Application_OnEnd* procedures, save a new copy of the global.asa file or stop and restart the Web server.

Script Debugger is a powerful and elegant tool, but it's hardly the only way to debug ASP pages. You can accomplish a lot by coding and testing in small increments, and by coding *Response.Write* statements that display values you're curious about. Script Debugger is nevertheless a very attractive tool. If you need it, it's probably worthwhile to set up the required environment.

Chapter Summary

This chapter presented a number of tools and techniques for testing, diagnosing, and correcting Web databases pages. It concluded with a brief introduction to Microsoft Script Debugger, which provides interactive debugging of browser-side and server-side script code.

This book has explained the fundamentals of creating database applications that clients access via the World Wide Web. Its approach has been practical rather than theoretical, compact rather than broad. I hope this approach has been useful, and that you're now prepared to create applications of your own. Best wishes and good luck with your site.

Index

Page numbers in italics refer to figures, tables, or code listings.

Jim Buyens is the senior PC-LAN administrator for AG Communication Systems, a leading provider of telephone switching equipment and software. An early proponent of TCP/IP connectivity, he administers a worldwide corporate network that includes more than 50 Microsoft Windows NT servers and more than 2000 client personal computers. He was an early champion of World Wide Web applications for intranet use, and he administers a corporate Web site at *www.agcs.com*.

Jim received a Bachelor of Science degree in computer science from Purdue University in 1971 and a Master of Business Administration from Arizona State University in 1992. When not administering a network or writing books, he enjoys traveling and attending professional sports events—especially NHL hockey. He resides with his family in Phoenix.

The manuscript for this book was prepared using Microsoft Word 2000. Pages were composed by Microsoft Press using Adobe PageMaker 6.52 for Windows, with text in Stone Serif and display type in ITC Franklin Gothic. Composed pages were delivered to the printer as electronic prepress files.

Cover Designer:	Girvin	Branding & Design
Interior Graphic Designer:	James D. Kramer
Interior Graphic Artist:	Rob Nance
Principal Compositor:	Barb Runyan
Principal Proofreader:	Patricia Masserman
Indexer:	Richard Shrout

MICROSOFT LICENSE AGREEMENT

Book Companion CD

IMPORTANT—READ CAREFULLY: This Microsoft End-User License Agreement ("EULA") is a legal agreement between you (either an individual or an entity) and Microsoft Corporation for the Microsoft product identified above, which includes computer software and may include associated media, printed materials, and "online" or electronic documentation ("SOFTWARE PRODUCT"). Any component included within the SOFTWARE PRODUCT that is accompanied by a separate End-User License Agreement shall be governed by such agreement and not the terms set forth below. By installing, copying, or otherwise using the SOFTWARE PRODUCT, you agree to be bound by the terms of this EULA. If you do not agree to the terms of this EULA, you are not authorized to install, copy, or otherwise use the SOFTWARE PRODUCT; you may, however, return the SOFTWARE PRODUCT, along with all printed materials and other items that form a part of the Microsoft product that includes the SOFTWARE PRODUCT, to the place you obtained them for a full refund.

SOFTWARE PRODUCT LICENSE

The SOFTWARE PRODUCT is protected by United States copyright laws and international copyright treaties, as well as other intellectual property laws and treaties. The SOFTWARE PRODUCT is licensed, not sold.

1. **GRANT OF LICENSE.** This EULA grants you the following rights:

   a. **Software Product.** You may install and use one copy of the SOFTWARE PRODUCT on a single computer. The primary user of the computer on which the SOFTWARE PRODUCT is installed may make a second copy for his or her exclusive use on a portable computer.

   b. **Storage/Network Use.** You may also store or install a copy of the SOFTWARE PRODUCT on a storage device, such as a network server, used only to install or run the SOFTWARE PRODUCT on your other computers over an internal network; however, you must acquire and dedicate a license for each separate computer on which the SOFTWARE PRODUCT is installed or run from the storage device. A license for the SOFTWARE PRODUCT may not be shared or used concurrently on different computers.

   c. **License Pak.** If you have acquired this EULA in a Microsoft License Pak, you may make the number of additional copies of the computer software portion of the SOFTWARE PRODUCT authorized on the printed copy of this EULA, and you may use each copy in the manner specified above. You are also entitled to make a corresponding number of secondary copies for portable computer use as specified above.

   d. **Sample Code.** Solely with respect to portions, if any, of the SOFTWARE PRODUCT that are identified within the SOFTWARE PRODUCT as sample code (the "SAMPLE CODE"):

      i. **Use and Modification.** Microsoft grants you the right to use and modify the source code version of the SAMPLE CODE, *provided* you comply with subsection (d)(iii) below. You may not distribute the SAMPLE CODE, or any modified version of the SAMPLE CODE, in source code form.

      ii. **Redistributable Files.** Provided you comply with subsection (d)(iii) below, Microsoft grants you a nonexclusive, royalty-free right to reproduce and distribute the object code version of the SAMPLE CODE and of any modified SAMPLE CODE, other than SAMPLE CODE, or any modified version thereof, designated as not redistributable in the Readme file that forms a part of the SOFTWARE PRODUCT (the "Non-Redistributable Sample Code"). All SAMPLE CODE other than the Non-Redistributable Sample Code is collectively referred to as the "REDISTRIBUTABLES."

      iii. **Redistribution Requirements.** If you redistribute the REDISTRIBUTABLES, you agree to: (i) distribute the REDISTRIBUTABLES in object code form only in conjunction with and as a part of your software application product; (ii) not use Microsoft's name, logo, or trademarks to market your software application product; (iii) include a valid copyright notice on your software application product; (iv) indemnify, hold harmless, and defend Microsoft from and against any claims or lawsuits, including attorney's fees, that arise or result from the use or distribution of your software application product; and (v) not permit further distribution of the REDISTRIBUTABLES by your end user. Contact Microsoft for the applicable royalties due and other licensing terms for all other uses and/or distribution of the REDISTRIBUTABLES.

2. **DESCRIPTION OF OTHER RIGHTS AND LIMITATIONS.**

   - **Limitations on Reverse Engineering, Decompilation, and Disassembly.** You may not reverse engineer, decompile, or disassemble the SOFTWARE PRODUCT, except and only to the extent that such activity is expressly permitted by applicable law notwithstanding this limitation.

   - **Separation of Components.** The SOFTWARE PRODUCT is licensed as a single product. Its component parts may not be separated for use on more than one computer.

   - **Rental.** You may not rent, lease, or lend the SOFTWARE PRODUCT.

   - **Support Services.** Microsoft may, but is not obligated to, provide you with support services related to the SOFTWARE PRODUCT ("Support Services"). Use of Support Services is governed by the Microsoft policies and programs described in the user manual, in "online" documentation, and/or in other Microsoft-provided materials. Any supplemental software code provided to you as part of the Support Services shall be considered part of the SOFTWARE PRODUCT and subject to the terms and conditions of this EULA. With respect to technical information you provide to Microsoft as part of the Support Services, Microsoft may use such information for its business purposes, including for product support and development. Microsoft will not utilize such technical information in a form that personally identifies you.

- **Software Transfer.** You may permanently transfer all of your rights under this EULA, provided you retain no copies, you transfer all of the SOFTWARE PRODUCT (including all component parts, the media and printed materials, any upgrades, this EULA, and, if applicable, the Certificate of Authenticity), **and** the recipient agrees to the terms of this EULA.

- **Termination.** Without prejudice to any other rights, Microsoft may terminate this EULA if you fail to comply with the terms and conditions of this EULA. In such event, you must destroy all copies of the SOFTWARE PRODUCT and all of its component parts.

3. **COPYRIGHT.** All title and copyrights in and to the SOFTWARE PRODUCT (including but not limited to any images, photographs, animations, video, audio, music, text, SAMPLE CODE, REDISTRIBUTABLES, and "applets" incorporated into the SOFTWARE PRODUCT) and any copies of the SOFTWARE PRODUCT are owned by Microsoft or its suppliers. The SOFTWARE PRODUCT is protected by copyright laws and international treaty provisions. Therefore, you must treat the SOFTWARE PRODUCT like any other copyrighted material **except** that you may install the SOFTWARE PRODUCT on a single computer provided you keep the original solely for backup or archival purposes. You may not copy the printed materials accompanying the SOFTWARE PRODUCT.

4. **U.S. GOVERNMENT RESTRICTED RIGHTS.** The SOFTWARE PRODUCT and documentation are provided with RESTRICTED RIGHTS. Use, duplication, or disclosure by the Government is subject to restrictions as set forth in subparagraph (c)(1)(ii) of the Rights in Technical Data and Computer Software clause at DFARS 252.227-7013 or subparagraphs (c)(1) and (2) of the Commercial Computer Software—Restricted Rights at 48 CFR 52.227-19, as applicable. Manufacturer is Microsoft Corporation/One Microsoft Way/Redmond, WA 98052-6399.

5. **EXPORT RESTRICTIONS.** You agree that you will not export or re-export the SOFTWARE PRODUCT, any part thereof, or any process or service that is the direct product of the SOFTWARE PRODUCT (the foregoing collectively referred to as the "Restricted Components"), to any country, person, entity, or end user subject to U.S. export restrictions. You specifically agree not to export or re-export any of the Restricted Components (i) to any country to which the U.S. has embargoed or restricted the export of goods or services, which currently include, but are not necessarily limited to, Cuba, Iran, Iraq, Libya, North Korea, Sudan, and Syria, or to any national of any such country, wherever located, who intends to transmit or transport the Restricted Components back to such country; (ii) to any end user who you know or have reason to know will utilize the Restricted Components in the design, development, or production of nuclear, chemical, or biological weapons; or (iii) to any end user who has been prohibited from participating in U.S. export transactions by any federal agency of the U.S. government. You warrant and represent that neither the BXA nor any other U.S. federal agency has suspended, revoked, or denied your export privileges.

DISCLAIMER OF WARRANTY

NO WARRANTIES OR CONDITIONS. MICROSOFT EXPRESSLY DISCLAIMS ANY WARRANTY OR CONDITION FOR THE SOFTWARE PRODUCT. THE SOFTWARE PRODUCT AND ANY RELATED DOCUMENTATION ARE PROVIDED "AS IS" WITHOUT WARRANTY OR CONDITION OF ANY KIND, EITHER EXPRESS OR IMPLIED, INCLUDING, WITHOUT LIMITATION, THE IMPLIED WARRANTIES OF MERCHANTABILITY, FITNESS FOR A PARTICULAR PURPOSE, OR NONINFRINGEMENT. THE ENTIRE RISK ARISING OUT OF USE OR PERFORMANCE OF THE SOFTWARE PRODUCT REMAINS WITH YOU.

LIMITATION OF LIABILITY. TO THE MAXIMUM EXTENT PERMITTED BY APPLICABLE LAW, IN NO EVENT SHALL MICROSOFT OR ITS SUPPLIERS BE LIABLE FOR ANY SPECIAL, INCIDENTAL, INDIRECT, OR CONSEQUENTIAL DAMAGES WHATSOEVER (INCLUDING, WITHOUT LIMITATION, DAMAGES FOR LOSS OF BUSINESS PROFITS, BUSINESS INTERRUPTION, LOSS OF BUSINESS INFORMATION, OR ANY OTHER PECUNIARY LOSS) ARISING OUT OF THE USE OF OR INABILITY TO USE THE SOFTWARE PRODUCT OR THE PROVISION OF OR FAILURE TO PROVIDE SUPPORT SERVICES, EVEN IF MICROSOFT HAS BEEN ADVISED OF THE POSSIBILITY OF SUCH DAMAGES. IN ANY CASE, MICROSOFT'S ENTIRE LIABILITY UNDER ANY PROVISION OF THIS EULA SHALL BE LIMITED TO THE GREATER OF THE AMOUNT ACTUALLY PAID BY YOU FOR THE SOFTWARE PRODUCT OR US$5.00; PROVIDED, HOWEVER, IF YOU HAVE ENTERED INTO A MICROSOFT SUPPORT SERVICES AGREEMENT, MICROSOFT'S ENTIRE LIABILITY REGARDING SUPPORT SERVICES SHALL BE GOVERNED BY THE TERMS OF THAT AGREEMENT. BECAUSE SOME STATES AND JURISDICTIONS DO NOT ALLOW THE EXCLUSION OR LIMITATION OF LIABILITY, THE ABOVE LIMITATION MAY NOT APPLY TO YOU.

MISCELLANEOUS

This EULA is governed by the laws of the State of Washington USA, except and only to the extent that applicable law mandates governing law of a different jurisdiction.

Should you have any questions concerning this EULA, or if you desire to contact Microsoft for any reason, please contact the Microsoft subsidiary serving your country, or write: Microsoft Sales Information Center/One Microsoft Way/Redmond, WA 98052-6399.

Proof of Purchase

0-7356-0966-7

Do not send this card with your registration.
Use this card as proof of purchase if participating in a promotion or rebate
offer on *Web Database Development Step by Step*. Card must be used in conjunction
with other proof(s) of payment such as your dated sales receipt—see offer details.

Web Database Development Step by Step

_____

WHERE DID YOU PURCHASE THIS PRODUCT?

_____

CUSTOMER NAME

mspress.microsoft.com

Microsoft Press, PO Box 97017, Redmond, WA 98073-9830

OWNER REGISTRATION CARD   *Register Today!*   0-7356-0966-7

Return the bottom portion of this card to register today.

Web Database Development Step by Step

_____   _____   _____

FIRST NAME   **MIDDLE INITIAL**   **LAST NAME**

_____

INSTITUTION OR COMPANY NAME

_____

ADDRESS

_____

_____   _____   _____

CITY   **STATE**   **ZIP**

                                    (   )

_____   _____

E-MAIL ADDRESS   **PHONE NUMBER**

U.S. and Canada addresses only. Fill in information above and mail postage-free.
Please mail only the bottom half of this page.

start faster
go
farther

For information about Microsoft Press®
products, visit our Web site at
mspress.microsoft.com

Microsoft®